Blake's Human Form Divine

Blake's
Human Form Divine

ANNE KOSTELANETZ MELLOR

UNIVERSITY OF CALIFORNIA PRESS · BERKELEY · LOS ANGELES · LONDON

University of California Press
Berkeley and Los Angeles, California

University of California Press, Ltd.
London, England

Copyright © 1974, by
The Regents of the University of California

ISBN: 0-520-02065-0
Library of Congress Catalog Card Number: 72-161995

Printed in the United States of America
Designed by Jean Peters

for Ron

Contents

Plates

All illustrations are by William Blake, unless otherwise specified. The numeration of the illuminated books is based on Keynes and Wolf's *Census* of *William Blake's Illuminated Books* (New York, 1953).

ix

Acknowledgments

In my study of Blake's changing theory and use of form, I am deeply indebted to all previous Blake scholars; even where I disagree with them, they have given me valuable insights into Blake's art and have challenged my own readings of Blake. At least four of these critics gave me personal encouragement and help when I most needed it, and to these I give special thanks: to S. Foster Damon for introducing me to Blake; to David Erdman and Sir Anthony Blunt for guiding my dissertation researches; and to Morton Paley for reading this manuscript in its final draft and providing me with invaluable corrections and criticisms. Two other scholars provided intellectual and psychological support for which I will always be grateful, Carl Woodring and Herbert Lindenberger. Several colleagues read and kindly helped me to revise my manuscript: I am particularly indebted in this regard to Wilfred Stone, Donald Davie, John Bender, Robert Polhemus, Bliss Carnochan, Lucio Ruotolo, and Albert Gelpi. And finally, thanks must go to all those friends and students, too numerous to name, who have willingly listened to me talk of Blake, challenged my interpretations, offered their own insights, and generously enriched my intellectual and personal life. To the person who has made my life both possible and pleasurable, I lovingly dedicate this book.

In addition, I wish to acknowledge with gratitude the kindness of the following publishers and owners in permitting me to reproduce works in their possession: Brown University Press (for material reprinted in chapter 4); *Philological Quarterly* (for material reprinted in chapter 2); *Studies in English Literature* (for material reprinted in chapter 8); The Museum of Fine Arts, Boston (for Plate 65); the Trustees of the British Museum (for Plates 1, 2, 7, 9–13, 15–21, 23–25, 49–54, 56, 59, 61–63, 66, 67); the Dean and Chapter of Chichester Cathedral (for Plates 46–48); the Syndics of the Fitzwilliam Museum, Cambridge (for Plates 3–6, 34, 36); the Fogg Art Museum, Harvard University (for Plate 69); Sir Geoffrey Keynes (for Plates 35, 60, 75); Kunsthaus Zürich (for Plate 33); the Collection of Mr. and Mrs. Paul Mellon (for Plates 76–78, 80–86); the National Trust, Arlington Court (for Plate 68); the Pierpont Morgan Library (for Plates 70–74, 79); Mr. Lessing J. Rosenwald (for Plates 14, 22, 26, 27, 37, 38); and the Tate Gallery, London (for Plates 8, 28, 39–45, 55, 57, 64).

Lastly, I give heartfelt thanks to the two eager and conscientious typists who helped me prepare this manuscript, Barbara Epmeier and, especially, Evelyn Barnes, and to Jeanne Kennedy, who prepared the index.

Introduction

This study of Blake's visual-verbal art will focus upon the development of form in his work, both as a philosophical concept and as a stylistic principle. I have chosen to emphasize this aspect of Blake's art, which has not been previously examined at length, because the functions and purposes of form came to pose a critical problem for Blake's thought and art. I hope to show that in 1795, Blake was simultaneously rejecting as a Urizenic tyranny the outline or "bound or outward circumference" which reason and the human body impose upon man's potential divinity and at the same time creating a visual art that relied almost exclusively upon outline and tectonic means. This contradiction, which calls into question the nature and value of form, and specifically of the human form, became for Blake a profound philosophical issue, the dilemma of personal salvation itself. How can the individual achieve the divinity of which Blake believed he was capable while bound within a finite, mortal body? Contrarily, how can the divine artistic imagination survive and manifest itself in the mortal world, if not in bounded, perceptible forms? Blake's struggle to resolve these questions will be the subject of these pages.

I have begun my discussion of Blake's composite art with his early poetry, but it may be useful to the reader if I briefly anticipate here my later remarks on Blake's visual art so that the reader may keep Blake's poetic and artistic development simultaneously in mind. Stylistically, Blake's art is a central example of the late eighteenth-century neoclassical idiom known as romantic classicism. Romantic classicism may be defined briefly as an attempt to represent an ideal image, usually the human form, recaptured from heroic human figures depicted in classical sculpture and Greek vase painting. To depict this ideal image, romantic classicism developed a style consisting of outline drawings or engravings of the human figure, usually nude or clothed in clinging draperies, and placed in an abstract, timeless setting. This emphasis on strong contours and linear rhythms entailed a de-emphasis, even an elimination, of plastic modelling, illusionistic shading, strong coloring or chiaroscuro, and real-istic environments. Blake's artistic practice, as we shall see, reflects an enthusiastic commitment to both the theory and the practice of such a neoclassical idiom, a style of pure outline drawing most widely known to art historians, perhaps, in John Flaxman's illustrations to classical au-thors. For Blake, as for his mentors—Flaxman, Fuseli, Cumberland, even Michelangelo—visual style is above all a matter of outline, of an image realized almost entirely through a strong, clear, bounding line.

When Blake published his first illuminated poetry in 1789 with the hope of achieving commercial success as a book-maker, he adopted for his purposes both the example of medieval illuminated manuscripts and the popular book-illustrating style of Thomas Stothard. Nonetheless, Blake's neoclassical orientation remains apparent in the sharpened out-lines, careful framing and closed or tectonic compositions of the designs for *Songs of Innocence.* The visual emphasis upon closure and a bounding line is paralleled in the philosophical content and metrical structure of these songs. Both visually and poetically, these lyrics present a closed or self-sufficient religious vision in which God is man and man is, at least potentially, divine.

Between 1790 and 1795, however, Blake's poetic vision and philosoph-ical principles came into conflict with his visual style. Philosophically, he began to question the social and political implications of a commitment to a self-sufficient religious vision. Since this closed vision had been visu-ally associated with the framed compositions and bounding lines of

Blake's early art, this also brought into question the nature and value of outline. Blake explicitly identified this bounding line with reason in *The Marriage of Heaven and Hell* (1793): "Energy is the only life and is from the Body and Reason is the bound or outward circumference of Energy." While still using strong outlines in his art, Blake, in the poems which follow *The Marriage,* mounted an increasingly hostile attack on the activities of reason in eighteenth-century English society; the domination of reason is identified with political tyranny, psychological oppression, sexual frustration, and the stifling of the imagination or "poetic genius." With the failure of the French Revolution to liberate French and English society, Blake grew pessimistic. In 1795, he depicted the material world and the mortal human body as the domain of Urizen, the tyrant reason. Blake's poetic denunciation of both the physical human body and of the bounding line or enclosed form as the work of an oppressive reason thus conflicted directly with his artistic reliance upon strong outlines and the human figure. Despite his philosophical questionings, Blake remained artistically committed to the conventions of romantic classicism, as the Tate Gallery color prints and the famous designs of the *Ancient of Days* and *Albion Rose* show. The conflict between his philosophical theory and artistic practice, between his philosophical rejection of the human body and his aesthetic glorification of the human figure, posed a profound problem for Blake. The concluding chapters of this book will attempt to trace Blake's poetic and artistic solutions to this problem.

A Note on Methodology

In writing this book, I have made three basic methodological assumptions. I have followed David Erdman, Morton Paley, and Sir Anthony Blunt in taking a chronological approach to Blake's poetry and art.[1] Unlike Robert Gleckner, who argues that Blake's verses must be read not only as individual poems but also as "contributions to the formulation of a system upon which their *full* meaning largely depends," [2] and Northrop Frye, who claims that the "main outlines" of Blake's personal mythic system were "in his mind from a very early age" [3] and that "anything admitted to [Blake's] canon, whatever its date, not only belongs in a unified scheme but is in accord with a permanent structure of ideas," [4] I believe that Blake's thought and symbols changed, developed, and even contradicted themselves in the course of his sixty-nine years. Blake was, after all, a human being, subject to the same changes of heart and mind that plague and enrich us all.

1. David Erdman, *Blake: Prophet Against Empire,* rev. ed. (Garden City, N.Y., 1969); Morton Paley, *Energy and the Imagination* (Oxford, 1970); Sir Anthony Blunt, *The Art of William Blake* (New York, 1959).

2. Robert Gleckner, *The Piper and the Bard* (Detroit, 1959), p. 34, his italics.

3. Northrop Frye, *Fearful Symmetry* (Princeton, 1947; second edition, Boston, 1962), p. 182.

4. *Ibid.,* p. 14.

xix

In studying the development of form in Blake's work, I have further assumed that the poetry and art are integrally related, sometimes illustratively, often contrapuntally, but always conceptually. I have tried to move beyond Northrop Frye's introductory essay and Jean Hagstrum's analysis of Blake's composite art in relation to the "ut pictura poesis" tradition to show that Blake's art not only serves as border, background color, illustrative scene, visualized metaphor and semantic illumination for his poetry, [5] but is also a *formal* unity with the poetry. Although I have had to separate my discussions of Blake's poetic form and verbal subtleties from my discussions of the development of his artistic style for the purposes of critical analysis, I have tried to show throughout that Blake's designs and text cannot be understood independently of each other. The compositional form of a design, whether tectonic (closed) or atectonic (open), is its philosophical meaning, or at least the boundaries within which its meaning must be defined. [6] The important theoretical work of Rudolph Arnheim and E. H. Gombrich has persuaded me that visual artists unconsciously or consciously structure their perceptions of the external world in terms of compositional configurations or forms. [7] Numerous studies of artists'

5. Northrop Frye, "Poetry and Design in William Blake," *Journal of Aesthetics and Art Criticism* 10 (September 1951):35–42; Jean Hagstrum, *William Blake, Poet and Painter* (Chicago, 1964), see especially pp. 3–18.

6. The terms 'open' and 'closed' form are taken from Heinrich Wölfflin's classic *Principles of Art History* (tr. M. D. Hottinger, London, 1932; New York: Dover Books, 7th ed., n.d.): "What is meant [by closed form] is a style of composition which, with more or less tectonic means, makes of the picture a self-contained entity, pointing everywhere back to itself, while, conversely, the style of open form everywhere points out beyond itself and purposely looks limitless, although, of course, secret limits continue to exist, and make it possible for the picture to be self-contained in the aesthetic sense" (p. 124). Wölfflin goes on to describe a tectonic composition as one that is perfectly balanced around a central axis, in which horizontal and vertical directions dominate the picture, and where edge lines and corner angles are felt to bind, frame and re-echo the composition (p. 125). In contrast, the atectonic composition is usually based on a diagonal thrust that negates or at least obscures the rectangularity of the picture space (p. 126).

7. Rudolph Arnheim argues for this view in his study of art in relation to gestalt psychology, *Art and Visual Perception* (Berkeley and Los Angeles, 1954). As Arnheim summarizes on page 64, "In the arts, . . . the elementary form patterns carry the core of meaning." E. H. Gombrich also argues that the artist's visual perception is based not so much on his perception of the "real world" as on his exploration of what Gombrich calls "the language of art" or style, a learned "system of schemata" or vocabulary of forms and images inherited from previous artists (in *Art and Illusion: A Study in the Psychology of Pictorial Representation*, 2d ed. re-set, New York, 1961,

preparatory drawings seem to confirm this: the artist first sketches out
the basic pattern, or "geometry," of a design, then fills in the minute
particulars as he works on the finished picture. When Blake moves from
the severely closed forms of the *Songs of Innocence* designs to the more
open forms of some of *The Marriage of Heaven and Hell* designs, he is
making a fundamental philosophical statement about his perception of
the relation of Innocence to Energy. More minutely, Blake's choice of
script for the title pages, first of *Songs of Innocence* and then of *Songs
of Experience,* in itself contains Blake's general attitude to these two
"Contrary States of the Human Soul." The word "Experience" is set in
hard, block, Roman, capital letters like prison bars across the page; the
word "Innocence" is written in a flowing script, with a small piper leaning against the "I." Although both type sets are closed and regular, the
state of Innocence contains far more freedom and playful exuberance than
the state of Experience. Even more importantly, the word "songs" on both
title pages bursts into arabesques of flames or flower stems. In both of
these closed worlds, artistic creation can expand and enrich the human
mind.

Finally, I have assumed that the meaning of individual figures, objects,
or gestures within a design depends first on the general geometry or composition of the picture, second on the iconography present in the picture,
and third on the recurrence of similar gestures in other designs. Here, it
has been useful to me to distinguish between the content and the configuration of Blake's designs, between what Erwin Panofsky has called the

---

pp. 53–58, 76–78). Gombrich summarizes his influential theory that "All art origi-
nates in the human mind, in our reactions to the world rather than in the visible
world itself . . ." (p. 76) in his discussion of the nature of caricatures:
"All artistic discoveries are discoveries not of likenesses but of equivalences which enable us to see reality in terms of an image and an image in terms of reality. And this
equivalence never rests on the likeness of elements so much as on the identity of responses to certain relationships. We respond to a white blob on the black silhouette of
a jug as if it were a highlight; we respond to the pear with these crisscross lines as if
it were Louis Philippe's head" (p. 345).
Gombrich here implies that the arrangement and construction of the basic forms, images, or relationships of dark and light or of line and space in a work of art take pre-
cedence over its iconography in determining our primary responses to and comprehension of the content or significance of the work. It is in this sense that I am arguing
that form is meaning in a work of visual art.

iconography [8]—the artist's systematic use of certain objects as symbols (in Blake's art, for instance, within a certain chronological period of his development, such objects as books, chains, nets, webs, crowns, and compasses are all symbols of Urizenic reason or the oppressions of the female will)—and artistic motifs, the repetition of configurations or gestures which are determined primarily by the geometry or composition of the design, but which may take on a symbolic meaning from their iconographic environment. Once the identity of, say, Urizen has been established by his iconographic accoutrements (book, crown, net, and so forth), one might also argue that his particular gesture—crouching down, crawling, spreading his arms over a prostrate figure—further exemplifies his closed or oppressive mind. I have come to believe that the geometry and the iconographic elements of a design are more reliable guides to its meaning than its repetition of human gestures from other designs. An artist as obsessed with the human form as Blake was is necessarily limited to an anatomically permissible vocabulary of gestures (although Blake used every available stylistic device of contortion and elongation to expand this vocabulary to its utmost). It is on the basis of this chronological approach and this art historical methodology that I have attempted to describe the "meaning" or iconology of Blake's composite, visual-verbal art and to define his changing attitudes to the value and function of form, and particularly of the human form, both in his own art and in life itself.

Some closing remarks on notation: since the pagination, the coloring, and even the details of Blake's designs differ in the various copies of Blake's illuminated books, I have tried to note the particular copy I am describing in cases where variations occur. The numeration of the copies and of individual plates follows that given in *William Blake's Illuminated Books: A Census,* compiled by Geoffrey Keynes and Edwin Wolf 2nd (New York, 1953). In general, I have followed those copies most accessible to the general reader, the Micro Methods microfilms and the rather more expensive Trianon Press facsimiles (indicated in my text as,

8. Edwin Panofsky clarifies this content/style distinction at length in his introductory chapter to *Studies in Iconology* (Oxford, 1939; rev. ed., New York: Harper and Row, 1962).

respectively, MM and TP).[9] All quotations by Blake are from David
Erdman's *The Poetry and Prose of William Blake* ([Garden City, 1965];
cited in my text as E). The plates reproduced in this volume are cited in
bracketed, italicized, Arabic numerals.

9. The limited editions of Blake's illuminated poems published for the Blake
Trust by the Trianon Press are available from Bernard Quaritch's of London; the
Micro Methods microfilms are available from Micro Methods Limited, Bradford Road,
East Ardsley, Wakefield, Yorkshire, England.

ONE

Innocence: The Closed Form

Innocence, as it is presented in Blake's *Songs of Innocence* and in his earlier poems and tracts, is a self-contained religious vision which sees God as man and man as, at least potentially, divine. To live in Innocence is to know that God resides both within oneself and without, that every living thing is holy, and that heaven and earth are potentially one. In these early works, Blake accepts and builds on the Antinomian interpretation of the New Testament, the Pauline doctrine that faith can achieve a new realization of Christ's vision in an age of love and spiritual liberty when God is in man. The *Songs of Innocence* (1789) depict such a new age, a time when God is manifest in man and the natural, spontaneous acts of man instinctively create a world of love and freedom in which the seeming evils of climate, disease, and death are rendered painless by the inner strength of faith. The conviction that man has become divine thus guarantees for the man of Innocence an intellectual and psychological security, a spiritual condition of liberty, love, and peace. This radical immanental Christianity, as Blake presents it in his early songs and tracts, is not a limited or necessarily naïve view of the world; rather, it is the moral basis upon which any radical reconstruction of society must

build. As David Erdman says, the social purpose of the *Songs of Innocence* is to create the "foundations of an imaginatively organized and
truly happy prosperity." [1]

In the sense that Blake's vision of Innocence looks toward the realization of an idyllic, unchanging, and self-sufficient society in which man's
spiritual needs are completely satisfied, the vision itself constitutes a closed
world. Its closed and self-sufficient nature means, of course, that aspects of
the "real" world, of eighteenth-century English life as Blake knew it, have
been excluded. This exclusion need not mean that the spiritual message of
the *Songs of Innocence* is either untrue or inadequate as a religious faith.
However, it does arouse a feeling of tension in the reader: how are we to
relate, how did Blake himself relate, to this closed or self-sustaining vision? I think that Blake resolves this tension in two ways: first by providing an image of human divinity to which one can whole-heartedly assent;
second by showing how such an image may be realized on earth, in English society.

In detailing the artistic and poetic means with which Blake constructs
the closed world of Innocence, I shall refrain from discussing Innocence in
relation to Blake's concept of Experience until later chapters. The *Songs
of Innocence* were printed in 1789, five years before the combined *Songs
of Innocence and of Experience* appeared in 1794; and even after 1794,
Blake continued to issue *Songs of Innocence* as a separate book, although
as far as we know he never issued *Songs of Experience* independently.[2]
This suggests that Blake wished his readers to consider Innocence in its
own terms, apart from *Songs of Experience*. And since other critics have
very ably defined the role of Innocence within Blake's mature system,[3] I
shall approach Blake's work chronologically, focussing first upon the char-

1. Erdman, *Blake: Prophet against Empire,* rev. ed. (Garden City, N.Y., 1969), pp.
126—27.

2. The *Census* of *William Blake's Illuminated Books* (ed. Geoffrey Keynes and
Edwin Wolf 2nd, New York, 1953, p. 11) lists twelve copies (J-U) of *Songs of Innocence* printed separately after 1794. E. D. Hirsch, Jr. has argued forcefully for an independent, chronological reading of the *Songs of Innocence* (in *Innocence and Experience:
An Introduction to Blake,* New Haven and London, 1964, chapter 2).

3. See Northrop Frye, *Fearful Symmetry* (Princeton, 1947), pp. 235—45; Robert F.
Gleckner, *The Piper and the Bard* (Detroit, 1959); and Harold Bloom, *Blake's Apocalypse* (London, 1963), pp. 39—51, among others.

Plate 1. "The Shepherd," from *Songs of Innocence and of Experience,*
Copy B (MM).

acteristics and implications of the closed image of Innocence in his earliest works.

The religious vision of the *Songs of Innocence* draws both on the traditional imagery of the religious pastoral and on the image of innocence as moral virtue presented in Blake's earlier *Poetical Sketches* (1783) to portray an earthly Eden where the innocent man is "the ark of God." [4] In "The Shepherd," the mortal shepherd evokes the heavenly shepherd of Psalm 23. Just as the ewes reply to the "lambs innocent call," so the shepherd responds to the needs of his flock and God answers the prayers of man. And all achieve peace, for "they know when their Shepherd is nigh" (E 7). Here, a spiritual fusion of man and God is implied both in the inclusive pronoun ("they" can include lambs, ewes, and mortal shepherd) and in the capitalization of shepherd (which thus includes both the mortal and the divine shepherd). Suggestively, a large, brightly colored bird, possibly a bird of paradise, flies above the shepherd in the upper left hand corner [*Plate 1*]. A similar fusion of lamb-child-piper-Christ, of man and God, occurs in "The Lamb" [*Plate 2*]. The lamb's "clothing of delight" and "tender voice" can also belong to the child; and both can be seen as the creation of the God who became both child and lamb. Again, the ambiguity of the pronoun reference seems calculated: "We [piper or child or animal?] are called by his name." Indeed, such an ideal fusion of animal, man, and God in a world without divisions seems presupposed by the structure of the poem: the poem itself is a rhetorical question, a closed question that demands the answer contained in the second stanza. The closed form of the poem, a catechistic question and answer, implies that the universe in which such a dialogue could take place is also closed; in other words, the world of Innocence includes all that one need know of man's relation to God. Blake's design emphasizes this sense of completeness: two trees with spreading branches intertwine around and between the stanzas to frame the entire pastoral scene of lamb and child into a single unit.

This idyllic world of Innocence is limited neither to children nor to

4. Compare Blake's 1789 annotation to Lavater's 533rd aphorism: "man is the ark of God the mercy seat is above upon the ark cherubim guard it on either side & in the midst is the holy law" (E 585). E. D. Hirsch, Jr. has discussed the nature of Innocence in the *Poetical Sketches* (*Innocence and Experience*, pp. 23–24).

Plate 2. "The Lamb," from *Songs of Innocence and of Experience,* Copy B(MM).

childish pleasures. That adults can and should share the joys of Innocence is implicit in both the texts and the designs of these songs. In "The Ecchoing Green," Old John actively participates in the joys of the girls and boys; although he is now too old to run and leap across the green, he feels such intense pleasure as he watches the children that he "does laugh away care" (E 8).[5] Throughout these designs, adults join in the children's pleasures: the mother watches or listens to the two children on the title page; fashionably dressed young men and women sing the "Laughing Song"; and the piper who actually creates these songs and brings the glad tidings of man's potential divinity is fully grown in the frontispiece. Nor are the pleasures of Innocence limited to those of a child. Sexual delights are implicitly celebrated in these songs, I believe. The infant whose very essence is a happiness which its mother shares is itself created by a previous joy, the sexual act itself. This fusion of emotional and sexual pleasure is further suggested by the design for "Infant Joy": the mother-Madonna shows the child-Christ to a Psyche-winged girl-soul within the petals of a large, vibrantly red flower. Both the form of the petals, curving flame-shaped points, and the vivid red of the blossom suggest the red rose of fiery passion and imply that this child, this embodiment of essential joy, is the fruit of sexual ecstasy.[6] More speculatively, I would argue that natural procreation and growth are again associated with human sexuality in "The Blossom." Here the "happy blossom" is both the flower that gladly comforts the sparrow and the robin and also the lovely winged maiden pictured in the design. The "happy blossom" greets the sparrow and the robin who, I would like to suggest tentatively, might be seen metaphorically as her two lovers. The sparrow has traditionally been associated with

---

5. For an application of a systematic approach to "The Ecchoing Green" which leads to a very different reading of the condition of Old John, see Robert Gleckner, *The Piper and the Bard*, pp. 92–93.

6. Joseph Wicksteed also associated the red blossom with the opened womb of the mother, although he saw the child as not yet born but only two days past conception. The fact that the second speaker (the mother) can see the child's smile (l. 10) would seem to contradict Wicksteed's interpretation; *Blake's Innocence and Experience* (New York, 1928), pp. 123–25. Jean Hagstrum also says that "the flame-flower and the pendant bud suggest sexual experience and birth"; *William Blake, Poet and Painter* (Chicago, 1964), p. 6. But see Raymond Lister, *Blake Newsletter* 6 (Summer, 1972), p. 19, for a list of eight copies of "Infant Joy" colored differently.

the phallus and lechery in English literature and slang.[7] In this context, note that the sparrow, "swift as arrow," pierces the blossom's "cradle narrow" (vagina?) and that the robin achieves what may be sexual orgasm, "sobbing sobbing," near her bosom. The happy blossom welcomes not only these natural companions or "lovers" but also the child who is the fruit of these sexual experiences and whom she cradles near her bosom in the design. In the design, the maiden is seated with her child upon tongues of flame shooting out from a column of green or red-gold fire. Some scholars have associated this spreading stalk of fire (which is particularly powerful in Copy AA, MM [8]) with a phallus.[9] The presence of several neoclassical *putti* or "winged loves" upon the flame-tongues may support this association. Finally, in the first design for "The Little Girl Lost," a poem originally published in *Songs of Innocence,* the symbolically seven-year-old lovely Lyca's "sleep" is identified as the embrace of a fully mature woman with her lover. The delights of Innocence seem to be sexual as well as spiritual.

Both the prosody and the illustrations of these songs emphasize the closed, completed nature of Blake's world of Innocence. The songs are carefully constructed, tightly controlled lyrics. Alicia Ostriker has listed the characteristically closed-in aspects of Blake's lyric form: the almost chantlike verbal repetitions, the high frequency of assonance and alliteration, the strong accentual rhythms and short stanza patterns of the nur-

7. The sparrow as an emblem of lechery appears in Chaucer's description of the summoner in the general prologue to *The Canterbury Tales:* "As hoot he was and lecherous as a sparwe" (l. 626) and in Shakespeare's *Measure for Measure,* where Lucio, concerning the seemingly austere Angelo, says "Sparrows must not build in his house-eaves, because they are lecherous" (III, ii, 177–178). That this usage of "sparrow" to signify lechery survived through the nineteenth century is shown in Albert Barrère's and Charles Leland's *A Dictionary of Slang, Jargon, and Cant* (1890) where "sparrow catching" is defined thus: "going out *sparrow catching* is for a girl to go out for the purpose of finding a lover" (1890; Detroit, 1967, p. 281). The more general association of the word "bird" with the phallus is given in the *Dictionary of Slang & Its Analogues, Past and Present,* by John S. Farmer and W. E. Henley, where the fifth meaning for "bird" is cited thus: "(venery)—The *penis*" (rev. ed. [New York, 1966], 1:226).

8. Because the coloring differs markedly from copy to copy, I have usually refrained from suggesting that colors carry symbolic meaning in Blake's designs, unless other textual or iconographic evidence seemed to warrant such a suggestion.

9. Both Irene Chayes and Jean Hagstrum have seen the flame-stalk in "The Blossom" design as phallic (in *Blake's Visionary Forms Dramatic,* p. 231, and *Blake, Poet and Painter,* pp. 79, 82, respectively).

sery rhyme which give a "crooning, hypnotic" effect, and the prevalence of monosyllabic feet, especially at the beginning of a line.[10] The use of short, simple sentence structures (for example, "I have no name.") transforms the single unit of the line into the unit of perception; thus the line as such is "vivid, compact, complete, a moment of vision," [11] wholly self-contained. Further, Blake uses the pause in these lyrics of Innocence to add symmetry to simplicity: the pause in the songs normally divides the line exactly in half. This symmetry is reinforced by the even distribution of stresses, especially in the distichs of the four-beat line. Nonetheless, within this tight, closed, stanzaic world, Blake experimented widely with "more meters than were dreamt of in the current prosodic philosophy." [12] Iambic lines, trochaic lines, and anapestic lines—and ingenious combinations, inversions, and substitutions of all three feet—enabled Blake to achieve tremendous rhythmical complexity and precision within a structurally closed form.

The illustrations further strengthen this image of the world of Innocence as an ideal realization of the infinite or divine within the finite. The setting of these songs is most often portrayed as a pastoral arcadia, as heaven on earth. Trees and vines flourish beside meadows, blue streams, and cottages (as in the designs for "The Lamb" [*Plate 2*] and Copy C.TP, the title page, "The Shepherd" [*Plate 1*], and others); children play on meadows and open fields while parents or nurses watch benevolently ("The Ecchoing Green," Plate 1, and "Nurse's Song"); shepherds watch over their flocks ("The Shepherd" [*Plate 1*]), and the child plays beside the lamb ("The Lamb" [*Plate 2*], "Spring," Plate 2). Night brings not merely wolves but also protecting angels and the helpful glowworm ("Night," "A Dream"), and day is a time for song, dance, feast, and laughter ("Nurse's Song," "The Ecchoing Green," and "Laughing Song").

This conception of an enclosed world under the protection of a kindly guardian or benevolent deity is reinforced by the consistently tectonic constructions and framed forms of these designs.[13] The compositions are clas-

10. Alicia Ostriker, *Vision and Verse in William Blake* (Madison, 1965), pp. 49–54.
11. *Ibid.*, p. 58.
12. *Ibid.*, p. 61.
13. For Heinrich Wölfflin's classic definitions of open and closed form, see my Note on Methodology, footnote 6.

sically balanced, occasionally even symmetrical (e.g. "Laughing Song"). They are carefully framed—luxuriant flames or foliage arch over the top of at least nineteen of these plates (as in the title page, frontispiece, "The Lamb," or "The Ecchoing Green," Plate 1), while the bottom is often defined by a stream ("Introduction," "The Ecchoing Green," Plate 2, both Copy C.TP), a plot of land ("The Shepherd," "Nurse's Song") or a creeping vine or flame ("The Divine Image," "The Blossom"). Vertically, the text is usually framed by foliage, vines, flames, or even a design as complex as the intertwined vine of "Introduction" (a design possibly taken from the Mortuary Roll of Abbot Islip).[14] The sky, when it appears, is filled in with the title, text, birds, stars, moon, flying angels, or flame-like foliage.

The figures and objects in these designs are clearly outlined in a sharply drawn, relief-etched line. Blake significantly changed the popular book-illustration, decorative style of Thomas Stothard and Salomon Gessner [15] which he chose for this first attempt at commercial book-making. Blake imposes on Stothard's pastoral scenes, cherubic children and wraith-like figures consistently sharper contours, more form-revealing clothing, more emphatic linear rhythms and more purely decorative elements such as birds, twining foliage and figures floating in abstract spaces between the text. In these designs, Blake's line not only defines the contours of the human body but also flows through patterns of flames, vines

14. Jean Hagstrum, who bases his interpretation of the designs for the *Songs of Innocence* on their supposedly dialectical or ironic position in Blake's fourfold system, sees their intertwined border motifs as "snaky," destructive vines of Experience; *Blake, Poet and Painter,* pp. 6, 80. This interpolation of the later symbols of Experience into Innocence seems iconographically questionable. The intertwined vines on the borders of "Introduction," *Songs of Innocence,* for instance, may be based on the first design of the Mortuary Roll of Abbot Islip which Blake could have seen either as an art student in the Westminster Abbey Chancery, on exhibition at the Society of Antiquaries in 1784, or in the workshop of James Basire where the Islip roll was engraved between 1784 and 1808 for the Society of Antiquaries publication in 1808. This design pictures the Abbot beneath an arch of intertwining vines strikingly similar to Blake's; the vines blossom into a sunflower labeled *prudentia,* a lily labeled *pietas,* a thistle labeled *sapientia,* and a violet labeled *spes.* The entire design is a tribute to the Abbot's Christian virtue and charity and might have been used by Blake to suggest true medieval Christian virtue and innocence.

15. To compare Blake's style with that of Salomon Gessner, see Gessner's engravings for his *New Idylles,* trans. W. Hooper (London, 1776); for Stothard, see Sir Anthony Blunt, *The Art of William Blake* (New York: Columbia University Press, 1959), pp. 10, 39, 48, and Plates 12b, 17a.

and branches around and between the text, enclosing both text and scene in a single, framed image.

In addition to their tectonic form, the content of these designs also suggests the presence of a realized divinity within a self-sufficient world. Heaven is not distinguished from earth: angels walk openly among men ("Night," Plate 2) and God or the father is at hand to rescue little lost boys ("The Little Boy Found").[16] The source of poetic inspiration is not a transcendent glory or light but a human child in a cloud (frontispiece). God as protector walks the earth both as Christ and as parent-nurse-shepherd: the mother of the little black boy bends toward him with as much love and concern as Christ ("The Little Black Boy," Plates 1 and 2). Throughout the *Songs of Innocence* illustrations, man is the divine image—there is no visual distinction between children on earth and children in heaven, between the mortal shepherd and the divine, between man and God.

It would be a mistake, I think, to take the framed, balanced structure of these lyrics and designs to be Blake's consciously ironic dismissal in 1789 of Innocence as naïve, unrealistic, or "closed-off." [17] Even though three of these songs—"Holy Thursday," "Nurse's Song," and "The Little Boy Lost"—appeared in Blake's earlier satire on eighteenth-century drawing-room society, *An Island in the Moon* (1784), they are not necessarily the butts of Blake's satire. And even though these particular songs are sung by such foolish visitors to Blake's print-shop as Obtuse Angle and Mrs. Nannicantipot as well as by the cynical Quid (who has been

16. In contrast to Thomas E. Connolly and George R. Levine who insist that the adult figure in the design for "The Little Boy Found" is the child's mother ("Pictorial and Poetic Design in Two Songs of Innocence," *PMLA* 87 [May 1967]:263), I would argue that this figure is a deliberate iconographic fusion of Christ (who often appears in Blake's art wearing a long white gown girdled beneath distinctly defined breasts, as in Plate 2 for "The Little Black Boy" or *The Rout of the Rebel Angels*, 1808) and the child's earthly father. As everywhere in these designs, there is no visual distinction between God and man. Cf. John Grant's persuasive refutations of this article in *Blake Newsletter* 1 (October 1, 1967):7–9 and 2 (September 15, 1968):29–32.

17. Harold Bloom has characterized Innocence as a vision of "imaginative incompleteness": "The garden of natural childhood was both vision and illusion, poem and deception" (*Blake's Apocalypse* [Garden City, N.Y., 1963], p. 51). But David Erdman, E. D. Hirsch, Jr., and W. H. Stevenson have argued against an ironic reading of Innocence as a "deception" in the *Songs of Innocence* in *Blake*, pp. 117, 126–30; in *Innocence and Experience*, pp. 3–46, and in *Blake: Annotated English Poets* (London, 1972), p. 53, respectively.

identified with Blake himself [18]), it does not necessarily follow that the songs themselves, like others in the manuscript, are silly, sentimental statements. It is at least possible, as Northrop Frye has argued,[19] that Blake's satire here is directed against the singers and the society they represent and not against the content of these three songs. Perhaps, within *An Island in the Moon,* Blake is using the simplicity, the clarity, and the holy vision of these lyrics of Innocence to satirize the confusion, obscurantism, and rambling nonsense propagated by Obtuse Angle, Mrs. Nannicantipot, Steelyard, Inflammable, and the other members of the Establishment who gathered at Blake's home in 1784. Perhaps the closed form of these lyrics is a calculated attack on the digressive, disordered conversations of this company; and thus Innocence, as it is presented in these songs, is the agent rather than the object of the satire. Certainly in *An Island in the Moon* itself, the singing of these simple songs reduces the garrulous company to silence, perhaps of admiration or personal embarrassment or an even more damning boredom. After Obtuse Angle's rendition of "Holy Thursday," "they all sat silent for a quarter of an hour" (E 453)

18. Erdman, *Blake,* p. 98.

19. Northrop Frye has emphasized the satirical intent of these songs and has seen them as attacks on the world presented in the "Gargantuan nightmare" of *An Island in the Moon (Fearful Symmetry* [Princeton, 1947], pp. 192, 237). While acknowledging Frye's insight, David Erdman still insists that the songs sung by Obtuse and Mrs. Nannicantipot reflect and thereby condemn the limitations of the singers' minds (Erdman, *Blake,* pp. 121–26). Erdman is surely right to emphasize the limitations of Obtuse Angle's overly "roseate," pious view of the orphans singing in St. Paul's as living proof of English society's public benevolence, when the hunger, maltreatment, and desperate loneliness of these orphans were well known; but his conclusion, that their song is only the "trembling cry" described in the "Holy Thursday" of *Songs of Experience,* is not necessarily warranted. Blake could acknowledge the evils of English orphanages and still believe that these children's innocent songs reverberated in "harmonious thunderings the seats of heaven among" (E 13). By sustaining their faith in their own holiness, these children both saved their own souls and implicitly damned "the guardians of the poor" who are spiritually beneath them and often, indeed, their enemies. Blake here satirizes not the innocent faith of the children, but the failure of society to recognize and "cherish" their holiness. Thus, Innocence, in these three lyrics, is the agent rather than the object of satire or irony.

Moreover, Martha England's study of Blake's debt to Samuel Foote's *Tea in the Haymarket* for the structure and content of *An Island in the Moon* implicitly supports a reading of these songs as non-ironic, satirical attacks on society. Noting that Foote's plays usually made room for genuine sentiment within their overall satirical structure, Miss England discusses these three songs as sincere, show-stopping songs of childhood which emphasize an increasing threat *to* Innocence rather than a denunciation of it; "Apprenticeship at the Haymarket?" *Blake's Visionary Forms Dramatic,* ed. D. V. Erdman and J. E. Grant. (Princeton, 1970), pp. 17–18, 23–24.

until Mrs. Nannicantipot, inspired by this song, sings an old favorite of her mother, "Nurse's Song." And after Quid's singing of "The Little Boy Lost," "nobody could sing any longer, till Tilly Lally plucked up a spirit & he sung" (E 454).

Nevertheless, as many critics have rightly pointed out, such poems as "The Chimney Sweeper," "The Little Black Boy," and "Holy Thursday" beg a fundamental question about the relation of Blake's vision of Innocence to the manifest social evils of eighteenth-century England (specifically, to the exploitation of child labor, the blatant racism of the slave trade, and the oppressive treatment of orphans). The question, of course, is whether Innocence as it is presented in the *Songs of Innocence* as a whole can deal effectively with these problems. Or is Innocence necessarily an evasion of such evils and thus both morally irresponsible and psychologically inadequate? Because these three poems acknowledge the existence of such social diseases but do not show how the child's vision of Innocence can cure or eliminate them, some of Blake's critics seem to conclude that he was condemning Innocence as incapable of ending social, political, and even psychological corruption.[20]

I believe this argument distorts both the intention and the effect of the *Songs of Innocence.* It seems unlikely to me that Blake would devote sixteen poems to the thankless task of setting up an elaborate straw man— the vision of Innocence—only to undercut it ironically in three poems. Rather, as the piper (who, as the acknowledged author of these songs, should be identified with Blake himself, especially since he is given Blake's profile and broad forehead in the frontispiece) says in "Introduction," these are "happy songs" which "every child may joy to hear." Both in text and in design, these songs present an ideal, or "divine," image of the child and man of Innocence as he could be, as he is born to be, but not usually as he is. Blake's *Songs of Innocence* should be read as religious prophecies, not as descriptions of beautiful childhood delusions.

The social purpose of these songs, then, is to construct a utopian image of a paradise on earth that shall come into being as soon as all men, individually and communally, realize their potential divinity and affirm that

20. Harold Bloom's discussion of "The Little Black Boy" points toward such a conclusion (*Blake's Apocalypse,* pp. 24, 48–51).

everything that lives is holy, and that the virtues of delight—mercy, pity, and love—can create a heavenly society of mutual trust, harmony, freedom, and peace for all living men, women, and children. Seen in this way, "The Chimney Sweeper," "The Little Black Boy," and "Holy Thursday" do not ironically condemn Innocence as morally or psychologically inadequate; rather, they suggest that Innocence is a religious vision of such power that it can psychologically sustain one even among such acknowledged social atrocities. The moral self-sufficiency of this vision of God as man, then, becomes a source of strength for the physically oppressed. Knowing that you can become God ensures your spiritual security and peace. Little Tom Dacre's dream of a sweep's paradise where "he'd have God for his father & never want joy" (E 10) enables him to endure even the worst afflictions of his job—soot-covered body and lungs, open and festering sores, poor food, long hours, frequent illnesses, and early death. The last two lines of "The Chimney Sweeper" need not be read as upholding the status quo; rather, they celebrate Blake's belief that the consciousness that one is potentially divine can bring joy and peace even to the most oppressed. "Tho the morning was cold, Tom was happy & warm,/So if all do their duty, they need not fear harm" (E 10). "Duty," here, should be read in the broad sense Blake intends in his annotation to Lavater's 539th aphorism. Lavater wrote: "A great woman not imperious, a fair woman not vain, a woman of common talents not jealous, an accomplished woman, who scorns to shine—are four wonders, just great enough to be divided among the four quarters of the globe" (E 585). In 1789, Blake commented on this passage: "Let the men do their duty & the women will be such wonders, the female life lives from the light of the male. see a mans female dependents you know the man" (E 585). Both here and in "The Chimney Sweeper," Blake uses "duty" to mean one's loyalty or commitment to one's capacity for divinity; one's obedience to that inner desire or command which urges us to fulfill, in our individual actions and characters, God's holy will and love.[21]

That Blake was personally committed to this self-fulfilling vision of Innocence in which God is human, man divine, is further supported by his

---

21. Blake uses the word "duty," again in this sense in his final comment on Lavater's *Aphorisms:* "for he who hinders another omits his own duty at the time" (E 590).

unqualified assertions in his prose tracts, *There Is No Natural Religion* and *All Religions Are One;* by the equation of innocence with moral virtue in the earlier *Poetical Sketches;* and by his subsequent affirmations of Innocence in *The Book of Thel* and *Tiriel.* In *There Is No Natural Religion* and *All Religions Are One,* Blake attempted to analyze logically the source and nature of Innocence. Assuming as his starting point Locke's conclusion in *An Essay Concerning Human Understanding* that all our moral beliefs, including our idea of God, are complex ideas made up entirely of the simple ideas we receive from specific physical sensations and reflection upon those sensations, Blake argued clearly that Locke's premise necessitates the conclusion that man's perceptions and desires must then be limited to objects of sense. However, Blake believed that it is a fact that men do desire objects that they have not perceived and do have experiences not caused by external stimuli. This proved to Blake's satisfaction that, in contradiction to Locke's assertion that man has no innate ideas, man does possess an innate spiritual capacity that Blake calls "the Poetic or Prophetic character." In the second series of *There Is No Natural Religion,* Blake continued this strictly logical argument. Since man is "not bounded by [sense] organs or perception," he is capable of knowing "more" than the sum total or "ratio" of what he has already known. If this were not the case, if Locke were correct, then the desire to know more than one has already experienced would be the cry of a mistaken soul. For Locke had argued that all the materials of reason and knowledge are derived wholly from "experience" and that "When the understanding is once stored with these simple ideas, it has the power to repeat, compare, and unite them, even to an almost infinite variety, and so can make at pleasure new complex ideas. But it is not in the power of the most exalted wit or enlarged understanding, by any quickness or variety of thought, to *invent* or *frame* one new simple idea in the mind, not taken in by [sensation]." [22] Blake countered with the argument that, since men do desire to know more than they have experienced and do desire to possess infinite knowledge, they must have some innate idea of the infinite:

22. John Locke, *An Essay Concerning Human Understanding,* in *The English Philosophers from Bacon to Mill,* ed. E. A. Burtt (New York, 1939), pp. 248–9, 253.

VII The desire of Man being Infinite the possession is Infinite & himself Infinite

Application. He who sees the Infinite in all things sees God. He who sees the Ratio only sees himself only.

Therefore God becomes as we are, that we may be as he is. (E 2)

Since Locke had reduced "the many" (complex ideas) to "the few when possess'd" (simple ideas) and had argued that God was a complex idea which could not be directly perceived by the senses,[23] Blake logically concluded that then man could desire the infinite, God, only if he had some innate idea of this infinite. Further, if man desired the infinite without being able to possess it, "despair must be his eternal lot." Since Blake assumed that men do not in fact live in despair, it follows that they must have perceived the infinite both in their own selves and "in all things." As Blake concluded in *All Religions Are One:* "Principle 4. As none by travelling over known lands can find out the unknown. So from already acquired knowledge Man could not acquire more. therefore an universal Poetic Genius exists" (E 2). Innocence, as Blake defined it in these tracts, is the presence of God in man, both as a potential mode of being (I can become God) and as a mode of vision (I see as God sees; I see the infinite in all things).

In his earlier *Poetical Sketches* (1783), Blake frequently equated innocence with the supreme moral virtue. In the lovers' paradise where "Love and harmony combine," the singer finds that "like gentle streams beneath our feet/ Innocence and virtue meet" (E 405). And he greets his maiden "Like as an angel glitt'ring in the sky,/ In times of innocence, and holy joy" where "Each field seems Eden, and each calm retreat;/ Each village seems the haunt of holy feet" (E 407). Although, as E. D. Hirsch, Jr., notes,[24] these early poems seem to associate innocence with the benefits of a conventional moral probity—the maiden who wears innocence "like a rose" also has "honour" on her brows and "the jewel health" on her neck (E 457)—they also anticipate the image of Innocence presented in the *Songs of Innocence:* the image of an inner spiritual vision that transforms the barren external world into an earthly paradise. The "direful monster," winter, is vanquished by a smile from heaven in

23. *Ibid.,* pp. 294–305.   24. Hirsch, *Innocence and Experience,* pp. 23–27.

"To Winter"; and in the "Song by an Old Shepherd," virtue, truth, and innocence are "a winter's gown/ So clad, we'll abide life's pelting storm/ That makes our limbs quake, if our hearts be warm" (E 457). In contrast to the discontented life of the melancholy man in "Contemplation," a wise use of humility and contemplation will lead one out of the "city's smoak" to pastoral plains and silent woods where "true joys descend": ". . . delights blossom around; numberless beauties blow; the green grass springs in joy, and the nimble air kisses the leaves; the brook stretches its arms along the velvet meadow, its silver inhabitants sport and play; the youthful sun joys like a hunter rouzed to the chace; . . . Like a triumph, season follows season, while the airy music fills the world with joyful sounds" (E 433). The ills of nature and society are rendered both bearable and insignificant by the inner light of moral faith and the divine vision. The pale youth in "The Couch of Death," who has sustained his belief in the inner presence of God despite his own sufferings, dies in an ecstasy of vision: "The sorrowful pair lift up their heads, hovering Angels are around them, voices of comfort are heard over the Couch of Death, and the youth breathes out his soul with joy into eternity" (E 433).

Throughout these poems and tracts, Blake is drawing both on the seventeenth-century English Antinomian interpretations of the New Testament [25] and on the Pauline doctrine that faith can create a new age of love and spiritual liberty when God is fully realized *in* man. Although Blake was probably not directly involved in an English Antinomian sect before 1789,[26] he did attend the General Conference of Swedenborgians in London in April, 1789, and it is quite likely that he was influenced by Emanuel Swedenborg's discussion of innocence in his *Heaven and Hell* which Blake read in the 1784 edition, probably in 1787–88. Swedenborg concluded that "it is so appointed, that man, during the time of his infancy, should have the external form of innocence, and when old,

---

25. For a study of Blake's debt to the English Antinomians and to "The Everlasting Gospel" of Joachim of Flora, see A. L. Morton, *The Everlasting Gospel* (London, 1958).

26. The myth that Blake's parents were Swedenborgians has been exploded by David Erdman; "Blake's Early Swedenborgianism: A Twentieth Century Legend," *Comparative Literature* 5 (1953):247.

its internal form" and that insofar "as any angel is in Innocence, so far is he under the divine leadings and influence, and so far in Heaven or, in other words, so far is he principled in goodness and truth." [27] In 1789, when he published his first illuminated poems, the *Songs of Innocence,* Blake was under no compulsion to deny the ultimate value and beauty of "the divine image":

> And all must love the human form,
> In heathen, turk, or jew.
> Where Mercy, Love & Pity dwell
> There God is dwelling too.
>
> (E 13)

Through the comparatively prosperous and peaceful, postwar 1780s, Blake could believe that the closed image of Innocence guaranteed one both the psychological security of knowing that everything that lives is innately holy and a moral stance that spiritually protects one from the corruptions of society even as it implicitly condemns those evils. But under the pressure of the political events of 1789–90, Blake's attitude toward the value of a closed, static vision of a realized human divinity gradually changed.

27. Emanuel Swedenborg, *A Treatise Concerning Heaven and Hell, and of the Wonderful Things Therein, as Heard and Seen* (London, 1784), pp. 163–64.

TWO

Innocence and Experience: Good and Evil Closed Forms

In the poetry written after *Songs of Innocence,* Blake began to acknowledge that a closed form could have negative as well as positive implications. The intuitive faith in their innate holiness successfully protected the chimney-sweep, the little black boy, and the orphans singing in St. Paul's at least from all spiritual harm and sustained their commitment to the practice of the virtues of pity, mercy, and love. But man is capable of creating closed images or myths that deny rather than include the divinity of man. On the one hand, John Locke had argued that the human mind is originally a blank slate (*tabula rasa*) which is then furnished entirely by physical sensations and reflection upon those sensations. On the other hand, the Augustinian (originally Platonic) tradition inherited by the eighteenth-century churches in England conceived of man as divided between two opposing entities: body, or matter; and rational mind, or soul. Augustinian Christianity held as dogma that man is born with original sin and that this inherent moral weakness cannot be rectified through man's own unaided efforts and can never in fact be entirely eliminated.[1]

---

1. For a discussion of Augustinianism in the eighteenth century, see Donald Greene's "Augustinianism and Empiricism: A Note on Eighteenth Century English Intellectual History," *Eighteenth Century Studies* 1 (1967–68):33–68.

At the risk of being absurdly schematic, we might say that the tension between the Lockean and the Augustinian views was resolved in the compromise of a limited or constitutional monarchy. Even so, the authority of
the monarch remained theoretically absolute, as Samuel Johnson powerfully argued in *Taxation No Tyranny,* and this meant that the king was
still potentially a tyrant. It was another side of Locke's thought, his belief
that property is a determining factor in politics, that, together with the
facts of economic power in eighteenth-century England, ensured that the
Crown stood at the apex of a thoroughly hierarchical society. And mean-
while the Augustinian temper of religious and moralistic thinking enforced moral and legal codes that, as Blake saw it, prohibited sexual fulfillment, spontaneous emotional expression, and creative freedom. In *The
Book of Thel* and *Tiriel,* two poems begun in 1789–90 when George
III's first attack of "madness" (or acute porphyria [2]) threatened England's
political stability with the regency crisis, Blake tried to distinguish between the benevolently closed world of Innocence—which realizes the
fusion of God and man—and what he saw as the malevolently closed
world of hierarchism—the vision of man defined by St. Augustine and
Locke and imposed on England by a seemingly tyrannical and lunatic
king,[3] a vision that rigorously denies man's potential divinity and the

2. George III's disease has been diagnosed as acute porphyria, a disorder of the nervous system, by Ida Macalpine and Richard Hunter; *George III and the Mad-Business*
(New York, 1969).
  3. Blake, of course, shared the popular as well as the Whig view of George III as the
stubborn denier of all civil liberties (his ministry had refused to seat John Wilkes as
the member of Parliament from Middlesex and then imprisoned Wilkes in 1768); the
oppressor of national freedom (George III always regarded the American colonists as
ungrateful rebels who should be harshly punished); and the calculating advocate of the
increased "influence" (and even "prerogatives") of the Crown in English politics. Although such eloquent apologists for George III as Lewis Namier and J. H. Plumb have
persuasively acquitted him of "calculated tyranny" (in *Crossroads of Power* [London,
1962], chap. 9 and *The First Four Georges* [London, 1956], chap. 4, respectively),
even Plumb has to admit that the "myth that George III was intent on restoring a
Stuart despotism was not the fabrication of later historians but a widespread belief that
grew out of the conflict with Wilkes and America" (p. 111). For a view of George III
close to Blake's own, one should consult Edmund Burke's *Thoughts on the Causes of
the Present Discontents* (London, 1770), Horace Walpole's *Memoirs of the Reign of
George III* (London, 1894), or W. E. H. Lecky's Whig *History of England in the Eighteenth Century* (New York, 1882). Lecky concludes that George III was "a sovereign of
whom it may be said without exaggeration, that he inflicted more profound and endur-
ing injuries upon his country than any other modern English king. Ignorant, narrow-
minded, and arbitrary, with an unbounded confidence in his own judgment and an ex-

rights of the individual. In both poems, I will argue, self-preservation within the closed world of Innocence is affirmed as the necessary initial response to the onslaught of such oppression. In other words, the child or adult of Blakean Innocence who has become conscious of his own holiness must vigorously reject all physical, intellectual, and psychological attempts to deny his innate goodness and categorically refuse to participate in any act or system of self-repression.

The Book of Thel, engraved in 1789 with the exception of the last plate and motto which were not engraved before 1791,[4] affirms the purpose and value of a life lived in the pastoral arcadia of the *Songs of Innocence.* I believe that the first five plates of this poem celebrate the capacity of the closed and completed vision of Innocence to respond satisfactorily to the human anxieties roused by the mutability of nature, by death, by the loss of the self. Thel's questioning of the world around her serves to examine and expand Blake's image of Innocence by showing that it has the complexity and power to cope with natural as well as spiritual evils and to give order and significance to human life. But the fact that many critics have seen the return of Thel to the Vales of Har on Plate 6 as a sign of Thel's spiritual defeat and of the failure of her Innocence to cope with the adult demands of experience [5] points directly at the obvious ambiguities of the text on Plate 6. Between 1789 and 1791, during the time when he was probably writing and illustrating *Tiriel,*[6] Blake

---

travagant estimate of his prerogative, resolved at all hazards to compel his ministers to adopt his own views, or to undermine them if they refused, he spent a long life in obstinately resisting measures which are now almost universally admitted to have been good, and in supporting measures which are as universally admitted to have been bad" (vol. 3, p. 15). W. R. Fryer has offered new arguments for the Burke/Whig view of George III in "King George III: His Political Character and Conduct, 1760–1784: A New Whig Interpretation," *Renaissance and Modern Studies* 6 (1962):68–99.

4. David Erdman, ed., *The Poetry and Prose of William Blake* (Garden City, N.Y., 1965), p. 713: "A changed style of script [specifically, the direction of the g-seraph] in these two plates shows them to have been etched no earlier than 1791–Plate 6 presumably replacing an earlier version, the Motto perhaps an afterthought."

5. See, for instance, Harold Bloom, *Blake's Apocalypse* (Garden City, N.Y., 1963), pp. 51–62; David Erdman, *Blake: Prophet Against Empire,* rev. ed., (Garden City, N.Y., 1969), pp. 132–37; Northrop Frye, *Fearful Symmetry* (Princeton, 1947), pp. 232–37; and Michael Tolley, "*The Book of Thel* and *Night Thoughts,*" *Bulletin of the New York Public Library* 69 (1965):375–85.

6. G. E. Bentley, Jr., dates *Tiriel* to 1789, although he notes that "none of our evidence would very convincingly contradict a date as much as, perhaps, four years on either side of this one." The fact that the line deleted from *Tiriel* (l. 370) appears in the

became increasingly disturbed by the negative potentialities of a closed vision. Both *Tiriel* and the conclusion of *The Book of Thel* portray the cruelties of an oppressively closed system. And both poems beg the question whether a spiritually enlarging but wholly self-validating closed system may not be impotent to inhibit or destroy such oppression. I shall discuss both *The Book of Thel* and *Tiriel* at some length to show Blake's struggle to separate the valid advantages from the limitations of a self-sufficient religious faith.

The setting of *The Book of Thel* is the pastoral arcadia portrayed in the text and designs of *Songs of Innocence.* It is a harmoniously echoing green world in which nature, animals, children, and adults are all united in a chorus of praise, for "they know when their Shepherd is nigh," both within and without themselves. Thel herself is both the adolescent shepherdess pictured on the title page [*Plate 3*] and the youngest of the daughters of Mne Seraphim. She is the bearer, like all men, of potential divinity, hence the possible reference to the Hebraic gods and the Christian angels in "Mne" (perhaps a deliberate feminization of "Bne") and "Seraphim." Thel is portrayed as a real person, fully fleshed. She is not literally an unborn "soul," [7] who would probably be surrounded by a cloud as is the "soul" of Innocence—the child in a cloud—which inspires the piper on the frontispiece of *Songs of Innocence.* Metaphorically, however, Thel's growth in the poem from a child to a woman is equivalent in significance and creative development to the entrance of the soul into a mortal body. Thel is a maiden of Innocence, living in a world populated by flowers and sheep. The Vales of Har are here pictured as an earthly paradise of blossoming vines, flowers, leafy trees, and fertile gardens. Moreover, Thel's Greek name (thêlo means "I wish," "I will"), coiled

---

motto of Thel actually suggests a dating for *Tiriel* prior, not to 1789 as Bentley argues, but to 1791, the earliest date at which the motto could have been engraved, if Erdman's surmise about Blake's change in the g-seraph is correct; G. E. Bentley, Jr., ed., *Tiriel* (Oxford, 1967), p. 51. David Erdman now supports the date of 1790 (*Blake,* p. 131n.)

7. S. Foster Damon, *William Blake* (Boston, 1924), pp. 75, 310. I am persuaded that Damon has confused the tenor and the vehicle of the metaphor here. As in Wordsworth's "Ode: Intimations of Immortality," the growth of the individual (Thel) from childhood through puberty into adulthood is compared to the passing of an unborn soul from heaven into a mortal body. But whereas Wordsworth portrays this as a fall or descent of the soul, Blake sees it as a process of enrichment and growth.

Plate 3. *The Book of Thel*, Title Page, Copy G(MM).

tresses, and simple, draped robes associate her with the perfect virgin of classical culture.[8] By 1789 Blake was already under the influence of George Cumberland's and John Flaxman's enthusiastic adulation of Greek art and may well have used these Greek motifs in *The Book of Thel* to link the sacred vision of Innocence to their ideal images of antiquity. In style as well, the designs for *Thel* adopt a neoclassical idiom: heroic male nudes appear (e.g. the cloud), clearly outlined and floating in non-illusion-istic spaces.

Thel, however, as the illustrations show, is passing through puberty; she is on the verge of womanhood and has become aware of the changes in her own body and in the world around her, of the mutability of forms. Not knowing what she will become in the future, Thel is aware only of the loss of her present self and laments what she fears is a finished and useless life. Thel has a more complex consciousness than was found in the *Songs of Innocence;* whereas the chimney sweeper sees natural and social evils as inexorable realities, to be borne and overcome by duty and faith, Thel asks why seeming evils exist in the world around her. Throughout the poem, Thel questions the world around her—a world of personified natural objects that radiate an inner spiritual life or holiness. The poem proceeds as a symbolic debate in which Thel's limited child vision of her-self and all transient objects as useless is gradually expanded into a recog-nition of the spiritual value and divine function of these objects. In other words, Thel's questioning of the purpose and meaning of life in the vales of Innocence leads to a deeper understanding and affirmation of the na-ture of Innocence. The closed form of Innocence here proves sufficiently expansive to include the entire cycle of human life, death, and infinity. It may be significant that the weeping-willow branch arching over the title

8. I think Jean Hagstrum wrongly identified Thel as one of the sterile daughters of memory (Mnemosyne), as a symbol of "classical culture and all its attendant and related evils and limitations" (*William Blake, Poet and Painter* [Chicago, 1964], p. 87n), by reading Blake's much later (1820) attacks on Greek art back into his conception of Thel. Certainly, in 1799, and probably earlier, Blake associated Greek forms with the ideal outlines of visionary art, as is evidenced in his letters to Trusler and George Cum-berland in August 1799; *The Complete Writings of William Blake,* ed. Geoffrey Keynes (London: Nonesuch, 1957), pp. 792, 793, 795. For other positive uses of Greek echoes in Blake's early poetry and art, see Kathleen Raine, "Some Sources of *Tiriel,*" *Huntington Library Quarterly* 21 (1957):1–20; and Collins Baker, "The Sources of Blake's Pictorial Expression," *Huntington Library Quarterly* 4 (1940–41):362.

on the title page [*Plate 3*] resembles a rounded tombstone engraved with Thel's name. Standing before it, Thel can see her future only as the death of her body and self. But Thel's error is already hinted in the fact that the willow is a living tree, not an inanimate stone. Thel's seeming grave plot will eventually be revealed as the entrance into a larger, more abundant life, as the flying figures and exuberant red blossoms blooming at its foot suggest.

Thel first laments the transiency of nature, asking "why fades the lotus of the water?" and compares herself to a "parting cloud." Since she can neither escape nor see beyond her present bodily form, she reconciles herself to a gentle "sleep of death." (Thel's sense of a threat to her life may be illustrated by the eagle who hovers over the tiny figures of leaping male, mother and child, reclining male, and warrior with shield and sword at the top of Plate 2. Significantly, however, these figures are not frightened or disturbed by the eagle; indeed the upper left male figure seems almost to welcome it.) But the lotus of the waters—the lily who identifies herself as "a watry weed"—gives the first answer to Thel's despair. Although her life is brief, she lives in joy, "clothed in light, and fed with morning manna," and when she fades away, she goes to "flourish in eternal vales" (E 3-4). Her death is only a metamorphosis; she exchanges one form for another. This lily, who is personified in the design for Plate 3 (Copy G, MM), as a beautiful woman, robed in white, who hovers like a lily blossom over the green leaves of the lily stalk, joyfully accepts both life and death, for she lives under the hand of the God who "walks in the valley." Like the child of the "Introduction" to *Songs of Innocence,* she "smild in tears." And Thel sees that the lily, no matter how brief her life, does perform a valuable service: her perfume revives the milked cow, her wine purifies the bees' honey, and her flowers nourish the innocent lamb.

But Thel still sees no purpose to her own life and compares herself to "a faint cloud kindled at the rising sun" that vanishes without a trace. Immediately, the cloud appears as the handsome male "bright form" with opened arms pictured on Plate 4 [*Plate 4*] and possibly also on the title page [*Plate 3*] and on Plate 2 in the upper left corner. He reiterates the twofold answer of the lily. He tells Thel that the creatures of the air are nourished by his substance and that when he vanishes, "It is to tenfold

III.

Then Thel astonish'd view'd the Worm upon its dewy bed.

Art thou a Worm? image of weakness. art thou but a Worm?
I see thee like an infant wrapped in the Lillys leaf:
Ah weep not little voice, thou canst not speak. but thou canst weep;
Is this a Worm? I see thee lay helpless & naked : weeping,
And none to answer, none to cherish thee with mothers smiles.

The Clod of Clay heard the Worms voice, & raisd her pitying head;
She bowd over the weeping infant. and her life exhald
In milky fondness. then on Thel she fixd her humble eyes.

O beauty of the vales of Har. we live not for ourselves.
Thou seest me the meanest thing, and so I am indeed;
My bosom of itself is cold. and of itself is dark,

But

Plate 4. *The Book of Thel*, Plate 4, Copy G(MM).

life, to love, to peace and raptures holy." He metamorphoses, first, into the "light wings" of blue-white vapor pictured on Plate 4 [*Plate 4*] and then blends, "link'd in a golden band," with the "fair eyed" dew, and both bear food to the flowers. Not only does the cloud, throughout his natural cycle, have an essential role in the nourishment and preservation of nature, but he also experiences in the fulfillment of this function the total delight and ecstasy of sexual union. This implication is sharpened by the possible personifications of the cloud and the dew as the boy seizing the girl on the title page [*Plate 3*]. That these figures might be the cloud and the dew is supported both by the fact that the boy's position is a mirror image of the cloud's on Plate 4 and by the fact that they emerge from two large red blossoms. These figures thus may be the cloud and the dew who, having linked themselves in love and marriage, bear food to all their "tender flowers."

Thel, however, still sees no purpose in her own life, and utters her last lament: "And all shall say, without a use this shining woman liv'd/ Or did she only live. to be at death the food of worms." Again, her vision of the world is expanded, for the cloud replies:

> Then if thou art the food of worms. O virgin of the skies,
> How great thy use. how great thy blessing; every thing that lives,
> Lives not alone, nor for itself. . . .

> (E 5)

The illustration reveals Thel's enlarged vision, for the worm summoned before her astonished eyes and open arms on Plate 4 [*Plate 4*] is a tiny child, "wrapped in the Lillys leaf." Thel begins to recognize her given role; she is to care for another rather than herself, and to "feed" this worm. Rejecting her earlier despair, Thel articulates her new knowledge:

> . . . Alas! I knew not this, and therefore did I weep:
> That God would love a Worm I knew, and punish the evil foot
> That wilful, bruis'd its helpless form: but that he cherish'd it
> With milk and oil. I never knew; and therefore did I weep. . . .

> (E 5)

Anticipating Thel's ultimate function, the clod of clay protectively reaches toward the worm-baby and tells Thel that "we live not for ourselves." The illustration for Plate 5 shows Thel seated behind the clod and the worm. The clod, personified as a lovely, naked woman (the mature woman and mother Thel is to become) lies beside the worm (pictured as a naked human baby), tenderly hovering beside it, ready to answer the child's every call. Thel has learned that in the world of Innocence, everything is loved and cherished and everything has a unique and worthwhile function. In this sense, *The Book of Thel* repeats Blake's contemporaneous annotation to Lavater's 630th aphorism:

It is the God in *all* that is our companion & friend, for our God himself says, you are my brother, my sister & my mother . . .

God is in the lowest effects as well as in the highest causes for he is become a worm that he may nourish the weak

For let it be remembered that . . . everything on earth is the word of God & in its essence is God. (E 588–9)

With this knowledge, Thel is prepared to enter the future, to die from childhood and be born into womanhood. The clod opens her "house," promising Thel that " 'tis given thee to enter, / And to return." Thel can face both the future and death, secure in the belief of Innocence that every creature on earth is holy; that man's purpose on earth is to reproduce, nourish, and love every creature; and that beyond earth and life is a greater peace in heaven. This, at least, would seem to be the implication of the poem if the 1789 version ended with Plate 5: that the closed vision of Innocence, emphasized by the consistently tectonic designs and by the enclosing weeping willow framing the title page [*Plate 3*], is large enough to include heaven and earth; the natural cycles of plants, animals, and elements; and all the metamorphoses of the human body in a single vision of a universal divinity.

I suspect that the final plate Blake added or would have added to the poem in 1789 was very different from the Plate 6 we now have. Responding to David Erdman's suggestion that the original ending of *Thel* might have been an "Innocence" version,[9] I would speculate that in 1789, Blake

9. I find myself agreeing with Erdman's "unverifiable" hypothesis about *Thel:* "In dates of etching (and presumably of composition) the last plate and the Motto are quite certainly of a later time than the rest of the poem. The last plate must have replaced an earlier plate or plates, something hardly to have been undertaken unless some important change was involved. Question: What was the original *Thel* like, i.e., how did it end? Mightn't it have been an 'Innocence' version, the new ending producing an 'Experience' version—and the Motto made for the latter?" *Blake Newsletter* 2 (September 15, 1968):24. I will deal with the implications of this change for the entire poem later.

might well have presented Thel entering her grave plot under the clod's guidance. There she would find the maggots or worm-babies whom she had been led to expect and would eagerly give her body (first the milk of her breast and then her entire body) to feed and nourish this life cycle. In this process, she would also experience the ecstasy of sexual union with a lover, to whom she would also give her body freely and joyously, just as Oothoon later offers her body and soul "of sweet delight" to Theotormon. As lover and mother, Thel would find herself "link'd in a golden band" both with the regenerative earth and with the God who "walks in the valley" and would thus discover the joy and peace of her older sisters. She would then return to the Vales of Har, prepared for sexual experience and an adult Innocence and filled with the conviction that God cherishes her both in life and death.

Between 1789 and 1791, the earliest time he could have engraved the last plate and motto for *The Book of Thel,* I think Blake was working on the unpublished manuscript and drawings of *Tiriel.* In *Tiriel,* a poem that admittedly did not engage Blake's imagination to the highest degree (as is evidenced both in the grotesquely flaccid, pseudo-antique figures of the drawings and in the unfinished and occasionally incoherent plot development and verse), I believe that Blake began to explore the negative aspects of a closed form or vision. The reading of *Tiriel* I wish to offer here, placed in this context of Blake's increasing uncertainty about both the social and the aesthetic implications of a closed form or system, is highly speculative. My emphasis on the positive over the negative aspects of the Vales of Har differs to some degree from previous readings of *Tiriel.* Nonetheless, I offer it here both because this reading seems at least plausible given the text and the designs (I hope my quotations will support this) and because such a reading of *Tiriel* concisely illustrates the transition that I see Blake making from *Songs of Innocence* to *The Marriage of Heaven and Hell.*

In the unpublished manuscript and drawings of *Tiriel,* Blake poses the "cage of Har," or self-sufficient Innocence, against the barren, geometric columns, doors, and pyramids of Tiriel's sterile, academic kingdom of the west.[10] Tiriel's kingdom is both closed in and oppressive. The severe, un-

10. Mary S. Hall and Nancy Bogen have traced the names, behavior, relationships, and groves of Tiriel's "lawless race" and western kingdom to the Cuthites, the Ama-

decorated walls of Tiriel's palace, seen in Drawings 1, 7, and 8, are physical counterparts of the mental walls of Tiriel's mind. Seven years before the poem begins, Tiriel ruled his sons with cruel, malicious laws; two years later, they rebelled in order to return to a time of Innocence. The "eternal delight" of Tiriel's sons is suggested, as G. E. Bentley, Jr. notes, both by their "richly sculptured" houses which appear in the untraced Drawing 9 and by the crowns of bay leaves (the poet's laurels) and vines (the Dionysian celebrant's garland) on two of the sons' heads in Drawing 1.[11] Although Tiriel's curses finally destroy one hundred of his sons, the five years of their freedom, when Tiriel and Myratana were banished to the desert, may have been a period of great pleasure and peace.

Despite his great power to inflict pain and death on his children, Tiriel is destroyed; at the end of the poem, he lies dead at the feet of Har and Heva or, in Drawing 12, at the feet of Hela. The tyranny of Tiriel, the law imposer and accuser, has been razed by its innate corruption and sterility. Tiriel finally recognizes that his repressive reign of deceit, slander, discontent, and despair enslaves not only the ruled but the ruler as well. One law for the lion and the patient ox, he sees, is oppression. He knows now that hypocrisy is "the idiots wisdom" (Bentley, l. 386), that his own curses and restrictive laws have consumed his paradise of the west and transformed his own once beautiful body into "a reptile form / A worm of sixty winters creeping on the dusky ground" (l. 363). Although Tiriel attributes his downfall to Har, whom he condemns as the "mistaken father of a lawless race," we know that he has only himself to blame. Significantly, Blake deleted from Tiriel's statement on page 14 the phrases he would later use for the motto of *Thel* and the questions of the voice of sorrow on Plate 6. This language, as we shall see in both *The Book of Thel* and *Visions of the Daughters of Albion,* becomes the rhetoric of revolution; there, it is used explicitly to condemn all limited forms. But Tiriel is neither revolutionary nor penitent. Although he recognizes

---

zonian tribes of Mauritania in westernmost Africa, and specifically to Cadmus, the Egyptian founder of the oppressive academia at Athens, "a place of exercises and science," as described in Jacob Bryant's *New System* in *"Tiriel:* Blake's Visionary Form Pedantic" and in "A New Look at Blake's *Tiriel,*" *BNYPL* 74 (1970):166–76 and 153–65, respectively.

11. *William Blake, Tiriel: Facsimile and Transcript of the Manuscript, Reproduction of the Drawings, and a Commentary on The Poem,* ed. G. E. Bentley, Jr. (Oxford, 1967), p. 18.

that his hypocrisy has destroyed "the immortal spirit" (l. 387), he remains trapped in his maliciously closed vision and dies cursing Har in "thirsty" serpentine hissings. Such a closed mind, chained to closed palaces and legal systems, here ends by destroying both itself and everything over which it gains power.

The "cage of Har," the alternative to Tiriel's frozen kingdom of the west offered in the poem, is presented more positively. Both in the text and the drawings, the Vales of Har appear as the earthly pastoral Eden of the *Songs of Innocence.* In the drawings, the Valley of Har is a rural meadow, shaded by trees and abundant grapevines and watered by a clear stream in which Har and Heva bathe; in the poem, it is a "pleasant garden" where milk and fruits are plentiful and where birds sing. Further, as G. E. Bentley, Jr. has noted, the names of Har and Heva mean "mountain" (in Hebrew) and "Eve"; [12] Har, like Adam, is the father of all mankind (Mnetha asks, incredulously, "are there then more people/ More human creatures on this earth beside the sons of Har" (ll. 106–7) and Tiriel, having falsely denied filial relationship to Har, hastens to reassure her, "No more . . . but I remain on all this globe"); and the Valley of Har, like Eden, is located geographically to the east of Tiriel's palace in Egypt. Bentley even links the mountain that borders Har's Eden, most clearly marked in Drawing 10, to Mount Pisgah from which Moses saw the Promised Land. [13]

The Valley of Har, both in the poem and the illustrations, resembles the land of Innocence. Har and Heva are like two children—"Playing with flowers & running after birds they spent the day/ And in the night like infants slept delighted with infant dreams" (ll. 60–61). They are two adults who have preserved the vision of Innocence into old age: in the illustrations, they swim happily in the clear stream, play on harps, and sleep peacefully. [14] They are protected both by "he that leadeth all" (l. 56), the divine shepherd who guides Tiriel to Har, and by Mnetha, that memory that preserves the vision of the past and guards against present evils. In Drawing 4, Mnetha is garbed in a richly patterned gown, shiny black slippers, and a checkered headcap which, as G. E. Bentley, Jr. observes, resemble the garb of the benevolent, protecting nurses and mothers

12. *Tiriel,* ed. Bentley, p. 3.   14. Drawings 2, 5, 11, respectively.
13. *Ibid.,* p. 12.

in the designs for the title page of *Songs of Innocence,* "Nurse's Song," and "The Ecchoing Green." [15] Finally, Har and Heva embody the divine love that welcomes and nourishes all life. As Hela knows, Har and Heva never hate or curse others, as Tiriel does, for "they are holy & forgiving filld with loving mercy / Forgetting the offences of their most rebellious children" (ll. 303–4). Their vision of mercy, love, and peace can survive even the curses of Tiriel; by the end of the poem, Tiriel is dead and Hela, in the final drawing, has been freed from the vicious serpents that Tiriel planted upon her brow. Like lovely Lyca in "The Little Girl Lost" (who is also, symbolically, "seven" years old in the text but revealed in the illustrations as a grown woman), Hela has escaped from seven years of slavery in Tiriel's land of death, that dark night in which Lyca too was "lost," into the gentle sleep of Har and Heva, the visionary sleep of innocent love, sensual enjoyment, and peace.

Thus, to follow some critics in condemning Har and Heva out of hand as a timid, senile old couple seems too extreme—they are clearly portrayed in Drawings 2, 6, and 11 as a beautiful young woman with long, flowing hair and a white-haired and bearded but muscular, physically youthful man. Nonetheless, the isolated "pleasant gardens" of Har are clearly under attack in the poem. Har and Heva are too easily frightened: they run "weeping like frighted infants for refuge in Mnethas arms" (l. 64) when the blind Tiriel appears at their gates, although their instinctive revulsion from Tiriel *may* be the proper response to such tyranny. And Tiriel clearly regards Har as a decrepit old man to whom he cannot speak openly lest he destroy both Har and Heva with "joy & grief" (l. 118 *del*). "I am not of this region, said Tiriel dissemblingly / (Fearing to tell them who he was because of the weakness of Har *del*)" (ll. 100–1).

Moreover, the *King Lear* echoes throughout the poem reinforce the identification of Har's great cage with Lear's beautiful but escapist fantasy in Act V, scene iii. Heva urges Tiriel to remain in their happy valley:

> Thou shalt not go said Heva till thou hast seen our singing birds
> And heard Har sing in the great cage & slept upon our fleeces.

(ll. 132–3)

15. *Tiriel,* ed. Bentley, p. 37.

And Lear urges Cordelia:

> . . . Come, let's away to prison:
> We two alone will sing like birds i' the cage:
> When thou dost ask me blessing, I'll kneel down,
> And ask of thee forgiveness; so we'll live,
> And pray, and sing, and tell old tales, and laugh
> At gilded butterflies. . . .

(V, iii, 8–13)

Neither Har's nor Lear's songs can prevent the vicious jungle battles raging around them: Tiriel's hundred children have all been "in their beds . . . cut off in one night" (l. 275); and Cordelia, Lear, Goneril, Regan, Edmund, and Gloucester will all die before the play's "promised end." By the end of *Tiriel,* both the evil closed world of Tiriel's kingdom of "one law" and the good closed world of Har's green gardens have been undermined—the first because of its blatant cruelty and self-destructiveness, the second because of its failure to prevent the tortures of Tiriel. Although Har and Heva welcome all wanderers into their divinely guarded arcadia, although their commitment to a vision of love preserves them, as it preserves the little chimney sweep, from all spiritual harm, they remain "in the great cage" of Har, cut off from the kingdom of the west by "the gate of the lower garden" (l. 351) and Mnetha's "sharp & winged" arrows of death which drive off all enemies. Har and Heva never venture out of their enclosed garden; they in no way try to prevent the tyrannies of Tiriel or to aid his enslaved sons. By withdrawing into an isolated garden of Innocence, Har and Heva permit manifest social evils to continue.

Returning to Plate 6 of *The Book of Thel* with this greater awareness of both the virulent evils of Tiriel's closed kingdom and of Har's inability to prevent them, Blake tried to interpolate into *Thel* his growing conviction that Innocence must both preserve its own integrity and also pit itself directly against the evils of tyrannical lawgivers. The obvious ambiguities of the final plate of *Thel* are the predictable result of Blake's not very successful attempt to fit new conceptual material into an already established but no longer adequate plotline and illustration. (I suspect that the design on Plate 6 was conceived and probably even engraved in 1789; only the text was changed in 1791.) [16]

16. Blake on at least one other occasion changed the text of an already engraved plate over a year after he had completed the original poem. The final four lines etched

The world Thel finds when she accepts the clod's invitation to enter her own grave and 'die' from her present self into her future self is not the adult world of Innocence she had been led to expect; she finds no worms or babies to nourish. Instead, Thel enters the world of Tiriel's kingdom of the west, a world of imprisoning forms, ensnaring roots, dark clouded valleys, and the agonies of the dead and dying. Sitting beside her own grave plot, she hears the voice of her sorrowing future self, lamenting the torments she will suffer if she enters this fallen world. The voice is rhetorically identified with that of the cursing Tiriel, and reflects the agony of a self trapped in the repressive social mores and intellectual absolutism of eighteenth-century England. Tiriel had demanded:

And why men bound beneath the heavens in a reptile form [,]
A worm of sixty winters creeping on the dusky ground [?]
[Some nostrild wide breathing out blood. Some close shut up
[In silent deceit. poisons inhaling from the morning rose
[With daggers hid beneath their lips & poison in their tongue
[Or eyed with little sparks of Hell or with infernal brands
[Flinging flames of discontent & plagues of dark despair
[Or those whose mouths are graves whose teeth the gates of eternal death
[Can wisdom be put in a silver rod or love in a golden bowl
[Is the son of a king warmed without wool or does he cry with a voice
[Of thunder does he look upon the sun & laugh or stretch
[His little hands into the depths of the sea to bring forth
[The deadly cunning of the scaly tribe & spread it to the morning (*bracketed lines deleted individually;* ll. 362–74).

Deleting all but the first two lines of this material because it implies an objection to these situations and thus a change or regeneration in Tiriel's tyrannical personality, Blake reassigned this rhetoric of revulsion to Thel's adult self.

Why cannot the Ear be closed to its own destruction?
Or the glistning Eye to the poison of a smile!
. . . .
Why a Tongue impress'd with honey from every wind?
Why an Ear, a whirlpool fierce to draw creations in?
Why a Nostril wide inhaling terror trembling & affright
Why a tender curb upon the youthful burning boy?
Why a little curtain of flesh on the bed of our desire?
                                                                (E 6)

onto the original copperplate of Plate 2 of *America* were masked over in all subsequent copies but the two latest. For a complete history of this case, see G. E. Bentley, Jr., "The Printing of Blake's *America*," *Studies in Romanticism* 6 (1966):46–57.

These fearful and resentful questions of Thel's voice of sorrow define a world where love is coquetry (the eyelids or lashes are armed to ambush men); where slander, hypocrisy, fear, and lies ("creations") are rampant; and where sex is "curbed." Faced with Tiriel's unnatural world of malice, terror, and repression, so horribly opposed to the sensual delights and overflowing love of Innocence, Thel refuses to participate in its perversions and flees back to the Vales of Har.

Thel's flight has often been interpreted as a sign of her defeat, fear, or spiritual failure.[17] But such a reading denies both the structural development of the poem and the actual poetic and visual imagery of the final plate and the motto. Throughout the poem, the Vales of Har have symbolized a divine and wholly satisfying life, a life of love, responsibility for the helpless, sensual pleasure, and complete emotional security. Thel's descent into her own grave plot signifies her willingness to give up her childish body and self, to enter the future, and to accept the duties as well as the pleasures of a mature woman and mother. Prepared to realize this holy vision of adult Innocence, Thel neither can nor should tolerate the evil and unnatural repressions of this "land of sorrows." Her return to the Vales of Har, then, can be seen as a positive personal action, an action that completes the progression of the plot (from ignorance to knowledge to action) and conforms to the specific textual and visual imagery of the final plate. It is the action the poem itself has led us to expect; remember that the clod's invitation to Thel includes this promise: "Wilt thou O Queen enter my house. 'tis given thee to enter,/ And to return; fear nothing" (E 6). And I believe that the controversial last two lines and particularly the design on Plate 6 can be read as endorsing Thel's return to the Vales of Har. Some critics have assumed that Thel's "shriek" is a pitiful cry of fear or panic in the face of adversity. But Thel's "shriek" may also be an angry and forceful rejection of the evils of the "land of sorrows," a confident rejection that leaves her free to return to the holy life of Innocence. Thel's Greek name suggests that she is a woman of strong desires and will. And in two other instances in which "shriek(s)" appears in Blake's poetry of 1790–93, the word indicates a strong de-

17. But Mary Lynn Johnson has argued that the ending of the poem is possibly ambiguous in "Mne Seraphim, Beulah and *The Book of Thel,*" *JEGP* 69 (1970):258–78.

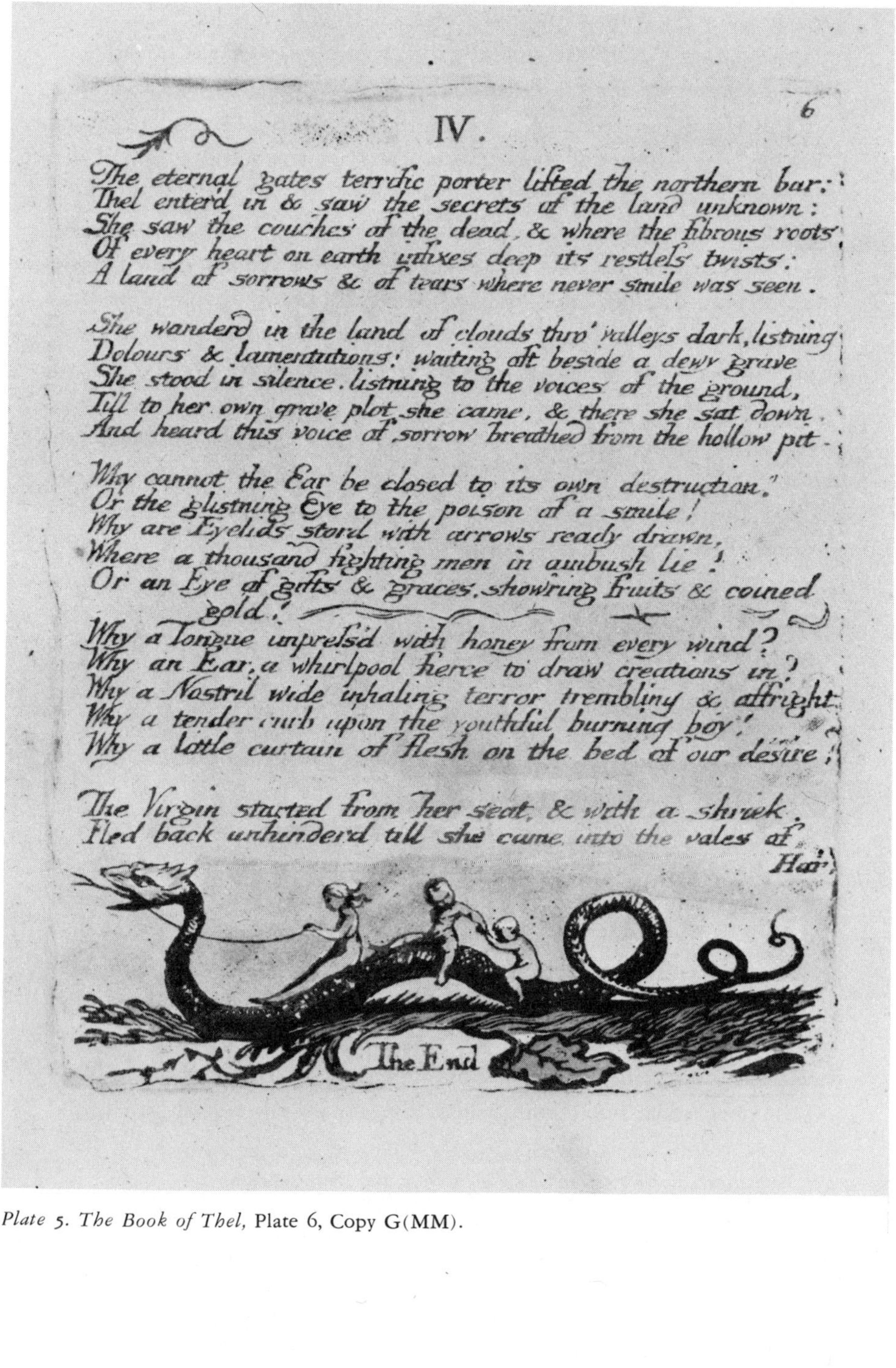

6

IV.

The eternal gates terrific porter lifted the northern bar:
Thel enterd in & saw the secrets of the land unknown:
She saw the couches of the dead, & where the fibrous roots
Of every heart on earth infixes deep its restless twists:
A land of sorrows & of tears where never smile was seen.

She wanderd in the land of clouds thro' valleys dark, listning
Dolours & lamentations: waiting oft beside a dewy grave
She stood in silence. listning to the voices of the ground,
Till to her own grave plot she came, & there she sat down.
And heard this voice of sorrow breathed from the hollow pit.

Why cannot the Ear be closed to its own destruction?
Or the glistning Eye to the poison of a smile!
Why are Eyelids stord with arrows ready drawn,
Where a thousand fighting men in ambush lie!
Or an Eye of gifts & graces, show'ring fruits & coined gold!
Why a Tongue impress'd with honey from every wind?
Why an Ear, a whirlpool fierce to draw creations in?
Why a Nostril wide inhaling terror trembling & affright.
Why a tender curb upon the youthful burning boy!
Why a little curtain of flesh on the bed of our desire?

The Virgin started from her seat, & with a shriek.
Fled back unhinderd till she came into the vales of Har

The End

Plate 5. The Book of Thel, Plate 6, Copy G(MM).

nunciation or rejection of an evil situation. Hela's "shrieks," which "appald the soul of Tiriel," are violent curses that demand Tiriel's death and the annihilation of his kingdom of the west, so that the gentle, loving Har and Heva may reign in peace (E 280). And in a line deleted from "London," the "shrieks of youths" voice the harlot's condemnation of the "marriage hearse" (E 719).

Much more importantly, the illustration on Plate 6 [*Plate 5*] suggests that Thel's shriek is, in effect, an affirmation of what she has learned in the Vales of Har. The final design shows three children—a young girl and two smaller children—gaily riding a large, bridled snake. I take this to be an emblem of the ability of Innocence to bridle or control the evils of the land of death, to overcome the restrictions of Tiriel's kingdom, and to reaffirm the wisdom of Innocence: "every thing that lives,/ Lives not alone, nor for itself" (E 5). This design appears again on Plate 11 of Blake's *America*, where Boston's angel (presumably Samuel Adams) indignantly denounces George III for his tyrannical and hypocritical reign in the names of pity, peace, honesty, and generosity—the very virtues extolled by the lily, the cloud, and the clod. Both in *America* and *The Book of Thel*, this design articulates the moral assumptions—the ethic of Innocence—in terms of which the speaker condemns and then rejects the evils in the world around him.

Thel, then, can be seen as having conquered death by reaffirming life. She has rejected coquetry and sexual restraints by returning to the Vales of Har where she will be a passionate lover like the ardent cloud on the title page and a devoted mother like the clod on Plate 5 and the woman holding her child on Plate 1. (Significantly, all of these female figures, plus the lily and the dew, very closely resemble Thel; in Copy O, TP, they all wear white dresses [except for the naked clod].) The sexual implications of this final illustration have been emphasized by Jean Hagstrum, who tentatively derives the design from a Priapian source and identifies the snake as a phallic symbol.[18] This suggests that Thel will not only reject the notion that sex is sinful; she will eagerly welcome her own sexual

18. Hagstrum, *Blake, Poet and Painter*, p. 89n and Plate XLIXA.

maturity without inhibition. Like her older sisters, the daughters of Mne Seraphim whom Cornelius Agrippa associated with Venus,[19] she will joyfully lead round her "sunny flocks," secure and lovingly productive in the mutable but holy world of Innocence. The evils of Tiriel's kingdom, of the smothering grave plot, can be avoided if one, like Thel, simply refuses (or wills not) to participate in them.

If this interpretation of the conclusion of *The Book of Thel* is at all tenable, then we might read the motto of the poem, which was also engraved after 1790, as a final summation of these themes:

> Does the Eagle know what is in the pit?
> Or wilt thou go ask the Mole:
> Can Wisdom be put in a silver rod?
> Or Love in a golden bowl?

> (E 3)

In this context, the motto suggests that we, like Thel, discover wisdom and love by knowing our own unique being and by appreciating the unique functions and experiences of every other creature. In order to understand the pit (Thel's grave of clay or "land of death"), we must ask not the eagle who soars in the skies (as on Plate 2), but the mole who has explored its depths and darknesses. But we need only *ask*—we need not ourselves participate in such evils. Similarly, Thel, in order to understand her nature and purpose fully, must enter the house of clay and confront the restrictions of Tiriel's kingdom with her own Innocence. Secondly, the motto implies that we learn love and wisdom only by refusing to restrict our conceptions of them, only by rejecting such conventional and limited equations as that of wisdom with the state rod of office or of love with the golden chalice of orthodox Christian ritual. As Blake annotates Swedenborg's *Divine Love and Divine Wisdom* (1788), only "Thought without affection makes a distinction between Love & Wisdom as it does between body & Spirit" (E 593). Love and wisdom are rather the intuition of the holiness of all life: "He who Loves feels Love descend into him & if he

19. Cornelius Agrippa, *Three Books of Occult Philosophy*, trans. John French (London, 1651), p. 243.

has wisdom may perceive it is from the Poetic Genius which is the Lord" (E 592).

Moreover, the structure of the motto, a series of questions, both duplicates Thel's questions and provides an emblematic form for the theme of the poem: one should ask questions that reveal an awareness of the infinite possibilities within the world of Innocence rather than give overly restrictive answers that enclose and thus limit understanding. Thel's return to the Vales of Har can be seen, then, as a "wilful," deliberate rejection of the self-imprisoned, sterile, and destructive way of life found in the "land of death," a land of silver rods and golden bowls, in favor of the potentially infinite wisdom, sexual delight, divine guardianship, and love found in the Vales of Har.

But Thel's return to the Vales of Har, however personally fulfilling for *her,* does not adequately satisfy the social conscience of the average reader. By articulating so vividly the "suffering & distress" of the voice of sorrow and the horribly unnatural perversions of Tiriel's kingdom (which Blake specifically associated with eighteenth-century English society under the rule of a recurrently lunatic King [20]), Blake inevitably arouses the reader's moral indignation. "Such evils must not continue!" the reader cries; and from this point of view, Thel's return is obviously evasive. I think that we can acknowledge the validity of our own socially conscious responses to Thel's return without imposing them on Blake's *original* conception of the poem, however. When Blake began this poem, he was primarily concerned with showing his readers how they could achieve a personal salvation through the divine vision of Innocence, by practicing mercy, pity, and love. But by 1791, Blake, like his modern readers, recognized that a morally responsible Innocence must actively try to destroy the evils of Tiriel's kingdom, lest those evils destroy the very possibility of Innocence. Therefore, in cataloging the evils of the land of sorrows, Blake adopted a rhetoric and tone of moral outrage calculated to arouse protest and rebellion; but since he did not wish to destroy the fine poem he had already written and illustrated, he preserved the conclusion demanded by the

---

20. Both David Erdman and Nancy Bogen have associated Tiriel with George III in, respectively, *Blake,* p. 135 and "A New Look," p. 163.

structure and imagery of his original poem, a conclusion that was in 1791 an inadequate response to the rhetorical demands of the voice of sorrow. In the illuminated poems that followed *Tiriel* and *The Book of Thel,* Blake gradually developed a more open, active version of Innocence, an Innocence that was capable of ending as well as just perceiving and avoiding the evils of psychic and social oppression.

THREE

Energy: The Open Form

Aware of the social limitations of a static, cut-off, and merely self-delighting myth, Blake specified in the poetry written after 1790–91 the steps that Innocence must take in order to sustain its own divinity, to protect others from social and psychological oppression, and to end social evils. To anticipate briefly my argument in this chapter, the man of Innocence must first achieve a conscious realization of his potential divinity, as do the piper, the adults and children of *Songs of Innocence,* and Thel. He must then reject all physical, intellectual, and psychological attempts to deny his innate holiness and categorically refuse to participate in any act of self-repression, as do Thel and, far less aggressively, Har and Heva. Having preserved his faith even in the face of doubt and overt hostility, he must then help others to realize their individual holiness and freedom. Blake depicts many ways in which this last mission can be achieved: by using the rhetoric of satire to expose and denounce "mind-forg'd manacles" (as does the bard of *Songs of Experience*); by asking open questions that reveal the limitations of the listener's understanding (as Oothoon does), by using one's liberated imagination to create aesthetic utopias that will inspire others to rebel against less perfect realities (as does the maker of the tyger); and by leading a political revolution that will destroy the institutions of oppression (as Orc does).

40

To end social evils, a static, closed Innocence must first transform itself into an active, assertive power. I believe that, in *The Marriage of Heaven and Hell* (1790–93), Blake traces this transformation of closed Innocence into that open, active force he calls Energy. Under the attacks of a rationalistic, dualistic, repressive society, argued Blake on the opening plate of this poem, man's innate holiness or Innocence must necessarily become more aggressive in its self-defense. Rintrah, the just man who has now been roused to prophetic wrath, once "kept his course along/The vale of death" (E 33) and sustained his conviction of Innocence in a post-lapsarian, mortal, mutable world.[1] Historically, this was the time when Christ, the new Adam, appeared to fulfill the Old Testament prophecies. But Rintrah has now been driven out of the fertile paradise of the Vales of Har into "barren climes." Deprived of his rightful heritage, the pastoral arcadia that his own faith "planted," Rintrah must now fight back and drive the "sneaking serpent" out of this earthly paradise. Blake identifies this sneaking serpent with the devourer reason who is embodied in the priests of the Christian Church, in the wily Jacob and in all the "lying children" of the godless tribe of Judah, whom Isaiah condemned as "children that will not hear the law of the Lord:/Which say to the seers, See not; and to the prophets, Prophesy not unto us right things, speak unto us smooth things, prophesy deceits" (*Isaiah* 30:9–10). Therefore Rintrah "roars & shakes his fires in the burdened air"; like the warrior from the tribe of Jesse whom Isaiah hailed, Rintrah will lead an army, "roar[ing] like young lions," against these lying children and destroy them with "burning" and "the flame of a devouring fire" (*Isaiah* 5:29, 9:5, 30:30). And, Blake asserts on Plate 3, referring to *Isaiah* 34 and 35, the rebellion of Rintrah against the descendants of the wily Jacob will be successful: "Now is the dominion of Edom [the descendants of Esau, the red-haired man of large appetites (*Genesis* 25:25, 30)][2] & the return of Adam into Paradise" (E 34).

1. I am here accepting the interpretation of the Argument put forth by Morton Paley, *Energy and the Imagination* (Oxford, 1970), pp. 261–62.

2. Although some critics have read "the dominion of Edom" as dominion *over* Edom, Blake is following common English and Biblical usage of the genitive here: dominion *of* in the sense of dominion *by*. Cf. 2 *Chronicles* 21:8: "In his [Jehoram's] days the Edomites revolted from under the dominion of Judah, and made themselves a King." Blake thus links the fate of Hadad and the Edomites who were deprived of their

In this Argument, Blake describes not only the history of western civilization since Jacob deprived Esau of his birthright but also the psychological history of every individual who permits the "mind-forged manacles" of an absolutist reason, an Augustinian conviction of original sin, or a Freudian superego to deny his innate holiness. In order to sustain or restore his psychic integrity, Blake argues, the man of Innocence must learn to fight against all attempts to repress or deny his potential divinity; he must embody the dynamic seeking of "eternal delight," which Blake calls Energy. Both the text and the designs of *The Marriage of Heaven and Hell* suggest that Blake's "Energy" is a more aggressive manifestation of that potential divinity which enables the innocent to perceive themselves and everything that lives as infinite. Four proverbs of hell proclaim the holiness of Energy, whether it be manifested as erotic delight, as a proud vision of the divinity of man, or as sublime or prophetic wrath:

> The pride of the peacock is the glory of God.
> The lust of the goat is the bounty of God.
> The wrath of the lion is the wisdom of God.
> The nakedness of woman is the work of God.
>
> (E 36)

Blake's identification of Innocence and Energy as modes of the same spiritual capacity or power is suggested even more clearly in the repetition of the conclusion of *There Is No Natural Religion* (b)—"Therefore God becomes as we are, that we may be as he is"—in the more emphatic assertions on Plates 11 and 16 of *The Marriage:* "All deities reside in the human breast" (E 37) and "God only Acts & Is, in existing beings or Men" (E 39).

To understand Blake's all-important concept of Energy, we must carefully analyze his central theoretical statements in *The Marriage:*

1. Man has no body distinct from his Soul for that calld Body is a portion of soul discernd by the five Senses, the chief inlets of Soul in this age.
2. Energy is the only life and is from the Body and Reason is the bound or outward circumference of Energy.
3. Energy is Eternal Delight.

---

lands and ruled by the kings of Israel (cf. I *Kings* 11:14–22) with the fate of Rintrah: both will now regain their heritage and dominion (power, rule) since "a new heaven is begun" (E 34).

In other words, Blake conceives of all being as force or power; both the physical and the spiritual realms are manifestations of this spiritual force. What men have been taught to perceive as fixed material bodies are only momentary images of this unbounded spiritual power, images imposed upon it by the limitations of the five senses. Blake's notion of the five senses as framing windows or "narrow chinks in the cavern" which limit the potential infinity of being to bounded, finite sense-data is very similar to Kant's concept of the "categories." Kant argued that the human mind inherently imposes forms or modalities, most notably of time, space, and causality, upon conscious experience and thus receives all its knowledge of the external world preshaped in terms of these categories. If man would expand his five senses, thus cleansing "the doors of perception" and annihilating such restrictive categories, Blake argues, then he would perceive that all so-called bodies are only images of a single spiritual power or soul, images that can be changed at will by the poetic genius or imagination. As Morton Paley has noted, Blake's denial of the dichotomy of soul and body had been anticipated in Joseph Priestley's *Disquisitions Relating to Matter and Spirit* (1777); as Priestley himself recognized, despite his professed materialism, one could equally well conclude from what he had written that all things are from the spirit.[3] And George Berkeley's famous thesis that *"esse is percipi"*, put forth in his *Treatise Concerning the Principles of Human Knowledge* (1710), also paved the way for Blake's assertion that the corporeal world exists only as objects of consciousness, a system of ideas or spiritual forces.

For Blake, this universal power or spirit could and always did move in two contrary or antithetical directions, towards expansion and towards contraction. Blake called the force which moves forward and outward Energy and further argued that this expanding force is "the only life." The word "life" is used here not as a descriptive term but as a value judgment. Blake believed that the self-aggrandizing psychic power which has traditionally been condemned as "sinful desire," the libidinal energy which for Blake as for Freud is "erotic in origin and . . . revolutionary in expression," [4] is the source of all the physical and spiritual experiences that are worth having.

3. Paley, *Energy and the Imagination*, p. 9.   4. *Ibid.*, 10.

Note that not only does Blake assert that Energy is the "only life" but that he also appropriates for this outward-moving power the very name of "energy," a term that by the eighteenth century had acquired positive and even deific connotations in theological and other writings. Energy was a fashionable cultword in the eighteenth century and was used as a term of approbation, albeit with varying meanings. Morton Paley has fully explored its usage during this period:

Energy . . . could have numerous meanings. In *Johnson's Dictionary,* these are divided into four groups. One—"strength of expression; force of signification; spirit; life"—is rhetorical. . . . Energy in this sense was frequently associated with the Longinian sublime, particularly with the language of the Old Testament. Another meaning, "faculty; operation," is the early scientific one, illustrated by John Ray's statement that "Matter, though divided into the subtilest parts, moved swiftly, is senseless and stupid, and makes no approach to vital *energy.*" Still another meaning, "power not exerted in action," may be considered a negative aspect of the definition closest to Blake's own usage: "force, vigour; efficacy; influence." [5]

Blake's concept of Energy clearly exploits the theological usage of the term; in the devotional writings of the seventeenth and eighteenth centuries, energy was often specifically associated with the operations of the divine will and the human soul. Henry More in his *Song of Soul* (1642) spoke of "Energie" as "the operation, efflux, or activity of any being: as the light of the Sunne is the energie of the Sunne, and every phantasm of the soul is the *energie* of the soul." *Johnson's Dictionary* cites other examples of this theological usage from Dryden, Grew, and Thomson (whose poetry Blake read and imitated in his earliest *Poetical Sketches*) as follows:

> Whether with particles of heav'nly fire
> The God of nature did his soul inspire;
> Or earth, but new divided from the sky,
> And pliant still, retain'd th'etherial *energy.*

> (Dryden)

God thinketh with operation infinitely perfect, with an omnipotent as well as an eternal energy.   (Grew)

> What but God!
> Inspiring God! who, boundless spirit all,

5. *Ibid.,* 5.

And unremitting *energy*, pervades,
Adjusts, sustains and agitates the whole.

(Thomson)

And Edward Young, in the *Night Thoughts* which Blake read by 1789 and echoed in *The Book of Thel*,[6] also speaks of the soul as "This particle of Energy divine" (*Night VII*, 824). Capitalizing on these theological usages of energy, Blake attempted rhetorically to persuade his readers that any force or energy directed toward the possession of greater sexual, political, or intellectual freedom is inherently good, even divine. The very word Energy is thus for Blake a term of highest praise, signifying that innate desire to achieve the vision of Innocence and realize the potential divinity inherent in every man.

Opposed to this constantly expanding, "life"-creating, pleasure-providing force of Energy is the contrary power which Blake calls reason. Reason moves inward and backward, seeking to dissect, analyze and catalogue infinite being into fixed, finite bodies, to limit sexual and mental experience, and to restrict the satisfactions and even the demands of Energy. Just as Energy seeks to expand into infinity, so reason seeks to contract to zero. As Blake notes in *The Marriage,* reason would cease to exist if Energy did not provide a counterforce of "ideas" upon which reason can work: "This is shewn in the Gospel [*John* XIV: 16–17], where he [Jesus] prays to the Father to send the comforter or Desire that Reason may have Ideas to build on, the Jehovah of the Bible being no other than he, who dwells in flaming fire" [i.e. Energy] (E 35). At its best, Blake's reason is similar to the Renaissance notion of intuitive reason or apprehension: a divinely inspired consciousness of the potential divinity of man which can be realized through the liberation of Energy. More often, however, Blake's reason manifests itself as discursive reason or comprehension which operates through deductive or inductive processes to establish absolute laws of being, laws which can then be enacted as repressive social codes.

Even though reason is potentially life-annihilating, Blake argues that both these antithetical forces are necessary: "Without Contraries is no

6. Michael Tolley, "*The Book of Thel* and *Night Thoughts*," *Bulletin of the New York Public Library* 69 (1965):375–85.

progression. Attraction and Repulsion, Reason and Energy, Love and Hate, are necessary to Human existence" (E 34). It is clear why reason needs Energy; without Energy, reason would cease to exist. In this sense, reason should regard itself as the servant or possession of Energy, as Blake's genitive suggests: "Reason is the bound or outward circumference *of* Energy" (italics mine). This is the role that reason plays in the *Songs of Innocence*, where questions, arguments, and learning all contribute to an expansion of innocent joy and the awareness of one's potential divinity. See, for examples, the questions in "The Lamb," the children's persuasive argument in "Nurse's Song" that they need not go to bed yet because "the little birds" and sheep are still awake, and the little black boy's learned conviction that he will eventually be loved by the English boy as well as by God.

But just as reason depends upon Energy, so Energy needs reason to survive. Blake recognizes that if his potentially infinite force, the creative activity of Energy, is to be kept in constant expansion, it must be constantly opposed. Only if conflict occurs, if reason relentlessly attempts to circumscribe, rein in, and diminish this potentially infinite Energy, will Energy be stimulated to new creative actions or "progression." As Blake says, "the Prolific [Energy] would cease to be Prolific unless the Devourer [reason] as a sea recieved the excess of his delights" (E 39). Blake's thought is thus dialectic: the thesis, Energy, is inevitably opposed by its antithesis, reason. Significantly, the resultant synthesis of Blake's dialectical process is an intensification of Energy. Thus, although reason serves to sustain the dialectical process, the process itself is an unceasing production of ever new, ever more creative Energy or "eternal delight." As David Erdman says, "Blake's theory admits of a true or necessary Reason as 'the bound or outward circumference of Energy' but leaves it no role in 'life' except to be pushed about." [7]

This dialectic is visually portrayed on the title page of *The Marriage of Heaven and Hell* [*Plate* 6].[8] The thesis, Energy, is imaged in the flames

7. David Erdman, *Blake: Prophet Against Empire*, rev. ed. (Garden City, N.Y., 1969), pp. 178–79.

8. W. J. T. Mitchell has offered a similar reading of this design ("Blake's Composite Art," *Blake's Visionary Forms Dramatic*, ed. David Erdman and John Grant [Princeton, 1970], pp. 63–66).

Plate 6. The Marriage of Heaven and Hell, Title Page, Copy I(MM).

bursting from the lower left corner and in the exuberantly embracing, flying figures everywhere in the lower section of the design. Its antithesis, reason, is imaged in the scene at the top of the design where, under barren, spiky trees, one couple walks side by side while another couple assumes a variation of the courtly love position Blake used in the design for "The Angel": the lady lying on the ground, the imploring lover kneeling beside her. In contrast to the passionate couples pictured below, these couples are not satisfying their sexual desires. The proper synthesis or "marriage" of Energy and reason is pictured, appropriately, in the section of the design devoted to Energy, the lower two-thirds. I believe that the large couple embracing in the lower center of the design represents the marriage of Energy (the woman emerging from the flames at the left) and reason (the man, who is colored darker in Copy D, TP, emerging from the "devouring" clouds at the right). Significantly, the triangular block of clouds in the right corner seems to define and further extend the diagonal upward thrust initiated by the flames; the devouring line of reason thus seems to strengthen rather than repress the control of Energy over the lower design. This suggestion is reinforced in Copy I, MM, where the flames of Energy glow upon the clouds immediately surrounding reason, implying Energy's domination over reason. In seeming to push back these dark clouds, Energy more vividly demonstrates not only its power to control reason but also its capacity to open up infinities of space, a suggestion emphasized by the clear blue, unfathomable sky in the center of the design in Copy I.

There is one other vital function that reason performs in addition to being a stimulus to Energy, a function that Blake's original formulation of reason emphasizes: "Reason is the bound or outward circumference of Energy." Reason is the force that draws a bounding line around Energy and thus makes possible the creation of an artistic image. (Note that Blake is here identifying reason with that very outline or bounding line upon which his neoclassical artistic style primarily depends.) Only when the expanding vector of Energy meets the contracting vector of reason can a stabilizing line be drawn and a form shaped. The *Songs of Innocence* had presented Blake's example of an ideal stabilized image, the "divine image" or manifestation of God in man. But by 1791, with the ever-growing strength of the Antijacobin alliance in England (encouraged by Edmund Burke's *Reflections on the French Revolution*), Blake feared that the force of reason was dominating the force of Energy in English society. The man of Innocence who in 1790 attempted to live within the closed, perfected psychological image of self-divinity would be called "naïve" or "mad" and taught instead that his body is finite and mortal, a corrupting envelope for his immaterial soul. Faced with this murdering dissection, argued Blake in *The Marriage,* the divine image must preserve its integrity by widening its borders, overwhelming all lesser images of man and accepting only those ultimate limits necessary to maintain its identity as an image. In this sense, Energy can be seen as the divine image in the act of expanding, as a development of Innocence.

Blake depicts Energy as a mode of Innocence in the fourth memorable fancy of *The Marriage,* where the angel of reason consigns the devil of Energy to his "eternal lot": a "cataract of blood mixed with fire" in the midst of which appears a "monstrous serpent" or Leviathan with a forehead "divided into streaks of green & purple like those on a tygers forehead" (E 40). The angel's vision of the devil's hell is both a vision of the triumph of Energy (both the serpent and the tyger are positive images of Energy in *The Marriage* and "The Tyger" [9]) and, more importantly, a vision of Innocence. As soon as the angel leaves, the devil finds himself "sitting on a pleasant bank beside a river by moon light hearing a harper" (E 41), back in the pastoral arcadia of the Vales of Har or the land of Innocence. When correctly seen as the devil sees them, the fiery head of Leviathan and the delightful song of the harper are aspects of the same vision of all life as holy; Innocence and Energy are a continuum of divine experience.

This philosophical development from Innocence to Energy in Blake's thought is paralleled by a shift in Blake's artistic and poetic style. Since Energy, the potentially divine force, is constantly expanding, it should present itself only in the most open and fluid of forms. Appropriately, the consistently tectonic, closed forms of the *Songs of Innocence* and *The*

9. "The tygers of wrath are wiser than the horses of instruction" (E 36). I will argue later that both the tyger in "The Tyger" and the vipers on Plate 15 of *The Marriage* symbolize positive aspects of the creative process.

Book of Thel give way to the more open, atectonic forms of the designs for *The Marriage.* Several of these designs defy narrow boundaries. Flames sweep into the lower left of the title page [*Plate 6*] from a source beyond the design, establishing a diagonal thrust that is continued by the dark clouds which seem to be rolling away, past the right edge. The woman flying in diagonally rising flames on Plate 3 stretches her arms wide in a gesture that points beyond the confines of the design; the eagle rising with the viper in his talons on Plate 15 spreads his wings to soar off the plate; and the youth seated on a skull on Plate 21 (Copy I, MM) looks up through the hungry clouds hovering overhead to a visionary sun beyond the design. In contrast, those figures who defy Energy or suffer the domination of reason are confined within tectonic forms. The couples at the top of the title page are enclosed by barren tree trunks and branches; Ugolino and his descendants [*Plate 16*] are symmetrically huddled together in a dark cell; and the crawling body of Nebuchadnezzar forms a rectangular box [*Plate 24*]. Nonetheless, all the designs for *The Marriage* adhere to a neoclassical idiom of clearly outlined human figures set in non-illusionistic spaces.

True to this vision of Energy as an open form, the structure as well as the content of Blake's Energy book, *The Marriage of Heaven and Hell,* scorns the limitations of a closed, rational system. The poetic structure of the work has been compared to Burton's *Anatomy of Melancholy* or Menippean satire,[10] both catch-all structures which, like that of *The Marriage,* defy logical categorization. Here, a parable-argument is followed by comments in both the author's and the devil's voices, followed by a memorable fancy which includes seventy proverbs of hell, followed by a history of religion, another memorable fancy, a prophecy of the millennium, a description of the creative process, an analysis of the nature of God, another memorable fancy, a digression on the achievements of various writers and philosophers, a fourth memorable fancy, and a concluding song of liberty, complete with chorus, all this illustrated by the author. The structure of the poem is open—new material could be inserted at almost any point—and yet the poem sustains a coherent unity. All the material illuminates, by parable or direct statement, the possible relationships

10. Harold Bloom, *Blake's Apocalypse* (Garden City, N.Y., 1963), p. 71.

of the creative imagination, or expanding Energy, to the circumscribing intellect, or reason. Blake has succeeded in creating a new form for his original ideas. As he defined the poetic process in his description of his printing house in hell on Plate 15, the poet/dragon-man, the fire-breathing man of Energy, first burns all the rubbish of old ideas, dead metaphors, stale clichés, and inhibiting conventions out of his head. He then fills his mind with new sensory delights: the "gold, silver & precious stones" brought by the vipers, those sensual pleasures that have been traditionally rejected as satanic or sinful. He then organizes this material into new images through the power of his eagle-imagination, which causes "the inside of the cave [head] to be infinite"; energetically executes these mental images as physical forms, aided by the "Lions of flaming fire," his physical strength and artistic tools; and finally casts them as the "Unnamed form" of this "poem" which men can find on the shelves of their libraries. Since Blake's vision is radically new, its physical form must also be radically new, hence never before named or known.[11]

The prosody as well as the structure of *The Marriage* is completely open. Since Alicia Ostriker has analyzed Blake's prosody at length, let me cite her metrical study of the Argument.

The "Argument" technically resembles, and may have had for inspiration, the freely rhymed choruses of *Samson Agonistes*. The difference is that Milton, attempting to parallel the effects of Greek drama in English, almost certainly was writing according to a set of self-imposed prosodic rules, while Blake almost certainly was trying to escape from rules.

Rintrah roars & shakes his fires in the burdened air;	7	[6]
Hungry clouds swag on the deep.	4	[4]
Once meek, and in a perilous path,	4	[4]
The just man kept his course along	4	[4]
The vale of death.	2	[2]
Roses are planted where thorns grow,	3	[4]
And on the barren heath	3	[3]
Sing the honey bees.	4	[3]

11. I have focused on the psychological aspects of Blake's extended metaphor for the creative process; as David Erdman notes, the metaphor works at the literal level of the techniques of copperplate engraving as well. The cave is the copperplate itself; the "chambers" are the various states of the engraving process. Thus the dragon-man is the

The principle is simple enough. Iambs, with the usual free metrical variations, are arranged in irregular line-lengths (as marked [my own scansions, which differ from Ostriker's, follow hers in brackets]) which correspond to the natural length of phrases. Rhyme is omitted, and the poem's melody depends altogether on the balance of the phrases and the vowel and consonant patterns within the lines. In acknowledgement of Blake's intentions and his influence, we might call this our first bit of English free verse.[12]

The rest of the poem is written in prose, in a style that depends heavily on the short, direct statement (used most effectively in the proverbs of hell) and occasionally shifts to the longer, Biblical cadences and syntactical constructions of the memorable fancies (as, for examples, in Ezekiel's history of the poetic genius on Plates 12–13 and the devil's account of the angel's destiny on Plates 19–20). *The Marriage* concludes with a song of liberty, arranged in the form of Biblical prose verses of widely varying lengths and metrical patterns.

If Energy is the power to achieve man's potential for infinite expansion and divine self-realization, then any restriction or limitation of Energy can become a denial of this potential divinity, and is therefore evil. Although Blake recognized that form and reason are both necessary to his dialectic, he increasingly feared that reason might become stronger than Energy and devour it entirely. The poetry written after 1790 virulently attacks the repressive physical, psychological, and social manifestations of a closed, rationalistic philosophy. Everywhere he looked during those tense years of the early 1790s when the French Revolution was becoming the Terror and England was preparing to go to war with France, Blake saw the oppressions and perversions of an authoritarian reason gaining the upper hand.

In his annotations to Swedenborg's *Divine Love and Divine Wisdom* (1788), Blake had accepted Swedenborg's notion that a celestial marriage of Love and Wisdom can occur whenever love or desire (Energy) inspires

engraver; his helping dragons are his tools; the viper "adorns" or illuminates the plate with colored inks and paints; the eagle actually organizes his poetic visions into the poetic text; the lions etch the combined designs and text onto the plate with their corrosive aqua fortis; and the "unnamed form" or plate is then inked and printed on paper and bound into books; "Postscript: The Cave in the Chambers," *Blake Essays for Damon,* ed. A. Rosenfeld (Providence, R.I. 1969), pp. 410–13.

12. Alicia Ostriker, *Vision and Verse in William Blake* (Madison, 1965), pp. 162–63.

reason to the understanding that God is man [13] and that everything that lives is holy. But to divorce reason from love and set it above love and the innocent affections as the final arbiter of spiritual truths, Blake felt, is to create a world riddled with the "errors of acquired folly" (*Annotations to Lavater*, 1789, E 589). Blake illustrated this distinction between a life of wisdom based primarily on the affections and a life of error based primarily on abstract reason in an annotation to Section 11 of *Divine Love and Divine Wisdom:* "Think of a white cloud. as being holy you cannot love it but think of a holy man within the cloud love springs up in your thought. for to think of holiness distinct from man is impossible to the affections. Thought alone can make monsters, but the affections cannot" (E 593). Only an abstracting reason divides the concept of man from the concept of God from the concept of cloud and, by thus splitting up human experience, paralyzes man's innocent responses to the unity and holiness of all being. It is this divided, dissected world constructed by thought alone which Blake attacks in the poetry published between 1793 and 1795. Since, during this period, subjugation to the limiting, fragmenting laws of reason seemed to Blake to be the common or shared "experience" of most men living in eighteenth-century Europe, he associates this state of oppression with the very word "Experience" both in the title for *Songs of Experience* and in the rejected motto for the *Songs of Innocence and of Experience:*

> "The Good [the passive] are attracted by Mens perceptions
> And Think not for themselves
>   Till Experience teaches them to catch
> And to cage the Fairies & Elves."

(E 490)

The physical aspects of this Experience, of this intellectual dissection and enclosure of the human psyche, are catalogued in the illustrations to *The Marriage of Heaven and Hell.* Chains literally bind the ankle of the flame-surrounded youth of Energy on Plate 4. Ugolino and his sons and grandsons, here identified with the "Giants who formed this world into its sensual existence and now seem to live in it in chains" (E 39), are hud-

13. Emanuel Swedenborg, *The Wisdom of Angels, concerning Divine Love and Divine Wisdom* (London, 1788): Sections 398–431.

dled in a narrow, dark prison cell (like the seven patriots who dared to oppose the state in Blake's *French Revolution,* E 283–5) on Plate 16. And man is physically reduced to a mad, crawling, bestial Nebuchadnezzar on Plate 24 (Copy I, MM). The most brutal result of an Augustinian or dualistic conception of the universe is physical slavery, as Blake proclaims in the text and illustrations for *Visions of the Daughters of Albion.* Blake had read Captain J. G. Stedman's *Narrative* recounting the cruelties and spiritual affronts of slavery in America and was personally acquainted with Stedman as well.[14] Blake's knowledge of the vicious black slave trade in America sharpens his image of Bromion's cave within whose cellars "sound like waves on a desart shore/ The voice of slaves beneath the sun, and children bought with money" (E 45) and his accompanying design of a naked, prostrate, perhaps beaten black man.

In the *Songs of Experience,* the four major psychological and social manifestations of a closed system where everything not forbidden is compulsory are: religious orthodoxy; political conservatism; codified social convention, most notably marriage; and intellectual absolutism. In a religious hierarchy that rigorously divides God from man and spiritual good from fleshly evil, any questioning of this dualistic hierarchy threatens the entire doctrinal structure and must be eliminated. Thus the priest in "A Little Boy Lost" of *Songs of Experience* literally kills the child who cannot comprehend an abstract God beyond the divine he perceives both within himself and in "the little bird/ That picks up crumbs around the door" (E 28). This poem implicitly affirms the little boy's vision of the identical holiness of man, nature, animal, and God, the very vision that underlies the *Songs of Innocence.* The *Songs of Experience* do not deny the validity of the visionary truth of Innocence.[15] Rather, they use the vi-

14. Erdman, *Blake,* rev. ed., pp. 230–33; Geoffrey Keynes, "William Blake and John Gabriel Stedman," *The Times Literary Supplement,* May 20, 1965, p. 400.

15. The continuing validity of the vision of Innocence in *Songs of Experience* is suggested by the fact that Blake chose to include two lyrics of Innocence, "The Little Girl Lost" and "The Little Girl Found," in *Songs of Experience;* subsequent editions of *Songs of Innocence* lack these two poems. Blake's image of a "lonely dell" of Innocence where Lyca finds sexual fulfillment (implied in the designs both by her embrace with her lover on Plate 1 and by her naked body, resting in Ingres' famous odalisque position, on the final plate) and a blissful harmony with man and nature is, in the context of *Songs of Innocence,* an appropriately enclosed, guarded place, which is nonetheless accessible to Lyca's parents. Looking back at these poems five years later, however, Blake recognized that although Lyca's vision was still a valid religious prophecy, the emphasis on the exclusive nature of Innocence, the presence of "the desart wild," and the exis-

sion of Innocence as the moral base from which to launch an energetic satiric attack upon those aspects of the eighteenth-century English social order that threaten Innocence. The "Two Contrary States of the Human Soul" posed against each other in *Songs of Innocence and of Experience,* then, are Innocence or Energy—the perception of the potential infinity in man and nature, and eighteenth-century Experience or the domination of reason—the denial of such a perception of the infinite.

Similarly, the king's power depends on a preservation of the status quo: regardless of the personal suffering involved, the soldier must fight and the child must labor under the worst physical conditions.[16] In "London," Blake denounces "How the Chimney-sweepers cry/ Every blackning Church appalls,/ And the hapless Soldiers sigh,/ Runs in blood down Palace walls" (E 27). And such a society sustains its stratifications only at the expense of individual fulfillment: Church and king join forces to prevent free love ("The Garden of Love"), to propagate the notion that sexual pleasure is evil ("The Sick Rose"), to impose the "marriage hearse" on all young lovers ("London"), to restrict emotion to "polite" discourse (thus perverting simple anger into murderous frustration, as in "A Poison Tree"), and to stifle the delights of mental warfare through the deadening stupor of tedious lessons in dreary rooms ("The School Boy"). Every sign of energy or exuberant physical activity is suppressed as a threat to the established system. In *America,* Albion's angel, King George III, predictably denounces the American Revolution as an attack on everything he values:

> . . . Then Albions Angel wrathful burnt
> Beside the Stone of Night; and like the Eternal Lions howl
> In famine & war, reply'd. Art thou not Orc; who serpent-form'd
> Stands at the gate of Enitharmon to devour her children;
> Blasphemous Demon, Antichrist, hater of Dignities;
> Lover of wild rebellion, and transgresser of Gods Law;
> Why dost thou come to Angels eyes in this terrific form?
>
> (E 52)

---

tence of parents seemingly in fear of or opposition to this vision were all more characteristic of a world dominated by reason and repression.

16. See Martin K. Nurmi, "Fact and Symbol in 'The Chimney Sweeper' of Blake's *Songs of Innocence,*" *BNYPL* 68 (April 1964):249–56, for a catalogue of the cruel working conditions actually imposed on five and six-year old chimney sweeps in Blake's lifetime.

The Human Abstract

Pity would be no more
If we did not make somebody Poor:
And Mercy no more could be.
If all were as happy as we:

And mutual fear brings peace.
Till the selfish loves increase.
Then Cruelty knits a snare
And spreads his baits with care.

He sits down with holy fears.
And waters the ground with tears:
Then Humility takes its root
Underneath his foot.

Soon spreads the dismal shade
Of Mystery over his head:
And the Caterpiller and Fly.
Feed on the Mystery.

And it bears the fruit of Deceit.
Ruddy and sweet to eat:
And the Raven his nest has made
In its thickest shade.

The Gods of the earth and sea.
Sought thro Nature to find this Tree
But their search was all in vain:
There grows one in the Human Brain

Plate 7. "The Human Abstract," from *Songs of Innocence and of Experience*, Copy B(MM).

In Blake's view, the most insidious threat to Innocence posed by the supporters of the oppressive status quo, however, is their calculated perversion of the language of Innocence, in which the child says exactly what he feels, in which knowledge and expression are one. This sincere language degenerates into the empty rhetoric of Experience, which manipulates the vocabulary of Innocence to divorce expression from feeling. In "The Human Abstract" [*Plate* 7], the poem opposed to "The Divine Image" in *Songs of Innocence,* Blake exposes how the rational mind which demands order, hierarchy, and a static system uses the very words and images of Innocence to sugar over its own cruelties and deceptions. Such a radical disjunction of meaning and language makes sincere human communication impossible. In "The Human Abstract," Blake focuses directly on the gulf between words and feelings in a system where language is a calculated perversion of meaning:

> Pity would be no more,
> If we did not make somebody Poor:
> And Mercy no more could be,
> If all were as happy as we;
>
> And mutual fear brings peace;
> Till the selfish loves increase.
>
> (E 27)

This poem is not, I think, a denunciation of mercy and pity, of the naïveté of Innocence, as it has often been read.[17] Rather, it is an implicit affirmation of the innocent heart which would pity the poor at the same time that it tried to alleviate their suffering. It is only the perverted heart of reason speaking here which justifies and sustains the existence of poverty by pointing out that it gives man an opportunity to demonstrate his charity. Pecksniff, that exemplar of selfish hypocrisy, has this rhetoric of Experience down pat. Sitting inside the coach on a frosty morning, he observes:

"For . . . if every one were warm and well fed, we should lose the satisfaction of admiring the fortitude with which certain conditions of men bear cold and

17. For such negative readings of the poem, see E. D. Hirsch, Jr., *Innocence and Experience: An Introduction to Blake* (New Haven, 1964), pp. 265–270, and Bloom, *Blake's Apocalypse,* pp. 142–43.

hunger. And if we were no better off than anybody else, what would become of our sense of gratitude, which," said Mr. Pecksniff with tears in his eyes, as he shook his fist at a beggar who wanted to get up behind, "is one of the holiest feelings of our common nature." [18]

The words "pity" and "gratitude," used in this way to legitimize the suffering within a hierarchical society rather than to profess a genuine emotional sympathy that would try to alleviate pain, have lost their original denotation; they no longer mean the same thing. Blake's later annotation to the title of Dr. Watson's book, *The Wisdom and Goodness of God, in Having Made Both Rich and Poor: a Sermon . . .* , points up just this abuse of language by the mind of reason: "God made Man happy & Rich but the Subtil made the innocent Poor/ This must be a most wicked & blasphemous book" (E 601).

How can a man of Innocence-become-Energy successfully oppose and end these evil oppressions of abstract reason? First of all, one must not retreat from them; one must remain in the world of Experience and try to save its victims. In *Visions of the Daughters of Albion,* Blake sends Oothoon, a fully mature Thel, back into the "land of death" to carry the vision of Innocence to her lover, Theotormon. En route Oothoon is raped by Bromion and consequently rejected as "impure" by the rationalist Theotormon. Blake's concern, however, is not with this plot (which he probably borrowed from Macpherson's *Oithona* where, significantly, Oithona's lover Gaul, unlike Theotormon, fights for her honor and defeats the rapist Dunrommath), but with the psychological responses of Oothoon, Bromion, and Theotormon to the limited categories of reason. The poem articulates the rhetoric of Energy which can survive amidst and eventually triumph over the oppressions of an abstracting and authoritarian reason.

And, again, as in *The Marriage of Heaven and Hell,* the rhetoric of Energy is based on an open form. But here this open form is placed in direct contrast to two closed minds, Bromion's and Theotormon's. The slave owner Bromion narcissistically and selfishly appropriates all experience —"Thy soft American plains are mine" (E 45). Not surprisingly, he confines himself to the syntaxes of the imperative command, the direct statement, and the rhetorical or closed question. "Behold this harlot here on

18. Charles Dickens, *Martin Chuzzlewit* (New York, 1965), p. 135.

Bromions bed," he commands Theotormon and then asserts, "Stampt with my signet are the swarthy children of the sun:/ They are obedient" (E 45). And Bromion's skillfully closed questions successfully impose his limited, dualistic social and intellectual system upon Theotormon. Bromion asks:

> Thou knowest that the ancient trees seen by thine eyes have fruit;
> But knowest thou that trees and fruits flourish upon the earth
> To gratify senses unknown? trees beasts and birds unknown:
> Unknown, not unperceived, spread in the infinite microscope,
> In places yet unvisited by the voyager. and in worlds
> Over another kind of seas, and in atmospheres unknown. . . .
>
> (E 47)

These questions have often been read as Bromion's sincere if futile attempt to understand Oothoon's world through rational categories. But these are rhetorical questions. Theotormon knows, says Bromion, that those trees he has seen can bear fruit; but how can he know, first, that there are trees and fruits which he has not perceived with his own senses and, even more unlikely, that there are senses which he does not possess? Bromion sharpens his mocking tone and secures Theotormon's rejection of Oothoon's vision by emphasizing that she spoke of "unknown" worlds, not just worlds that man has not yet perceived or that voyagers have not yet visited even "in the infinite microscope." Bromion erroneously assumes that infinity is bounded by the microscope, at least at one end. But Robert Gleckner has shown that Blake himself dismissed the microscope as a limited view of the world: "The microscope, the telescope, and all optical devices intensify the senses . . . without expanding them." [19] Further, in contrast to Bromion's idea of infinity as the mere mechanical extension of the given, Blake sees the ultimate regeneration of the senses as "a multiplication as well as [an] expansion and cleansing," as a return to a *communis sensus* "by which the senses could be united with each other, a kind of total synaesthesia reflective of total coinstantaneous perception." [20] Bromion drives in his narrow view with a pounding series of rhetorical questions, all presupposing (1) that the only possible emotions, thoughts,

19. Robert Gleckner, "Blake and the Senses," *Studies in Romanticism* 5 (August 1965):5.
20. *Ibid.*, p. 12.

or acts are those we have already experienced and (2) that the laws we have always accepted are absolute: "Is there not one law for both the lion and the ox?" (E 47). Such worlds as Oothoon describes are mere "phantoms of existence" from which religious doctrines of "eternal fire, and eternal chains" protect us.

To this diatribe, Theotormon cannot reply; he silently rejects Oothoon's vision. For Theotormon is trapped in the Lockean conception that all experience is reducible to concrete sense-data. All along he assumes that thoughts are made of "substances," that joys must grow in "gardens," that sorrows swim in "rivers," and that men escape "cold despair" only by closing themselves up in houses or, in the symbolism of the poem, in minds or *tabulae rasae* fed solely by the five senses (E 46–7).

Oothoon, throughout the poem, articulates the open vision of innocent Energy in an appropriately open syntax. She rejects abstract rational statements and instead speaks in suggestive poetic images. She distinguishes between two kinds of time: *kairos,* a "breaking day" in which "the nightingale has done lamenting" and the "lark does rustle in the ripe corn"; and *chronos,* a "deadly black" night in which day and night are barely distinguishable, in which day is "a bright shadow" and night "a sickly charnel house." [21] Oothoon perceives time as linear, as a progression toward an ultimate apocalypse or "last judgment" when all errors are consumed and man appears as he should be, infinite and holy. But Theotormon, trapped in his five senses, can perceive time in only two, equally limited, ways. Either time is a meaningless repetition of events, the same dull round over again—for him "the night and morn/ Are both alike: a night of sighs, a morning of fresh tears" (E 46). Or time is a degeneration, *kairos* in reverse: "Tell me where dwell the joys of

21. *Chronos* is "a mere aggregation or accidental sequence of events," time passing without ultimate significance, "one damn thing after another" as John Marsh puts it in *The Fullness of Time* (New York, 1952), p. 22. *Kairos* is the sense of the moment as having a significant relationship with a defined end of time, with an apocalypse or eternity. *Kairos* is the vision of time as ordered, with a beginning and an end, as a linear progression to which each moment contributes its necessary and valuable being. Blake envisions time as *kairos;* for him all passing moments move toward and derive their meaning from their relationship to the ultimate personal and social apocalypse. For further discussions of the concept of *kairos* in modern literature and in Blake, see Frank Kermode, *The Sense of an Ending* (Oxford, 1966); and Bloom, *Blake's Apocalypse.*

old! . . ./ That I might traverse times and spaces far remote and bring/ Comforts into a present sorrow" (E 47).

And Oothoon asks, not the closed questions of the rationalist who knows all the answers, but deliberately open questions that cannot be understood or answered within the framework of a dualistic or empirical system. This is a characteristic Blakean device: Blake often defines a mind or personality not by what he does but by the questions he is capable of asking. An open question which recognizes both the uniqueness of experience and the infinite number of possible answers reveals an open mind; a closed or rhetorical question which expects only one answer uncovers a closed mind.

Oothoon first asks, if the world were really limited to one day and night, if our five senses really opened upon the same given and unchanging world, how could the animals understand things man cannot? With which of our five senses does the tame pigeon measure out the expanse? Not only, she implies, do the animals have senses or abilities to use their senses in ways that we do not, but their senses differ even among themselves. True wisdom comes from knowing that each individual creature has unique functions and pleasures. Secondly, she asks, "How can one joy absorb another?" (E 47). She implies that not only is every joy unique but that all joys are "Holy, eternal, infinite!" (E 47).

Oothoon then moves into the rhetoric of social protest, the rhetoric of satire with which the more open vision of Energy denies and denounces the unnecessary limitations of reason. Having heard Bromion manipulate Theotormon into acquiescence, Oothoon now fully understands the mental vision that rules over "the land of death" and addresses it accordingly: "O Urizen! [Your Reason] Creator of men! mistaken Demon of heaven" (E 47). She then specifically attacks those kings and priests who take the tithes of the poor, who stifle true love in involuntary marriage bonds, who corrupt sexual desire into forced procreation (emphasized by the prostrate, possibly pregnant woman in the illustration for Plate 5, Copy P, MM). She powerfully denounces all religious and moral codes that teach a child to repress his natural instincts, that brand "virgin joy" with the name of whore, that hypocritically pervert sexual energy into "religious dreams and holy vespers" (E 48).

Plate 8. Visions of the Daughters of Albion, Tailpiece, Separate Plate, Tate Gallery.

Oothoon concludes with the syntax of triumph, the exclamation: "for everything that lives is holy!" (E 50). The final illustration shows her spirit in flames above the margined shore where the enslaved daughters of Albion, a Greek chorus of women still obedient to Bromion's rule, sit weeping. Although Oothoon has not saved Theotormon—the tailpiece (or frontispiece in some copies) [*Plate 8*] shows him still crouching around the "adulterate pair/Bound back to back in Bromion's cave" (an illustration of Plate 2:3–4)—she has nevertheless terrified Bromion (his face is contorted with horror and fear) and retained her own freedom (significantly, she wears no chains in the tailpiece; only Bromion is literally bound). She still affirms the motto of the poem: that "the eye sees more than the heart knows," that vision is infinite and not bounded by feelings, thoughts, or the five limited senses (in contrast to Bromion and Theotormon who can see only what their enclosed, paralyzed hearts have already known). In another sense, too, Oothoon sees more than the heart knows, for the title page shows her running between two realms, one of sunshine (Copy P, MM), rainbows, and dancing figures; the other of rain, storm, dark skies, black clouds, and fierce white-bearded men in flames or hurling thunderbolts. She sees both realms but refuses to let her heart "know" that the "land of death," of sexual, economic, and political oppression, is absolute or true. She sees it, not as given, but as one very limited way of life or pattern of thought.

It is not only the final exclamation, the tailpiece, and the motto of *Visions of the Daughters of Albion* that point toward a more open form or vision. The prosody of the poem is based on the septenary, a line that Blake used with such subtlety and variation that Alicia Ostriker has called it his "line of freedom." [22] In this poem, the septenary develops from the elegiac cadences of *The Book of Thel* into grander, more compelling Biblical rhythms. By drawing on all the traditional techniques of blank verse, by adding extensive variations on usual accenting and pause patterns, and by frequently using enjambment and extra light syllables, Blake here achieved tremendous prosodic liberation. However, even as Blake's visual iconography and poetic language denounce the limitations of Bromion's closed mind and society and affirm instead Oothoon's vision of the infinity of Energy and the imagination, his visual style returns to the closed, tectonic compositions characteristic of the neoclassical idiom. The designs for *Visions of the Daughters of Albion,* like those for *America* and *Europe,* generally avoid dynamic, baroque movements and rely instead on a rectilinear format and a stable horizontal-vertical axis. The

22. Ostriker, *Vision and Verse,* pp. 120–44.

continuing dependence of Blake's visual art upon strictly tectonic compositions and sharply outlined, clearly bounded human figures and objects creates a tension with his poetic attacks upon the limitations of a closed intellectual or social system. This tension, as we shall see, is not finally resolved until Blake's late art and poetry.

Although Oothoon demonstrated the power of the open rhetoric of Energy to survive and attack the restrictions of reason, she was not able to destroy those evils or to liberate Theotormon from a closed society and mind. In "The Tyger" and *America,* Blake suggests two ways in which an excessively closed form can actually be annihilated. Through art, the man of Innocence or Energy can create an image—a visual or verbal mythology or utopia—that enables him both to sustain his own vision and to communicate that vision to others. He can thus liberate others from the limiting forms or syntaxes of abstract reason and, by eliminating the popular support for evil institutions, eventually destroy them. "The Tyger" portrays the process through which Energy is given artistic form and is thus enabled to survive in the world of Experience. The glowing tyger is an image of Energy as it blazes forth in the land of death or rational oppression, the "forests of the night." Its creator is that God who is man, who is also, in this instance, the poetic genius or divine imagination. Only this divine creator has the physical strength ("the shoulder") to control his tools (the hammer, chain, anvil, and furnace of the blacksmith who works with the most recalcitrant materials of all, with iron and steel); the creative vision ("the art"); and the moral courage (the aspiring, daring wings of Icarus) to "seize the fire" of pure Energy that encompasses all being and burns from distant deeps to distant skies.

Such an omnipotent and daring artist can "smile" as the starlit night breaks into dewy dawn, as water tempers his star-sparkling steel, and his blazing sun-tyger eclipses the "starry hosts" of the tyrant Urizen (*America* 8:4). Confronted with this greater creation, the forces of reason fling down their spears in fear and defeat, and water heaven with tears of repentance, frustration, or hypocritical humility. This reading of the perplexing fifth stanza is supported by the extremely close parallel of a line in a poem written three to five years later, "When Klopstock England Defied." English Blake, as the daring defender of English poetry against the challenge of Klopstock's Miltonic *Messiah,* there rises from beneath the poplar tree in Lambeth and arouses his creative powers: "The Moon at that sight blushd scarlet red / The stars threw down their cups & fled" (E 491). Similarly, in Night V of *The Four Zoas,* the stars— identified by David Erdman as the counterrevolutionary armies at York-town and Valmy [23]—who are urged at the council of Urizen to deny God are overcome by God's power: "The stars threw down their spears & fled naked away" (E 337). By 1793, Blake had often associated stars with the oppressions of monarchy and with a Newtonian, mechanistic concep-tion of the universe. After the tyrannical king of France has invoked the scorn of his ancestors on the rebels in Blake's *The French Revolution* (1791), "his bosom / Expanded like starry heaven" (ll. 81–82, E 286). In "A Song of Liberty" (1793), the "gloomy king" leads his "starry hosts thro' the waste wilderness [where] he promulgates his ten com-mands" (E 43); and earth, in "Earth's Answer," denounces this same "Selfish father of men" as "Starry Jealousy" (E 18). Blake's association of the stars with Newton is anticipated in *The Marriage of Heaven and Hell,* where the "fixed stars" mark the void where the angel of reason is shown his destined place among the devouring monkeys (E 41). Later, of course, Blake would charge that "Newton numbered the stars" (in *A De-scriptive Catalogue,* 1809, E 524) and that "the Newtonian Voids be-tween the Substances of Creation" are "the Chaotic Voids outside of the Stars . . . measured by / The Stars" (*Milton,* 1804, E 137).

The creator of the tyger possesses, as all men do potentially, the daring imagination and the sublime wrath necessary to dominate the forces of reason. Man's expanding Energy can be channeled into an awe-inspiring, bounded artistic image, the fearful symmetry of this tyger. But the Energy of this tyger is a development of the Innocence of the lamb, as the contro-versial illustration indicates. The tyger is pictured as a gentle, brightly colored, striped, and peaceful beast (in Copies B [MM] and Z [TP]), a creature that fuses the loving gentleness of the lamb with the quiet power of Energy at rest.[24] When the murdering dissections of reason are annihi-lated, the tyger and the lamb will lie down together.

23. Erdman, *Blake,* p. 194.

24. C. O. Parsons has suggested that, in this design, Blake may have been making the traditional distinction between 'character' and 'expression' in eighteenth-century animal pictures. "An artist brings out an animal's *character* when he portrays the unimpas-

"Did he who made the Lamb make thee?" Blake's refusal to answer this question allows his readers two different responses. The response the reader chooses defines his own mentality as a man of Innocence or of reason. The reader who answers "Yes" perceives the continuity of Innocence and Energy as two modes of the holiness in man and nature. The reader who answers "No" is trapped in a closed, rationalistic system which can only divide and separate, which sees the tyger as totally different from the lamb and as a fearful, destructive, evil force. The syntax of the poem, a series of questions, thus embodies the meaning of the poem: pure Energy can exist on earth; but it should resist overly closed, fixed forms, just as Blake's questions resist overly simplistic answers. Energy should always exist in tension with its form, in a "fearful symmetry" that threatens to explode into an infinitely expanding force at any moment, just as the pressure of Blake's vision against the syntax breaks the full-line questions of lines 7 and 8 into the half-line questions of lines 13 and 15. The artist alone is able to, *dares* to, fit Energy into form and draw the bounding line of reason around it, but Blake's fear of overly limiting or "framing" Energy permits him to use only the most open and fluid of rhetorical syntaxes.[25]

America a Prophecy (1793) celebrates the capacity of political and military revolution to destroy the closed institutions of reason. Orc, the spirit of revolutionary Energy born on the American plains in 1776, argues Blake, can cross the Atlantic sea in 1793 and bring life, liberty, and the pursuit of happiness to every British citizen shackled by the tyrannies of

---

sioned permanencies of his look and features and its *expression* when he reveals the agitated muscular action, instinct, and passion super-imposed on character by some emergency," noted Thomas Landseer in his *Twenty Engravings of Lions Tigers Panthers & Leopards* (London, 1823), Introduction. Blake may thus have intended to present his tyger's character in his design; its expression in his verse ("Blake's 'Tyger' and Eighteenth Century Animal Pictures," *Art Quarterly* 31 [1968]: 300).

25. But not the most open of visual designs. The disappointment that many readers have felt with the illustration for "The Tyger," despite its clarification of the spiritual identity of the tyger and the lamb, is caused, I suspect, by the fact that Blake was forced to re-use Stothard's illustrative style in this companion-volume to *Songs of Innocence*. Stothard's sentimental, decorative mode is by 1794 clearly inadequate to Blake's poetic vision. For two illuminating discussions of "The Tyger" which support this reading of the poem, see Morton D. Paley, "Tyger of Wrath," *PMLA* 8 (Dec. 1966): 540–51, and Fred Kaplan, "'The Tyger' and Its Maker: Blake's Vision of Art and the Artist," *SEL* 7 (Autumn 1967):617–27.

George III. If Orc succeeds, George III and the bishops of London and York will fall, the Anglican Church whose priests have systematically perverted sensual delight into "pale religious letchery" will be driven into "reptile coverts," and all the adherents of Urizen (Blake's personification of authoritarian reason) will eventually be annihilated, either through death or liberation. *America* ends with a triumphant prophecy of freedom. "The five gates" of the "law-built heaven" of Locke and the kings of France, Spain, and Italy are "consum'd, & their bolts and hinges melted" by the fierce flames of Orc, the force of Energy channeled into revolution (E 56).

However, when Blake published his small book of emblems, *For Children: The Gates of Paradise,* in 1793, he included no images of a successful political revolution or of a paradise regained on earth. Instead, he carefully distinguished between mortal or physical man and the immortal or spiritual man. Here the gates of paradise are open only to the spiritual man after the death of the physical body. The life of mortal man on earth is presented pessimistically, as a graveyard existence dominated by authoritarian reason, psychological oppression and physical suffering. Of course, the conventions of the emblem-book to some extent limited the visual statements which Blake could make. It would be difficult, though not impossible, to convey in such simple, small emblems the complexities of a viable program for political reform or an increasingly ambivalent response to the development of the French Revolution. Nonetheless, the fact that no image of a pastoral arcadia like that found in the *Songs of Innocence* designs appears in *The Gates of Paradise* suggests that Blake no longer felt confident that personal and social regeneration could take place on earth.

On the title page of *The Gates of Paradise,* one tiny flying figure points the way to a life of Innocence in paradise. But first, as the frontispiece shows, the mortal child or man must escape from his confining physical body. Job's question, "What is Man!", which appears on the frontispiece, is answered by the emblem itself [*Plate* 9]: man is born a worm-chrysalis, a physical body generated from the caterpillar on the oak leaf above it. The caterpillar reminds us of Blake's parasitical priests in the Proverbs of Hell who feed on the energy of the oppressed: "As the caterpillar

Plate 9. For Children: The Gates of Paradise, Frontispiece, Copy B.

chooses the fairest leaves to lay her eggs on, so the priest lays his curses on the fairest joys" (E 37). Here the material body similarly confines and devours the child's spiritual body and soul. This child-chrysalis is tightly swaddled, like the mentally and physically "bound" child in "Infant Sorrow." Nonetheless, the chrysalis suggests the possibility that this child will eventually metamorphose into a butterfly, winged and free.

But first it passes through a material existence. In the first emblem, the

Plate 10. For Children: The Gates of Paradise, Figure 1, Copy B.

child-chrysalis has become a mandrake-child [*Plate 10*]. Northrop Frye points out that the mandrake was traditionally thought to be the grotesque man-dragon generated by the earth from the fallen seed of a hanged man.[26] Since Blake had used a line from Donne's "The Progresse

26. Northrop Frye, "The Keys to the Gates," *Some British Romantics,* ed. J. V. Logan *et al.* (Athens, Ohio, 1966), p. 30.

2   Water

Published by W. Blake 17 May 1793

Plate 11. For Children: The Gates of Paradise, Figure 2, Copy B.

of the Soule" as a legend for the Notebook sketch on Page 85, he was surely aware of Donne's description there of mortal man as "a living buried man, [a] quiet mandrake" (St. XVI). Here the mandrake-child is plucked by its unnatural "mother" (the mandrake was also supposed to have the power to make barren women fertile) out of the earth under a

Plate *12. For Children: The Gates of Paradise,* Figure 3, Copy B.

Plate *13. For Children: The Gates of Paradise,* Figure 4, Copy B.

tree (mandrakes were thought to grow under gallows trees and near places of execution [27]) and swaddled in her apron. The original longer legend under this design in the Notebook (Page 63), "I found him beneath a Tree in the Garden," suggests that this child had begun its life in the Garden of Eden, in a spiritual paradise from which this false mother has pulled him into the fallen world.

This child then grows into the mortal man pictured on the next four emblems, a man wholly enclosed within "mind-forg'd manacles" and the four emblems of physical matter. Water pours over and around him in Figure 2 [*Plate 11*], confining him to a rocky shore beneath a leafless tree, like the chained earth "Prison'd on watry shore" in "Earth's Answer" or the brain-washed Theotormon isolated on his rocky shore on Plate 4 of *Visions of the Daughters of Albion*. His morose expression indicates that this is the despairing melancholy man suggested by the Notebook legend for this design (Page 95); the legend is Hamlet's suicidal wish ("O that the Everlasting had not fixed His canon gainst Self slaughter," *Hamlet* I, ii, 131–2). In the next emblem, Earth presses down on this same man, burying him in a dark grave [*Plate 12*]. The Notebook legend for this design, "Rest, rest perturbed spirit" (Page 93), links this man with the ghost of old Hamlet, condemned to wander "unhousel'd" and "unanel'd" through the fires of purgatory (*Hamlet, I, v, 181*). And the Air also presses around him in heavy, swagging clouds [*Plate 13*] like the "hungry clouds" which try to devour Rintrah in the Argument for *The Marriage of Heaven and Hell*. The accompanying legend in the Notebook (Page 94), "Thou hast set thy heart as the heart of God" (*Ezekiel* XXVIII: 6), links this huddled figure with the Prince of Tyre, the powerful ruler who, because he has taken too much pride in his wealth and intelligence, is brought low by Jehovah. Thus this figure of Air depicts man under the oppression of a jealous God or an authoritarian ruler. The fourteen stars behind this figure further suggest the presence of Newton's or Urizen's "starry floor" and indicate the additional domination of a devouring reason.

27. Geoffrey Keynes notes this superstition in his commentary on Blake's *Gates of Paradise* (Trianon Press facsimile, London, 1968, p. 10). References to Blake's Notebook are to *The Note-book of William Blake called the Rossetti Manuscript,* ed. Geoffrey Keynes (London, 1935); the page numbers are Blake's own.

Plate 14. For Children: The Gates of Paradise, Figure 5, Copy D.

At length for hatching ripe
he breaks the shell
6
Publish'd by WBlake 17 May 1793

Plate 15. For *Children: The Gates of Paradise*, Figure 6, Copy B.

But the fiery element in man, his Energy, enables him to rebel against such material and mental prisons [*Plate 14*]. This suggestion is subtly reinforced by Blake's use of his famous *Glad Day* or *Albion Rose* figure —the naked youth with open arms, erect torso and wide-spread legs [*Plate 37*]—for his figure of Fire. The *Albion Rose* figure is an icon for Innocence as it expands into Energy, as it throws off all manacles and strikes forth as revolutionary liberation.[28] Here he carries his spear and shield; he is ready to enter battle, as flames roll past him. The Notebook legend (Page 91) from *Paradise Lost,* "Forthwith upright he rears off the

28. See my discussion of this figure in chapter 4.

Pool/ His mighty stature," identifies him as Milton's fallen Satan who raises himself on the vast wastes of Pandemonium, eager to try once again to overthrow a repressive deity and to assert his own divinity:

> Forthwith upright he rears from off the Pool
> His mighty Stature; on each hand the flames
> Driven backward slope their pointing spires, and rowl'd
> In billows. . . .
>
> (*Paradise Lost*, I, 221–4)

Inspired by this proud desire or Energy, the immortal soul can break through its physical body. Like a butterfly emerging from its cocoon, a young child with tiny wings steps out of an eggshell onto a cloud in Figure 6 [*Plate 15*]. The legend, which also appears under the Notebook design (Page 69), is from Dryden's translation of Chaucer's *Knight's Tale*:

> So Man, at first a Drop, dilates with Heat,
> Then form'd, the little heart begins to beat;
> Secret he feeds, unknowing in the Cell;
> *At length, for Hatching ripe, he breaks the Shell,*
> And struggles into Breath, and cries for Aid;
> Then, helpless, in his Mother's Lap is laid.
> He creeps, he walks, and issuing into Man
> Grudges their Life, from whence his own began;
> Retchless of Laws, affects to rule alone,
> Anxious to reign, and restless on the Throne:
> First vegetive, then feels and reasons last;
> Rich of three Souls and lives all three to waste.
>
> (Dryden, transl. Chaucer's *Knight's Tale:*
> "Palamon and Arcite," iii, 1066–1077;
> italics mine).

Unlike Chaucer's corrupted man, however, Blake's child escapes the evils of the physical body. In the next emblem [*Plate 16*], a naked young child flies away from a prostrate body on the ground. Allowing for the diminishment of perspective, these two naked young bodies might be identical; perhaps the flying child is the immortal soul or spiritual body escaping from its physical body. An older youth runs up, hat in hand, eyes wide

Plate 16. For Children: The Gates of Paradise, Figure 7, Copy B.

open. Perhaps he is trying to catch this flying figure in his hat, as Blake later caught the fairy who dictated *Europe* to him (E 59). Or perhaps he is only expressing his amazement at what he sees. The Notebook legend for this design (Page 19) may help to clarify its meaning for Blake:

> Ah luckless babe born under cruel star
> And in dead ashes bred,

Full weenest thou what sorrows are
Left thee for portion of thy livlihed
                    (a corruption of Spenser's
                    Fairie Queene, II, ii, 2)

This older youth, like Sir Guyon when he finds the orphaned baby Ruddymane (the personification of original sin), sees mortality as inescapable
sin and suffering. All men are born under cruel stars (which Blake associates with reason), separated from paradise, and condemned to live in
misery, evil, and despair. Like Guyon, the older youth here may recognize
that mortal life is terrible and that the only salvation lies in escaping the
mortal body.

The next two emblems explore the possibility of an escape from the oppressions of the body and of reason during one's mortal life. In Figure 8, a
naked youth with curly hair points a spear at an old man who is seated
on a massive stone block or throne, sword in hand, in a posture of despair
[*Plate 17*]. The legend identifies this youth as Absalom, the young rebel
who fought for justice ("Oh that I were made judge in the land, that
every man which hath any suit or cause might come unto me, and I
would do him justice!", II *Samuel* 15:4) and marched against his father
David (the legend "My Son! My Son!" is David's cry of woe [29]). Possibly
this Absalom figure will be able to overthrow and even destroy the oppressions of reason and political tyranny; here, the old man with long
white hair and beard closely resembles the figure of Albion's Angel or
George III as he appears on Plates 4 and 8 of *America.* But Absalom
himself, we recall, finally became as oppressive as his father [30] and died in
defeat, hung by his long hair from a tree. Yet the hair of this youth is
short and he may thus be able to avoid Absalom's death.

The lovers, standing arm in arm, gazing at the heavens, and the tiny
figure preparing to climb a ladder to the moon in Figure 9 [*Plate 18*]
also hold out the hope that, even on earth, man may be able to escape his
psychological prisons and satisfy his desire for infinite pleasure and vision.
The legend "I want! I want!" vividly articulates man's demand for com-

29. First noted by Chauncey Brewster Tinker, *Painter and Poet* (Cambridge, Mass.,
1939), pp. 111–12.
30. Morton Paley points out that Absalom metaphorically becomes his father when
he seizes David's house and goes into David's concubines (II *Samuel* 16:21); *Energy
and the Imagination,* p. 83.

Plate 17. For Children: The Gates of Paradise, *Figure 8, Copy B.*

plete satisfaction which in *There is No Natural Religion* (b) demonstrated his divinity: "The desire of Man being Infinite the possession is Infinite & himself Infinite" (E 2). And David Erdman has pointed out that this design is a subtle satire on James Gillray's cartoon showing the En-

Plate 18. *For Children: The Gates of Paradise*, Figure 9, Copy B.

Plate 19. *For Children: The Gates of Paradise*, Figure 10, Copy B.

glish patriots, represented by Charles Fox of the Whig opposition, sinking so deep in the slough of despond that they will never see the promised land of "Libertas." Fox's "straight Gate or the way to the Patriot's Paradise" is clearly closed, for from Gillray's gate there is no way to reach the moon; the ladder set up by Fox is patently too short.[31] Blake's ladder, in direct contrast, reaches all the way to the moon: by traversing the starry heavens (which have been associated with the depressed Air, tyrannical reason, and Ruddymane or original sin in these designs), Blake's true patriot can achieve both physical freedom and psychological satisfaction.

But the possibility that such an escape from political or intellectual oppression can take place on earth, within the physical body, seems to be rejected in the following emblem [*Plate 19*]. Here Blake's visionary

31. David Erdman, *Blake*, rev. ed., pp. 202–05.

Plate 20. *For Children: The Gates of Paradise,* Figure 11, Copy B.

climber of Figure 9 has apparently fallen off his ladder into the sea where
he is drowning with no help in sight. Desire alone, even the power of
fiery Energy, here seems inadequate to free mortal man from the manacles
of his material body and the psychological oppressions of an absolutist political, social, or intellectual system. This design may thus be a cruel demonstration of the axiom Blake thought he had disproved in *There is No
Natural Religion* (b): "If any could desire what he is incapable of possess-
ing, despair must be his eternal lot" (E 2). The despair of this drowning

Plate 21. For Children: The Gates of Paradise, Figure 12, Copy B.

figure is also forced upon the youth in Figure 11 [*Plate* 20]. This winged youth who races eagerly towards the sun has his wings held and clipped and his desires frustrated by an old man with spectacles and closed eyes. In this oppressive world, all revolutionary thinkers are viciously tortured and immured in dungeons by the King and the Church. In Figure 12, Ugolino and his sons and grandsons who trusted the established church have been maliciously condemned, like the Little Boy Lost of *Songs of Experience,* to the gallows of a jealous, judging Priesthood [*Plate 21*]. Ugolino can only cry out in horror and despair, "Does thy God O Priest

Plate 22. For Children: The Gates of Paradise, Figure 13, Copy D.

take such vengeance as this?" Blake used a very similar scene of Ugolino and his descendents dying in prison to illustrate his statement in *The Marriage of Heaven and Hell* that "The Giants who formed this world into its sensual existence and now seem to live in it in chains, are in truth, the causes of its life & the sources of all activity, but the chains are, the cunning of weak and tame minds" (E 39).

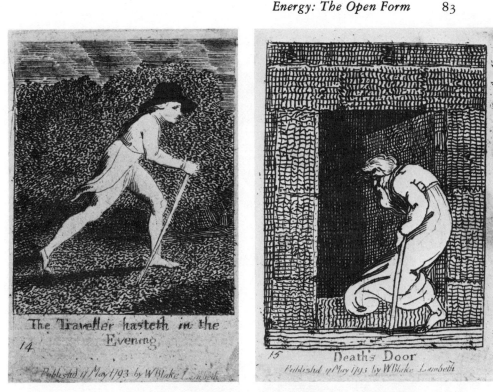

Plate 23. For Children: The Gates of Paradise,
Figure 14, Copy B.

Plate 24. For Children: The Gates of Paradise,
Figure 15, Copy B.

In this vale of oppression and fear, the only hope lies in death. In Figure 13 [*Plate 22*], the resurrected body of a dead old man rises before his astonished mourners. Pointing to heaven with his left arm, he assures them that, as the legend says, "Fear & Hope are—Vision." Out of the fears and sufferings of man's mortal life arises a vision of salvation, the faith that we shall arise after death as spiritual bodies and return to paradise. As the Notebook legend confirms, "What we hope we see" (Page 61). Man has two alternatives, then, as the simpler legend on the early proof copy of Figure 13 says, to "Fear or Hope," to live oppressed by the fears endemic to our mortal existence or to hope for and believe in a spiritual salvation after death. Trusting the old man's vision, both young and old, both the middle-aged traveller in Figure 14 [*Plate 23*] (who earlier appeared as Lockean man trapped in "the same dull round" of already ac-

Plate 25. *For Children: The Gates of Paradise,* Figure 16, Copy B.

quired sense-experience on Plate 7 of *All Religions are One*) and the crippled old man in Figure 15 [*Plate 24*], hasten in the evening towards
Death's Door.

The final emblem depicts the death of man's physical body. The traveller, still holding his staff and wrapped in a winding sheet or hooded robe,
crouches in a grave beneath the roots of a tree, beside two barely visible
buried heads [*Plate 25*]. A large worm coils around his body. This is
Job's worm of corruption, as the legend indicates. Tormented by the death

of his children, the loss of his property, and the boils upon his body, Job desires only to die and join the worms in his tomb: "I have said to corruption thou art/ My father to the worm thou art/ My mother and my sister" (*Job* XVII:14). The mortal body must be given to death, but the spiritual body or soul of man, as Figure 13 showed, can still escape to paradise.[32] Interestingly, Blake did not include among his published emblems all those Notebook sketches which depict the spiritual body entering the Gates of Paradise (Page 41) or reuniting with friends or relatives in heaven (Pages 31, 35). The emphasis in this emblem-book is rather on the sufferings of the mortal life than on the delights of an afterlife in heaven; seemingly, here, there is little hope for a successful political or intellectual revolution which will restore paradise on earth or redeem the physical body of man.[33]

By 1794, Blake seems to have become pessimistic about the possibilities of a successful political revolution in Europe. The poem *Europe* (1794) ends far less triumphantly than *America*. We do not see the victory of the fiery Orc but only his first appearance in the dawn sky over France, while Los has only begun to summon his sons to "the strife of blood" and the conquest of the repressive female will (Enitharmon) that has ruled Europe for eighteen centuries. The visual images of despair that accompany this poem—the ancient of days ruling the universe with number, weight and measure (frontispiece, Copy K [*Plate 34*]); the assassin hiding in his cave (Plate 1); the deathwatch on Plate 7; the scaly, crowned warrier-king on Plate 5—have not yet been transformed or annihilated in the redemptive "strife of blood." On Plate 15, Los leaves the burning city carrying his wife on his back and holding his child by the hand. The design reminds us of traditional portrayals of Aeneas, leaving Troy with Anchises on his back and Ascanius beside him. But the new Rome or utopian state which Los will found lies far in the future.

---

32. Keynes has also argued that "the object of the emblems has been to remind Man of his melancholy progress from birth to death, but it is only the material body that is surrendered to the worm. The vision on Plate 13 has given the hope of immortality to the Traveller on his journey" (Commentary, *The Gates of Paradise*, p. 19).

33. John Beer also sees these emblems as an example of the eighteenth-century Graveyard school's pervasive melancholy and pessimism, of its vision of mortal life as completely wretched, and of salvation as the resurrection of the spiritual body after the death of the physical body (*Blake's Humanism*, Manchester, 1968, p. 232).

At some point in 1794, Blake acknowledged the failure of the French Revolution and the increasing unlikelihood that a successful political revolution would occur at this time. Four lines which appear at the bottom of Plate 2 in the earliest extant copy of *America* (watermarked 1794) reveal Blake's disillusion with the capacity of armed revolution to overthrow tyranny:

> The stern Bard ceas'd, asham'd of his own song; enrag'd he swung
> His harp aloft sounding, then dash'd its shining frame against
> A ruin'd pillar in glittring fragments; silent he turn'd away,
> And wander'd down the vales of Kent in sick & drear lamentings.

(E 51)

As many subsequent revolutionaries have learned, the attempt to realize a utopian society through the limited mechanisms of war can corrupt the ideals for which Energy fights; the means compromise and finally destroy the ends; and the ideologist is left in a crisis of doubt.[34] Recognizing that if Energy goes into battle it must necessarily restrict itself to specific strategies and battlefields, that it may destroy innocent lives and deny moral values, Blake suffered the moral crisis of the "true believer" later documented in Wordsworth's *Prelude* (1805, Bks. IX, X, XI), Dostoevski's *The Possessed,* Malraux's *Man's Fate,* and Koestler's *Darkness at Noon.* He too witnessed the historical degeneration of revolutionary Energy into "mind-forg'd manacles." Rather than creating more open, liberated minds and systems, Energy devoted its powers to the service of oppression and closed forms. The French Revolution was passing through the Terror toward Bonapartism: Danton was executed on April 5, 1794, having himself expelled the Girondists from the Assembly; and Robespierre was killed on July 28, only a month after he deposed the Goddess of Reason and established the worship of the supreme being at a ceremony in the Champs de Mars.[35]

Responding to these historical realities, Blake changed his attitude toward Energy in the Lambeth poems of 1794–95. As Morton Paley has shown, Orc, the embodiment of revolutionary Energy, is transformed from

34. Morton Paley fully discusses this corruption of Energy during war in his chapter on the Lambeth Books, "Heroic Fatality," in *Energy and the Imagination*, pp. 61–88.
35. For a detailed analysis of Blake's response to the French Revolution, see Erdman, *Blake*, parts 3 and 4.

a divine savior into an increasingly ambivalent figure in *Europe, The Book of Ahania,* and *The Book of Urizen.* Throughout these poems, "Orc appears variously as divine child, human fire, demon and serpent." [36] This contradictory imagery reveals Blake's new awareness of the paradoxical potentialities of Energy. On the one hand, revolutionary Energy can liberate all men from "mind-forg'd manacles" and free them to realize their potential divinity. On the other hand, revolutionary activity can commit one to such time-bound strategies as lying and murder, strategies that compromise and finally deny one's utopian goals, and thus betray Energy to the repressive cycle of history in which Orc inevitably becomes Urizen. By 1795, Energy no longer seemed to Blake an intrinsically divine, liberating force. He now presents Energy more neutrally, as pure power, a power that can function as a Nietzschean will-to-power that inevitably leads to the authoritarian repression of the weak by the strong. With this revaluation of Energy comes the shift in Blake's image of Satan and the serpent. The satanic hero of *The Marriage,* the divine rebel and possessor of infinite desire, now becomes the subtle satanic serpent, the embodiment of Energy directed solely toward calculated oppression and the satisfaction of a self-aggrandizing ego, who appears most strikingly in *Vala* and *Milton.*[37]

The Book of Urizen (1794) and the Tate Gallery color prints develop this negative concept of Energy and the graveyard pessimism of *The Gates of Paradise* into an anti-utopian vision. *The Book of Urizen* presents a world in which reason totally dominates the imagination and Energy becomes the agent of repressive jealousy, a world where every conceivable form, even the human body itself, becomes an instrument of enslavement. To convey the full horror of his nightmare, a vision of the future that Blake felt was all too possible during what he saw as the insane, tyrannical reign of George III and William Pitt, Blake created what is probably the first literary anti-utopia. Blake's *Book of Urizen* goes beyond the genre of satiric utopia practiced by Jonathan Swift and Samuel Butler. Rather than depicting an imaginary world that is an inversion,

36. Paley, *Energy and the Imagination,* p. 74.
37. Morton Paley traces this shift in Blake's poetic imagery of Satan and the serpent (*ibid.,* pp. 154–57).

parody, or grotesque variation of reality—the technique employed in *Gulliver's Travels* and *Erewhon*—Blake presents what he believes to be a real psychological possibility. Blake's *Book of Urizen* is prophecy, not unrealizable fantasy, in Blake's sense of the word prophet. "Every honest man is a Prophet he utters his opinion both of private & public matters Thus If you go on So the result is So He never says such a thing Shall happen let you do what you will. a Prophet is a Seer not an Arbitrary Dictator." [38] Thus it may be Blake, rather than H. G. Wells who has been credited with it, who initiated the great genre of anti-utopian "science fiction" in which, as Mark Hillegas points out, "the fundamental principle is prediction or extrapolation, from existing knowledge and conditions, of things to come." [39]

In *The Book of Urizen,* Blake constructs an all-too-human hell from which no escape seems possible, in which the divine vision of Innocence and the liberating progression of Energy seem totally lost, in which the forces of reason conquer the human world. In 1794 Blake saw this nightmare becoming a reality: the French Revolution was failing, Pitt was still Prime Minister, and English politics were becoming increasingly conservative and oppressive. The proclamation against seditious writings had been issued in 1792; in December of that year the English militia was called up, and in February 1793 France declared war against England. And out of the troubles in Ireland came not only George III's stubborn refusal to grant Catholic Emancipation, but also a lukewarmness about religious tolerance in England.[40] Only four years later, Blake cried in alarm and anger, "To defend the Bible in this year 1798 would cost a man his life" (E 601). Blake's growing fear for his personal freedom and safety may have been directly responsible for the increasing obscurity of his early prophetic books, *America* (1793), *Europe* (1794), and *The Song of Los* (1795). In his need to hide his political radicalism from the authorities, Blake was forced to use the very mystery and secrecy he had denounced so lucidly in *Songs of Experience.* Thus in form as well as con-

---

38. Annotations to Bishop Watson's *An Apology for the Bible,* 1798, E 606–7.
39. Mark Hillegas, *The Future as Nightmare* (New York, 1967), p. 9.
40. See Erdman, *Blake,* chaps. 9–15, for Blake's attitude toward English politics at this time.

tent, Blake's poetry of 1794–95 presents the triumph of an uncontrolled and wholly repressive reason. In both *The Book of Urizen* and in Blake's most famous paintings, the Tate Gallery color print series, human life is created by Urizen, the demiurge of reason. Innocence and expanding Energy no longer exist on earth.

Blake's personal "Bible of Hell" parodies the creation myths of both *Genesis* and Milton's *Paradise Lost* as it recounts the origin of reason and Energy and the fall of Energy. Throughout *The Book of Urizen*, Blake identifies the creation and growth of rational man with the suppression of holy Energy. Significantly, Blake here abandons the septenary, the "line of freedom," and instead chooses for his base line a trimeter, usually anapestic but occasionally lapsing into iambs. This brief line, reinforced by frequent repetitions of such negative abstractions as "horror," "unknown," "unseen," "dark," "closed," and "brooding," defines a frighteningly "mechanical, metronome-like monotony of repeated action and reaction, in a situation where the conscious individual has lost control of his fate." [41] Alicia Ostriker notes another effect of this appropriately closed, self-sustaining line. The trimeter in this poem gallops along, creating the impression of unstoppable momentum, of an inexorable power that overwhelms all opposition. "The accretive sentence structure, the jaw-jamming consonants, and the deep vowels of 'Sund'ring, dark'ning, thund'ring, . . . asunder rolling' [E 71]" also combine with this meter to increase the "sense of a massive weight exerting itself against some great resistance." [42] Both in prosody and in imagery, the relentless pressure of an enclosing form or metrical line annihilates imaginative or rhythmic freedom.

Moreover, the designs for the poem fall into rigorously closed, tectonic forms. Several are structured around a single human form centered on a vertical axis that divides the design symmetrically, so that the left half is an almost perfect mirror image of the right half. On the title page, Urizen sits with both shoulders hunched forward, both knees drawn up to his chin, in the exact centers of the open book of hieroglyphs beneath him and the stone decalogue behind him (Copy G, TP) [*Plate 26*]. Heavy, leafless tree trunks arch over him from both sides of the decalogue. This rigid bilateral symmetry is strikingly underlined by the fact that Urizen

41. Ostriker, *Vision and Verse*, p. 166.   42. *Ibid.*, pp. 164–65.

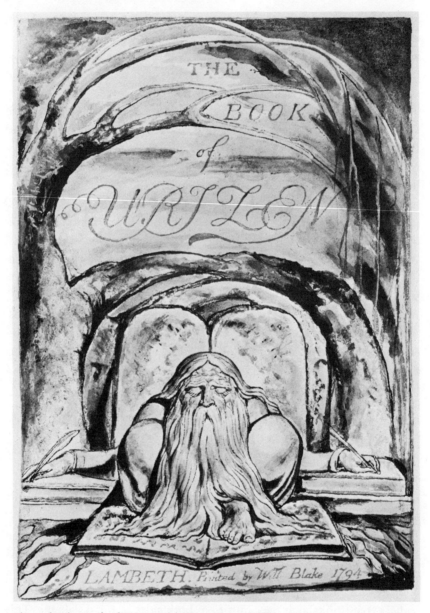

Plate 26. The Book of Urizen, Title Page, Copy G(TP).

writes with *both* hands on the identical piles of books at his right and left. This bilateral symmetry is repeated on Plate 5, where Urizen holds his book of mystery open with both outstretched arms; on Plate 6 (Copy G, Plate 7) where the central cruciform figure falling in vertical flames and wrapped round by a snake is flanked on each side by a serpent-coiled figure grasping its head with both hands; on Plate 16 (G 14) where Los huddles in flames, both knees drawn up to his chin, both hands clasped behind his head, both brows wrinkled in terror; on Plate 17 where Los bends over the globe of blood, both hands pressed to his head, and his veins streaming symmetrically around the globe; on Plate 22 (G 11) where Urizen squats weeping, both wrists and both ankles fettered by heavy chains; and finally, on Plate 28 (G 27) where Urizen sits enmeshed in a net of heavy ropes dropping from both hands.

This visual impression of rigid closure is intensified by the frequent repetition of two specific configurations. One, the crouching figure, first appears on Plate 7 (G 9) where Los, huddled and howling in flames, anticipates both the crouching skeleton of Urizen on Plate 8 (G 10) [*Plate 27*] and Urizen bent down beneath a mass of rocks on Plate 9 (G 4). This crouching-figure motif appears again on Plates 11, 16, 19, 22, 24, and 28 (G 13, 14, 19, 11, 24, 27 respectively). The second major configuration—a figure rising, falling, or pushing an obstacle with arms outstretched and legs bent—appears on at least six designs. On Plate 10 (G 12) a nude man (Los?) struggles to lift a massive stone off his head; on Plate 12 (G 6) Urizen rises through the water with arms lifted; on Plate 13 (G 15) a nude woman (Enitharmon?) pushes two cloudbanks apart with outspread arms; on Plate 14 (G 8) a nude man (Los?) hurls himself down through the clouds; on Plate 20 the child Orc is flung downward through flames with his arms outstretched and his legs bent; and finally, on Plate 27 (G 23) Urizen rushes upward and inward, his hands upraised. The sense of strict enclosure and static balance conveyed by these designs is underlined by the oppressive rectangularity of Plate 26, where a child stands rigid in prayer and a dog howls before a massive, paneled, closed wooden door. Even the flames in these designs, rather than thrusting themselves off the plates, obediently follow the vertical and horizontal frames of the designs, as on Plates 2, 6, 7 (G 9), 11 (G 13), 14

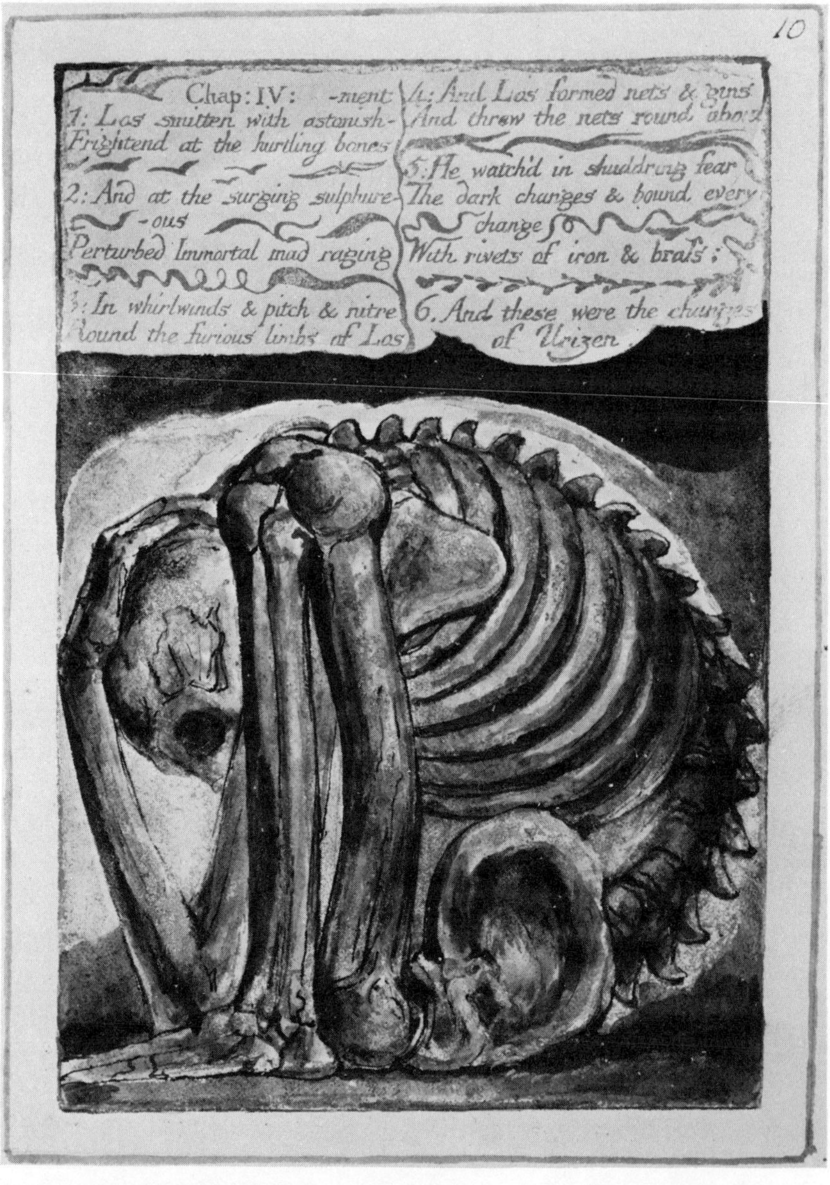

Plate 27. The Book of Urizen, Plate 8, Copy G(TP).

(where the flames actually seem to burn *inward,* toward the huddled, howling Los in the center), 18 [*Plate 38*], and 20. Only on Plate 3, where an Eternal (possibly Los, the eternal prophet) flees in horror from Urizen's self-enclosed "abominable void," do the flames push off the upper left-hand corner of the design, although the nude figure racing with open arms here seems curiously static in comparison with the dynamic torsion of Blake's earlier figures of Energy in *The Marriage of Heaven and Hell* (for example, Plates 3, 4, 14). Together, the rigid symmetry, limited configurations, and strictly tectonic compositions of these designs for *The Book of Urizen* construct a wholly self-enclosed, self-referential, bounded visual universe.[43]

Structurally, since this is a regressive, degenerative action, the poem moves backward in three actions: first, Urizen's creation of the universe; then the preceding creation of Urizen himself, who is separated off from Los; and finally, the original conflict within Los which resulted in that separation. Urizen (the limiting *horizen* seen by *your reason*), that "Creator of men! mistaken Demon of heaven" (E 47) whom Oothoon identified with the rationalistic tyrant Bromion, is an anthropomorphic incarnation of reason, political tyranny, rigid legalism, and moral hypocrisy [*Plate 26*]. He is Blake's personified voice of rational Experience, the counterpart of the voices of Innocence and Energy: the child and the shepherd, Thel, Oothoon, and the poet or rebel in flames. The world Urizen constructs in a parody of Satan's creation of pandemonium and God's cre-

---

43. Robert Simmons' ingenious and provocative essay, *"Urizen:* The Symmetry of Fear," extends this visual symmetry to the poem's conceptual structure: the dualisms of subject/ object and mental/physical (reason and the senses, religion and nature); the use of the Narcissus myth; and the parallelism of opposites as well as identities in the verbal texture. Although I will argue for a tripartite rather than quadripartite narrative structure in the poem, I am persuaded by Simmons that Urizen's universe is constructed on the law of symmetry. As Simmons observes: "It is symmetry itself—the generalizing and abstracting habit of reducing the world to similars and opposites, ups and downs, lefts and rights, rights and wrongs—that crystallizes the symmetrical world of the isolated, lowest common denominator, solely quantitative, fallen senses. Being symmetrical, this world is also predictable and universal, a world of futurity and fixity. Man's birth is accompanied by the inevitable symmetry of his death. A symmetrical world links joy with pain, love with hate, master with slave, desire with dread. In the world of Urizen, symmetry is both the sign and the seal of fear." *Blake's Visionary Forms Dramatic,* ed. David Erdman and J. E. Grant (Princeton, 1970), p. 165. Simmons goes on to point out that, from the point of view of the Eternals, this symmetry appears grotesque, even laughable (p. 167).

ation of the world is a self-enclosed vacuum, a "wide world of solid obstruction" carved out of the "petrific abominable chaos" which the Eternals shun. It is the by now familiar world of rational Experience which is ruled by religion and mystery, by

> Laws of peace, of love, of unity:
> Of pity, compassion, forgiveness.
> Let each chuse one habitation:
> His ancient infinite mansion:
> One command, one joy, one desire,
> One curse, one weight, one measure
> One King, one God, one Law.

(E 71)

Significantly, in this nightmare world, the human form itself becomes an incarnation of reason. Blake defines Urizen's "dark globe" in anatomical imagery:

> And a roof, vast petrific around,
> On all sides He fram'd: like a womb;
> Where thousands of rivers in veins
> Of blood pour down the mountains to cool
> The eternal fires beating without
> From Eternals; & like a black globe
> View'd by sons of Eternity, standing
> On the shore of the infinite ocean
> Like a human heart strugling & beating
> The vast world of Urizen appear'd.

(E 72)

Urizen's creation takes on the form of the human body, while Urizen himself, as we see in the second action of the poem, is molded by Los from "a clod of clay" (E 73) into a human skeleton. Blake here pictures the creation of the human form itself as a fall from infinity into a closed rationalism. No one can escape this fate: whoever bears a mortal body is automatically cut off from the infinitely expanding Energy of the Eternals. Whereas Blake had earlier defined the body as "a portion of Soul discernd by the five senses" (E 34), he now pictures the body as fixed, finite matter, inexorably bounded by the five senses and the circumscribing force of reason. Mortal man is now born with original sin, those "Seven deadly Sins of the soul" which only the eyes of the Eternals can see truly as "enormous forms of energy;/ . . . In living creations . . ./ In the flames of eternal fury" (E 71).

The creation of Urizen himself from the ribs of Los is, of course, a parody of the creation of Eve from the ribs of Adam. But Urizen is originally only a potentiality, a mere embryo, "Cold, featureless, flesh or clay"; not until Los, here acting both as the nourishing female womb and as the artistic creator, provides "nets & gins" can Urizen begin to take shape. Urizen's growth, as Carmen Kreiter has shown, meticulously follows the eighteenth-century theory of human embryological development taught by Dr. John Hunter.[44] Here, reason completely usurps the human form: the changes of Urizen bring him, first, a skeleton (spine, rib, and bones); then a heart; then brain, nerves, and eyes; ears, nostrils; stomach; throat and tongue; and, finally, limbs. The resultant anatomy, meagerly fleshed, is pictured on Plate 8 (G 10) [*Plate 27*]. The seven changes of Urizen are thus the seven ages of man as well as a parodied seven days of creation. And Los, too, shrinks into the human form, while

> All the myriads of Eternity:
> All the wisdom & joy of life:
> Roll like a sea around him,
> Except what his little orbs
> Of sight by degrees unfold.

(E 76)

Both Los and Urizen are now ensnared in the dark narrow void of the human body, "Cut off from life & light frozen/ Into horrible forms of deformity."

With the binding of Urizen into a human form, Blake achieves a visual and poetic image for fallen Experience itself, for that authoritarian reason which is antithetical to love and liberating Energy. Urizen embodies the deceit and sexual repression of Thel's "land of death," the economic slavery and intellectual empiricism of Bromion, the political oppression of Albion's angel, the false dualism and predestinarianism of Swedenborg, and all the evils denounced in *Songs of Experience*. This old man, white haired, white bearded, crouched over the brass book of mystery [*Plate*

44. Carmen S. Kreiter, "Evolution and William Blake," *Studies in Romanticism* 4 (Winter 1965):110–18.

26]—a striking parody of the Christian God depicted in medieval and Renaissance art—personifies to Blake every aspect of the limited rational mind.

Why was Los also reduced to a bounded human form? Beginning with chapter 5 of *The Book of Urizen,* Blake explains how Los, the poetic imagination or divine vision within man (a masculine version of the voice of Innocence) can be dragged down into the sordid world of Experience. Blake's explanation for the defeat of the poetic genius is psychologically subtle. As Blake had argued in "The Tyger," the poetic imagination must always struggle to reconcile expanding Energy with a bounded form or "fearful symmetry," without limiting Energy too much. The imagination is the final arbiter of the contrary and conflicting but equally valid demands of Energy and reason. The imagination thus constantly runs the risk of arbitrating unfairly, of creating an image that is too open and unstructured to be comprehensible or an image that is too closed and limited to be original or interesting. At some point in his artistic career, Los made the latter mistake: he imagined the excessively limited, symmetrical form of Urizen. Los then, in all innocence, felt pity for the sufferings of this grotesque progeny:

> He saw Urizen deadly black,
> In his chains bound, & Pity began
>
> In anguish dividing & dividing
> For pity divides the soul.
>
> (E 76)

But Los's pity or compassion for Urizen leads Los to sympathize with Urizen, to participate in the psychology of his enemy and feel some identification or communion with this grotesquely limited creature. By so doing, Los schizophrenically tears himself in two; he becomes devourer as well as prolific, hater as well as hated, finite as well as infinite. In sympathizing with Urizen, Los's heart comes to "know" evil. Thus reason becomes the stronger power in Los, weakening his Energy and integrity and driving him to ever more fragmented self-division. The emotion of pity, the force which originally alienated Los from his Energy, now itself divides off into a "globe of life blood" and a separate, branching, "fibrous" female form.

With this final disjoining of the two human sexes, man's fall from eternity into the limited mortal body is completed. The Eternals recoil in horror from these human forms and carefully exile them to Urizen's rational kingdom:

> They began to weave curtains of darkness
> They erected large pillars round the Void
> With golden hooks fastend in the pillars
> With infinite labour the Eternals
> A woof wove, and called it Science.
>
> (E 77)

"Science" here is that "self-destroying beast formd Science" (*Four Zoas*, IX, 120: 70) depicted as Nebuchadnezzar and his companion Newton in the Tate Gallery color prints and denounced by Boston's Angel (Samuel Adams) on Plate 11 of *America:* "Till pity is become a trade, and generosity a science,/ That men get rich by" (E 54). This is science as seen by Urizen: the ratio of the five senses, an empirical and dissecting categorization of all human experience, rather than the "eternal science" (*Ahania* 5:34, E 88) or true knowledge of man's potential divinity.

The human form as such has now been denied this divine vision. Within this fallen world, the sexes are antagonistic and perverted— Enitharmon taunts Los "in perverse and cruel delight"—and procreation only proves their perversity: "Eternity shudder'd when they saw,/ Man begetting his likeness,/ On his own divided image" (E 78). Orc, the embodiment of revolutionary Energy, is now the product of human generation, a fallen child who is easily chained within the world of reason. His Energy is cruelly and successfully repressed by his father's jealousy and his mother's authoritarianism. As the "shadowy" daughter of Enitharmon laments in the preludium to *Europe* (1794), all her children, born in Innocence, are now enclosed in the human form and condemned to mental, moral, and physical slavery.

> Ah mother Enitharmon!
> Stamp not with solid form this vig'rous progeny of fires.
>
> I bring forth from my teeming bosom myriads of flames.
> And thou dost stamp them with a signet, then they roam abroad
> And leave me void as death. . . .
>
> (E 60)

To assume the human form, then, is to enter the land of Urizen and leave forever the realm of eternal vision. Blake's parody of *Genesis'* seven days of creation now insists that the generation of the human form *is* the fall:

> Then the Inhabitants of those Cities:
> Felt their Nerves change into Marrow
> And hardening Bones began
> In swift diseases and torments,
> In throbbings & shootings & grindings
> Thro' all the coasts; till weaken'd
> The Senses inward rush'd shrinking,
> Beneath the dark net of infection.
>
> Till the shrunken eyes clouded over
> Discernd not the woven hipocrisy
> But the streaky slime in their heavens
> Brought together by narrowing perceptions
> Appeard transparent air; for their eyes
> Grew small like the eyes of a man
> And in reptile forms shrinking together
> Of seven feet stature they remaind
>
> Six days they shrunk up from existence
> And on the seventh day they rested
> And they bless'd the seventh day, in sick hope:
> And forgot their eternal life.
>
> (E 81–82)

Seemingly, Blake offers a moment of hope at the end of *The Book of Urizen*—Fuzon, a modern day Moses and a man of fire, calls together those few remaining children of Urizen who have not totally lost their sight and hearing and leads them out of the "pendulous earth," called Egypt, into the promised land. But the poem ends, not with their successful exodus and arrival in Israel, but with the "salt ocean" rolling "englob'd" around Urizen's kingdom. The implication is that Fuzon's followers may have been drowned in the Red Sea; but even if they escaped, no one else will be able to follow them.

And in *The Book of Ahania* (1795), Fuzon becomes a surrogate Orc figure who willingly succumbs to Urizen's powers. Fuzon begins as a figure of revolutionary Energy—he is associated with Satan, with Moses as liberator, with Prometheus—and challenges Urizen-Jehovah:

Shall we worship this Demon of smoke,
Said Fuzon, this abstract non-entity . . .
So he spoke, in a fiery flame. . . .

(E 83)

But, as Morton Paley has shown, Fuzon quickly casts out Ahania or pleasure, sets himself up as a new dictator, and is then crucified on the tree of
mystery; Energy is once again reduced to a Urizenic will-to-power.[45]

Moreover, Blake's poetry of 1794–95 consistently depicts the human
body as a physical prison that confines and inevitably prevents Energy
from expanding to infinity. In *Europe,* Blake denounces both the degeneration of religion ("golden Verulam" is replaced by Albion's king's "serpent temple") and the creation of the human form as signs of man's fall
from the divine vision:

. . . when the five senses whelm'd
In deluge o'er the earth-born man; then turn'd the fluxile eyes
Into two stationary orbs, concentrating all things.
The ever-varying spiral ascents to the heavens of heavens
Were bended downward; and the nostrils golden gates shut
Turn'd outward, barr'd and petrify'd against the infinite.

Thought chang'd the infinite to a serpent; that which pitieth:
To a devouring flame; and man fled from its face and hid
In forests of night; then all the eternal forests were divided
Into earths rolling in circles of space, that like an ocean rush'd

And overwhelmed all except this finite wall of flesh.
Then was the serpent temple form'd, image of infinite
Shut up in finite revolutions, and man became an Angel;
Heaven a mighty circle turning; God a tyrant crown'd.

(E 62)

The accusation that the human form manifests the dominion of Urizen is
made again at "the tables of Eternity" in *The Song of Los* (1795):

(Night spoke to the Cloud!
Lo these Human form'd spirits in smiling hipocrisy War
Against one another; so let them War on; slaves to the eternal Elements). . . .

(E 66)

And *The Book of Los* (1795) ends with a final condemnation of the
human form as the incarnation of Urizen:

45. Paley, *Energy and the Imagination,* pp. 81–86.

> . . . here Urizen lay
> In fierce torments on his glowing bed
> Till his Brain in a rock, & his Heart
> In a fleshy slough formed four rivers
> Obscuring the immense Orb of fire
> Flowing down into night: till a Form
> Was completed, a Human Illusion
> In darkness and deep clouds involved.
>
> (E 93–94)

In such a hell, nothing that is human or mortal can become divine or infinite. Man can return to the divine vision only by rejecting his physical form, by being "raised a spiritual body," as "To Tirzah," a poem added to *Songs of Experience* around 1805, concludes. Innocence cannot survive in such a world: man must deny his mortal body to enter heaven. As Blake had argued in *The Gates of Paradise,* only death can save man from human evil, from suffering and despair.

Merely articulating this terrifying anti-utopian vision must have given Blake some freedom, some control over his private nightmare—as Wordsworth knew, a "timely utterance" can give even a thought of genuine despair and madness some relief. But simply painting a possibly exaggerated picture of how man and life on earth must be when Innocence no longer exists, when reason rules absolutely and the human body itself is an instrument of oppression, does not solve the real problem Blake faced. To ensure that both he and his readers should not succumb to the forces of rationalism rampant in eighteenth-century England, Blake had to offer a positive alternative, a viable utopia that could triumph over all Urizenic tyrannies. He had to answer, for all men rather than for the artist alone, the problem first posed in "The Tyger": How can Energy, which is potentially infinite and divine, be preserved within a bounded form or an intellectual system without being perverted into a repressive will-to-power? Predictably, Blake sought the answer among the formal patterns he understood best, the images of his own painting and engraving. Significantly, the development of Blake's artistic style during this period (1773–95), which I shall trace in detail in the next chapter, moves toward ever more neoclassical designs. To reconcile this increasingly bounded and tectonic art with his philosophical condemnation of boundaries, Urizenic systems and the physical human form is the struggle Blake undertook in *Vala,* or *The Four Zoas.* In the convoluted rethinkings and revisions of that manuscript, as I shall show in chapter 5, we can trace the ground of Blake's five-year battle with despair, a contest from which he finally emerged with a triumphant reconciliation of form and infinity, of reason and Energy, of man and God.

FOUR

Romantic Classicism and Blake's Art, 1773-1795

From his apprentice work to his mature style, Blake's art developed steadily within the idiom of eighteenth-century neoclassicism. Both his teachers and his personal friends and mentors encouraged him to imitate antique art, from casts, drawings and engravings available in England. But as we shall see, Blake's personal adaptation of the neoclassical style tends to emphasize the contours of the human figure at the expense of its mass, to reduce a three-dimensional sculpture to a two-dimensional design, and to exaggerate linear rhythms. Outlines, abstract linear patterns, and, with only a few exceptions such as the designs for *The Marriage of Heaven and Hell* discussed earlier, strongly tectonic compositions control Blake's art. For his subject-matter, Blake focused more and more fixedly on one particular motif, the naked human body. In his illuminated poetry and in his paintings, he gradually distinguished two symbolic human figures: the open-armed youth in flames who signifies the poet or rebel—the figure of Innocence become Energy—and the crouching, aged man with white hair and beard who represents the lawmaker or priest—the figure of rational Experience. Interpreted in light of this fairly consistent iconography, Blake's Tate Gallery color-print series reflects Blake's philosophical condemnation of the human form. But this very condemnation is presented in visual terms that glorify the human form: the figures in the Tate Gallery series are uniformly large, muscular, and heroic. As we shall see, Blake's linear, tectonic style and visual glorification of the human body implicitly contradict the rejections of the human form and all closed systems voiced explicitly in *Europe, The Book of Urizen, The Book of Ahania,* and *The Song of Los,* and symbolically in the Tate Gallery color prints. By more closely studying the development of Blake's style and personal iconography and by noting the aesthetic practices and theories of his time which greatly influenced him, we can better understand why Blake was forced into such a contradiction.

THE DEVELOPMENT OF BLAKE'S STYLE

As an apprentice engraver, Blake's early style was predictably eclectic. He experimented with many of the major artistic idioms of the late eighteenth century: the neoclassical return to antique sculptures and vase painting; the Society of Antiquaries' engravings of severely delineated, Gothic forms; the large, muscular figures and historical scenes of the grand style derived from Raphael and Michelangelo; the sentimental pastorals of eighteenth-century rococo; the sublime subject matter defined by Burke and most often found in the poetry of Dante, Shakespeare, and Milton; the documentation of contemporary persons and events (Blake drew an occasional portrait and painted allegorical scenes of the triumphs of Pitt and Nelson). Despite these heterogeneous influences, as we shall see, Blake quickly formed a distinctly personal style. He aligned himself with the neoclassical school's emphasis on outline and the human figure, and rejected complex baroque movements, rococo decoration, strong coloring, and Dutch-Flemish realism. Blake was strongly encouraged to move in this direction, of course, by the purist aesthetic theories of his closest colleagues and friends, James Barry, George Cumberland, John Flaxman, and Henry Fuseli and by the magnificent example of Michelangelo. He soon became one of the proponents of romantic classicism, an idiom heavily based on outlines, flat planes, attenuated figures, clinging draperies, and nonillusionistic settings. His final style, which is paralleled most closely by the severely linear illustrative modes of Flaxman and Asmus Jakob Carstens, moves toward contemporary abstract constructions. Large, elongated, precisely outlined figures float through flattened, unperspectived spaces; illusionistic settings, color and modeling are absent; linear rhythms completely control Blake's compositions, as in the art nouveau which he anticipated.[1]

Blake's earliest known engravings already reveal his characteristic linearity and his interest in the human form. Although his knowledge of anatomy and his facility with the graver are immature and his figures, as a result, static, flabby, and blurred, Blake's obsession with muscle delineation and clinging draperies is already clear. His *Joseph of Arimathea* (a line engraving done in 1773 when Blake was apprenticed to James Basire and based on Salviati's copy of Michelangelo's lower right-hand figure in *The Crucifixion of St. Peter* in the Pauline Chapel) manifests Blake's early fascination with an abstract human form and with sharp, defining lines (especially evident in the nervous, broken, rococo waves).

Blake's tendency to emphasize linear rhythms and the human outline also appears in the draperies and flattened masses of his engravings of the Westminster Abbey medieval effigies of Edward III, Queen Philippa, Aveline of Lancaster, Henry III, and Richard II and his queen for Richard Gough's *Sepulchral Monuments of Great Britain* (1786); in the classical figures of Abraham, Lot, Joseph, and Joshua based on Raphael and Rubens which he engraved for *The Protestant's Family Bible* (1781); and in his famous design known as *Glad Day* (1780 [*Plate* 37]). Here Blake broadens and flattens the firm plastic modeling of his source, a Roman bronze unearthed at Herculaneum. Blake's preparatory drawings for the *Glad Day* engraving, now in the British Museum,[2] sharply unmask his unfamiliarity with anatomy (the jointure of shoulder and arm in the front view drawing is extremely awkward, and the jointure of right leg to pelvis is not defined), as well as his disposition to reduce a sculptured, three-dimensional figure to a linear, two-dimensional design.

Blake's natural inclination to linearity appears even in his early, other-

1. See Robert Schmutzler, "Blake and Art Nouveau," *Architectural Review* 118 (August 1955):90–97.
2. Reproduced in Sir Anthony Blunt, *The Art of William Blake* (New York, 1959), Plates 6c, 7c.

wise faithful imitations of both his friend Thomas Stothard's illustrative style and the grand manner of history painting practised by Joshua Reynolds, Benjamin West, James Barry, Gavin Hamilton, and Angelica Kauffmann.

Stothard's pastoral settings, soft sweet faces, and wraith-like figures float through Blake's engravings for the frontispiece to Commins' *An Elegy Set to Music* (1786), for Joseph Ritson's *A Select Collection of English Songs,* and most obviously for *Songs of Innocence.*[3] Old John in "The Ecchoing Green" mimics Stothard's elegantly dressed men in his fashion plates for *The Lady's Poetical Magazine* (1781); and Blake's shepherd with crook [*Plate 1*] echoes Stothard's own drawing of *The Shepherd* (which Blake actually engraved in 1780). But Blake characteristically adds greater linear definition to Stothard's figures. Whereas Stothard's puppets have no muscles to speak of and are draped in flowing or bulky form-concealing garments, Blake's piper of Innocence (frontispiece) has a firmly outlined chest, pelvis, and leg muscles and wears a skin-tight, form-revealing leotard. Indeed, this garment is worn by almost all the male figures in the designs for *Songs of Innocence*—the shepherd, the singer of "Laughing Song," the boys in "The Ecchoing Green" and "Nurse's Song" designs—and it functions throughout these designs to define and celebrate the lineaments of the masculine human form.

In his episodes from early British history, Shakespeare, and the Bible (all subjects recommended by Burke as suitable for the sublime style), Blake followed contemporary history painters in their predilection for large idealized figures, rhetorically grouped configurations, static attitudes, and "morally elevating" events. We find Blake painting James Barry's examples of "general and perfect" nature—episodes from Shakespeare's *King Lear* and the *Book of Job*[4]—as well as watercolor scenes from English history (1775–89) that clearly demonstrate moral precepts. His *Death of Earl Godwin* illustrates the divine vengeance on murderers; the *Keys of Calais* teaches the quality of mercy; *Edward and Elenor* (in which Queen Elenor sucks the poison from Edward's wound) instructs self-sacri-

3. *Ibid.,* pp. 20, 39, 47–49.
4. James Barry, R. A., *Lectures on Painting,* ed. Ralph N. Wornum (London, 1848), p. 118.

Plate 28. The Penance of Jane Shore in St. Paul's Church, Tate Gallery.

fice and heroism; *Jane Shore* [*Plate 28*] and *Queen Emma* both picture
the triumph of modesty and innocence over hypocritical sexual morality
and the false accusations of envy.[5]

Stylistically, however, Blake's history paintings prefer a more strictly
neoclassical rhetoric of simplified outlines, flat planes, and tectonic compositions to the elaborate draperies and illusionistic settings of Angelica
Kauffmann and James Barry. His *Jane Shore* (1778–79) [*Plate 28*] is
organized symmetrically. A flattened, strictly balanced, two-dimensional

5. See Blunt, *Art of William Blake,* pp. 8–9.

pattern almost eliminates the illusion of depth.[6] Jane's central position on the left is balanced by the dark-bearded, burly guard at the center-right; the head of another guard with a plumed hat, appearing between their shoulders, forms the apex of an equilateral triangle defined by their three heads and is, moreover, at the vertical center of the picture. These three central figures are compositionally flanked by two paired figures and backed by an undifferentiated mass of guards. The static grouping is further emphasized by the checked pattern on the floor that defines the balanced placing of these pieces as though on a checkerboard. The modeling of Jane's figure is flat and planar, although the stylized, clumsy folds of her robe at least mark the curves of her left hip and right thigh. The burly guard, like the piper, wears a closely fitted leotard that sharply outlines his chest and thigh muscles. The configurations in both *Queen Emma* and *Edward and Elenor* [7] are also repetitive, two-dimensional, and rhetorically static. Again, pictorial movements are severely limited to a horizontal-vertical axis: in *Queen Emma,* all the figures stand upright, while the rectilinear movements of *Edward and Elenor* are interrupted only by the diagonal lines of the poisoned arrow held by an attendant, the flow of the water-bearers' dark robes, and the leaning Elenor above.

Blake's natural tendency toward a two-dimensional, nonillusionistic rendering of the grand style is further developed in *A Breach in a City* (1784), *Joseph and his Brethren* (1784), and *The Complaint of Job* (1785, [*Plate* 29]), based on James Barry's *Job* (1777). Both thematically and stylistically, *A Breach in a City* presents an abstract statement on the miseries of war rather than a description of a specific historical event.[8] The disposition of the figures is rigidly rectilinear and adheres closely to the horizontal and vertical axes of the picture frame. The figures themselves are unnaturally attenuated. The dead warrior in the foreground is elongated beyond the capacities of the human frame, and the kneeling woman beside his head is abbreviated into a simplistic, curvilinear rhythm. Both the figures and the setting have been unnaturally re-

6. For an illuminating discussion of this painting, see Robert Rosenblum's unpublished doctoral dissertation, "The International Style of 1800: A Study in Linear Abstraction" (New York University, 1956), p. 102.

7. Reproduced in Blunt, *Art of William Blake,* Plates 4b, 5a.

8. See Rosenblum, "International Style," p. 103. Reproduced in Blunt, Plate 8b.

Plate 29. The Complaint of Job.

duced to flat, abstract patterns of line and value, although, as Robert Rosenblum notes, the work does carry "overtones of a natural space in its suggestion of recession and in the gravitational pull implied by its horizontal format," [9] as well as in the perspectival diminishment of the figure wandering outside the breached walls.

The suggestion of a natural spatial environment has been further lessened in both the Joseph and the Job scenes. Here the figures are almost reduced to linear, purely decorative designs: their bodies, even the grandiose forms of Job and his three comforters, are merely flat areas of light and dark placed in a crowded two-dimensional plane. The rhythms of the pictures are linear: the circular line flows down from Joseph's raised left arm through the embracing figure of Benjamin at his feet to the arching back of the kneeling brother at the far right. This circularity is further

9. *Ibid.*, p. 104.

emphasized by the massed grouping of the kneeling brothers who fill in the bottom half of the circle and by the kneeling, bent figure in the center whose body repeats in itself the larger compositional circle. Similarly, *The Complaint of Job* [*Plate* 29] is held together and compositionally cemented by the echoing rhythms of the drapery and arched backs of the three comforters. The basic composition is that of a vertical line tangential to an oval; the upright, seated figure of Job at the left forms a vertical pole, beside which the wife and three comforters are pressed into an oval accentuated by their bent heads, arched backs, and the flowing lines of the foremost comforter's robes. This simple geometrical pattern is made more interesting by the *S* lines of the drapery over Job's right leg and foot and of the drapery flowing from the first comforter's left knee along his thigh and left arm to his left shoulder. The linear flow, however, is not strong enough to compensate for the empty rhetoric of Blake's grandiose, static bodies or the bland, almost sweet facial expressions; and the picture itself is finally a dull, almost academic exercise in the grand style of eighteenth-century English history painting.

Although Blake exhibited a consistent tendency to linearize and two-dimensionalize the two major styles he used in the late 1780s—the grand style and Stothard's illustrative mode—he had not yet liberated himself from their flaccidity and oversweet pastoralism. Neither of these modes was as yet a satisfactory vehicle for Blake's personal vision of man and nature presented in his poetry. The violent if incoherent curses of the aged, wracked Tiriel become almost ludicrous when read in conjunction with the grand manner illustrations Blake did for the poem.[10] Tiriel appears as a balding man with a short white beard, dressed in a Greek toga; Har is a surprisingly youthful old man with flowing white hair and beard and a grandiose but flatulent body; Heva's young body is flattened and empty; and Mnetha is a static figure, twice oddly clothed in an elaborately printed fabric made up in the eighteenth-century fashion. This interjection of contemporary dress fashions into the otherwise consistently classical postures and dress of these figures seems almost grotesque. The figures themselves are inflated, weak forms, and their facial expressions are confined to total blankness or exaggerated horror or fear. These flaccid, pseudo-

10. See G. E. Bentley, Jr.'s edition of the text and designs of *Tiriel* (Oxford, 1967).

antique figures derived from the grand style of history painting fail to sustain Blake's more forceful poetic language. But also reflected in these designs is Blake's characteristic tendency to stress the linear contours of the human figure at the expense of its muscular plasticity, to set his figures in nonillusionistic, abstract spaces, and to compose them into limited rectilinear or triangular patterns. These designs thus reveal Blake's development toward a more flexible and powerful visual idiom, an idiom built on outlines, linear rhythms, tectonic compositions, and abstract spaces.

Similarly, Stothard's delicate pastoralism and fashionable drawing-room personnel, which Blake used reasonably effectively in the *Songs of Innocence* illustrations, a few years later proved inadequate to the satiric statements of the *Songs of Experience*. The child leading the crippled old man in the design for "London"; the kneeling, expressionless priest and adolescents in the design for "The Garden of Love"; the perturbed, melancholy face of the old man beneath the net in "The Human Abstract"—all are disappointingly sweet, sentimental images in comparison with the fierce condemnatory tone of the poems themselves. Even the intentionally innocent tyger in some copies looks too much like a stuffed toy to be a wholly persuasive lamb. In several of these designs, Blake's line is so weak and his coloring so haphazard that details of the designs are obscured; only in a few copies of "The Chimney Sweeper" in *Songs of Experience*, for instance, is it apparent that the tiny soot-covered boy carries a sweep's brush in his right hand. Perhaps aware that both the grand manner and the illustrative styles would prove inadequate to his purposes, Blake channelled his increasing technical proficiency into the development of a more mature, personal, and responsive medium based on strong linear rhythms and sharply outlined, idealized human figures.

Blake's mastery of an abstract linear style was both a personal inclination and the predictable result of his extensive exposure to this neoclassical idiom. Dora and Erwin Panofsky have more precisely defined this idiom as romantic classicism: "Romantic in that an idea unattainable for the present tended to be mistaken for a reality believed to have existed in the past, doctrinaire [classical] in that nevertheless (or, perhaps for this very reason) a passionate effort was made to regain this Paradise Lost by means of scientific reconstruction rather than creative assimilation." [11] In its search for a precise representation of the ideal images of the past, romantic classicism developed its own style: engravings consisting of outlines without either color or modeling which had previously been used only for preliminary sketches or scientific and diagrammatic illustrations. Examples of this pure outline engraving appear on the plates of Morghen's *Principi del Disegno tratti dalle piu eccelenti statue antiche,* published in 1786, and in Tischbein's edition of engravings of William Hamilton's antique vases, published from 1791 onward.[12] This style was practiced in Rome by the Danish-German neoclassicist, Asmus Jakob Carstens (whose art closely parallels Blake's style, although the two artists knew nothing of each other,[13] and thus testifies to the pervasiveness of romantic classicism) and in England by Blake's mentor, John Flaxman. This style quickly gained universal popularity in the late eighteenth century, partly because it was less expensive than mezzotint or cross-hatched etching, partly because it

gave tangible expression not only to the ontological superiority accorded to the line in the theory of cognition (had not Thomas Aquinas asserted that the relation between image and prototype rests on *figura* rather than *color* because 'if the color of anything is depicted on a wall, this is not called an image unless the figure is also depicted' [*Summa theologiae,* I, qu. 35, art. 1, c.]?), but also to the aesthetic superiority accorded to it in all idealistic theories of art, and to the metaphysical superiority accorded to it by every type of Platonism.[14]

Frans Hemsterhuys wrote in 1769 that simple line drawings retain more of the "godlike fire of the first conceived idea than paintings." [15] And, the

11. Dora and Erwin Panofsky, *Pandora's Box,* rev. ed. (New York: Pantheon Books, 1962), p. 85.

12. See David Irwin, *English Neoclassical Art* (London and Greenwich, Conn., 1966), p. 61.

13. As Robert Rosenblum points out in "British Art and the Continent, 1760–1860," in *Romantic Art in Britain: Drawings and Paintings 1760–1860,* Exhibition Catalogue, ed. Frederick Cummings and Allen Staley (Philadelphia Museum of Art, 1968), p. 12, both Carstens and Blake invented private mythologies to replace the dead myths of the Establishment which they vehemently rejected; and both did so in a "Michelangelesque style of heroic figures that soared through flattened, abstract spaces."

14. Panofsky, *Pandora's Box,* p. 91.

15. See J. G. van Gelder, *Dilettanti en Kunstwetenschap* (Wormerveer, 1936), p. 20.

Panofskys conclude, "reduced to pure contours, the visible world in general, and the precious relics of antiquity in particular, seemed to assume an unearthly, etherial character, detached from the 'material' qualities of color, weight and surface texture." [16]

Blake had encountered this pure outline engraving style in D'Hancarville's *Collection of Etruscan, Greek, and Roman Antiquities from the Cabinet of the Honorable William Hamilton* (Naples, 1766–67), perhaps when he was a student of engraving at the Royal Academy. To simulate the appearance of red-figure Greek vases, D'Hancarville printed his plates in black ink on an orange-red ground. As on his Greek models, his figures are constructed solely with a sharp, fine black line, a line that defines the contours of the human body, delicately indicates the musculature, sketches in the most important facial features, and carefully delineates the drapery, fold by fold. Blake scrupulously copied several figures from D'Hancarville's plates in two surviving pencil drawings.[17] In addition to D'Hancarville's famous volumes, Blake could have seen early examples of this outline engraving style on the first three plates of Thomas Martyn's and John Lettice's *The Antiquities of Herculaneum,* Volume I (London, 1773), and on Page 383 of the sixth volume in this series, *De' Bronze di Ercolano* (Naples, 1771), where we see depicted in sharp outline a child riding a phallus. This particular volume may thus be the source not only for Blake's Glad Day figure as noted by Sir Anthony Blunt, but also for the final plate of *The Book of Thel.*

In addition to being exposed to outline engravings, Blake was encouraged to imitate a purist linear style by such extremely close friends as George Cumberland, Henry Fuseli, and John Flaxman. Inspired by the aesthetic theories of these neoclassicists, Blake associated the outline form with that pure form that they all thought to be the most authentic embodiment of the primitive mind's cognition of the divine. Blake had engraved at least one plate for Jacob Bryant's *A New System* in 1776 and was familiar at this time with Bryant's theories of the primal unity of mankind, of a single aboriginal tribe and language from which all con-

16. Panofsky, *Pandora's Box,* p. 91.

17. Blake's pencil drawings are in the British Museum Print Room: #1867-10-12-207 is copied from Volume II, plate 68, of D'Hancarville's *Collection;* #1867-10-12-208 is copied from Volume III, plate 36.

temporary civilizations have descended.[18] As Blake said much later, in 1809, "The antiquities of every Nation under Heaven . . . are the same thing as Jacob Bryant, and all antiquaries have proved. . . . All had originally one language, and one religion, this was the religion of Jesus, the everlasting Gospel" (*A Descriptive Catalogue,* V, E 534). This notion of a syncretic mythology and aboriginal civilization was accepted by other antiquarians of Blake's day. James Barry's first lecture "On the History and Progress of Art" at the Royal Academy in 1782 digresses at length on the descent of all modern civilizations from the lost tribes of the Atlantides; [19] and similar theories were propounded by Abbot Pezron in *The Antiquities of Nations* (London, 1706) and by Jean Sylvain Bailly in *Letters upon the Atlantis of Plato* (London, 1801). Since Blake believed the human imagination to be holy, the simplest and clearest expressions of the imagination are closest to God. As he wrote later to Dr. Trusler on August 23, 1799:

To Me This World is all One continued Vision of Fancy or Imagination & I feel Flattered when I am told So. What is it sets Homer Virgil & Milton in so high a rank of Art. Why is the Bible more Entertaining & Instructive than any other book. Is it not because they are addressed to the Imagination which is Spiritual Sensation & but mediately to the Understanding or Reason Such is True Painting and such (was) alone valued by the Greeks & the best modern Artists. (E 677)

At this time Blake clearly identifies Greek art as the first authentic creations of the imagination. He enthusiastically urged his friend George Cumberland to continue his "divine" imitations of antique forms: "Go on, if not for your own sake, yet for ours, who love & admire your works; but, above all, For the Sake of the Arts. Do not throw aside for any long time the honour intended you by Nature to revive the Greek workman-

18. See Nancy Warshaw Bogen's unpublished master's essay, "Jacob Bryant and William Blake" (Columbia University, 1962), for a study of the influence of Bryant's *A New System* on Blake's *The Book of Thel,* as well as her study of *Tiriel* in relation to Bryant cited above.

19. Barry discusses the history of civilization in his *Lectures on Painting,* p. 64n, thus: "Even these Ethiopian predecessors of the Egyptians seem themselves to have derived their knowledge from a still more ancient people—from the Atlantides, those Titanic descendants of Ouranus, whose celebrity is unfortunately but too conspicuous in the ancient poets and historians; and who left their names so inscribed or identified with the sun, planets, and the other constellations of our hemisphere, as to give an additional turpitude and malignity to Sabaism, or idolatrous stellar worship."

ship. I study your outlines as usual, just as if they were antiques" (August 26, 1799, K 795).

George Cumberland's influence on Blake's thought and style has perhaps not been sufficiently appreciated. Not only did Cumberland suggest the method of illuminated printing that Blake used—Cumberland's article on "A New Mode of Printing" appeared in *A New Review with Literary Curiosities and Literary Intelligence* in 1784 [20]—but he also encouraged Blake to engrave in a completely linear "antique" style. Cumberland had returned from Greece and Italy in 1784 with a portfolio of drawings of fifth-century B.C. Greek vases and sculpture and Italian Renaissance paintings, frescoes, and sculptures.[21] In these drawings Cumberland invariably used a sharp and severe, if uncertain, line; a clear, if occasionally awkward, figural outline; and a flat, two-dimensional plane. Exactly when Cumberland and Blake met is not known, but they shared common friends in 1780 and it is probable that Blake saw these drawings in the 1780s.[22] Certainly Blake and Cumberland had become close friends by December 6, 1795, the date of Blake's first extant letter to Cumberland. Throughout this period, Cumberland was ardently advocating Greek art and civilization as a model for England. In *Some Anecdotes of the Life of Julio Bonasoni . . . to Which Is Prefixed, A Plan for the Improvement of the Arts in England* (London, 1793), Cumberland set up an appreciation of Greek art as the ultimate criterion of taste and achievement and urged English artists and thinkers to imitate the Greeks, "for whatever people content themselves with a lower ambition than to equal the Greeks at the highest period of art, will be found to be wandering from perfection, instead of approaching towards it." [23] And when Cumberland commissioned Blake to engrave several of his drawings for his *Thoughts on Outline,* Blake responded enthusiastically, both to Cumberland's designs and to his ideas: "I congratulate you, not on any achievement, be-

20. *A New Review with Literary Curiosities and Literary Intelligence,* ed. Henry Maty (London, 1784), 14:318–19.

21. George Cumberland, *Outlines from the Ancients* (London, 1829), pp. iv–xxiv.

22. For evidence of Blake's friendships with Thomas Stothard, George Cumberland and John Flaxman in the early 1780s, see G. E. Bentley, Jr., *Blake Records* (Oxford, 1969), pp. 18–20, 362.

23. George Cumberland, *Some Anecdotes of the Life of Julio Bonasoni* (London, 1793), p. 7.

Think you, the happy in the shades below
Or see your tears, or listen to your woe?

Petronius. Ephesian Matron.

Design'd & Eng.ᵈ by G. C. Publish'd Jan.ᵗ 1 1795

Plate 30. Cumberland, *Thoughts on Outline*, Plate 17.

cause I know that the Genius that produces these Designs can execute them in any manner. . . . Now you will, I hope, shew all the family of Antique Borers that Peace & Plenty & Domestic Happiness is the Source of Sublime Art, & prove to the Abstract Philosophers that Enjoyment & not Abstinence is the food of Intellect" (December 6, 1795; K 790). Having received the published book in 1796, Blake again urged Cumberland to "Go on. Go on. Such works as yours Nature & Providence, the Eternal Parents, demand from their children: how few produce them in such perfection: how Nature smiles on them: how Providence rewards them" (December 23, 1796; K 791).

Blake's execution of Cumberland's designs reveals his own commitment to Cumberland's linear style. In contrast to Cumberland's own engravings, where the lines are often wavering, uneven, and broken [*Plate 30*],

PSYCHE DISOBEYS

From an original Invention by G. Cumberland Esq.ʳ by W. Blake   Published   as the   November 5. 1794

Plate 31. Cumberland, *Thoughts on Outline,* Plate 12.

Blake's plates (Pls. 12–16, 18–19, 23) smooth out the line into a strong, firm flow [*Plate 31*]. Blake de-emphasizes Cumberland's flesh bulges and awkward attempts at muscular definition and stresses instead the flow of outline along an entire torso or limb (whereas Cumberland's line is bumpier, less rhythmic). In addition, Blake usually lifts Cumberland's rather heavy, sagging buttocks and sweetens his facial expressions. Blake's admiration of Cumberland's subjects and his marked improvement of Cumberland's style suggests that Blake himself may have drawn as well as engraved the one design which Cumberland confesses is not his own. Blake's technical mastery of outline engraving is demonstrated again in the four highly accomplished plates he engraved in 1794 for the third volume of James Stuart's and Nicholas Revett's *Antiquities of Athens.* In contrast to the rather heavy-handed muscular definition and bumpy contours of his colleague, T. Skelton, Blake's line is firm, clear, and smooth;

his musculature delicately indicated; and his contours a single, harmonious, flowing line.

Both his letters and engravings confirm Blake's endorsement of Cumberland's belief in "the inestimable value of chaste outline." [24] Cumberland felt that there could be no true art without outline, that sculpture is all outline, and that outline is the basis of Greek art. Cumberland defines outline not as a simple line, but as a bounding form: the best bounding form is a *"fine, firm, flowing,* and *faint"* line, as in da Vinci and Raphael. After noting the necessity of a precise style and rhythmic composition (in which the lines flow from one to another), Cumberland concludes that "A fine, simple Outline may possess grace, action, expression, character, and proportion." [25] Although Blake himself did not voice his commitment to outline until his annotations to Reynolds' *Discourses,* written between 1798 and 1809,[26] we have seen that clear bounding lines and linear rhythms dominate his earliest works. The title page for *The Book of Thel* (1789) [*Plate 3*], for instance, not only depicts a Greek shepherdess with a Greek name but also emphasizes the linear flow of the overarching willow tree, of the involuting flowers (possibly Greek acanthus) at the lower right, and of the elaborate script of the title itself through which tiny flying figures interweave. And Blake's illustration for "Infant Joy" strikingly emphasizes his early obsession with an arabesque line and a two-dimensional plane: the flowing petals, curved stem, and flame-pointed leaves of the large red passion flower all create an abstract, nonillusionistic design.

Blake's two closest friends at this period, John Flaxman and Henry Fuseli, further encouraged him to develop his linear style into ever purer outlined forms. As Blake commemorated their friendship in a letter-poem "To My Dearest Friend, John Flaxman":

I bless thee, O Father of Heaven & Earth, that ever I saw Flaxman's face.
Angels stand round my Spirit in Heaven, the blessed of Heaven are my friends
    upon Earth.

24. Cumberland, *Thoughts on Outline, Sculpture, and the System that Guided the Ancient Artists* (London, 1796), p. 1.
    25. *Ibid.,* p. 33.
    26. This is the date suggested by David Bindman, "The Dating of Blake's Marginalia to Reynolds," *Burlington Magazine* 108 (October 1966):522.

When Flaxman was taken to Italy, Fuseli was given to me for a season. . . .

(September 12, 1800; E 680)

John Flaxman, two years Blake's senior, probably introduced Blake into the home of the Reverend and Mrs. A. S. Mathew where both men visited regularly after 1770. At this time Flaxman was designing and making wax models of antique vases for the cameo wares of Wedgwood and Bentley and spending his free time drawing scenes and characters from Homer, Aeschylus, and Hesiod; he painted his *Oedipus and Antigone* and a *Venus and Cupid* during these years.[27] In 1787 Flaxman began a seven-year residence in Italy where he sculpted Ovid's *Fury of Athamus* as well as a *Cephalus and Aurora* and drew outline designs from Homer, Aeschylus, and Dante (engraved in 1792–93 and published in 1793, 1795, and 1802 respectively).[28] Throughout his life, as his lectures and works demonstrate, Flaxman was committed to a neoclassical aesthetic that revered Greek art above all and established simplicity, truth to an ideal nature, a clear outline, and an internal harmony or linear rhythm as the ultimate criteria of artistic perfection. To Flaxman, Greek art represented the highest achievement of the ideal style, which he defined as "a representation of the human form, according to the distinctions of sex and age, in action or repose, expressing the affections of the soul . . . and selected from such perfect examples as may excite in our minds a conception of the supernatural."[29]

Flaxman's early drawings and sculptures describe a pure, idealized image in a severely linear style. Flaxman consciously rejected the compositional complexity of the seventeenth and eighteenth centuries and the rich variety of spatial, luminary, and atmospheric values of postmedieval art. In his illustration for *The Prayer of the Daughters of Danaus,* Flaxman reduces his composition to "a heraldic grid of rectilinear rhythms, in which the archaic triad of cult statues presides with rigid and absolute authority."[30] Flaxman deliberately minimized any three-dimensional illu-

27. John Flaxman, *Lectures on Sculpture* (London, 1829), p. 9.
28. G. E. Bentley, Jr., "Notes on the Early Editions of Flaxman's Classical Designs," *BNYPL* 68 (May–June 1964):277–307, 361–80.
29. Flaxman, *Lectures on Sculpture,* p. 200.
30. Robert Rosenblum, *Transformations in Late Eighteenth-Century Art* (Princeton, 1966), p. 161.

Plate 32. Flaxman, *The Descent of Discord,* illustrations for Homer's *Iliad,* engraved by Thomas Piroli.

sion by eliminating all background and perspective lines. In fact, Flaxman's style is founded on the exclusive use of a fine, continuous outline, an outline that is reproduced with scrupulous precision and regularity in Thomas Piroli's engravings of his works [*Plate 32*].

Flaxman's style is probably the most complete summary of the idiom of romantic classicism. Flaxman rigorously rejected the illusionistic art of the seventeenth century for "a conceptual, linear art founded upon basic symbols of reality rather than upon illusions of it, an art whose severity of means and expression suggests a pure and early phase of image-making." [31] For Flaxman, as it became for Blake, romantic classicism was both a conscious rejuvenation of art after the corruptions of the baroque and Dutch-Flemish realist styles and a "vehicle for the evocation of, on

31. Rosenblum, "International Style," p. 3.

the one hand, a remote, heroic past of pristine simplicity and, on the other, a comparably unworldly vision of fantastic legends or Christian piety." [32] The linear rhythms, flat planes, and impersonal normative statements of Flaxman's style are thus an analogy for the primitive purity and truth of the heroic scenes he illustrates.

That Blake knew and admired Flaxman's work is clear not only from his letters and other biographical records but also from Blake's artistic works. Blake often borrowed motifs, configurations, and anatomical studies from Flaxman. Sir Anthony Blunt has pointed out Blake's use of the open-armed woman poised on her left foot (from a 1783 Flaxman wash drawing now in the Fitzwilliam Museum) in his *The Good and Evil Angels Struggling for Possession of a Child*.[33] Interestingly, Blake places this figure (transformed into a blind youth in the final Tate Gallery color print [1795, *Plate 43*]) on a more severely rectilinear plane (both his arms and his right leg stretch along a straight horizontal line). In his later illustration for Dante, *The Hypocrites with Caiaphas,* Blake borrowed the hooded monks and the crucified Caiaphas from Flaxman's design for Dante's *Hypocrites.* Blake also used a reduced version of Flaxman's thirteen circling female figures in *The Ninth Sphere* (an illustration to Dante) in the eight women circling with interwoven arms in an oval on Plate 43 of *Milton.* More importantly, Blake imitated Flaxman's austere, simple mode of pure outline engraving. Blake's engravings for Cumberland's *Thoughts on Outline* clearly demonstrate Blake's competency in and preference for this purely linear engraving style.

With Flaxman and Cumberland, Henry Fuseli was the contemporary who had the most considerable impact on the development of Blake's aesthetic theory and linear style. Blake recognized his debt to Fuseli in an epigram (c. 1808):

> The only Man that eer I knew
> Who did not make me almost spew
> Was Fuseli he was both Turk & Jew
> And so dear Christian Friends how do you do.
>
> (E 498)

32. *Ibid.*, p. 123.
33. Blunt, *Art of William Blake*, p. 42; the Flaxman drawing is reproduced on Plate 32c.

Although Fuseli had first come to England in 1764, Blake probably did not meet him until several years after Fuseli's Italian sojourn (1770–78). As Blake said, "When Flaxman was taken to Italy [in 1787], Fuseli was given to me for a season." That "season" ended in mutual disaffection by 1810, but by that time Blake had been thoroughly exposed to Fuseli's *Sturm und Drang* style, his admiration for Rousseau's celebration of emotion and primitivism,[34] and his ardent defense of classical art and art theory.[35] Fuseli enthusiastically endorsed Winckelmann's almost religious adoration of Greek art. He had translated Winckelmann's *Reflections on the Painting and Sculpture of the Greeks* into English in 1765 and was completely persuaded, as were so many of Winckelmann's readers, that Greek art—and especially the sculpture and vase painting of the sublime or grand style (Phidias and his contemporaries, fifth century B.C.) and of the beautiful style (Praxiteles to Lysippos, fourth century B.C.)—was the supreme achievement of human culture. Winckelmann had located the essential perfection of Greek sculpture in its fusion of a careful observation of nature and the human body with the perfect proportions, flowing lines, clear outlines, and vigorous expressions of ideal art. It was Winckelmann's insistence that sublime art presents the naked, preferably male, body in a moment of energetic action or intense emotional stress—or in the moment of serene tranquility that follows such heroic exertions—together with Winckelmann's almost mystical evocation of the spiritual ecstasy embodied in these classical sculptured forms that most influenced Fuseli and, through him, Blake. Reading Winckelmann's superbly lyrical adoration of the Apollo Belvedere (a statue that Winckelmann incorrectly assigned to the Phidian period), Fuseli and Blake must have been persuaded that this figure truly embodied the human form divine:

This statue surpasses all other representations of the god. . . . An eternal springtime, like that which reigns in the happy fields of Elysium, clothes his body with the charms of youth and softly shines on the proud structure of his limbs. To understand this masterpiece you must fathom intellectual beauties and become, if

---

34. Fuseli had articulated his commitment to Rousseau's teachings in his *Remarks on the Writing and Conduct of J. J. Rousseau* (London, 1767).

35. Eudo Mason has summarized Fuseli's classical aesthetic in his introductory notes in *The Mind of Henry Fuseli* (London, 1951), p. 222.

possible, a divine creator; for here there is nothing mortal, nothing subject to human needs. This body . . . is animated by a celestial spirit. . . . His lofty look, filled with a consciousness of power, seems to rise above his victory and gaze into eternity. . . . In the presence of this miracle of art I forget the whole universe and my soul acquires a loftiness appropriate to its dignity. From admiration I pass to ecstasy, I feel my breast dilate and rise as if I were filled with the spirit of prophecy. . . .[36]

Fuseli's *Lectures on Painting, Delivered at the Royal Academy,* March 1801, enthusiastically proclaimed Winckelmann's doctrines of beauty: "The imitation of the ancients was, *essential, characteristic, ideal.* The first cleared nature of accident, defect, excrescence; the second found the stamen which connects character with the central form; the third raised the whole and the parts to the highest degree of unison. . . . the art of the Greeks possessed in itself and propagated, like its chief object, Man, the germs of immortality." [37] Throughout these lectures, Fuseli maintained that painting should depict only the ideal, heroic human figure, classically proportioned, preferably nude or draped in the Grecian style, expressively engaged in a morally elevating action, and placed in a timeless setting.

Since Blake acquired his own copy of Fuseli's translation of Winckelmann's *Reflections* in the 1770s and had almost certainly discussed with Fuseli Winckelmann's more famous *History of Ancient Art,* these books may have strongly influenced several of Blake's most important ideas concerning art theory and his own practice. Winckelmann's assertion that ideal beauty approximates the divine on earth—"The highest beauty is in God," [38] he wrote, and again, "Sensual beauty furnished the painter with all that nature could give; ideal beauty with the awful and sublime; from that he took the *Humane,* from this the *Divine*" [39] —parallels Blake's insistence that the poetic genius perceives and creates the human form divine. Blake certainly responded, in statement and in practice, to Winckelmann's demand that modern painters create a my-

36. This is a rather free translation from Winckelmann's *The History of Ancient Art Among the Greeks* by Hugh Honour in *Neo-Classicism* (Baltimore: Penguin, 1968), p. 60.

37. *Lectures on Painting,* ed. H. G. Bohn (London, 1847), p. 348.

38. Johann Joachim Winckelmann, *The History of Ancient Art Among the Greeks,* trans. G. Henry Lodge (London, 1850), p. 43.

39. Winckelmann, *Reflections on the Painting and Sculpture of the Greeks,* tr. Henry Fuseli (London, 1765), p. 14.

thology similar to the Greek myths. Such a mythology, said Winckelmann, gives art "its most eminent prerogative, the representation of invisible, past and future things." [40] Blake's own prophetic books created a new mythological system based on an eclectic fusion of the various myths collected by Richard Payne Knight and Jacob Bryant; and Blake later defended this practice with the statement that "the Greek Fables originated in Spiritual Mystery & Real Vision. . . . The nature of my Work is Visionary or Imaginative it is an Endeavour to Restore. . . . The Golden Age" (*A Vision of the Last Judgment*, 1810, E 545).

Stylistically, too, Blake followed Winckelmann's precepts for Greek art: an emphasis on outline, accentuated by clinging drapery, with a corresponding de-emphasis on color—"the essence of beauty consists, not in color but in shape" [41]—and a denial of realistic, perspective space. In addition, Blake may have chosen to draw and engrave the Laocoön because Winckelmann selected this sculpture as "an image of the most intense suffering" endured by "the determined spirit of a great man who struggles with necessity and strives to suppress all audible manifestations of pain"; [42] he may have derived his use of the compass (in *The Ancient of Days*, among other works) partially from its appearance on the title page of Winckelmann's *Reflections* (in the Fuseli translation), where it symbolizes the proportions of classical art; and he may have taken his image of Vala, the personification of nature as seen by a mind lacking the capacities for vision, from Winckelmann's eulogy of the *zeitgeist* of freedom embodied in Greek art:

Art claims liberty: in vain would nature produce her noblest offsprings, in a country where rigid laws would choak her progressive growth, as in Egypt, that pretended parent of sciences and arts: but in Greece, where, from their earliest youth, the happy inhabitants were devoted to mirth and pleasure, where narrow-spirited formality never restrained the liberty of manners, the artist enjoyed *nature without a veil*. [43]

Despite Fuseli's enthusiasm for Winckelmann, his own aesthetic theory emphasized the expressive qualities of art far more than Winckelmann who had seen in the most sublime examples of antique art "eine edle Ein-

---

40. *Ibid.*, p. 62.
41. Winckelmann, *History of Ancient Art*, p. 40.
42. *Ibid.*, p. 165.
43. Winckelmann, *Reflections*, p. 9; my italics.

falt und eine stille Grösse"—a noble simplicity and a calm grandeur. Fuseli insisted that "Expression alone can invest beauty with supreme and lasting command over the eye." [44] In his own art, Fuseli consistently chose classical subjects with particularly fantastic or horrific aspects, such as *Dion Seeing a Female Spectre Sweep His Hall* or *Ulysses Killing the Suitors.* And Fuseli's style, developed during the years he spent in Italy visiting churches and drawing from Michelangelo's Sistine Ceiling and the *Horse-Tamers* of Monte Cavallo, is both linearly stylized and highly expressive. His Italian drawings are more monumental, severe, and schematic than his earlier works, but they sustain his predilection for a pictorial *Sturm und Drang* drama. Fuseli sought to convey his passionate apprehension of life and his private obsessions through violent, distorted figural attitudes, strong chiaroscuro, and striking diagonal compositions.[45] In *The Witches Show Macbeth the Descendants of Banquo* (*in a Mirror*) (dated 1773–79, [*Plate 33*]), for instance, we see Fuseli's characteristically strong, nervous outline and muscular curvature in the central, dominating figure of Macbeth. His penchant for dramatic compositions is apparent both in the violent chiaroscuro—the pale descendants on the left and the brightly lighted contours of Macbeth's body are hurled against the blackened, spread arms of the hovering witch or angel of death, Macbeth's black cloak, and the dark masses of struggling figures on the right—and in the vigorously diagonal movements of Macbeth's right arm and spear, which are heightened by the foreshortening of Macbeth's torso. This fusion of classical outlines and expressionist compositions also occurs in Fuseli's pen, ink, and wash drawing of *Standing Figure of Man in Profile* (1773–79). Here the figure of the man standing on his right leg, his left arm supporting his head and leaning on his raised left leg, is a stylized version of the figure of Klytius on the Meidias Vase in William Hamilton's collection.[46] Fuseli has lengthened the legs, arms, and neck of this figure; thickened the torso; and drawn the entire figure with a strong, sharp, nervous line and an excessively heavy outline. Both the figure and the space in which it is placed are two-dimensional: the

44. Mason, *Mind of Henry Fuseli*, p. 301.
45. See Frederick Antal, *Fuseli Studies* (London, 1956), pp. 30–34.
46. Reproduced in *ibid.*, Plates 24a, b.

figure has no modeling or plastic qualities but is rather presented as a nonillusionistic collection of flat areas of light and dark. Here Fuseli's line dictates rather than follows the human form, constructing purely geometric patterns.

Both Fuseli's linear style and his expressionist techniques—his spatial irrationality, his denial of scale, his melodramatic chiaroscuro, his diagonal compositions, and his invention of violently contorted, elongated or foreshortened human figures—exerted a heavy influence on the development of Blake's own abstract linearism and inclination for heroic, nonillusionistic figures. Blake's figure of David in *David and Goliath*, of *Pestilence*, and of the running youth in flames in *The Book of Urizen*, Plate 3, are all based on Fuseli's earlier drawing of *Achilles at the Funeral Pyre of Patroclus*. Blake may also have borrowed his familiar figure of Urizen—the old bearded man with outstretched arms—from Fuseli's drawing of Jupiter Pluvius in *The Fertilization of Egypt*, which Blake engraved for Darwin's *Botanical Garden* in 1791. On the other hand, since this particular figure is already distinctly formulated on Plate 4 of Blake's *All Religions Are One* (1788–90), it is possible that Fuseli took this figure from Blake.[47] Similarly, Fuseli could have borrowed his figure of a horizontally flying, winged old man whose form-fitting robe curves around his feet, which Paul Ganz calls *The Spirit of Night* and dates 1808,[48] from Blake's figures of God in *God Creating Adam* (1795, [*Plate 39*]) or of Enitharmon weeping over Orc(?) on Plate 3 of *Europe* (1794). The flow of the drapery and the repeated horizontal lines of body and wings are uniquely Blakean motifs; in contrast to Fuseli's diagonal movements and angular rather than curvilinear drapery folds. Some of Blake's most striking images, however, are derived directly from Fuseli. The leaping figure with leg drawn up, arm raised, and frame thrust dramatically sidewards who appears both on *Europe* 9 and *Jerusalem* 32 [46] [*Plate 83*] is copied from Fuseli's Roman Sketchbook design for

47. Albert Roe argues that both the drawing (in the British Museum) and the engraving of *The Fertilization of Egypt* were created by Blake (in "The Thunder of Egypt," *Blake Essays for Damon*, ed. A. Rosenfeld [Providence, R.I., 1969], pp. 160, 444–45). But Michael Tolley insists that Fuseli originated this figure of the old man (in "The Auckland Fuselis," *Blake Newsletter* 3 [Dec. 15, 1969]:51).

48. Paul L. Ganz, *The Drawings of Henry Fuseli* (London, 1949), Plate 106.

the death of Sarpidon (1778). And Fuseli's Sketchbook design for Juliet leaning over Romeo is the source for the long-necked woman with hanging head and circling arms who appears as Eve in Blake's *The Body of Abel found by Adam and Eve.*

Fuseli's influence on Blake, and vice versa, has been argued back and forth. Frederick Tatham and Gilchrist support Fuseli's overwhelming debt to Blake, putting great emphasis on the probably apocryphal statement by Fuseli that "Blake is d..m good to steal from!" [49] Eudo Mason, in his attempt to redress the balance, quotes Stothard, Cunningham, and Robert Hunt who all saw Blake as Fuseli's pupil.[50] Certainly, Fuseli had developed his mature style before he met Blake; and Blake was strongly attracted by his linear style, his nonillusionistic and dramatic scenes, and his mannerist compositions and configurations. On the other hand, several of Fuseli's later works, done after 1795, include that peculiar arabesque, continuous line, that almost abstract flow of drapery and body limbs, that rectilinear construction (as opposed to Fuseli's earlier diagonal compositions), and the delicate color and tones that are the touchstones of Blake's personal style. Blake's impact on Fuseli certainly amounted to more than the "Attitude or . . . idea . . . here and there" that Eudo Mason allows him.[51] On this issue, however, Sir Anthony Blunt is probably wise to suggest that it is futile to argue the question of indebtedness,[52] and it is sufficient here to note that Fuseli's style and influence did much to encourage Blake's own predilection for strong linear rhythms and expressively attenuated figures.

Blake's style and especially his subject matter were perhaps even more extensively molded by the art of Michelangelo, the man whom both Blake and Fuseli believed to be the most sublime of painters.[53] Blake hailed Michelangelo as the "supreme glory" of Italian art (E 535) and as the exemplar, along with Raphael, Shakespeare, Milton and the best of

49. Quoted by Mason, *Mind of Henry Fuseli*, p. 50.
50. *Ibid.*, pp. 51–53. For some Blake borrowings from Fuseli, see J. A. Wittreich, Jr., "A Note on Blake and Fuseli," *Blake Newsletter* 3 (June 15, 1969):3–5.
51. *Ibid.*, p. 52.
52. Blunt, *Art of William Blake*, p. 41.
53. Giorgio Melchiori has discussed Fuseli's debt to Michelangelo in *Michelangelo nel Settecento Inglese* (Rome, 1950), pp. 81–86; this book also contains a useful chapter on Blake's response to Michelangelo.

Plate 33. Fuseli, *The Witches Show Macbeth the Descendants of Banquo,* Kunsthaus Zürich.

antique art, of "perfect and eternal" inspiration (E 535). So many scholars have noted Blake's overwhelming artistic debt to Michelangelo that I need not dwell upon it here.[54] It will suffice to remind ourselves of the three fundamental characteristics that Blake derived from Michelangelo. Stylistically, Blake was primarily influenced by Michelangelo's use of a sharp, incisive contour or outline in both his painting and his sculpture. An early painting like the *Doni Madonna* vividly demonstrates the dependence of Michelangelo's pictorial style upon an unusually sharp, clean

54. See Blunt, *Art of William Blake,* pp. 4, 35, 73; Melchiori, *Ibid.;* Roger Fry, *Reflections on British Painting* (London, 1934), pp. 85–88; Hagstrum, *Blake, Poet and Painter,* pp. 39–41.

line. The etched outline of the Madonna's head, arms and feet, the sharply
defined rhythms of the rather heavy drapery and the nervous but precise
contour of the Christ-child's body all show that in Michelangelo's early
art, form is basically a product of contour. The patchy chiaroscuro and
rather arbitrary anatomy of the nudes in the background only underline
Michelangelo's primary concern with a melodic line.[55] Michelangelo's
early sculpture—the Rome *Pietà*, the Bruges *Madonna*, the *Bacchus*,
the *David*—also reveals an obsession with linear rhythms and contours.
Here, too, form or mass emerges from the superimposition of clearly
drawn profiles or outlines (which Michelangelo actually drew on the faces
of the marble block). Not until 1506, with the Pitti *Madonna*, the *St.
Matthew* and the sculptures for the tomb of Julius II does Michelangelo's
style move toward a new ideal of mass rather than contour. Erwin Panofsky has concisely characterized the style of Michelangelo's middle period
as (1) the condensation of the sculptural unit into a compact mass which
strictly isolates itself from the surrounding space; (2) a sharp accentuation
of "the basic directions of space," of horizontal and vertical lines and of
frontal and orthagonal planes; and (3) the use of this rectangular system
not as a static but as a dynamic principle.[56] Michelangelo's pictorial style
combines this new emphasis on mass, achieved through a broadly applied
chiaroscuro now closely united to anatomical realities, with a still sharply
defined contour. The massive, broadly modeled figures in the Sistine
Chapel frescoes are bounded with a line which "never for a moment loses
its delicious pulsation and clear definition of form." [57] In his final period,
in the Pauline Chapel frescoes and the Milan *Pietà*, Michelangelo rejected
his former emphasis on mass for an art of greater linear elegance constructed from even stronger contours and almost weightless forms. Thus,
all of Michelangelo's art demonstrated to Blake the necessity of a clear,
sharp outline.

Secondly, Michelangelo's art provided Blake with a subject: the heroic
or ideal human figure, modeled in gigantic proportions and with accentuated muscular definition, preferably in the nude. Both the style of

55. Frederick Hartt, *Michelangelo: Paintings* (New York, 1964), pp. 66–70.
56. E. Panofsky, *Studies in Iconology* (New York: Harper Torchbooks, 1962), pp. 172–73.
57. Hartt, *Michelangelo: Paintings*, p. 106.

Blake's human figures and the central position they occupy in all his mature art are derived from the imposing images of man and God that dominate Michelangelo's painting and sculpture. The Sistine Chapel frescoes alone provided Blake with an enormous vocabulary of human gestures and movements, singly or in groups, upon which he drew for many of his compositions. And Michelangelo's late sculpture (the Medici Chapel figures, the *Victory,* the Florence and Milan *Pietàs*) and painting (the Pauline Chapel frescoes) extended this vocabulary even further by adding such early sixteenth-century mannerist distortions as elongations, foreshortenings, and attenuations.

Thirdly, Blake followed Michelangelo's late art in placing these ideal, heroic figures in nonillusionistic spaces. *The Crucifixion of St. Peter* lacks a stabilizing ground plane or localizing perspective. As Frederick Hartt comments, these "figures emerge from nowhere, cut off at the waist by the frame, so that the space moves disconcertingly forward to include us." [58] The result is that the whole scene seems to be floating in a dream world. This same effect of massively modeled figures floating in an unreal space occurs even more vividly in the Sistine Chapel *Last Judgment.*

In attempting to define the precise nature of Michelangelo's influence on Blake's art, we must remember that Blake knew Michelangelo's work only through the drawings at Windsor Castle [59] and the copies, engravings, and casts of the master's art available in London during his lifetime. It is more than likely that Blake never saw an original Michelangelo work and knew even the Windsor Castle drawings only secondhand, in copies. When we examine the engravings Blake is most likely to have found in the Library of the Royal Academy, where we know he studied the prints of Michelangelo (E 628), and elsewhere, three important facts emerge. Almost invariably, the engravings lose much of the three-dimensionality, the volume and massivity achieved by the subtle chiaroscuro of Michelangelo's mature painted figures. The cross-hatching technique used by Michelangelo's engravers, Marcantonio Raimondi, Nicholas Beatrizet,

58. *Ibid.,* 154.

59. For a catalogue of the original Michelangelo drawings at Windsor Castle in the eighteenth century, see A. E. Popham and Johannes Wilde, *The Italian Drawings of the XV and XVI Centuries in the Collection of His Majesty the King at Windsor Castle* (London, 1949), pp. 244–69.

Adamo and Giorgio Ghisi, Baptista de' Cavalieri, Martinus Rota, and Michele Lucchese, to name only the most widely known and prolific, almost necessarily stresses the contours and linear rhythms of Michelangelo's art at the expense of his subtle chiaroscuro, calculated lighting effects, and plastic modeling. Adamo Ghisi's widely distributed engravings of the Sistine Chapel *ignudi,* for instance, consistently reduce the torsion and tension of Michelangelo's dynamic nudes to static, two-dimensional outlines. Michelangelo's powerfully bulging muscles here become mere spider webs of linear rhythms, as in Ghisi's rendering of the nude at the left above the Cumaen Sibyl. Moreover, these engravings often place Michelangelo's figures in undefined or unreal spaces, omitting his carefully designed architectural environments. Ghisi's *ignudi* are set upon isolated boxes in empty spaces; while Beatrizet's engraving of the *Pietà* for Vittoria Colonna adds a grandiose and arbitrarily confining architectural frame. Casts or engravings of Michelangelo's sculptures almost always omitted the architectural setting, thus creating the impression that these were wholly ideal forms, divorced from time and space. Finally, we must remember that all the drawings, prints and casts Blake could have seen were in black and white, not color. This may explain why Blake tended to overlook Michelangelo's carefully planned and rich color schemes (Blake hailed Michelangelo for subordinating color to form, E 520, 536, 640); it may also have encouraged Blake's personal dislike for Venetian coloring effects.

In addition to taking on almost whole cloth the basic characteristics of Michelangelo's style as refracted through the prints and casts he knew, Blake frequently borrowed specific gestures, configurations, and motifs from Michelangelo's works. Blake's Newton is based on the *Abia* in the Sistine Chapel lunette; his Joseph of Arimathea is copied from the lower right-hand figure in *The Crucifixion of St. Peter,* and his scaled jailor in the design for *Europe,* Plate 13, is taken from the Roman soldier at the lower left; the falling horse and chariot wheel in the design for Plate 5 of *The Marriage of Heaven and Hell* are borrowed from Michelangelo's first and final versions of *The Fall of Phaeton,* as are the enrooting women in the *Jerusalem* designs.

In imitating Michelangelo's art so closely, Blake was of course following the taste of his age; by the late eighteenth century, Michelangelo was widely considered to be a "perfect painter." [60] Jonathon Richardson, as early as 1719 in his *Argument in Behalf of the Science of a Connoisseur,* had praised Michelangelo for his combination of "greatness" and "grace"; and on December 10, 1790, Sir Joshua Reynolds closed his famous series of *Discourses* before the Royal Academy with his eulogy of Michelangelo as the "exalted founder and father of modern art, of which he was not only the inventor, but which, by the divine energy of his own mind, he carried at once to its highest point of possible perfection." [61] William Hayley's *Essay on Painting* (1778) which Blake almost certainly read includes the following typical paeon to Michelangelo:

> Inflamed by Genius with sublimest rage,
> By toil unwearied, and unchilled by age,
> In the fine frenzy of exalted thought,
> Gigantic Angelo his wonders wrought;
> And high, by native strength of spirit rais'd
> The mighty Homer of the pencil blazed.

Since Michelangelo was widely hailed in England as the artist who revived the antique style, it was easy for Blake to combine his imitation of Michelangelo's style and subject matter with his philosophical commitment to the neoclassicism of Cumberland, Flaxman, and Fuseli.

In addition to the influences of Michelangelo and romantic classicism, the English Gothic style strongly stimulated Blake's linearism. In his brilliant study of the "Englishness" of English art, Nikolaus Pevsner has shown that a fascination with abstract geometric or curvilinear surface patterns is characteristic of English architecture, painting, sculpture, and decorative art. Medieval English churches, funeral monuments, and illuminated manuscripts of 1290–1350 are constructed either in the perpendicular style—an angular, geometric, repetitive, spacious, clear, matter-of-fact style—or in the decorated style—the capricious, illogical style found in the flowing tracery of East Anglia parish churches; the

60. John Steegmann, *The Rule of Taste from George I to George IV* (London, 1936), p. 102.
61. Sir Joshua Reynolds, R. A., *Discourses,* ed. Roger Fry (London, 1905), p. 410. Blake, of course, regarded Reynolds' admiration of Michelangelo as hypocritical (E 504).

willful curves and countercurves of the north portal of St. Mary Redcliffe, Bristol; the elaborately sinuous embroidery known as *Opus Anglicanum;* and the undulating line of fourteenth-century manuscripts based on the Utrecht Psalter. Both styles, however, are nonillusionistic and linear for, as Pevsner points out, "both styles are anti-corporeal or disembodied, in the sense of a negation of the swelling rotundity of the body. Perpendicular denies it with angular planes, angular towers, long, thin, wiry, sinewy lines, Decorated also with long, also with thin, but with flaming or flowing lines. But both are unfleshly, both linear." [62]

Blake had first imitated English medieval art when he drew sketches of the medieval tombs in Westminster Abbey for Basire's plates in Richard Gough's *Sepulchral Monuments in Great Britain* (1786). Blake's engravings of Henry III, Aveline of Lancaster, Queen Philippa, Edward III, and Richard II and his queen, all exhibit a strict adherence to the strong, clear, simple lines of the effigies. The faces are sharply outlined, the features strongly defined (in a style similar to that of Holbein), and the hair carefully delineated, lock by lock. Blake's engravings make no attempt to model the surface of the face: they are strictly two-toned, unshaded, and totally flat, two-dimensional designs.[63] This concern with a delicate, sure line and a meticulous rendition of detail also controls Blake's engravings of the entire monument of Aymer de Valence in which every arch, spire, and tracery is sharply picked out.

Blake's delight in Gothic figures and designs was doubtless promoted by Flaxman and Fuseli, both of whom blended Gothic motifs into their neoclassical idioms.[64] Flaxman had also studied Westminster Abbey closely and copied Gothic figures and designs into his Morley monument in Gloucester Cathedral (1784) and into the set of medieval chessmen he designed for Wedgwood in 1785. Flaxman may also have shown Blake his drawings based on European medieval art: he sketched the Gothic architecture at Dieppe, Rouen, and Lyons and carefully analyzed Italian tre-

---

62. Nikolaus Pevsner, *The Englishness of English Art* (London, 1956; paper, 1964), pp. 133–34.
63. See Paul Miner for a comparison of Blake's plates with photographs of the effigies: "The Apprentice of Great Queen Street," *Bulletin of the New York Public Library* 67 (1963):639–42.
64. Irwin, *English Neoclassical Art*, pp. 87–94, 99–102.

cento and quattrocento painting. The Middle Ages also appealed to Henry Fuseli, who used Gothic subjects in *The Oath of the Rütli* (1779–81) and *Thor Battering the Serpent Midgard* (1792). And Blake also admired the drawings of Albrecht Dürer, whose angular lines, attenuated figures, allegorical landscapes, and medieval literary subjects further stimulated Blake's preference for linear rhythms and sharply outlined, elongated figures. As we shall see in Blake's late art, these seemingly contradictory Gothic and neoclassical idioms can be successfully united.

While working in Westminster Abbey, moreover, Blake might well have seen the illuminated medieval manuscripts housed in the Westminster Chancery House library. The fourteenth-century Lytlington Missal, for instance, would have drawn his eye, not only to the interaction of text and design which he later imitated in his own illuminated books, but also to medieval English linear drawing style. The Lytlington designs— both the borders of foliage, animals, angels, shields, tiny figures of the prophets, monks or court attendants, and the full-page scenes of the crucifixion, the Madonna, and the king and queen—are drawn in a thin, spiky, angular pen line. The watercolors, red, blue, gold, were added later. The Mortuary Roll of Abbot John Islip which Basire engraved for the Society of Antiquaries is also illustrated with austere outlines set in two-dimensional spaces. Blake may also have seen the more elaborately colored illuminated manuscripts housed in the British Museum after 1802; in addition, the famous Bedford Hours would have been available to him in John Johnson's print shop [65] and he could have gained access to the Queen Mary's Psalter displayed in Montague House after 1759. Both these well-known manuscripts are illuminated with a delicate, careful, precise line that defines every detail. All scenes and figures are presented two-dimensionally and nonillusionistically; perspective and spatial definition are absent or irrational; color is applied in flat, abstract areas with no reference to a defined light source; configurations and designs are severely geometrical and tectonic. Pevsner has accurately described the figures in the Queen Mary's Psalter as "long and slender, their heads are exceedingly small, their bodies attenuated and swaying, their outlines sinuous.

65. Jean Hagstrum, *William Blake, Poet and Painter* (Chicago, 1964), pp. 31–33.

There are no real backgrounds, just a diapering perhaps, and no clearly directed actions. This is a world of disembodied bodies, almost spectres, moving weightlessly, . . . with inscrutable expressions in their oddly boneless faces." [66] Such illuminated manuscripts provided Blake with both a model for his own bookmaking and a stylistic technique: the pen and ink delineation of flat, linear forms that are subsequently filled in with watercolor.

Blake's interweaving of poetic text and visual design in his illuminated printing was almost certainly inspired by such medieval illuminated manuscripts. Jean Hagstrum has convincingly argued for such an influence, and has defined this influence in three categories—illustration, decoration, and illumination. Yet he may have overlooked some of the complexities both of Blake's intertwining of text and design and of the medieval page.[67] Blake's designs can function in at least five ways: (1) to illustrate directly a given text, as in "The Lamb"; (2) to clarify an event described in the text, as in "The Tyger," where the gentle tyger is shown to be no more fearful than a lamb; (3) to present additional thematic commentary or amplification, as in "The Little Girl Lost," where seven-year-old Lyca's "sleep" is unmasked in the design as the embrace of a mature young woman with her lover and thus identified as the holy sexual experience of Innocence; (4) to make an ironic commentary on the accompanying text, as on Plate 51 of *Jerusalem* [*Plate 84*], where Albion's worship of the divine Trinity of Rahab-Vala, Hyle, and Scofield is revealed as a false idolatry for the fallen gods of the Deists, the female will, accusing law, and despair; and finally (5) to tell an independent story or to provide an analogue in a different spatial, temporal, or psychological dimension, as in the full-page designs for *Europe* that portray the physical manifestations —the onslaught of plague, death, and the funeral bell—of the mental imprisonment and torture described in the poem. David Erdman has compared this fifth technique to a "cinerama" of "color-motion-music pictures" which creates, when filled in with the text, an almost "four-dimensional mental screen." [68]

66. Pevsner, *Englishness of English Art*, p. 132.
67. Hagstrum, *William Blake*, pp. 1–20, 31–33, *passim*.
68. In "America: New Expanses," *Blake's Visionary Forms Dramatic*, ed. D. V. Erdman and J. E. Grant (Princeton, 1970), p. 93.

Such subtle and complex counterpoint between design and text did not originate with Blake, although he developed this technique to its most sophisticated form. The illuminated borders of the Queen Mary's Psalter often introduce the artists' own versions of Biblical stories or theological doctrine. Here the fall is caused by the machinations not of a serpent as *Genesis* states, but of several mischievous devils; Cain and Abel's dispute arose not over a sacrifice, but over a hockey game; and Noah's wife has to trick Noah into telling her of the flood with a magic potion. Similarly, the Queen Mary's Psalter decorations often present secular scenes that have no direct relation to the Biblical text but rather tell their own story of a Christian life lived in the Middle Ages or of the temptations (depicted as grotesque or humorous little creatures) that plagued medieval man.[69]

By 1795, Blake had successfully fused these three major influences—the romantic-classical outlines of D'Hancarville, Cumberland, Flaxman, and Fuseli, the incisive contours and heroic nudes of Michelangelo, and the linearism of English Gothic monuments and manuscripts—into a mature style, a linear style based on strongly defined outlines; idealized, heroic figures that soar through irrational, two-dimensional spaces; a lack of textural richness; and a reliance upon closed, tectonic compositions. Following Flaxman rather than Fuseli, Blake rejected the dramatic chiaroscuro, foreshortening and diagonal compositions characteristic of the baroque period. As early as 1788, Blake had denounced the baroque tastes of Georg Moser, the Swiss keeper of the Royal Academy. Blake later recalled the incident:

I was once looking over the Prints from Rafael & Michael Angelo. in the Library of the Royal Academy Moser came to me & said You should not Study these old Hard Stiff & Dry Unfinished Works of Art, Stay a little & I will shew you what you should Study. He then went & took down Le Bruns & Rubens's Galleries How I did secretly Rage. I also spoke my Mind . . .
   I said to Moser, These things that you call Finished are not Even Begun how can they then, be Finished? The Man who does not know The Beginning, never can know The End of Art. (E 628)

69. For other examples, see Lillian Randall, "Exempla as a Source of Gothic Marginal Illumination," *The Art Bulletin* 39 (June 1957):97–107.

Instead, Blake now favored compositions constructed with extreme geometric regularity, with static patterns of circles and squares. The linear abstraction of Blake's mature style is further accentuated by his choice of medium. Rather than working with oils which were used in the eighteenth century to capture natural colors, shading, and textures and thus create an earthbound illusionism, Blake limited himself to pen and ink, watercolor, and tempera—all media that provide a nonillusionistic, purely pictorial surface.[70]

These qualities of Blake's mature style are fully manifested in what is perhaps Blake's most famous print, *The Ancient of Days,* the frontispiece to *Europe* (1794, [*Plate* 34]). Here Blake has totally rejected a natural space: the figure of the creating demiurge is placed flatly in a two-dimensional circle that floats in an abstract space. The body, as Rosenblum notes, is "tightly compressed against the picture surface, underlining the flatness of the design and paralleling the contortive postures of much sixteenth century mannerist painting." [71] Blake's mature insistence on sharply defined contours and pure geometric designs becomes even clearer when we compare this 1794 relief etching of *The Ancient of Days* with an earlier watercolor now in the possession of Sir Geoffrey Keynes [*Plate* 35]. In the later finished design, Blake has lengthened the wind-blown hair and beard into more rigorously horizontal lines; darkened and defined the clouds around the circle into longer, flatter planes; and sharpened the lines of the beard under the nose—all to accentuate the lateral grids of the design. He has more exactly centered the head of the kneeling man in the circle and corrected the diagonal thrust of the right knee into a precise radius from the circle's center. He has thus accentuated the geometrical composition—a circumscribed square whose hypotenuse is laid on the radius of the surrounding circle. Moreover, the linear contours have been strengthened throughout; the smoother rhythms are particularly noticeable in the elimination of the compass handle and in the clearcut definition of the right foot which is hidden in shadow in the early water color. Blake has also flattened the coloring in the later design into single-value areas, using a palette of deep blue, red, white, and even, in

70. Rosenblum, "British Art," p. 12.
71. Rosenblum, "International Style," p. 105.

Plate 34. The Ancient of Days, from *Europe*, Copy K(MM).

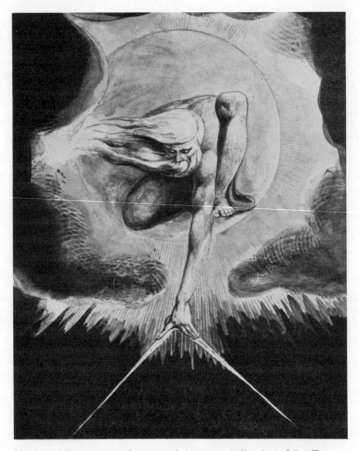

Plate 35. The Ancient of Days, early version, Collection of Geoffrey Keynes.

the Whitworth Gallery copy, a gold that heightens the effect of an abstract medieval image. Here, as everywhere, the heroic human form dominates Blake's mature art: his compositions are conceived as patterns of static or moving idealized human figures, often defined by swirling, clinging draperies. Artistically, then, Blake has made a total commitment to abstract outlines, geometric designs, and the contours of the human body as the vehicles of aesthetic beauty.

STYLE VERSUS ICONOGRAPHY [72]

Thus Blake's mature visual style contradicts the symbolism of the illuminated poetry he wrote in 1794–95. Artistically, he uses the human figure, abstracted outlines, and closed forms to convey the clearly defined images of primal vision; poetically, he condemns the human body and all limited, rational, abstract systems as tools used by Urizen to enclose and destroy holy Energy. The iconography that Blake developed in his illuminated books and color prints between 1789 and 1795 tried to resolve this contradiction by distinguishing between the closed, rational, evil forms of Urizen and the open, expanding forms of poetic genius. But since Blake used the same visual style and media to paint both evil and good images, his normative attitudes often blur. He portrays the fallen human form with the same precision, linear rhythm, incisive contour, and grandeur as the divine human form. Inevitably, as we can see in the Tate Gallery color-print series done in 1795, symbolic content and style conflict in Blake's art: his iconographic condemnation of the human form as fallen and corrupt contradicts his visual affirmation of these magnificent Michelangelesque figures.

Although Blake often drew on traditional sources for both his visual compositions and his iconography,[73] the meaning of his designs usually depends directly on the accompanying text and occasionally contradicts its actual source. Milton's golden compasses, for instance, with which God the Creator imposed "number, weight and measure" on the universe [74] and which often appear in medieval manuscripts and Renaissance paintings as the instrument of the omnipotent, benevolent creator, become for Blake a tool of the demiurge, the Ancient of Days, who restricts Energy

72. Since some readers may not be familiar with these art historical terms, let me in simple terms distinguish them thus: stylistic analysis is the study of the way an image is presented, how it looks; iconography is the study of the meaning or symbolism of the image. See Erwin Panofsky's *Studies in Iconology* (Oxford, 1939), chap. 1, for more precise and detailed definitions.

73. See Sir Anthony Blunt, "Blake's 'Ancient of Days'—The Symbolism of the Compasses," *Journal of Warburg Institute* 2 (1938–39):53–63; "Blake's Brazen Serpent," *Journal of Warburg & Courtauld Institutes* 6 (1943):225–27; "Blake's Pictorial Imagination," *Journal of Warburg & Courtauld Institutes* 6 (1943):190–212; Hagstrum, *Blake, Poet and Painter*, pp. 23–75; Piloo Nannavutty, "Blake and Emblem Literature," *Journal of Warburg & Courtauld Institutes* 15 (1952):258–61.

74. In *Paradise Lost*, Bk. VII, ll. 226–31.

into arbitrary and stultifying forms. To understand the meaning of Blake's designs, then, we must study both the development of his visual symbolism in his own art and the context of these same symbols in his poetry.

Blake's two major visual symbols represent the two sides of what he sees as the fundamental antagonism in the human psyche and in society: on the one side, that contracting, circumscribing reason that subordinates the individual to the general and attempts to construct a society based on hierarchy, moral strictures, and political repression governed by a tyrant or an oligarchy; and on the other side, that expansive Energy or divine imagination that expresses itself socially as candid sexuality, political rebellion, and artistic creation. Blake visually personifies each of these two psychic forces or states of mind. The enclosing mind of reason is depicted as an old but virile, white-haired, white-bearded man, usually clothed in a white robe and often seated in a crouching position over a scroll or decalogue; whereas the expanding mind of Energy is pictured as a naked youth, frequently surrounded by flames, often running or standing with open arms or carrying a hammer.

We first see the old man in Blake's *All Religions Are One* (1788–90), where he appears on the title page and again above Principle 1, Plate 4, as the creating God, his arms spread open above the clouds. Here he personifies the poetic genius and is clearly based on traditional images of God or the Hebraic prophets: on the title page, he is seated beside a stone tablet or decalogue inscribed with the title of the tract. An angel hovers overhead. Blake uses this figure again in this conventional way in the illustration for "The Voice of the Ancient Bard" in *Songs of Experience,* where the white-haired, white-bearded, old man holding the harp represents the bard of the Welsh triads (as in similar depictions of the bard by Fuseli, Barry, and John Martin). In the designs for Blake's *Tiriel* (1790), however, the white-haired and white-bearded man is associated both with Har, the holy father who has preserved the divine vision of Innocence, however ineffectually, and with Tiriel himself, the cursing demagogue of oppressive law.

This confused iconography is finally clarified on Plate 11 of *The Marriage of Heaven and Hall* [*Plate 36*], where Blake traces the history both of religious oppression and of his own image of reason: the original vi-

The ancient Poets animated all sensible objects
with Gods or Geniuses, calling them by the names and
adorning them with the properties of woods, rivers,
mountains, lakes, cities, nations, and whatever their
enlarged & numerous senses could perceive.
   And particularly they studied the genius of each
city & country. placing it under its mental deity.
   Till a system was formed, which some took ad-
vantage of & enslav'd the vulgar by attempting to
realize or abstract the mental deities from their
objects; thus began Priesthood.
   Choosing forms of worship from poetic tales.
   And at length they pronounced that the Gods
had orderd such things.
   Thus men forgot that All deities reside
in the human breast.

Plate 36. *The Marriage of Heaven and Hell*, Plate 11, Copy I(MM).

sions of the "ancient Poets" who saw living deities in every natural phenomenon were abstracted from the natural objects and erected into a hierarchical system formulated by the "Priesthood." Thus the bearded old man who once personified the divine creator, the poetic genius, was corrupted into an image of the law giver. The truly creative personifications at the top of Plate 11 (in Copy I, MM)—the sun rises as a woman with flaming hair; the earth is a lovely, tender woman here dressed in pink who gently nurses the plant or waves, pictured as a helpless baby; and, most importantly, the barren tree or towering wave in the center is a white-haired, white-bearded old man wearing a crown and carrying a sceptre (perhaps the personification, Neptune) [75]—have degenerated into the abstract image at the bottom of the plate. The single, rationalizing vision of the priesthood has abstracted the white-haired, bearded old man from the tree or wave and established him as a tyrant-God who now rules alone, his arms spread over dark clouds, oblivious to the naked prostrate woman beside him. Blake further links this image of the old man to the tyrant Nebuchadnezzar, the white-haired, white-bearded man crowned with golden spikes who crawls on the ground and looks back in abject terror, on Plate 24 of *The Marriage*.

The white-haired, bearded man reappears in *Visions of the Daughters of Albion* (1793) as Bromion, the slave-owning tyrant who affirms "one law for the lion and the ox" and who is chained in his cave of political oppression and social misery in the tailpiece [*Plate 8*]. The most specific association of this image with a closed mind in Blake's work by 1794 occurs in the illustration for "The Human Abstract" of *Songs of Experience* [*Plate 7*]. The poem articulates a mental state of selfish cruelty and Pecksniffian hypocrisy, which the illustration visually personifies. A white-haired and white-bearded old man, dressed in white, crouches beneath a net of heavy ropes on a rocky shore, hemmed in by dark waves, a barren tree, and drooping reeds. A frown contorts his brow, and tears flow from his eyes. The design visualizes the explicit personification of the text:

75. Details of the design differ markedly in various copies. In Copy D, TP, the face of the old man seems to reside within a large plant, the woman is naked, and the surrounding cave is omitted. Jean Hagstrum has also identified the image of Urizen as old, bearded king with traditional representations of Neptune (*Blake, Poet and Painter*, p. 106).

Then Cruelty knits a snare,
And spreads his baits with care.

He sits down with holy fears,
And waters the ground with tears:
Then Humility takes its root
Underneath his foot.

(E 27)

From 1793 on, this old, bearded man occurs frequently in Blake's designs and usually symbolizes an oppressive, rational mode of thought or a tyrannical political program. The old, crippled man in the design for "London" reveals the "Marks of weakness, marks of woe" left by "mind-forg'd manacles"; the old man with the book of law and spear, the old Nobodaddy ruling with arms spread in ironic blessing, and the old cripple entering death's door on Plates 4, 8, and 12 of *America* (1793) represent the political, religious, and social oppressions and murders of Albion's angel, George III; and the compass-wielding Ancient of Days [*Plate 34*] embodies the religious and political tyranny denounced in *Europe* (1794). This personification culminated, of course, in the designs for *The Book of Urizen* (1794) where the old, bearded man *is* Urizen, the creator of the abstract void and the ruler of a divided, limited man enclosed in the human form [*Plate 26*].

By studying Blake's various portrayals of Urizen as an old, bearded man, we can compile a fairly consistent list of the objects or situations usually associated with Urizen and thus emblematic of the closed mind. Such a list, garnered from both Blake's poetry and his art, includes nets [*Plate 7*], chains [*Plate 8*], briars, and spider webs; [76] all such severely rectilinear forms as tombs or horizontal corpses, closed doors, pyramids, and cradles; [77] all enclosed, circular forms, such as caves [*Plate 8*], crowns, embryos, and circles; [78] all limited human forms, such as the skeleton [*Plate 27*] or the partially formed body; [79] water, sea, and rain (tra-

76. See *Urizen*, Plate 28; *Visions of the Daughters of Albion*, tailpiece [*Plate 8*]; "The Garden of Love"; and Europe, Plate 12, respectively (plate numbers as given in Keynes-Wolf *Census*).

77. See *Songs of Experience*, title page; *Urizen*, Plate 26; *Tiriel*, Drawing 1 or *The Marriage of Heaven and Hell*, Plate 21, Copy D; "Infant Sorrow," respectively.

78. See *Europe*, Preludium, Plate 1; *Europe*, Plate 11; *Urizen*, Plate 17; and *Europe*, frontispiece [*Plate 34*], respectively.

79. See *Urizen*, Plates 8, 11, 24 and 25.

ditionally associated with materialism) [*Plate 11*]; [80] such malevolent or corrupting animals as the serpent, worm, vulture, dragon, and bat; [81] and finally, such predictable accoutrements of a rationalistic, oppressive tyrant as the compass, book, scroll, or decalogue [*Plate 26*]; scales; sword, and spear.[82]

In opposition to the old, white-bearded, robed figure of Urizen stands Blake's icon for the open, intuitive mind of creative Energy, the youthful male nude with open, welcoming arms. Blake evokes the Greek idealization of the nude rather than the alternative Gothic condemnation of the sinful naked body. Like both the "grand works of ancient art" he so admired, the Farnese Hercules, the Medici Venus, and the Apollo Belvedere (E 522), and Michelangelo's middle-period nudes, Blake's nudes enthusiastically affirm the naked body as both the perfection of physical beauty and the revelation of the divine spirit. As Blake knew, the Greeks felt that the body and the spirit were one; "the Venus, the Minerva, the Jupiter, the Apollo," said Blake in 1809, ". . . are all of them representations of spiritual existences . . . to the mortal perishing organ of sight; and yet they are embodied and organized in solid marble" (E 532). Blake's earliest imitations of these ideal marble forms embody the doctrine, stated in his *Marriage of Heaven and Hell,* that "Man has no Body distinct from his Soul for that calld Body is a portion of Soul discernd by the five Senses" (E 34).

Blake's nudes are always in motion, never static. The Greeks had prized the prowess and grace of their athletes and heroes; and their artists had frequently painted and sculpted nude figures arrested at moments of great physical exertion, as in the famous Diskobolus of Myron.[83] For Blake, as for the Greeks, the male nude, captured at an instant of perfectly balanced motion, incarnates Energy. The nude figure known as Glad Day

80. See *Visions of the Daughters of Albion,* tailpiece [*Plate 8*], title page, Plates 4 and 8; *Urizen,* Plate 12; or *The Gates of Paradise,* Emblem 2 [*Plate 11*].

81. See *Europe,* title page; *America,* Plate 1; *Visions of the Daughters of Albion,* Plate 3, where Theotormon's eagle rends Oothoon's flesh like a carrion bird its prey; *America,* Plate 4; and *Europe,* preludium, Plate 1, respectively.

82. See *Europe,* frontispiece [*Plate 34*]; *Urizen,* Plate 5; *Urizen,* title page [*Plate 26*]; *America,* Plate 5; *America,* Plates 5 and 4, respectively.

83. I am heavily indebted to Sir Kenneth Clark's *The Nude: A Study in Ideal Form* (Garden City, N.Y., 1959) for this comparison of Blake's nudes with their Greek sources.

Plate 37. Glad Day, or *Albion Rose from where He Laboured at the Mill with Slaves,*
Collection of Lessing J. Rosenwald.

and titled in Blake's later caption *Albion Rose from Where He Labourd at the Mill with Slaves,* is Blake's first successful expression of human Energy [*Plate 37*]. Blake here transforms the static geometric figure of perfect "Vitruvian" man diagrammed in Scamozzi's *Idea del' architettura universale* into a kinetic image that radiates vitality, Innocence, and creativity by drawing on the Dionysiac motion of his second source, the front and rear engravings of a bronze sculpture of a Bacchic dancer in *De' Bronze di Ercolano* (1767–71; reproduced in Blunt, Plates 6a, 6b). Significantly, Blake shifts the center of his Vetruvian man downward; Blake's human circle radiates from the loins and genitals rather than from the navel. He further adds torsion and expression to the figure. Blake's naked youth stretches out his arms, not solely for convenient measurement, but as a gesture of eager acceptance; his right leg is extended, not to fit a circumscribed circle, but to balance him as he strides across the hilltop. The colorwheel that radiates from his chest in the 1794 color print further manifests his creative powers: he is the light source for all the colors in the spectrum. In Blake's line engraving based on the 1780 design and probably engraved c. 1800, Albion's open legs bestride a bat-winged insect and a segmented worm. Possibly this configuration represents the triumph of Albion or holy Energy over the oppressions of reason (associated with bats on *Europe* 1) and of the physical body (associated with the worm on the final emblem of *The Gates of Paradise* [*Plate 25*]). Furthermore, in order to accentuate the muscular tension and movement of the human form, the Greeks were often forced to distort the body or to add draperies that extended or sharpened bodily gestures. Blake also used these devices: his mannered elongations and elaborate, swirling draperies sharply reveal the Energy and creativity contained in the human form.

"Energy is Eternal Delight," and Blake's nudes are calculated to both arouse and express erotic desire. Kenneth Clark reminds us of what Blake must have known perfectly well, that "no nude, however abstract, should fail to arouse in the spectator some vestige of erotic feeling even though it be only the faintest shadow—and if it does not do so, it is bad art and false morals." [84] Blake's male and female nudes repeatedly adopt the tra-

84. *Ibid.,* p. 29.

ditional attitudes of sexual ecstasy—the head thrown back, the body unbalanced or floating, the draperies whirling in excited rhythms—to celebrate the lineaments of gratified desire.

Borrowing from antique models and Michelangelo the ideal forms he admired so much, Blake gradually evolved a powerful image for Innocence and Energy—the heroic male nude with outstretched arms, captured in moments of passionate desire and vigorous movement. Outstretched arms are also a traditional icon, as Janet Warner reminds us, both of the "Cross, a symbol of divinity rich with associations of self-sacrifice or death and regeneration" and of creativity, as in Michelangelo's *God Creating Adam* or Raphael's God in the designs for the Vatican Loggie.[85] Having articulated this icon in the 1780 design, *Glad Day,* Blake crowded the illustrations for *Songs of Innocence* with similarly open-armed, energetic children and adolescents: the piper's Muse, the child floating in a cloud in the frontispiece, spreads his arms, palms upward, in welcome; the child on its mother's lap reaches out toward the horizon in the first design for "Spring"; three of the *putti* on the flame in the "Blossom" design dance with open arms; and the leader of the "Laughing Song" opens his arms, in a backwards version of the Glad Day figure, in joy and delight. This open-armed, joyful acceptance of all experience as holy occurs again on Plate 4 of *The Book of Thel* [*Plate 4*], where Thel welcomes her responsibility to be "the food of worms" with arms spread in delight over the tiny infant resting on the ground. Her eager acceptance is accentuated by the draperies that swirl around her feet as she rushes toward the child. Oothoon also embodies this exuberant welcoming of sexual and imaginative experience in *Visions of the Daughters of Albion:* on the last plate of the poem, she rises in flames over the daughters of Albion as they crouch upon the rocky shore, her arms spread open in blessing. Her naked beauty and accepting gesture reveal the open mind of Innocence which looks on all life as holy, which loves every object for its unique and infinite capacities.

This open-armed nude specifically embodies Energy and poetic creation

85. Janet Warner, "Blake's Use of Gesture," *Blake's Visionary Forms Dramatic* (Princeton, 1970), p. 177. Mrs. Warner goes on to identify this image as a revelation of the inherent divinity of man and also to point out that Blake uses this gesture in parodic or demonic as well as positive contexts (pp. 179–88).

in *The Marriage of Heaven and Hell.* A running, open-armed maiden in flames is identified with "the Eternal Hell," "the active springing from Energy," on Plate 3. On the following plate, the maiden becomes a handsome youth, chained by the ankle in flames over the sea (as Oothoon was chained in a flame-shaped wave on Plate 4 of *Visions*), who reaches out with wide-spread arms while the fiercely struggling, open-armed child is held back by the restraining arms of another youth. In this early version of Blake's famous color print *The Good and Evil Angels Struggling for Possession of a Child* (compare [*Plate 43*]), the chained youth and the child assume similar attitudes: their legs are spread and their arms open. Both the chains of the adolescent youth and the arms of the parent are reason's attempts to repress Energy. This naked youth, the emblem of Energy, appears again in *The Marriage of Heaven and Hell* designs as the devil from hell on Plate 10 and as the triumphant speaker who sits upon a skull, gazing up, on Plate 21; and in female guise, as the "cherub with his flaming sword" who soars in flames with outstretched arms over the corpse on Plate 14. This figure of Energy is further identified with Orc, the embodiment of revolutionary Energy, in *America,* Plate 1, where the child Orc is chained to the ground in a cruciform position similar to the Glad Day figure, and again on Plate 10 where Orc, kneeling in flames with open arms, triumphantly conquers Urizen by usurping the gesture and position of the so-called heavenly Father who precedes him on Plate 8. The naked youth as creative Energy culminates in the figure of Los, the poetic imagination incarnate, who appears on the final plate of *The Song of Los* as a naked youth crouched over a ball of flame, his hammer clutched to his breast. In *The Book of Urizen,* Los variously appears as an open-armed figure racing through flames (Plate 3), standing in flames with hammer in hand (Plate 18 [*Plate 38*]), or as a crouching youth who, although still surrounded by the flames of Energy, has begun to degenerate into a huddled or shrunken Urizenic body (on Plates 7 and 11 [G 9, 13]). In the full page design on Plate 21, Los has taken on the chains, envy, and repressive hostility of Urizen.

Intertwined with this figure of the open mind of Innocence and Energy are such emblematic objects as flames, often appearing in an *S*-shaped de-

Plate 38. The Book of Urizen, Plate 18, Copy G(TP).

sign, much like Hogarth's line of beauty [*Plate* 6] [86] and flamelike foliage, flowers, or waves [*Plate* 3];[87] curling branches and vines, often weighted with Bacchic grapes; [88] brightly-colored, nonpredatory birds; [89] the radiant dawn or rainbow, traditional emblems of newborn hope and the covenant with God; [90] the tools of artistic creation, such as anvil and hammer [*Plate* 38]; and, most often, naked figures in open-armed, running, flying, or embracing positions [*Plate* 6]. These images are Blake's visual shorthand for the prolific, for Energy, for sensual and mental liberation, for the completely open mind and joyously gratified body.

TATE GALLERY COLOR PRINTS

In the light of this fairly consistent iconography, the meaning of Blake's famous Tate Gallery color-print series leaps into focus. Blake first identified eight of these large color prints in his debtor-creditor correspondence with Thomas Butts on July 5 and September 7, 1805: "4 Prints Viz 1 Good & Evil Angel 2 House of Death 3 God Judging Adam 4 Lamech" and "4 Prints Viz 1 Nebuchadnezzar 2 Newton 3 God Creating Adam 4 Christ appearing." [91] In addition to these eight prints, the Tate Gallery possesses two others, *Hecate* and *Pity;* and the last two, similar to these in style and color, size and date, are the *Satan Exulting over Eve* (in the collections of Gregory Bateson and John Craxton) and the *Naomi Entreating Ruth* (in the Victoria and Albert Museum and the collection of Geoffrey Keynes). All these color prints are dated 1795 (which may refer to the time when they were conceived rather than the date of execution) and should therefore be seen in conjunction with Blake's illuminated poetry of that year. Although Blake chose his subjects from literary works as

86. See "The Divine Image," "The Blossom" and Plate 10 of *America*.
87. See *Songs of Innocence*, title page; "Infant Joy;" and *Visions of the Daughters of Albion*, Plate 4, respectively.
88. See "The Lamb" [*Plate* 2]; "The Ecchoing Green," Plate 2; or *America*, Plate 15.
89. See the title page of *Songs of Innocence and of Experience;* "The Shepherd" [*Plate* 1]; or the swan on Plate 11 of *America*.
90. See *America*, Plate 7 (Copy M, TP); and *Visions of the Daughters of Albion*, title page.
91. *The Letters of William Blake*, ed. Geoffrey Keynes (London, 1956), pp. 150–151.

diverse as the Bible, Milton, Shakespeare, and his own poetry, all illustrate themes that he had discussed in his own work of this period. Even
though Blake himself did not set these paintings into any particular order,
perhaps because he hoped to sell them individually, I believe that they
fall into a coherent series. The order in which I shall discuss them seems
to me to clarify their meaning.

Like Blake's "Bible of Hell," *The Book of Urizen,* these prints portray
the creation of man, the formation of the mortal body, as a denial of
human divinity.[92] Here again, Urizen reigns as the demiurge of an anti-
utopian nightmare, systematically imprisoning man within the stifling
forms of the human body and rational categories. Stylistically, Blake
again uses the conventions of romantic classicism: strong outlines, heroic
human figures, emphatic linear rhythms, and severely tectonic compositions. Here, these rigidly closed compositions seem to intensify the claus-
trophobic nature of Urizen's fallen, limited kingdom. Interestingly, Blake
increases the textural density of his medium and the richness of his coloring by using tempera for these color prints. Perhaps this was a deliberate
attempt to accentuate the earth-bound materialism of Urizen's fallen
world; perhaps it was only a desire on Blake's part to create more monumental, commercially successful paintings.

In the first print, *God Creating Adam* (or *Elohim Creating Adam*
[*Plate 39*]), the Elohim is identical with Blake's figure of Urizen in *The
Book of Urizen.* God has the same face, the same long nose and heavy eye-
brows, the same white hair and beard, the same white robe and muscular
body as Urizen (compare *Urizen,* title page [*Plate 26*], plates 5, 9); and
his creation, like Urizen's, is molded from a clod of clay into a human
body (Adam's head and right arm have not yet been fully formed). The
large red worm winding its tightening, restricting coils around Adam's
body shows that this creation is a fall from eternity into mortality, into
the world of physical generation and despair depicted both in *For Children: The Gates of Paradise,* where the worm appears on the last emblem,
coiled round the huddled figure buried in the tomb [*Plate 25*], and on

92. These prints are reproduced in *The Works of William Blake in the Tate Gallery,*
ed. Martin Butlin (London, 1957), Plates 8–13. Blunt has offered a similar interpretation, *Art of William Blake,* p. 58.

Plate 39. God Creating Adam, Tate Gallery.

Plate 25 of *Urizen,* where three figures are trapped in the coils of a large winged worm. The worm coiling around Adam's cruciform body clearly signifies the constriction of his holy Energy into a limited material body. Adam's fall into a finite, circumscribed form is paralleled in the strictly mathematical composition of the print, a series of straight horizontals (God's body, hair, and wings, and Adam's torso) counterpointed against the left-right diagonals of God's and Adam's arms and set against a half circle, the setting sun.

The next print in the series, *Satan Exulting over Eve,* further demonstrates that this creation is indeed a fall. The repetition, in reverse direction, of a winged figure hovering over a prostrate body now wrapped round by a serpent encourages the association of this Satan with God, this Eve with Adam. Eve's eating of the forbidden fruit (the apple lies beneath her right hand) and guilty recognition of her own sinfulness is equivalent to God-Urizen's molding of the human body; both are an expulsion from paradise or Innocence. The serpent is specifically associated with the fallen world of reason in *Europe, Urizen,* and *Ahania.* The serpent is linked to the "snaky hair" of the female will, the "ancient temple serpent-form'd" of repressive, institutionalized religions and the general restrictions of reason ("Thought chang'd the infinite to a serpent") in *Europe;* and although Morton Paley suggests that the huge coiling serpent of the title page may be an ambiguous symbol of renewal as well as degeneration,[93] the poem ends with Los rearing his head in "snaky thunders" clad and the apocalypse unrealized (E 59, 62, 65). On Plate 6 of *The Book of Urizen,* serpents coil around the falling immortals. In *The Book of Ahania* (1795), the serpent is a completely negative image. The serpent is now one of those "fell monsters" produced by Urizen's perversely "dire Contemplations":

> . . . some [of these monsters] aloft flew in air

> Of these: an enormous dread Serpent
> Scaled and poisonous horned
> Approach'd Urizen even to his knees
> As he sat on his dark rooted Oak.

(E 84)

And, in *Vala,* written a few years later, Urizen

> . . . knew that weakness stretches out in breadth & length he knew
> That wisdom reaches high & deep & therefore he made Orc
> In Serpent form compelld stretch out & up the mysterious tree. . . .

(E 349)

Satan's shield, spear, and green bat wings further reveal his consanguinity with the militant, despotic Urizen.

The expulsion itself occurs in the next print, *God Judging Adam* (the print formerly called *Elijah,* but shrewdly retitled by Martin Butlin, [*Plate* 40]),[94] where Adam's fall is seen both in his willingness to obey Urizen (before whom he stands with bowed head) and in his physical

---

93. Paley, *Energy and the Imagination,* pp. 79–81.
94. Martin Butlin, "Blake's 'God Judging Adam' Rediscovered," *The Burlington Magazine* 107 (February 1965):86–89.

Plate 40. God Judging Adam, Tate Gallery.

similarity to Urizen—both figures have identical white hair, beards, and physiques. (Blake often used this pictorial device of repeated features and figures to unmask the spiritual identity of two seemingly separate characters, as Joseph Wicksteed has pointed out in his discussion of Job's identity with God in Blake's illustrations for *The Book of Job*).[95] Adam's limited vision which cannot see beyond Urizen's abstract, rational world is emphasized by the limitations and strict repetitions of line and color in the print: the vertical lines of Adam's right leg and torso are repeated in God's back and legs and in the horse's front left leg; the horizontal line of

95. Joseph Wicksteed, *Blake's Vision of the Book of Job* (London, 1910), Plate 2 and *passim*.

God's knees and thighs, emphasized by the stone book upon his lap, are repeated in the horse's back and in Adam's bowed head and shoulders, the left-right diagonal of the horse's upper rein runs directly parallel to God's extended, judging arm and sceptre; and the entire scene is flatly placed against the circle of flames of God's chariot on the right. Significantly, here the flames of Energy are completely confined to the fixed circle of God's chariot; Energy has now become mere will to power and works as the wheels of God's carriage and the tools of his oppressive policies. God's robes fall in flat vertical folds; and the colors of the design are based on a limited palette—the black-yellow-reds of the horse and flames and the contrasting white bodies of God and Adam.

The results of this Urizenic creation, this fall from eternity into the limited human body and mind, are pictured in the next six prints. Adam is imprisoned in a mental and physical world ruled by Urizen, a world of political tyranny, rationalism, superstition, total repression of Energy, sickness, and death. *Nebuchadnezzar* embodies the consequences of the oppressive policies of the tyrant who, like Bromion in *Visions of the Daughters of Albion,* imposes "one law for the lion and ox" (as the caption under the reversed Nebuchadnezzar on Plate 24 of *The Marriage of Heaven and Hell* emphasizes) and is thus one aspect of the Urizen who rules with

> One command, one joy, one desire,
> One curse, one weight, one measure
> One King, one God, one Law.
>
> (E 71)

Fixed within this bestial, degenerate, crawling body, Adam/Nebuchadnezzar knows only his own impotence and fear; his face is distorted with terror. The design itself is appropriately confined to a central rectangle (bounded by Nebuchadnezzar's back, right arm, left palm, left knee, and right knee and thigh) placed against a large triangle formed by two intersecting wheat sheaves. Interestingly, the visual source for this design, John Mortimer's drawing of *Nebuchadnezzar Recovering his Reason* (etched in 1781), specifically links this bestial tyranny with reason. *Newton* [*Plate 41*], the companion to *Nebuchadnezzar,* even more clearly embodies the limited, rationalistic philosophy that is derived solely from

Plate 41. Newton, Tate Gallery.

empirical sense data. Blake denounced this epistemology in *The Song of Los:*

> Thus the terrible race of Los & Enitharmon gave
> Laws & Religions to the sons of Har binding them more
> And more to Earth: closing and restraining:
> Till a Philosophy of Five Senses was complete
> Urizen wept & gave it into the hands of Newton & Locke.

(E 66)

The limitation of Newton's vision is underscored by the fact that he looks *downward* rather than up to heaven, by his use of compass and geometric diagram (the instruments used by the Ancient of Days to construct the fallen world of *Europe*), and by his environment. The dark blue-green

Plate 42. Hecate, Tate Gallery.

coloring and the lichen-covered rock suggest the bottom of a cave and may link Newton to Plato's deluded men who see only the reflected shadows of truth; [96] the dark coloring may also indicate night. Like Newton's mind, the composition itself is severely restricted—here, to a series of intersecting triangles: the triangular hill on the left, the triangle formed by the lower legs together with the left arm of Newton of which his head forms the apex (this triangle is filled in by the white cloth hanging behind Newton), the triangle outlined by the rock and calves of Newton's legs, the compasses, and the triangle actually drawn on the scroll.

The threefold figure of Hecate [*Plate 42*] is a traditional emblem of

96. John Gage has further identified Newton's cave with "the 'dark chamber' which formed the setting for his optical experiments" in "Blake's *Newton*," *Journal of the Warburg and Courtauld Institutes* 34 (1971), p. 373.

witchcraft, superstition, and mystery, as in Shakespeare's *Macbeth* where her brew includes many of the figures in Blake's color print:

> Eye of newt and toe of frog,
> Wool of bat and tongue of dog,
> Adder's fork and blind-worm's sting,
> Lizard's leg and owlet's wing.

(IV, i, 14–7)

Hecate's realm is further described by Puck in *Midsummer Night's Dream:*

> Now the hungry lion roars,
> And the wolf behowls the moon:
> Whilst the weary ploughman snores,
> All with weary task fordone.
> Now the wasted brands do glow,
> Whilst the screech-owl, screeching loud,
> Puts the wretch that lies in woe
> In remembrance of a shroud.
> Now it is the time of night
> That the graves all gaping wide,
> Every one lets forth his sprite,
> In the church-way paths to glide:
> And we fairies, that do run
> By the triple-Hecate's team,
> From the presence of the sun,
> Following darkness like a dream,
> Now do frolic. . . .

(V, i, 378–94)

Blake's *Hecate* is specifically linked with Urizen's rule of religious mystery and fear. Like Urizen on the title page and Plate 5 of *The Book of Urizen,* she crouches over a book of unintelligible hieroglyphs, and over her head hovers the bat-winged spectre of abstract reason or, rather, that authoritarian attitude which masks as reason. Hecate's traditional menagerie—the owl, the frog or lizard, the ass—gather round her. Moreover, the ass is eating a bat-winged plant or fungus. Blake's choice of a female witch to illustrate the theme of superstition and mystery may suggest that the female causes the fall.

All three aspects of Urizen's repressive rule—political oppression, rationalism, and superstition—are summarized in the more general state-

Plate 43. The Good and Evil Angels Struggling for Possession of a Child, Tate Gallery.

ment of *The Good & Evil Angels Struggling for Possession of a Child* [*Plate 43*] which depicts the corruption of all Energy into Urizenic will to power. This design originally appeared, in reverse, at the bottom of Plate 4 of *The Marriage of Heaven and Hell* where it illustrated the "errors" of "All Bibles or sacred codes," the denial of life-expanding Energy and the glorification of reason. The "Evil Angel" (or devil) of Energy was there chained in flames, as was Oothoon in the *Visions of the Daughters of Albion,* Plate 4; the "Good Angel" of reason prevented the child from reaching the sun, the source of infinite energy. But in this later, reversed use of the design, Blake depicts his post-1793, pessimistic vision of energy. The naked man chained in flames is now blind, and his left arm seems to reach directly toward the child (rather than stretching beyond the child, as in the earlier design). As happened to Los in *The Book of Urizen,* creative Energy has been devoured by reason and perverted into an instrument of oppression. The creative or revolutionary impulse is now distorted into a blind fury that seems to attack the very child (Orc?) it should protect. And this young child, like Orc, flees in terror from this perverse will-to-power with open arms and kicking legs, toward the sun. But he is held in the arms of a well-intentioned male good angel who, like the guardian nurses and mothers of *Songs of Experience* or like Enitharmon in *The Book of Urizen,* tries to protect or "swaddle" the child from this fiendish energy. Lest we be tempted to see the beautiful male nude on the right solely as a savior or rescuer who mercifully shields the child from the cruelties of the blind evil angel, we should remember the title of the print. Both figures are angels, Blake's familiar word for the servants of reason, of "sacred codes," absolutist systems, and political empire. George III is Albion's angel in *America.* Moreover, both angels struggle for "possession" of the child; both see the child, as Bromion would, as a piece of property, to be owned and controlled. The "Good Angel's" rescue of the child will not guarantee the child the freedom he desires. Moreover, the sun in the print is setting and has already half disappeared beyond the horizon [ourizein], although it was blazing well above the horizon in the *The Marriage* design; no holy, life-expanding Energy is left untrapped in this perverted world. The human body itself now contributes to the perversion of Energy into mere will to power and thus to the strengthening of rational or authoritarian repression.

The physical results of the fall are depicted in the next two prints, *The Lazar House* and *Lamech and His Two Wives. The Lazar House* or *House of Death* [*Plate* 44] is based on Milton's famous description in *Paradise Lost* (Bk. XI: 477–93) of "maladies/ Of ghastly Spasm, or racking torture" over which "triumphant Death his Dart/ Shook, but delaid to strike, though oft invok't/ With vows, as thir chief good, and final hope." The horizontal corpses of the strong man, the beautiful man, and the ugly man lying on the mat at the lower left; [97] the vertical figure of suicidal despair, dagger in hand, at the right; and the ironically blessing arms of a blind Urizen-God which horizontally cover the scene

97. Thus identified by John Grant, "You Can't Write About Blake's Pictures Like That," *Blake Studies* I (Spring 1969):196.

Plate 44. The House of Death, Tate Gallery.

and rain down spears—all unmask the physical disease and suffering hurled upon man by Urizen's imprisonment of the human spirit in a mortal, bodily form. The other immediate result of the fall, of course, was murder and death; and Blake returns to the Bible, not to the too well-known tale of Cain and Abel but to the *Genesis 4* account of Lamech's murder of a man, to illustrate this theme in *Lamech and His Two Wives.* Here, the tomblike rectilinear grid of the vertical bodies and horizontal murdered corpse is broken only by the slight curves in the robes of Lamech and his two wives.

The cause of man's fall, of Energy's or the imagination's submission to the closed rule of reason, is the natural pity one man feels for another. As

Plate 45. *Pity,* Tate Gallery.

Blake explained in *The Book of Urizen,* Los divided and fell because he took pity on Urizen shut up in the void:

> He saw Urizen deadly black,
> In his chains bound, & Pity began,
>
> In anguish dividing & dividing
> For pity divides the soul.

(E 76)

Blake acknowledges the positive aspects of pity in the print of *Naomi Entreating Ruth,* where Ruth clings sympathetically to Naomi while Orpah abandons her mother-in-law. However, the negative results of compassion are suggested in the more complex print, *Pity* [*Plate 45*], which is drawn from Shakespeare's description of pity in *Macbeth:*

And pity, like a naked new-born babe,
Striding the blast, or heaven's cherubin, hors'd
Upon the sightless couriers of the air,
Shall blow the horrid deed in every eye,
That tears shall drown the wind.

(I, viii, 21–6)

Here, the mother of the newborn child (who closely resembles the new-born Orc plunging through flames on Plate 20 of *The Book of Urizen*) seems to be dying in childbirth. The division of mother and child, the result of "Man begetting his likeness,/ On his own divided image" (E 78), causes separation and death. Thus, this print also includes Macbeth's "horrid deed," the murder of Duncan and the breaking of all familial ties and social bonds. Significantly, in both prints, pity is associated with women (the child is received by the hands of a woman). As in *The Book of Urizen,* where pity specifically takes the female form of Enitharmon, Blake implies that the traditional virtue of the "gentle sex" can become a subtle trap of the female will. By encouraging the imagination and heart to "know" and empathize with its implacable enemies, feminine compassion undermines the integrity and strength of creative Energy. Again, in these prints, Blake's vision is presented in strict geometrical patterns: vertical lines control the *Naomi Entreating Ruth;* horizontal lines dominate *Pity.*

The final print of the series, which may have been added after 1795 when Blake was illustrating the Bible for Butts in 1799–1806, the *Christ Appearing to the Apostles After the Resurrection* (now in the Yale Gallery of Fine Arts), repeats the solution to the problem of man's fall into a limited human body which Blake offered in *The Gates of Paradise.* As later in "To Tirzah," the lyric added to *Songs of Experience* around 1805, the fallen mortal body must be "Raised a Spiritual Body." Both Christ and man must forsake the mortal body in order to attain spiritual perfection and regain paradise. This traditional Christian conception of the resurrection of a spiritual body after physical death is Blake's immediate solution to the problem posed by the Tate Gallery color prints. In the revisions of *Vala,* undertaken after 1805, however, Blake wrestles again with this problem: if form, especially the human form, is a sign of man's fall from eternity into the limited, closed world of Urizenic Experience; and if, on the other hand, an austerely neoclassical style based on tectonic compositions, abstract linear rhythms, clear outlines, and heroic Michelangelesque nudes (a style Blake used especially effectively in the Tate Gallery color-print series) is the most authentic articulation of antique, divine images; then Blake is at the same time rejecting and affirming form, and especially the human form. His finest designs both iconographically denounce the creation of the human body as a separation from eternity and thus as an unmitigated evil; and visually portray that same human body as an ideally beautiful, heroic, Michelangelesque form. Philosophically, Blake could not reconcile this intellectual condemnation of the human body as the denial of man's divinity with his aesthetic practice in the Tate Gallery color prints. The magnificence of these heroic, idealized human figures—one thinks especially of the *Newton,* often chosen by unsuspecting physicists to illustrate their textbooks—belies the intellectual denunciation of the human body articulated in Blake's iconography. Perhaps Blake's shrewd insight into Milton's *Paradise Lost* also applies to him: Blake was of the human body's party without knowing it (E 35). This conflict compelled Blake to develop his iconographic distinction between the fallen human body confined within Urizenic categories and the liberated human body that radiates Innocence and Energy into a philosophical distinction between the corrupted human body and the human form divine.

FIVE

Vala, or The Four Zoas: Blake's Concept of Form, 1795-1810

In 1795 Blake's poetry and color prints had presented a very pessimistic vision of the human condition. Man is born into a corrupting physical body; his imaginative vision is impaired by the mind-forged manacles of reason, a repressive conscience, and a conviction of the necessity of law; his hope for salvation is frustrated by his corporeal nature and his inability to believe wholly in a spiritual afterlife. It had therefore become increasingly imperative for Blake, both as a poet-prophet and as a man, to show the way out of this living hell, the way to realize one's potential divinity within the fixed limits of mortality.

From the bibliographic tangle that separates the first fair copy of *Vala* from the much expanded, heavily revised, and perhaps unfinished "final" version of *The Four Zoas* we can, I think, extricate Blake's developing solution to this problem. The question posed by *The Book of Urizen* and the Tate Gallery color prints—if annihilation of outline (formlessness, the dissipation of Energy into entropy, or Urizen's abstract void) is evil and if containment within a given form (specifically, the human body) is

165

evil, what possible salvation can mortal man achieve?—is here stated, restated, and at last tentatively resolved.

Although such noted scholars as David Erdman, G. E. Bentley, Jr., and H. M. Margoliouth have assiduously grappled with the complexities of the *Vala*, or *The Four Zoas*, manuscript,[1] their efforts have as often undermined as supported each other. Although all three editors agree that the poem was probably composed in at least three chronological layers, their conclusions concerning which layer came first, which section belongs to which layer, and when each layer was substantially composed differ significantly. As a result, there is not yet a sufficiently reliable chronology for my study of Blake's developing concept of form to rest upon. Therefore, I have had to draw my own conclusions from both the manuscript and the readings of these editors and have often, I fear, chosen that arrangement of the text that most clearly reveals the theme with which I am primarily concerned. That Blake was struggling with the problem of form I do not doubt; and I hope that frequent quotations from the text will manifest this. Further, the conclusions I reach in this chapter concerning Blake's final concept of the human form divine in *The Four Zoas* are strongly supported by Blake's later poetry and art where the same concept is repeated and expanded. In this chapter, I shall attempt to isolate only two separate versions of the manuscript, corresponding roughly, I hope, to the first fair copy of *Vala*, probably completed by 1805, and the "final" version of the poem known as *The Four Zoas* which was effectively finished by 1810. Comparison of these two versions reveals a striking shift in Blake's attitude to the human body and to bounded forms in general.

DATING THE MANUSCRIPT

H. M. Margoliouth has suggested that the original version of *Vala* may have been a two-hundred-line composition written in 1797 and then

---

1. David Erdman, ed., *The Poetry and Prose of William Blake* (Garden City, N.Y., 1965) and "The Binding (Et cetera) of *Vala*," a review of Bentley, Jr., published in *The Library* 109 (1964):112–29; G. E. Bentley, Jr., ed., *William Blake: Vala or The Four Zoas* (Oxford, 1963); and H. M. Margoliouth, ed., *William Blake's Vala* (Oxford, 1956).

treated as a "Preludium" or prologue to the poem proper (similar in purpose to the preludia that preface *America, Europe,* and *The Book of Urizen*).[2] Margoliouth identifies this two-hundred-line poem as "Text A" and prints it in an appendix to his edition of *Vala* as part of the original Night I. Although it is by no means certain that this short poem was completed *before* a fair copy of all nine *Nights* (Bentley conjectures that the date 1797 on the title page of *Vala* was added when Blake finished copying out a poem of about 2,100 lines, structured, as the title page indicates, as "A DREAM of Nine Nights" [3]), it is interesting to study it separately from the Nights as an early capsule statement of Blake's concept of form in 1797. My discussion of these two hundred lines is based on Margoliouth's "Text A" with corrections from the textual notes of Erdman's edition of Blake's *Poetry and Prose.*[4]

The composition of *Vala, A Dream of Nine Nights* may have been completed in brief by 1797 as Bentley surmises, but I find Margoliouth's suggestion that the bulk of *Vala* was written after Blake went to Felpham in 1800 more plausible. References in Blake's letters to his work "in a Land of Abstraction where Spectres of the Dead wander" (to Butts, 11 September 1801; E 685) suggest that he is at work on a poem suiting the description of *Vala* or *Milton.* Margoliouth has also noted that the accuracy of Blake's descriptions of the sea in the Tharmas passages in Nights III and IV was probably garnered from Blake's personal encounters with the ocean at Felpham.[5]

Further, the drawings of grotesque figures that appear in the margins of Night II, page 26; Night VI, page 70; Night VIIb, page 98; Night VIII, page 100; and Night IX, pages 134 and 136 [*Plates 49–53*] are similar to the medieval wood carvings on the misericords in Chichester Cathedral and St. Mary's Hospital, Chichester [*Plates 46, 47, and 48*]. Note especially the bat-winged, web-footed wyvern; the human-headed and armed bull; the dog-faced, serpent-tailed, winged creatures surrounding the old man; and the winged, four-legged, bull-headed monsters on the

2. Margoliouth, *William Blake's Vala,* p. xxiii.
3. Bentley, Jr., *William Blake: Vala,* p. 159.
4. All page references to *Vala* or *The Four Zoas* are based on the G. E. Bentley, Jr., transcription of the manuscript.
5. Margoliouth, *William Blake's Vala,* p. xxiv.

Plate 46. Misericord in Chichester Cathedral, Prebend of Highleigh.

Plate 47. Misericord in Chichester Cathedral, Prebend of Hova Villa.

Plate 48. Misericord in Chichester Cathedral, Prebend of Seaford.

misericords on the north side of the cathedral. (No such grotesque drawing appears on the pages of Night I or Text A, which may support Margoliouth's suggestion that this section was composed in 1797.) We know
that Blake visited Chichester (a town situated about seven miles from Felpham) by October 2, 1800, because he describes the city in a letter of that
date to Thomas Butts; in addition, we have two of Blake's landscapes of
Chichester from this period (one, showing the Church of St. Mary, is now
in the Tate Gallery). Since the misericords in both the cathedral and St.
Mary's Hospital are famous throughout England for their workmanship
and wit, it seems probable that Blake studied them closely and appreciated their fusion of fantasy and religion. Blake was already sympathetic
to Gothic art, as we know both from his apprentice work in Westminster
Abbey and from the influence of the English Gothic style on his later art.
These medieval depictions of the grotesque and the secular, these literali-
zations of the medieval conception of hell, would almost certainly have
appealed to him. Indeed, Blake may have found a direct analogy between
these attempts to picture fallen man and the monsters of hell and his own
efforts to articulate a Bible of hell, an allegorical picture of the fallen
human mind in eighteenth-century England's repressive society.

Granted that the absence of Chichester drawings cannot be used to
date an early (pre-1800) layer of *Vala* (Blake may not have drawn such
designs on Night I or Text A simply because they were not suitable to the
text at that point), their presence may possibly support a post-1800 dating
of pages where they seem to relate to, or better yet to suggest, some parts
of the accompanying text.[6] Without excessive forcing or ingenuity, I
think we can see all of these drawings as illustrations (and perhaps even
as inspirations) for images in the accompanying text. On page 26, the
grotesque drawings of the female (her vulva is pointedly outlined), web-

6. G. E. Bentley, Jr.'s conclusion (in *William Blake: Vala*) that the drawings were
added *after* the text was written (p. 158) does not seem convincing in all cases. Blake's
imagination was not irrefutably "first poetic and then graphic" (p. 158). After all, Blake
was trained as an artist and engraver rather than as a poet. Moreover, on pp. 19, 25,
37, 54, 64, 126, 132 and 134 [*Plate* 52], the text seems to have been written *over*
parts of the drawing. And Martin Butlin offers impressive evidence that on at least one
occasion a visual idea inspired a later poetic idea in *Vala* (in "The Literature of Art—
Blake's *Vala, or The Four Zoas* and a New Water-Color in the Tate Gallery," *The Burlington Magazine* 106 (August, 1964):381–82).

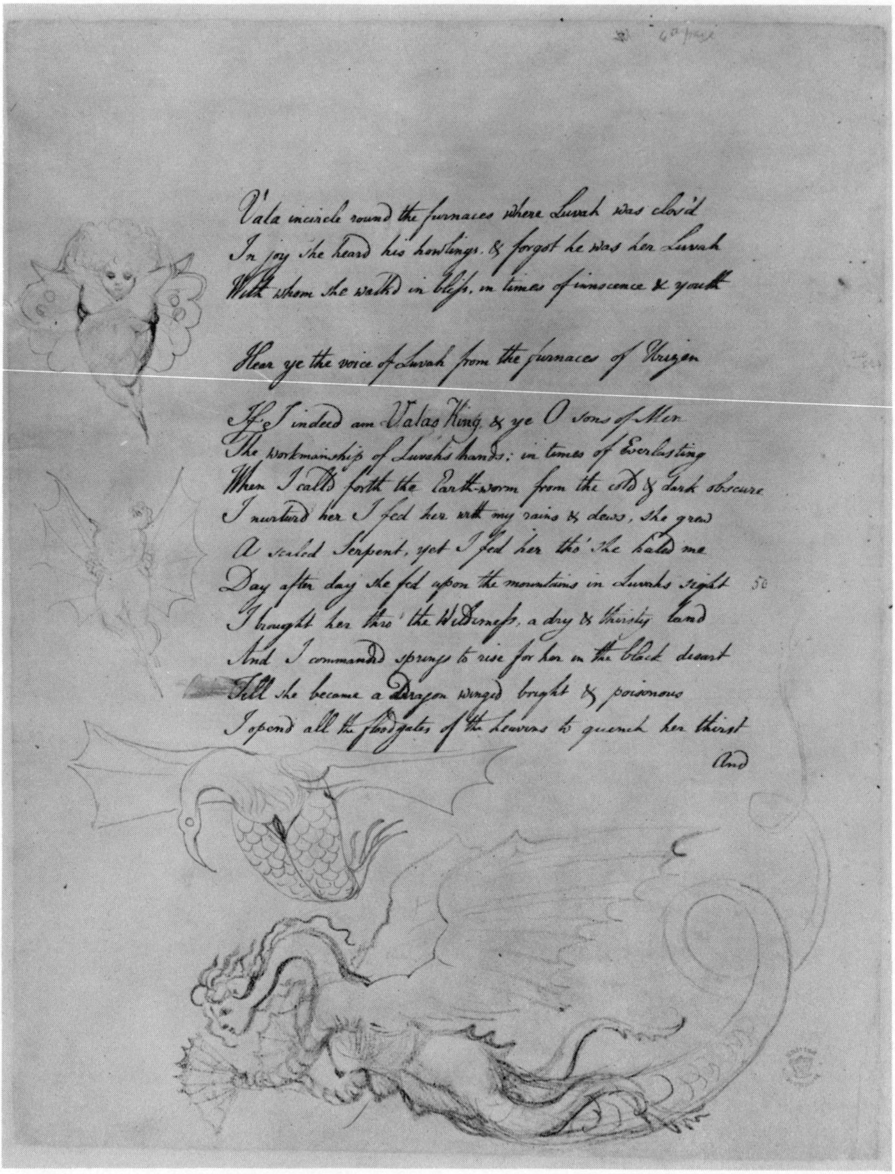

Vala incircle round the furnaces where Luvah was clos'd
In joy she heard his howlings, & forgot he was her Luvah
With whom she walkd in bliss, in times of innocence & youth

Hear ye the voice of Luvah from the furnaces of Urizen

If I indeed am Valas King, & ye O sons of Men
The workmanship of Luvahs hands: in times of Everlasting
When I calld forth the Earth-worm from the cold & dark obscure
I nurturd her I fed her with my rains & dews, she grew
A scaled Serpent, yet I fed her tho' she hated me
Day after day she fed upon the mountains in Luvahs sight 56
I brought her thro' the Wilderness, a dry & thirsty land
And I commanded springs to rise for her in the black desart
Till she became a Dragon winged bright & poisonous
I opend all the floodgates of the heavens to quench her thirst
                                                         And

Plate 49. *Vala*, Page 26, British Museum.

winged, swan-necked, fish-tailed creature at the bottom left and the female, human-faced, swan-necked, bat-winged, triple-breasted, web-handed, foot-less, and serpent-tailed creature at the bottom ([*Plate 49*], compare with the bat-wings, webbed feet and serpent-tail of the wyvern on the High-leigh misericord [*Plate 46*] and the bare-breasted mermaid on the Ear-tham misericord) both illustrate Luvah's accompanying description of his creation of Vala from an "Earthworm" through a "scaled Serpent" into a " [Dragon] winged bright & poisonous." This illustration is a remarkably accurate summary of eighteenth-century evolutionary theory: in the womb, the human embryo passes through the entire evolution of the human species from an amoeba, through reptile and bird, to a mammal.[7] Blake's two female creatures have collapsed the chronological stages of that development. Part reptile, part bird, part mammal, their grotesque appearances testify to Vala's perversion of a normal human embryo into a freakish serpent-dragon.

The human hands and feet so strangely attached to the batwinged alli-gator with open jaws at the bottom of page 70, Night VI ([*Plate 50*], compare with the human hands of the bull on the Hova Villa misericord [*Plate 47*] and the batwings and serpent-tail of the bird-footed monster on the Archdeacon's Stall) bear witness to the degeneration of Urizen's children in the abyss, those "ruind spirits" described in the first layer of text on page 70. Further, this drawing may actually have inspired the final revision of the text where the children are specifically described as

> . . . forms of tygers & of Lions dishumanizd men
> Many in serpents & in worms stretchd out enormous length
> Over the sullen mould & slimy tracks obstruct his [Urizen's] way
> Drawn out from deep to deep woven by ribbd
> And scaled monsters or armd in iron shell or shell of brass
> Or gold a glittering torment shining & hissing in eternal pain.
>
> (page 70:34—9)

The drawings on page 98, Night VIIb, and page 100, Night VIII, portray the cowled Prester serpent described on page 97 and the hooved, spec-trously bat-winged, bearded Urizen who summons the fallen "Synagogue

---

7. Carmen S. Kreiter, "Evolution and William Blake," *Studies in Romanticism* 4 (Winter 1965):111.

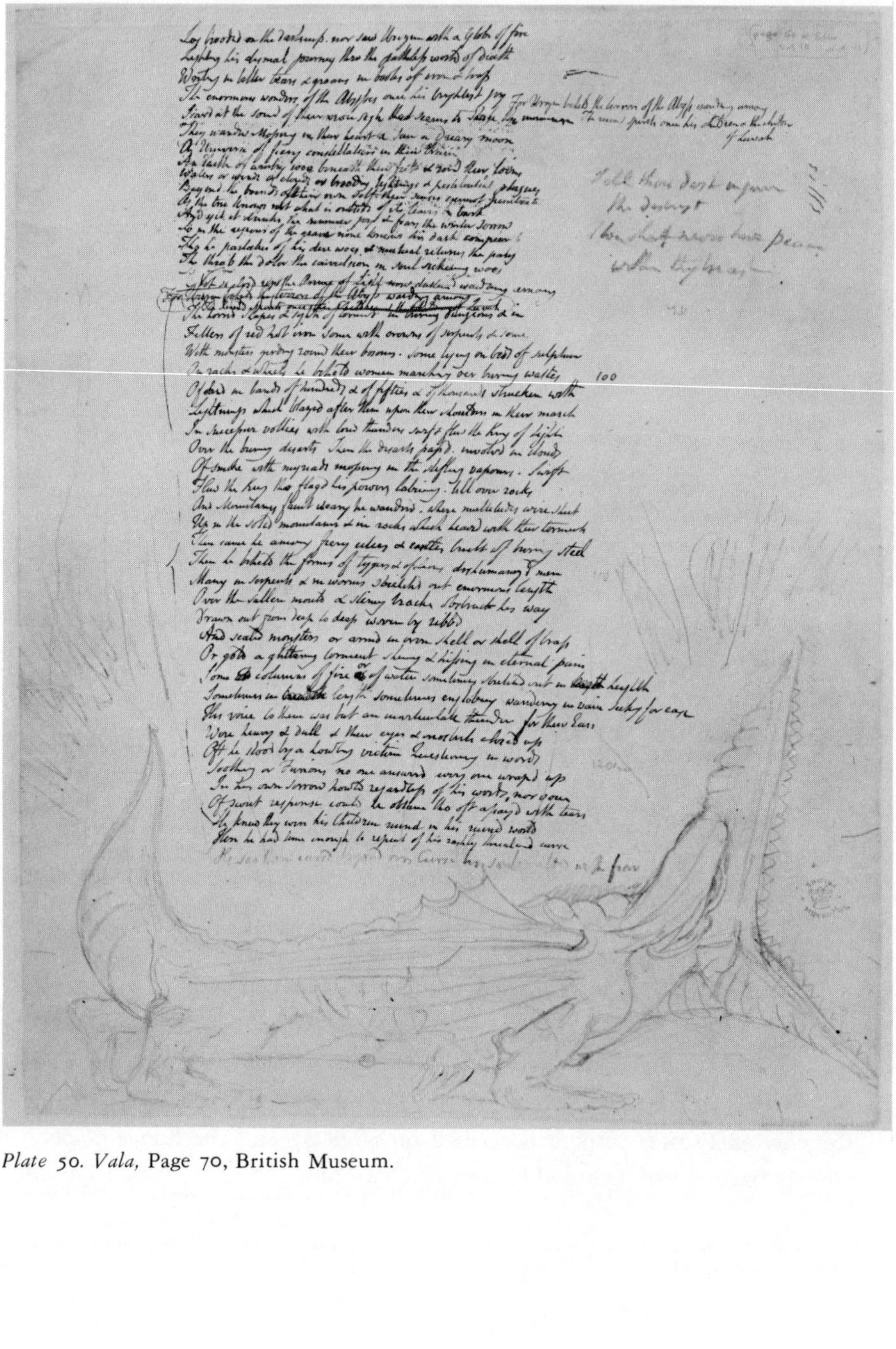

Plate 50. Vala, Page 70, British Museum.

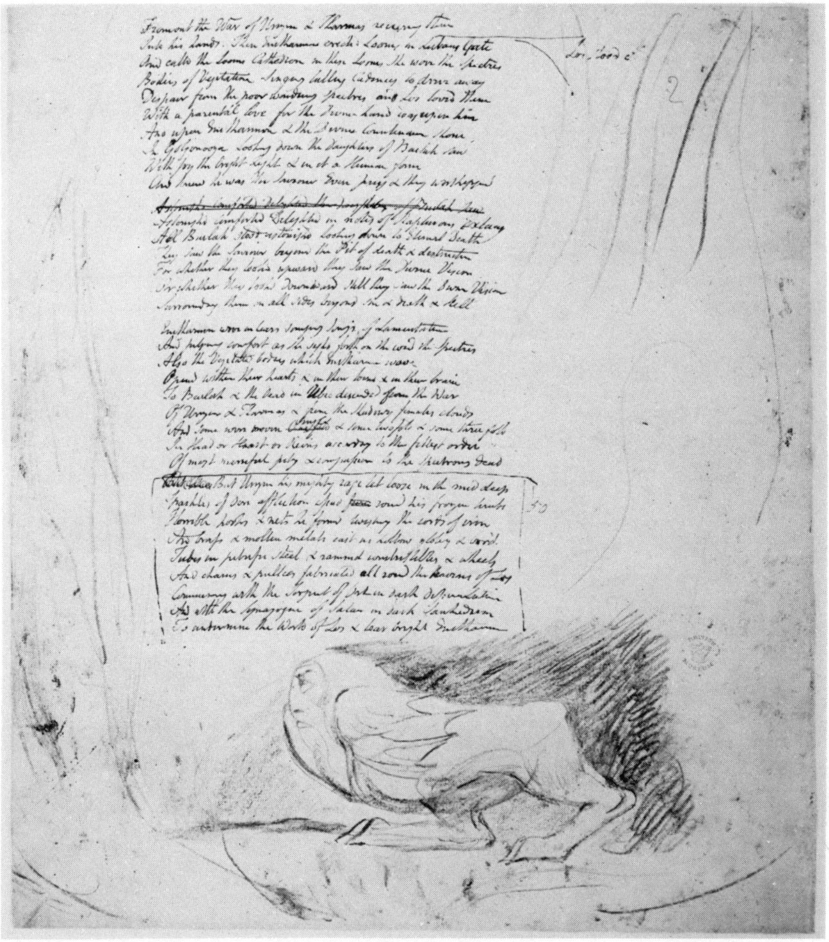

Plate 51. Vala, Page 100, British Museum.

of Satan in Dark Sanhedrim" on page 100 ([*Plate 51*], compare with the human head and hooves of the bull on the Hova Villa misericord [*Plate 47*] and the bearded centaur on the Middleton misericord).

Finally, on pages 134 and 136 of Night IX, the drawings again illustrate the accompanying text. The human-faced (with a startling resemblance to George III), bird-footed, winged, and serpent-tailed creature on page 134 ([*Plate 52*], compare with the serpent-tail, talons, and wings

Plate 52. *Vala*, Page 134, British Museum.

of the monster on the Archdeacon's Stall) recalls the grotesque image of
the fallen female will, Vala, on page 26 and here specifically represents
political tyranny and religious mystery, whose pomp and power are destroyed by the winnowing fan of the true human form, the generated

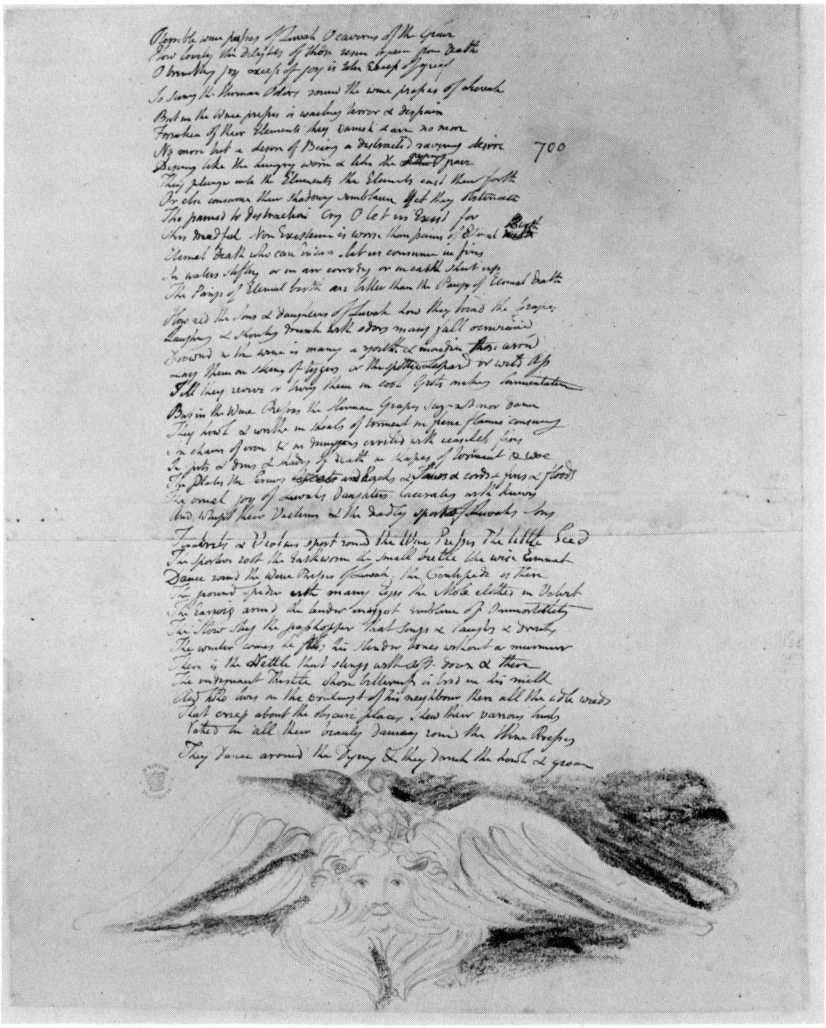

Plate 53. Vala, Page 136, British Museum.

body of the redeemed Tharmas. And the gentle-eyed, mustached, bearded, and winged face that appears at the bottom of page 136 ([*Plate 53*], compare with the smiling, bearded and mustached old man on the Seaford misericord [*Plate 48*]) may well be the "Eternal Man," the face of the resurrected Albion or Christ who watches over the wine pressing of Luvah and blesses the coming apocalypse. The lined waves of this man's beard closely resemble the outlined waves of Richard II's beard in Blake's engraving for Gough's *Sepulchral Monuments;* perhaps Blake associated this old man with that divinely anointed medieval king.

The close relationship of these drawings, both to the misericords in Chichester Cathedral and to their accompanying text, suggests that the pages in question, pages 26, 70, 98, 100, 134, and 136, may have been written after Blake visited Chichester in 1800. This supports the generally accepted dating of these pages, with the single exception of page 26. Here, the drawing may have been added after Blake wrote the text; or perhaps the bulk of even the earliest draft of *Vala,* beyond the "Preludium," was done between 1800 and 1803 at a period when Blake was working hard and enthusiastically on his illuminated poetry.

If these references to Blake's letters, sea descriptions, and drawings are meaningful, then we might tentatively assume, in the absence of more concrete evidence, that the first versions (and fair copies) of Nights II–VI, VIIa, VIIb, and IX, as well as the expanded version of Night I (the preludium plus the song at the feast of Los and Enitharmon [Margoliouth's Text A *] plus minor changes and revisions [Margoliouth's Text B]), were written between 1797 and 1805, with much of the work done during the Felpham years (1800–1803).

The final revision of the manuscript in which the title was changed to *The Four Zoas* and the poem itself greatly expanded (the present Night VIII was added and Night VIIa was almost doubled in length) was probably completed by 1810. The similarities in content and symbolism of *The Four Zoas* to Blake's other work of this period, most notably *Milton* (1804), *Jerusalem* (1804–20), and *A Descriptive Catalogue* (1810), support this dating, and perhaps an even later one, if we assume that *The Four Zoas* was never finally abandoned. This final text of the poem has been faithfully transcribed in Erdman's edition of Blake's *Poetry and Prose* and shall be used in my discussion. Again, I remind the reader that the following reading of *Vala* and *The Four Zoas* is highly tentative, based as it must be on an extremely confused and occasionally undecipherable text. As David Erdman, the most recent editor of this text, has concluded: "The complexities of the ms, in short, continue to defy analysis and all assertions about meaningful physical groupings or chronologically definable layers of composition or inscription must be understood to rest on partial and ambiguous evidence" (E 739).

VALA, 1795–1805

The epic account of man's fall into the generated human body and his eventual salvation that Blake set out to write in *Vala* was heavily indebted to Edward Young's *Night Thoughts*. Between 1795 and 1797, Blake drew 537 watercolor illustrations for Young's poem and, in the process, completely absorbed Young's vision of the human condition as a vale of tears from which only physical death can free us. Titling his poem *Vala, or The Death and Judgment of the Ancient Man, A Dream of Nine Nights,* Blake closely followed the epic structure of Young's nine Nights: a completely morbid account of man's unrelieved suffering on earth followed by a triumphant Christian vision of the resurrection, in which the mortal body, after death, enters into the eternal bliss of a spiritual afterlife. Blake's sympathy with Young's rejection of the mortal world is evident in many of his illustrations for Young: Blake consistently translates Young's poetic metaphors into precise visual images and often draws on his own iconography to expand Young's vision. In his design for Young's description of man as a "helpless Immortal! Insect infinite! A Worm! a God!" (Night I:79–80), for instance, Blake illustrated Young's idea with his own image of Innocence. A child with purple insect wings emerges from the green earth into golden sunbeams, his arms spread open in a gesture that manifests his realized divinity. But this child is destroyed. Blake captures Young's pessimistic vision of time and mortality as the prison of the divine soul in a striking visual image of despair on Page 79. A naked human figure with her right leg chained, her hands grasping her head, and her mouth open in horror is trapped within a huge yellow and black ouroboros, the traditional emblem of eternity that here symbolizes an unending cycle of serpentine perversion and oppression.

In many cases, however, Blake found it necessary to correct Young's explanations for man's mortal degeneration. Whereas Young attributed man's fall to his failure to obey the dictates of reason and to observe the degrees of the great chain of being and the laws of science, Blake sees these very demands for rational behavior, strict allegiance to social and political hierarchy, and the worship of science as the causes of man's downfall.[8] He illustrates Young's "Where *Sense* runs Savage, broke from *Reason's* chain,/ And sings false Peace, till smother'd by the Pall" (Night III, Page 81) with his own image of liberated sensuality, a naked joyful girl who is about to be trapped or smothered in a black pall thrown over her by a white-haired figure who reminds us of Blake's Urizen. Where Young praises the "Chain of Ages" or the great chain of being (Night VII, Page 322), Blake depicts it "as sinisterly dwarfing the tiny figures who clamber onto it from a lake of fire." [9] And Blake illustrates Young's affirmative "To rise in Science, as in Bliss,/ Initiate in the Secrets of the Skies" (Night VI, Page 227) with a figure who measures the heavens with a compass, just as his Ancient of Days [*Plate 34*] restricted the entire universe into "number, weight and measure."

Although Blake provided designs for Young's final affirmation of a Christian resurrection and afterlife, these designs are less powerful and compelling than his illustrations for the "fallen" world.[10] This suggests that although Blake fully agreed with Young's morbid vision of nature and the mortal body as wholly corrupt, he could not yet fully share Young's enthusiastic affirmation of spiritual redemption. Young's bitter

8. I am indebted to Morton Paley, "Blake's *Night Thoughts:* An Exploration of the Fallen World," in *Blake Essays for Damon,* ed. A. Rosenfeld (Providence, R. I., 1969), pp. 137, 150–51, and to Jean Hagstrum, *Blake, Poet and Painter,* pp. 122–23, for these observations. However, I find Paley's assumption that Blake had fully conceived the myths of both *Vala* and *The Four Zoas* before he began illustrating Young's *Night Thoughts* in 1795 questionable; his article rests on an earlier dating of *Vala* than has yet been demonstrated. Until a 1795–96 date can be firmly established for the bulk of *Vala,* commentators on the *Night Thoughts* designs might be on safer ground if they saw these designs as anticipations of or gropings toward the detailed myth and imagery of *Vala.* Blake's tendency to personify such negative abstractions as fortune, the tyrant life, and fame as women, often robed or crowned, may have suggested (rather than reflected) the personified summation of all such evils as the dark-robed, veiled lady he later named Vala. Such a development of an icon for Vala or nature would closely parallel the development of the icon for rationalism or Urizen from such earlier white-haired, bearded tyrants as Tiriel and Bromion (cf. my discussion of this iconography in chapter 4).

9. Paley, *ibid.,* p. 151.

10. Paley also makes this observation, *ibid.,* p. 140.

rejection of human life and suicidal desire to escape from human suffering must have been constantly present in Blake's mind as he composed *Vala:* forty-seven leaves of the poem were actually written on the proof sheets of Blake's forty-three engraved designs for *Night Thoughts*.[11]

At work on the early Nights of *Vala*, articulating a graveyard vision of human life, Blake often felt despair. The breakdown of the peace negotiations of 1796–97 between England and France had convinced Blake and many others of the intransigence of both parties. And with the coup d'etat of 18th Brumaire (November 7, 1799), a Bonaparte dynasty was established in France and the libertarian hopes of the Revolution crushed in the Napoleonic invasions of Austria and Italy which shortly followed. Several letters written between 1797 and 1802 voice Blake's fear that human evil had triumphed; that Innocence and the poetic imagination had been virtually annihilated in eighteenth-century Europe; and that Energy survived only in the demonic parodies of Napoleon, Pitt, and Nelson, all men who dedicated their considerable energies solely to the acquisition of absolute power for its own sake (or so Blake thought). He told Dr. Trusler on August 23, 1799, that "Merit in one [is] a cause of envy in another & Serenity & Happiness & Beauty a Cause of Malevolence" (E 676). Economic difficulties—"Even Johnson & Fuseli have discarded my Graver" (August 26, 1799, K 795)—intensified Blake's unhappiness, and in July, 1800, he confessed to Cumberland that he had been in "a Deep pit of Melancholy, Melancholy without any real reason for it, a Disease which God keep you from & all good men" (E 679). His first two years at Felpham were plagued with ill health, financial worries, and Hayley's jealousies; he saw himself as "a man who having Spiritual Enemies of such formidable magnitude cannot expect to want natural hidden ones" (January 10, 1802, E 687). These years of anxiety, "despondency," and physical discomfort ended climactically with a fraudulent deposition for assault and treason by John Scolfield, soldier, against William Blake on August 15, 1803.

The "Preludium" [12] and the first seven Nights of *Vala* present a

11. See Bentley, *William Blake: Vala*, p. 209, for a list of the *Night Thoughts* engravings used in *Vala*.

12. The surviving fragments of Blake's original preludium to *Vala* appear on pages 7, l. 19–p. 14, l. 5; pp. 17, l. 1–18, l. 9.

lengthy account of the first action in Blake's epic: the creation of man as the fall of man. As in *The Book of Urizen* and the Tate Gallery color prints, copulation and generation of the human body bring oppression, conflict, and murder into a world bound by empirical time and space. Man's inherent Energy is either dissipated into chaos and formlessness, stultified in a paralyzing, self-destructive, enclosed form, or perverted into sheer power drives. The opening lines of the "Preludium" are irretrievably lost, but the fragments retrieved by Erdman suggest that the poem originally began as the lament of Enitharmon for the loss of "Eternal Life" and the triumph of "Duty instead of Liberty" (E 740), a "terrible Sentence" which "shook the heavens with wrath" and roused the earth, the mountains, streams, and valleys, in "dismal fear" to marshal "in order for the day of intellectual battle" (E 739). The surviving lines of the "Preludium" [13] portray the generated human form already separated from a "perfect Unity" (page 3). "Tharmas Parent power [is] darkning in the West," while Enion, divided from Tharmas in "Jealous Despair," is almost annihilated: "I am almost Extinct & soon shall be a Shadow in Oblivion" (page 4:17–19, 24). Enion cannot survive as a "shadow": neither formlessness nor the creation of "the Auricular Nerves of Human Life" can restore man to eternity.

The separation of Tharmas and Enion into generated sexual bodies can lead only to further conflict. Enion creates from her own repressed desire for Tharmas a "Phantasm," a "shadowy human form winged," with whom she copulates and gives birth to Los and Enitharmon. These infants "sulk upon her breast," drinking up her energy to increase their own will to power until, "ingrate," they reject her "into Non Entity" and assume control over fallen, man-defined time and space. Enitharmon then rejects Los, accusing him of aiding their parents, and sings her dirge of death, a song of the sorrow of Vala who was abandoned by Luvah when he usurped the place of Urizen in the human brain. Los quarrels with Enitharmon; she then calls upon Urizen to destroy Los; Urizen descends triumphantly; and the pastoral world of Innocence and harmony is destroyed forever:

13. Margoliouth's Text B.

Where dwell the children of the elemental worlds in harmony.
Not long in harmony they dwell, their life is drawn away
And wintry woes succeed. . . .

(page 13:15–17)

The first fair copy of *Vala* begins with an epic invocation:

Los was the fourth immortal starry one . . .
. . . Urthona was his name
In Eden; in the Auricular Nerves of Human Life
Which is the Earth of Eden, he his Emanations propagated
Like Sons & Daughters, Daughter of Beulah Sing
His fall into Division & his Resurrection to Unity.

(page 3:9, 11; page 4:1–4)

This epic will recount the history of man's fall from a primal spiritual harmony or unity in which Energy and reason were married into a divided human form in which reason dominates and Energy is perverted into sheer will to power, and his difficult but ultimately successful return to eternity through the resurrection of the spiritual body. In the first seven Nights of the poem, Blake focuses on the evils that resulted from the fall; in the concluding Nights VIIa, VIIb, and IX, he celebrates a Christian afterlife in which man's sins are forgiven and the physical body is redeemed.

The evils portrayed in the first seven Nights of *Vala* are the evils denounced in *The Book of Urizen* and the color prints: sexual jealousy, perversions, and enforced chastity; rational abstraction; selfishness; violence (brutality, murder, war); the annihilation of imagination and love; the perversion of Energy and self-destroying despair. Night I describes the divisions of Tharmas, the generative power or principle of physical and psychic unity. In other words, Tharmas is the urge toward self-preservation, the natural instinct that coheres intellect, imagination, emotion, and behavior. The disintegration of Tharmas causes a general psychic fragmentation or anxiety that distorts all other relationships (sexual, fraternal, filial). Tharmas is estranged from Enion by jealousy and despair; she copulates instead with a "shadowy semblance" or fantasy-lover and mingles into a monster, "Half Woman & Half Spectre" (pictured as a screaming woman with a coiling serpent tail on page 7), which further divides into Los and Enitharmon. They in turn reject both their mother and each

other: "Alternate Love and Hate his breast; hers Scorn & Jealousy." War
rages around them and Enitharmon's only solution is more conflict:

> Then Enitharmon reddning fierce stretchd her immortal hands
> Descend O Urizen descend with horse & chariots
> The Human Nature shall no more remain nor Human acts
> Form the free Spirits of Heaven, but War & Princedom & Victory & Blood.
>
> (page 11:29, 31, 33–4)

The second Night portrays the triumph of abstract reason over the
imagination. Urizen encases fallen man in his empire built with mathematical precision and unyielding geometrical forms on the very edge of
nonexistence. The design at the bottom of page 25 shows Urizen as the
ancient of days, kneeling with his back to us, with opened compasses, controlling both the heavens and the earth. Even the galaxies are now

> Travelling in silent majesty along their orderd ways
> In right lined paths outmeasurd by proportions of number weight
> And measure. mathematic motion wondrous. along the deep
> In fiery pyramid or Cube. or unornamented pillar square
> Of fire far shining. travelling along even to its destined end
> . . . .
> Others triangular their course maintain, others obtuse
> Acute Scalene; in simple paths. but others move
> In intricate ways biquadrate. Trapeziums Rhombs Rhomboids
> Parallellograms. triple & quadruple. polygonic
> In their amazing hard subdued course in the vast deep.
>
> (page 33: 22–6, 32–6)

Even the human capacity for pity is annihilated. Although Los and Enitharmon retain the power of "contracting or expanding their all flexible
senses" (page 34:10), they cannot perceive the suffering of Enion or rec-
tify the evils of Urizen. In the third Night, Ahania tries to arouse Urizen's
pity and restore Enion and Tharmas, Vala and Luvah, Los and Enitharmon to harmony. But Urizen, the rigid moralist and repressor of Energy,
rejects Ahania's vision of love and mercy, of "sweet fields of bliss/
Where liberty was justice & eternal science was mercy" (39: 12–13), as
mere self-indulgence. Urizen perverts Ahania's plea for love and pity into
the dogmas of mystery, as the illustration on page 44 reveals. Urizen
groans in agony in the lower left-hand corner while a woman (Ahania?)

looks away, a spiked crown of tyranny upon her head and a Gothic trip-
tych spanning her loins. Urizen has replaced her uninhibited sexuality and
Energy with the repressive codes of mystery and moral chastity. Both
Enion and Ahania are now repelled to the very margin of nonentity,
"Substanceless, voiceless, weeping, vanishd" (46:2); such gentle female
passions as love, mercy, and pity cannot exist in a world confined within
hard, unyielding blocks and stones.

In Night IV, the human form itself has become an instrument of oppression. Tharmas rapes Enitharmon away from Los; she is left prostrate,
weeping and bleeding, with arms outstretched, as in the drawing on page
50, while Los is totally paralyzed. Los, in horror, tries to enclose the
"formless unmeasurable Death" of Urizen's frozen kingdom within a body
he can control, but his attempts only divorce him further from Enitharmon. Los now realizes that a bounding line is both necessary and evil: to
give form to Urizen, he must also pour "molten iron round the limbs of
Enitharmon" (53:16). The binding of Urizen becomes, once again, the
binding of Los—"he became what he beheld." In a quotation from *The
Book of Urizen,* Blake recreates the fallen human form: spine, ribs, bones,
heart, eyes, ears, nostrils, throat, tongue, limbs. Los's skeletal frame now
dances grotesquely over the abyss, separated irretrievably from the abandoned body of Enitharmon.

One possible salvation for the fallen, "shrunk up" human form is suggested in the opening lines of Night V. Los and Enitharmon have
"Shrunk into fixed space . . ./ Yet mighty bulk & majesty & beauty remaind but unexpansive"; "Their senses unexpansive in one steadfast bulk
remain" (page 57:12–13, 19). The key word is "unexpansive." Possibly
the fallen body could expand, perhaps infinitely, into a form that includes
all being. In *The Book of Thel* and *Visions of the Daughters of Albion,*
Blake taught that each physical sense is potentially infinite and unique.
"Does the Eagle know what is in the pit?/ Or wilt thou go ask the
Mole"; and Oothoon echoes this awareness of the uniqueness and holiness
of every creature's perceptions:

> With what sense does the bee form cells? have not the mouse & frog
> Eyes and ears and sense of touch? yet are their habitations.
> And their pursuits, as different as their forms and as their joys.

(E 46)

The sea fowl takes the wintry blast. for a cov'ring to her limbs:
And the wild snake, the pestilence to adorn him with gems & gold.
And trees. & birds. & beasts. & men. behold their eternal joy.
Arise you little glancing wings, and sing your infant joy!
Arise and drink your bliss, for every thing that lives is holy!

(E 49–50)

By liberating and expanding his senses, by experiencing the uniqueness of
being and the infinite pleasure of the holiness of life, perhaps fallen man
could overcome the limitations of his mortal body. But in Night V, still
trapped in a fallen world, man is not yet capable of such "an improvement of sensual enjoyment." And finally, in *Vala,* it is only by destroying
his material body and achieving a spiritual redemption that man can
overcome his mortal limitations. The promise of *physical* regeneration offered in Night V is not in fact fulfilled in this poem.

Instead, the senses of Los and Enitharmon continue to shrink up as
they turn against Orc, the child of their desire and "the King of rage &
death." Los finally nails Orc down in a parody of the crucifixion, "binding
around his limbs/ The dismal chain" (60:28–9). Los here anticipates
the completely oppressive old woman of "The Mental Traveller" who
feeds on the restricted Energy of the young child. Once man has fallen
from eternity into the human form, Blake implies, he can only become
more and more limited, repressed, and self-enclosed. Significantly, in the
drawing on page 60, the chain encloses the breast of the kneeling, full-
grown Los rather than the adolescent Orc who kisses the grown woman,
Enitharmon, seated on a nearby rock. It is Los, not Orc, who is truly
bound down. Orc's senses are newborn and as yet uncorrupted; they can
expand and contract at will. The forces of Energy, the demons, bring to
Orc

. . . the thrilling joys of sense to quell his ceaseless rage
His eyes the lights of his large soul contract or else expand
Contracted they behold the secrets of the infinite mountains
The veins of gold & silver & the hidden things of Vala
Whatever grows from its pure bud or breathes a fragrant soul
Expanded they behold the terrors of the Sun & Moon
The Elemental Planets & the orbs of eccentric fire.

(page 61:17–23)

But Orc remains chained, as the illustration on page 62 (an echo, in reverse, of *America,* Plate 1) shows; revolutionary Energy has been manacled by selfish jealousy and rational abstractions. Orc is now ready to learn the arts of war from Urizen, just as Sieyès had betrayed the ideals of the French Revolution to Napoleon and a dictatorship even more repressive and imperialist than that of the Bourbons.

Setting out to explore his kingdoms in Night VI Urizen meets only a threefold incarnation of himself. When seen through the shrunken eyes of Urizen, his three daughters immediately shrivel into fixed, limited forms: "They shrunk into their channels . . ./ Hiding themselves in rocky forms from the Eyes of Urizen" (68:3–4). In Urizen's realm, all things must mirror him. Like Tiriel's curse, Urizen's laws force his sons and daughters to propagate his doctrines, to "worship the obscure demon of destruction . . . & obey the violent." And the human form shrivels up still further, into "fish & monsters of the deep," into "monstrous forms" (69:12–13). Urizen's subjects are reduced to tortured prisoners in "Fetters of red hot iron," to pitiful bands of female soldiers "marching oer burning wastes," to "dishumanized men" whose "ears/ Were heavy & dull & their eyes & nostrils closd up." All have degenerated from even the normal human form to become the grotesque bat-winged alligator pictured on page 70 [*Plate* 50].[14]

Urizen, horrified by these misshapen freaks, casts himself into the void, trying to escape his own creations. But for Urizen, as for man, there is a limit to this physical degeneration: "The ever pitying one who seeth all things saw his fall/ And in the dark vacuity created a bosom of slime" (71:25–6) where Urizen rests his wearied limbs. But such rest only restores Urizen to his former vigorous self. The cycle of repression, exhaustion, rest, and renewed repression is unending: Urizen moves from chaos to void, from void to chaos, trapped in a "world of cumbrous wheels." To end this vicious circle, he arbitrarily chooses a spot on which to build his city, a city laid out in chartered streets by metallic instruments, a city whose citizens "shrunk away inward withring away." In this city, man's vision of heaven—his "eyelids expansive as morning & the Ears/ As

14. John Beer, *Blake's Visionary Universe* (Manchester, England, 1969), p. 349, also sees this figure as a monstrous perversion of Energy under Urizen.

a golden ascent winding round to the heavens of heavens" (73:36–7)
—fades away. Human passion (Luvah), reason (Urizen), and physical
and psychic unity (Tharmas) are all perverted; even the imagination
(Urthona) is enslaved by its spectre, that uncreative, arbitrary power
Coleridge called the "fancy." Conquered by his own spectre, fallen man
first fears

. . . old age, poverty, sickness, loneliness, and then [succumbs] to an omnipres-
ent anxiety, a nameless dread of death-in-life, of time as an oppressive burden
daily increasing in weight. . . . The Spectre is irresolute and dependent, colored
dismally blue in a parody of the color of imagination, shod and armored in iron as
befits a self-crippled and time-obsessed will. He is a cripple . . . but his strength
within any artist is a subtle and persistent reality.[15]

The next Night, the early draft of Night VIIa, recapitulates the conflict
between Orc and Urizen. Although David Erdman and Harold Bloom
correctly note that Night VIIa is "in at least some respects . . . an imaginative advance on VIIb" (E 876), their conclusion that Night VIIa was
"written later than and presumably to replace Night VIIb" (E 345) does
not necessarily follow. The early draft of Night VIIa thematically pro-
gresses from the conclusion of Night VI, Urizen's survey of his kingdom,
to Urizen's encounter with Orc and ends with Enitharmon's account of
the birth of Orc; Night VIIb begins with the nurturing of Orc by the
"shadowy Vortex" and ends with the war song of Urizen; the early version of Night IX begins with the "universal Confusion" of Urizen's war-
torn kingdom. This thematic sequence, which both Margoliouth and Bentley, Jr. present so persuasively in their editions of *Vala*, suggests that
Night VIIb was intended to follow Night VIIa; in effect, it was the original version of Night VIII.[16] The following hypothetical scenario
might then be possible: Blake, realizing that Night VIIb inadequately anticipated the apocalypse of Night IX, decided to write a much longer,

15. Harold Bloom, Commentary in David Erdman, ed., *The Poetry and Prose of
William Blake* (Garden City, N.Y., 1965), p. 813.

16. W. H. Stevenson both argues for this sequence of the two Nights VII and pro-
vides detailed examples of Blake's attempts to revise VIIb in line with VIII; *Blake
Newsletter* I (March 15, 1968):6–8. Morton Paley also regards the plot sequence of VI,
VIIa, and VIIb as persuasive evidence for the ordering I have followed (*Energy and the
Imagination*, Appendix B, p. 263). Most important, G. E. Bentley, Jr. offers significant
bibliographical evidence to support this sequence (*William Blake: Vala*, pp. 162–63).

more complex Night VIII. Anticipating this revision, he considered combining Night VIIa and Night VIIb into a single Night VII. But the new conception of form that appears in both the revised version of Night VIIa and Night VIII and the linking of the narrative at the end of the new VIIa with VIII (VIIa ends with the reunited Los and Enitharmon working together to save the dead; VIII begins with their efforts, after a brief introductory description of the council of God) made the plot line of Night VIIb irrelevant. Blake then tried to revise portions of Night VIIb to fit it back in between VIIa and VIII, but was never fully satisfied with the result. He left VIIb with the manuscript, probably planning to revise it or to omit it altogether. This scenario, unfortunately, offers no solution to the truly vexing question: Why did Blake write and preserve two Nights, *both* of which are titled Night VII? My hypothesis would require that Night VIIb was originally intended to be Night VIII—but there is no manuscript evidence for this. Perhaps Blake added the title "Night the Seventh" to VIIb only after he decided to write a longer Night VIII; but then why had he begun an untitled chapter? And why did he not revise Night IX to follow directly from VIII? Since my hypothesis does not answer these questions, I cannot find it very satisfactory; its only value lies in its consistency with the little stylistic and bibliographic evidence that we have. We know that Night VIIa was at one time stitched together with Nights IV–VI; Night VIIb was never stitched in with these earlier Nights. Although Erdman dismisses this evidence for an early grouping of Nights IV through VIIa by saying that Night VIIb was written *before* VIIa and *rejected* by the time Nights IV–VIIa were stitched,[17] it does not seem likely that Night VIIb ever followed Night VI directly. Night VIIb begins with the nurturing of Orc; Night VI ends with the chaotic reign of Urizen. This sequence omits the connection between Urizen and Orc, the very encounter Night VIIa supplies.

Whatever the actual chronological sequence of the two Nights VII may be, together they portray the total corruption of the human condition. Energy itself, the raging fires of Orc, is successfully fettered by Urizen's very ignorance. Urizen cannot understand the nature of Orc's power, the libidinal aggression that actively resists all mental and physical repression. Un-

17. Erdman, ed., *Poetry and Prose of Blake,* p. 737.

able to comprehend how Orc can continue to survive the fierce tortures imposed on him, Urizen assumes that Orc is sustained by a false vision of "Sweet bliss" or by Urizen's own satisfactions ("is thy joy founded on torments which others bear for thee?"). And Orc, although he knows that the violence of his resistance is caused simply by the excessive oppressions of Urizen, cannot forever avoid both the stone wall of Urizen's stupidity and the devious labyrinth of his subtle psychological tyranny. Hearing Urizen practice the fine art of hypocrisy—"Compell the poor to live upon a Crust of bread by soft mild arts/ . . . Smile when they frown, frown when they smile & when a man looks pale/ With labour & abstinence say he looks healthy & happy"—Orc too succumbs and shrinks into a serpent, resignedly restricting his potentially infinite Energy into a narrow "poisoned cup" (80:2, 10–11, 46). And the fall from Eden is complete: Orc's submission occurs simultaneously with the divorce of Los and Enitharmon and the reduction of Enitharmon to a disembodied shadow pursued by the grotesque spectre of Urthona/ Los. No escape from the "tubelike forms" of human arteries and the "deformed form" of the mortal body is possible.

And the fall into the human form inevitably gives rise to a universal holocaust. In Night VIIb, in a last desperate effort to liberate Energy from the excessively limited forms of reason, Orc rends his chains and rouses his lions to go forth in battle against the "dragons of the North," the troops of Urizen. In the bloodshed that follows, all the forces of liberty and divinity are destroyed: Luvah is crucified and laid in a sepulcher for 6,000 years; Orc is totally transformed into a monster of sin, the will to power incarnate—"No more remain of Orc but the Serpent round the tree of Mystery" (93:24); Enion, the mother of the best possible generated "form of life," is fragmented into a "formless indefinite" and strewn upon the abyss (93:26–7); and the pastoral world of Innocence is wholly ravaged (the sons of Urizen destroy the hourglass and burn the waterwheel because their workmanship is "like the workmanship of the Shepherd" [92:25]). The human form itself has been broken and scattered; the triumph of the dissecting Urizen is complete. All the faculties of man war against each other: Los, Orc, Tharmas, and Urizen wage an internecine slaughter; the very fruit trees and animals join in the bloody battle. Urizen's web of war and mystery now covers all the world, vibrating "torment on torment."

The only escape from this holocaust lies in the message brought by Vala, a weeping Magdalen. She writes the eternal promise on every tombstone: "If ye will believe your Brother shall rise again." Blake here accepts the traditional Christian solution to the fall of man, the solution celebrated in Young's *Night Thoughts:* man's fallen mortal body will be redeemed after physical death as a purified spiritual body. This is the triumph over rational Experience that Blake envisioned in "To Tirzah," the poem he added around 1805 to *Songs of Experience.* The domination of Tirzah, the mother of mortality and the consort of Urizen, can be overcome only by the dissolution of the mortal body. Echoing Jesus' rejection of Mary, his mortal mother, Blake affirms a spiritual rebirth only after death.

> Whate'er is Born of Mortal Birth,
> Must be consumed with the Earth
> To rise from Generation free;
> Then what have I to do with thee?
> . . . .
> The Death of Jesus set me free,
> Then what have I to do with thee?
>
> (E 30)

The accompanying design portrays the Christian resurrection of the body. An old man pours a reviving, baptismal water upon a corpse held by two women. This iconographic fusion of the descent from the cross and the raising of Lazarus is summed up in the lines engraved upon the old man's robe—"It is Raised a Spiritual Body." Mortal existence is totally evil; only through death can fallen man be freed from his corrupted human form and redeemed as a spiritual, purified body.[18]

In Night IX of *Vala,* probably composed to follow Night VIIb directly, this redemption of the fallen human body occurs on a universal scale. The Last Judgment begins when the eternal man awakes from physical death.

18. Blake's illustrations to Gray's "Elegy in a Country Churchyard," sketched between 1796 and 1798, also affirm physical death as a spiritual rebirth; see Irene Tayler's *Blake's Illustrations to the Poems of Gray* (Princeton, 1971), pp. 140–47, for a detailed analysis of Blake's visual critique of Gray's excessive pessimism in the "Elegy".

Horrified by the chaotic "war within [his] members" and remembering his former innocent delights, he turns angrily against Urizen who has perverted his spiritual form into a limited mortal body and a confused, deceived mind, threatening to destroy Urizen utterly if he does not repent. Urizen remorsefully abandons "dark mortality" and the hardened deformities by which he separated family from family (121:4, 14–6), shakes the hoary mantle of oppression off his shoulders, and rises, redeemed, "in naked majesty/In radiant Youth" (121:31–2). The eternal man then promises a spiritual resurrection after death to all:

> Behold Jerusalem in whose bosom the Lamb of God
> Is seen tho slain before her Gates he self renewd remains
> Eternal & I thro him awake to life from deaths dark vale
> The times revolve the time is coming when all these delights
> Shall be renewd & all these Elements that now consume
> Shall reflourish. Then bright Ahania shall awake from death.
>
> (122:1–6)

In the culminating apocalypse of *Vala,* man is redeemed. The innocents are resurrected; the evil are cast out; Christ appears in radiant clouds of glory. But the mortal body cannot yet enter the "Consummation"; it must first be transformed into a spiritual body. The sons of Urizen therefore drive the plow over the graves of the dead, sowing new seeds of "immortal souls." As the eternal man waits for the harvest of these spiritual bodies, he teaches Luvah and Vala how man should live during his fallen but necessary time on earth. Man must live in the pastoral idyll of Vala's gardens, secure in the knowledge that everything that lives will survive after death through the loving care of God. In contrast to the *Songs of Innocence* and *The Marriage of Heaven and Hell,* however, Blake here draws a rigid distinction between the physical and the spiritual, the mortal and the divine, time and eternity, earth and heaven. Man can now become God only *after* the annihilation of his physical body and his temporal life. Vala's song is less a lyric of Innocence than a hymn of a more orthodox Christian faith:

> Hah! shall I still survive whence came that sweet & conforting voice
> And whence that voice of sorrow O sun thou art nothing now to me
> Go on thy course rejoicing & let us both rejoice together
> I walk among his flocks & hear the bleating of his lambs

O that I could behold his face & follow his pure feet
I walk by the footsteps of his flocks come hither tender flocks
Can you converse with a pure soul that seeketh for her maker
You answer not then am I set your mistress in this garden
I'll watch you & attend your footsteps you are not like the birds
That sing & fly in the bright air but you do lick my feet
And let me touch your wooly backs follow me as I sing
For in my bosom a new song arises to my Lord.

(127:28–128:3)

Vala now seeks a Lord or maker who exists beyond rather than within herself.

The pleasures of this earthly idyll are portrayed in the accompanying illustration (page 128, [*Plate* 54]). Finished in blue, pink, and brown watertints and outlined in ink, the sketch shows a boy and girl playing with hands clasped over pebbles (Indian wrestling? pressing grapes?) at the left and a female flautist serenading a reclining woman dressed in bracelets, jester's shoes, and a cloth girdle which exposes her genitals, with a tamborine under her left hand. Sexuality, music, physical play—all are included in the delights of this "lower Paradise." These children know that their Lord and Maker will one day lead them through the valley of death into life everlasting. Then man shall cast off his vegetable covering, the veil that separates him from eternity, the sexual garment that divorces male from female, and be reborn as an immortal spiritual entity.

But first, man must endure the terrors and agonies of death; the harvested human grapes must be crushed in the wine presses of Luvah so that the pure human wine may be extracted and stand "wondering in all their delightful Expanses" (137:32). With the apocalyptic harvesting, man is reborn a spiritual body, purified, at peace. There is harmony both in heaven and on earth, for man knows that he will be redeemed from his fallen body after death. And now

. . . Urthona rises from the ruinous walls
In all his ancient strength to form the golden armour of science
For intellectual War The war of swords departed now
The dark Religions are departed & sweet Science reigns.

(139:7–10)

Here "sweet Science," the knowledge that man will be redeemed from sin after death if he practices the virtues of mercy, pity, and love, overcomes

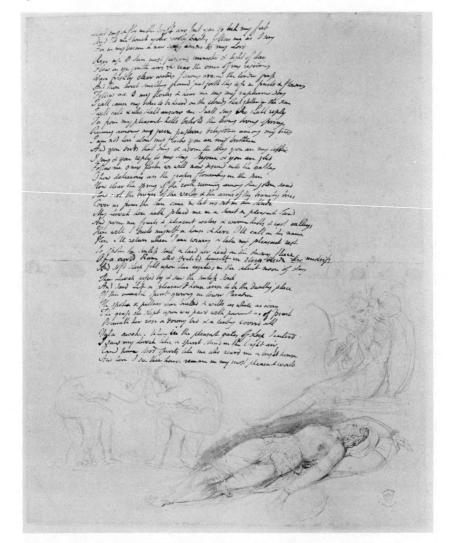

Plate 54. Vala, Page 128, British Museum.

the darker vision of eighteenth-century Augustinianism which insists that man is eternally corrupted to some degree by original sin.

But this orthodox Christian solution to the problem of the corrupted mortal body does not solve Blake's problem as a man or as an artist. As in

The Book of Thel and again in *Tiriel,* this solution permits manifest social evils to continue unabated. Moreover, even if every individual were
freed from social oppressions and enabled to play happily in this "lower
Paradise," he would still be trapped in a limiting, essentially corrupt
human body. In Blake's poetry, the generated human form still separates
man from God.

Yet during this very period (1795–1802) in which his poetry continues to present the human body as a barrier to man's realization of his potential divinity and to show all severely limited forms or rational systems
as evil, Blake's visual art relies on an increasingly limited vocabulary. In
the Bible illustrations which Blake painted for Thomas Butts between
1799 and 1805,[19] his compositions are generally based on very simple
geometric patterns. Mirror-image, bilateral symmetry appears both in the
overall constructions and in the configurations of minor elements in many
of these designs. Abstract figural contours are placed in hieratic compositions that are relieved only by linear rhythms. Colors fade into delicate
water-color washes; illusionistic details tend to disappear; human figures
function as much to define Euclidian shapes as to represent Biblical
events. Here, Blake's romantic classicism moves toward an abstract art
built on static geometric forms or bilateral symmetry, that very symmetry
which in *The Book of Urizen* designs he had identified with the mathematical world of reason. But we cannot suspect Blake of using symmetry
here to criticize or condemn these Biblical events; the range of subject-
matter is too diverse to submit to such a generalization.

Of the hundred or so illustrations reproduced in the exhaustive Trianon
Press catalogue of Blake's Bible illustrations that can be dated between
1799 and 1805 on the basis of inscription, provenance, Blake's letters, and
style, almost half have prominent symmetrical elements or are composed
in strict bilateral symmetry.[20] Three watercolors mentioned in Blake's letter to Thomas Butts (July 6, 1803) are striking examples of Blake's abstract, symmetrical patternmaking. In *The Death of the Virgin Mary*

19. Blake first mentions this series in a letter to Cumberland on August 26, 1799,
and later in letters to Butts on September 11, 1801, and on July 6, 1803 (K 795, K
808, K 824).
20. *Blake's Illustrations for the Bible,* ed. Geoffrey Keynes (Paris: Trianon Press,
1957).

Plate 55. The Death of the Virgin Mary, Tate Gallery.

[*Plate 55*], the resurrected Virgin stands stiffly at right angle to the horizontal boardlike corpse of Mary, who is bounded at head and feet by two kneeling angels in precisely corresponding attitudes. The scene is framed by a half-circle rainbow of seraphim, of which Mary's mortal body forms the diameter, her spiritual body the perpendicular radius. This geometric construction is underlined by the geometrical pattern along the side of Mary's bed which blocks out the bottom of the design. This circle-square structure is exchanged for an equally rigid diamond pattern in *The Sacri-*

Plate 56. The Sacrifice of Jepthah's Daughter, British Museum.

fice of Jepthah's Daughter [*Plate 56*]. Jepthah kneels before the altar, his arms raised in right-angled diagonals that form the bottom half of a diamond completed by two clouds of smoke that rise from the sides of the altar and meet above his daughter's head. The daughter herself is placed in the exact center of the diamond, on the altar, where she forms the vertical intersecting line of an upright isosceles triangle composed of wheat sheaves (or faggots). She is flanked at either side by musical instruments (a tambourine and a lyre) and the bowed heads of identically bending angels. An oppressive symmetry and repetitive verticals dominate the design

Plate 57. The Four and Twenty Elders Casting Their Crowns, Tate Gallery.

for *The Angel of the Divine Presence Clothing Adam and Eve with Coats of Skins.* The white-haired, six-toed, robed angel stands firmly erect, his hands encircling the hips of Adam and Eve who stand directly in front of him on either side, their heads bowed and hands folded in precisely corresponding configurations. At each side of the design, vertical altars spout vertically rising flames; the entire design is framed by vertical palm trunks whose branches arch in a half circle over the angel's head.

Symmetrical designs also appear in the Bible illustrations mentioned two years later in Blake's account of May 12, 1805, with Butts. In *Noah and the Rainbow,* Noah stands vertically with opened arms before a rectangular stone altar lifting pyramidically vertical flames, symmetrically balanced on each side by three kneeling figures, under a half-circle rainbow. Again, in *The Four and Twenty Elders Casting Their Crowns* [*Plate 57*], the elders throw down their crowns along the sides of an isosceles triangle based on a horizontal row of flaming angels' heads. God's radiant head forms the apex of the triangle, beneath a semicircular arch of the four beasts of the apocalypse and a rainbow. And in *Christ Girding Himself with Strength,* Christ is seated on an isolated stone step, flanked at each side by angels whose wings fall in a pointed Gothic arch over his head. Such frequent bilateral symmetry constructed around such simple geometric patterns increases the tension between Blake's philosophical rejection of limited physical forms and rational mathematical systems and his artistic obsession with severely limited forms and patterns. Blake had recognized but failed to resolve this conflict in *Vala.* If the human body and all closed rational systems are restrictive prisons that man eagerly hopes to escape after death, how can an artist use the human form or symmetrical geometric configurations affirmatively? Worse yet, how can the orthodox Christian, supported only by the promise of a distant spiritual afterlife, adequately cope with the real sufferings and social evils of life on earth? To look to death as a solution to the trials of life is, as Blake and many others have discovered, unsatisfying. Man must live on earth; and Blake was anxious to make that life as fulfilling, as divine, as possible. In the revisions that transformed *Vala* into *The Four Zoas,* Blake offered a more complex and more viable solution to this conflict between reason and Energy, form and infinity.

The Four Zoas, 1805–1810(?)

In *The Four Zoas,* Blake more fully develops the solution to the problem of form that had been anticipated in his poetry over a decade earlier.
External boundaries, however narrowly defined, are constricting only if
one psychologically accepts them as fixed and unchangeable. True vision
or belief in the potential infinity of all being can transform a concrete object into an expansive image, a metaphorical manifestation of the infinite
and eternal. If one sees form as restrictive, if one sees with the eyes and
through the categories of Urizen, then one is truly imprisoned, as is Theotormon. But if one sees with the eyes of Innocence, if one sees, as Oothoon
does, that "every thing that lives is Holy," then any given form can be
transformed into a metaphor or image of potential infinity and one is psychologically freed from all limiting conceptions of the self.

The pessimism that appeared in Blake's poetry, art, and letters from
1795 to 1802 now gives way in the final Felpham year (1802–1803)
to optimism. In several visionary moments, occurring most often during
the last Felpham year, Blake experienced what Morton Paley has identified as a religious conversion,[21] a conviction of personal redemption that
left him confident of his own powers as an artist and of the capacity of art
to save a fallen world. In the lyrics, prose, and letters written after 1803,
Blake's earlier pessimism is replaced by his growing confidence that one
can change one's psychological state by changing how one sees. Radically
different modes of perception create radically different personalities. "For
the Eye altering alters all" (E 476). But Blake does not merely
restate a simplistic relativism (different people see and respond to the
world differently; perception is subjective). Rather, he attempts to distinguish between true (infinite, divine) and false (limited) vision.
Blake characterizes true vision as that which perceives the holiness of
everything that lives; the man who sees the world with such eyes of
Innocence lives in joy and peace.

This capacity to perceive infinity within the finite is ironically
posed against fallen human vision in "The Mental Traveller" (c.
1803–1805). Structurally and thematically, of course, the poem is a

21. Paley, *Energy and the Imagination,* pp. 192–93.

closed circle, the endlessly repeating perversion of revolutionary Energy into Urizenic repression. But this circle is implicitly contained within a greater vision that passes through and beyond the limited vision of "cold Earth wanderers." Both Morton Paley and Irene Chayes have felt this double perspective, but they both insist that the larger perspective is present only ironically, never explicitly. Morton Paley locates this irony in the distance between what the "pseudo-naïve narrator" tells us, that this is a vision of an alien world, and what we know almost from the first lines, that this is a paradigmatic vision of *our* world.[22] And Irene Chayes attributes the sense of distance both to the peculiar flatness of the diction and to the pattern of the double circle that the narrator does not seem to anticipate; he describes events as if they were in simple linear progression and not until the very last line does he become aware of their eternal recurrence.[23] And both would agree that "it is no more the business of this poem to supply the missing perspective than it is that of Book IV of *Gulliver* to provide a corrective view of the Houyhnhnms." [24]

I would suggest, however, that at three points in the poem, the beginning, stanza 7, and stanzas 22–23, the larger vision is presented, both implicitly and directly. The narrator himself, the mental traveller, immediately implies that he has experienced a world where the sexes are not divided against themselves.[25] If he had not, there would be no need to distinguish between a "Land of Men" and a "Land of Men & Women," as he does in the opening lines. Here he suggests that it is possible to live as "men" in a world where sexual partners blend harmoniously in love and joy and fertile creativity. This suggestion is then momentarily realized even within the closed pattern of psychological and sexual antagonisms enacted by "cold Earth wanderers." When the baby boy grows up and throws off his mental and physical manacles and seizes the object of his desire, the rejuvenated woman old (the mother, society, or nature which has been impregnated with his Energy and can now blossom forth as a vital, creative wife or community),

22. *Ibid.,* pp. 123–24.
23. "Plato's *Statesman* Myth in Shelley and Blake," *Comparative Literature* 13 (1961):358–69.
24. Paley, *Energy and the Imagination,* p. 124.
25. John Sutherland locates the narrator in Eternity, "Blake's 'Mental Traveller,' " *ELH* 22 (1955):140.

> He plants himself in all her Nerves
> Just as a Husbandman his mould
> And she becomes his dwelling place
> And Garden fruitful seventy fold.
>
> (St. 7, E 476)

At this moment, masculine creative Energy and feminine form or body fuse in a wholly productive image, and the proper dialectical marriage of Energy and reason is achieved. When the male uses his imagination to transform his environment into a garden of Eden, and the female willingly becomes the dwelling place or physical garment of the man's vision, then the holy city of Jerusalem is built on this cold earth. But on our fallen earth, this vision does not endure; the forces of reason and narrow self-interest have become too powerful. The man quickly perverts his energies away from imaginative creation into the acquisition of material goods and power; he now feeds on the "gems and gold/ Which he by industry" has gotten and ignores his wife. And she, a woman scorned with "akeing heart," jealous of his work and angry at his indifference, now rejuvenates herself. She springs, a "Female Babe . . . of solid fire/ And gems & gold" from his own hearth, and eagerly takes a lover both to satisfy her own needs and to spite the aged host. Together, wife and lover drive out the old man and, as he goes, his now blinded eyes can see only the destruction of his once fertile "Garden & its lovely charms." This Orc-become-Urizen can see only Ulro, "for the Eye altering alters all"; everywhere he looks,

> The Senses roll themselves in fear
> And the flat Earth becomes a Ball
>
> The Stars Sun Moon all shrink away
> A desart vast without a bound
> And nothing left to eat or drink
> And a dark desart all around.
>
> (E 476–7)

All sexual relationships in this desert world are inevitably antagonistic; his maiden flees from him in fear and he pursues her futilely "night & day." They end where they began, he a frowning baby boy and she a weeping woman old; victim and victimizer.

It is at this point, when the cold earth cycle has substantially completed itself, that this fallen and endlessly recurring vision is explicitly overwhelmed by a greater vision. When one has gone through this cycle, either experientially or under the mental guidance of the traveller, one can fully comprehend its perversity and energetically choose to reject it. At this moment of total knowledge, and only then, when the entire cycle or Urizenic state has been completed and revealed, one can leap out of this closed circle and create with one's imagination a new Jerusalem.

> Then many a Lover wanders here
> The Sun and Stars are nearer rolld
>
> The trees bring forth sweet Extacy
> To all who in the desart roam
> Till many a City there is Built
> And many a pleasant Shepherds home.

> (st. 22–3, E 477)

At the very beginning of the cycle, before Energy has been perverted by reason or the female will, and at the very end, when the cycle has been revealed in all its monstrous destructiveness, the imaginative lover can reject this fallen pattern of human relationships and create his alternative vision of a holy city or pastoral cottage. But most men are now too frightened to seize the wayward babe and use his and their own immense Energy to create the lineaments of gratified desire; they flee in terror. Only the traditional institutions of repression are strong enough to capture and crucify the naked boy. Therefore, the cycle repeats itself and "all is done as I have told" (E 477).

In addition to love, pleasure, and self-fulfillment, true vision can bring liberation from the boundaries of time and space. This radical idea, which denies the Kantian epistemological assumptions most modern thinkers have shared, is not fully developed until *Jerusalem*. But in "Auguries of Innocence" (c. 1803) and in *The Four Zoas*, Blake anticipates his apocalyptic epistemology. The eyes of Innocence can respond positively to the devil's question, "How do you know but ev'ry Bird that cuts the airy way,/ Is an immense world of delight, clos'd by your senses five?" (E 35). They can see both the outward form and the inward infinity which it conveys but does not contain. They can see "a

World in a Grain of Sand/ And a Heaven in a Wild Flower/ Hold Infinity in the palm of your hand/ And Eternity in an hour" (E 481).
They can both value the beauty of the particular form (a wild flower)
and also see it as an image of holiness, a manifestation of infinity.

One learns to see this temporal and eternal flower both in nature and
in art. In the period 1803–10, Blake's letters reveal his increasing
awareness of the capacity of not only his own but of other artists' works
to articulate the divine vision of Innocence. Both his study of Romney's
paintings for Hayley's *Life of Romney* and his visit to the Truchsessian
Gallery in October 1804 confirmed Blake's growing confidence in the capacity of artistic form to manifest holy Energy. He enthusiastically hailed
the sublime vision of Romney's *Lear and Cordelia:* "An incomparable
production . . . and exquisite for expression" (May 4, 1804, K. 843). And
on October 23, 1804, he wrote ecstatically to Hayley:

For now! O Glory! and O Delight! I have entirely reduced that spectrous Fiend
to his station, whose annoyance has been the ruin of my labours for the last passed
twenty years of my life. . . . my feet and my wife's feet are free from fetters. O
lovely Felpham, parent of Immortal Friendship, to thee I am eternally indebted
for my three years' rest from perturbation and the strength I now enjoy. Suddenly,
on the day after visiting the Truchsessian Gallery of pictures, I was again enlightened with the light I enjoyed in my youth, and which has for exactly twenty
years been closed from me as by a door and by window-shutters. Consequently I
can, with confidence, promise you ocular demonstration of my altered state on the
plates I am now engraving after Romney, whose spiritual aid has not a little con-
duced to my restoration to the light of Art. . . . Dear Sir, excuse my enthusiasm
or rather madness, for I am really drunk with intellectual vision whenever I take
a pencil or graver into my hand, even as I used to be in my youth, and as I have
not been for twenty dark, but very profitable years. (E 702–3)

The collection of Count Joseph Truchsess, which was opened in London in August, 1803, for exhibition or sale to the public, remained in
Portland Place for almost two years. The collection, listed in the "Summary Catalogue of the Pictures now exhibiting and on Sale at the Truchsessian Gallery, New Road, opposite Portland Place (London, 1 June
1805)" included several works that would have demonstrated to Blake's
satisfaction that a severely tectonic, linear style can nonetheless convey
the innate holiness of man. When Blake visited the gallery in October
1804, he must have seen Holbein's *Portrait, Supposed To Be Luther's.*

Also there were several sixteenth-century Flemish interiors by P. Neefs, examples of French classicism by Poussin and Claude Lorrain, and religious subjects by such Italian masters as Ghirlandajo, A. Carracci, Guido Reni, Correggio, and Guilio Romano. Such a collection certainly appealed to Blake's own love for Biblical subjects; and the strong outlines of Holbein, together with the linear style, tectonic structures and specific details of Ghirlandajo, Poussin, and Neefs, would have confirmed for Blake the necessity of sharp lines, clear outlines and closed compositions to the creation of a truly sublime art.

By 1810, when Blake stopped work on the extensive revisions of *Vala* which transformed the poem into *The Four Zoas—The Torments of Love & Jealousy in The Death and Judgement of Albion the Ancient Man,* he had clarified the relation of the fallen world to eternity and suggested a possible reconciliation between physical form and infinity. The creation of the mortal body as such is no longer a fall; and death is no longer a necessary prerequisite for redemption. Rather, the fall occurs to each individual if, and only if, he contracts his imaginative vision, denies his mortal body as sinful flesh, and represses or perverts his Energy. The universe, as Blake shows us in *The Four Zoas,* is fourfold; and each man individually chooses the mental and physical state in which he lives.

These four states of being or levels of awareness are here called Eden, Beulah, Earth, and Ulro. Eden is the place of spiritual and psychic integration, where females sleep and "Males immortal live renewd by female deaths" (page 5:3), where all creatures are responsive to each other, "where the lamb replies to the infant voice & the lion to the man of years" (page 71:10), where all being can be seen as the single expansive form of one divine man, in whom Energy and reason are harmoniously reconciled. Just beneath Eden lies Beulah, "a mild & pleasant rest" where the human form is divided into male and female and the females rest from the labours of procreation. It is

> . . . a Soft Moony Universe feminine lovely
> Pure mild & Gentle given in Mercy to those who sleep
> Eternally. Created by the Lamb of God around
> On all sides within & without the Universal Man
> The Daughters of Beulah follow sleepers in all their Dreams
> Creating Spaces lest they fall into Eternal Death.
>
> (page 5:32–37)

Here, the human form is artistically created as an image in, but not confined to, time and space.

> The Daughters of Beulah beheld the Emanation they pitied
> They wept before the Inner gates of Enitharmons bosom
> And of her fine wrought brain & of her bowels within her loins
> Three gates within Glorious & bright open into Beulah.
>
> (page 20:1—4)

In Beulah, as in the *Songs of Innocence,* the created human form is not a limitation of the divine vision. Rather, these forms are temporal-spatial manifestations of that innocent vision that enables mortal man to perceive the holiness both within and beyond himself. They are "portions of Soul discerned by [but not limited to] the five Senses." In seeing an artistic image of Christ as both man and God, one is inspired to transcend his five senses and emulate the life of Christ. Beneath Beulah lies Earth, "the world of Tharmas," where "in the Auricular Nerves of Human Life" the mortal body is generated. This is the organic world bound by time and space, redeemed from eternal death or separation from eternity only by the limits of contraction and opacity set by Christ. Even further distanced from eternity is Ulro, the state created by Urizen. This is the void of the disembodied intellect or reason run amok, a world where the imagination is petrified into rock and sand, where the male and female forms are divided in torment and conflict, where every form is repressive and grotesque.

Blake now locates his complex myth of the fall and return within this fourfold universe. Blake now sees man, no longer as polarized between the two conflicting forces of Energy and reason, but as the reconciliation of four capacities (zoas) somewhat similar to the four Renaissance humors. Reason remains as one of these capacities: in its proper functioning, it helps one to comprehend and realize the divine vision of all life as holy. But Blake now clarifies his concept of divine Energy. Acknowledging that revolutionary Energy failed to save Europe in his times, that it was too easily perverted into mere will to power in the course of the French Revolution and the Napoleonic Empire, Blake now distinguishes between three psychic powers, capacities or energies in man. These are (1) the power that coheres one's psychic and physical behavior, the power of integrity or self-preservation as a distinct, harmonious image, the power which Freud called the ego and Blake calls Tharmas; (2) the emotions and sexual desires—in Freudian terms, the id, in Blake's myth, Luvah; and (3) the imagination (Blake's Urthona or Los). As Morton Paley emphasizes, the imagination now replaces revolutionary Energy as the primary power of salvation and the true sublime while "Christian brotherhood replaces revolutionary fraternity in Blake's thought as the agent of love among men." [26] In this optimistic recasting of his myth, reason is no longer the contrary (and potential destroyer) of divine Energy but rather the servant or vehicle of the divine imagination. The redemptive activity of the imagination now consists in creating ordered artistic images that integrate rather than divide the four zoas. Man falls from the paradise created by this redemptive imagination whenever his four basic psychic energies or zoas divide or come into conflict. Whenever any one zoa usurps full control over the human psyche, man becomes either a spectre (disembodied intellect or anxiety—the rule of Urizen or reason), a serpent (perverted emotional sublimation—the rule of Luvah or passion), a vegetating form (physical bestiality—the rule of Tharmas or instinctive self-preservation), a hermaphrodite (a false misunion of two opposites caused by the uncreative "fancy"—the rule of fallen Los-Urthona or the diseased imagination), or a "chaotic non-entity" (total schizophrenic disintegration and chaos [27]). But each man can escape these fallen conditions and return to Eden whenever he reintegrates his psychic forces, expands his imaginative vision, and perceives his innate holiness. In Blake's now more flexible myth, man can transcend the limitations of the human form in two ways. He can either completely destroy his mortal body through death and exchange his mortal form for a spiritual body; or he can transform his living mortal body into the human form divine, an expansive physical form that embodies and reveals man's holiness.

26. Paley, *Energy and the Imagination*, pp. 199, 154; also see chapter 8.
27. R. D. Laing's study of schizophrenia, *The Divided Self: An Existential Study in Sanity and Madness* (Baltimore, 1965), praises Blake's prophetic books as "the best description . . . in literature" of the self-body split basic to all schizophrenia. Laing interprets Blake's phrase "chaotic non-entity" thus: "When the 'centre' fails to hold, neither self-experience nor body-experience can retain identity, integrity, cohesiveness, or vitality, and the individual becomes precipitated into a condition the end result of which we suggested could best be described as a state of 'chaotic nonentity' " (p. 162).

In order to make his image of the infinite human form divine more convincing, Blake attempts to include within this image and this poem all historical times and spaces, all known persons, places, and events. Thus, in Night II, English rivers, Welsh mountains, European cities, Biblical events, and Druid rites are now involved in Urizen's conquests (page 25); and in Night VIII, we find numbered among the sons of Los and Enitharmon figures from every major historical epoch, from Blake's mythic Rintrah and the Old Testament Adam and Solomon to the Christian Paul, Luther, and Milton. Blake specifically draws analogies between his own myth and the Bible: numerous additions point out direct parallels between Urizen's fall and that of Satan, between the sons of Urizen and the twelve tribes of Israel, between the crucifixion of Luvah and that of Christ. In *The Four Zoas* Christ is the eighth eye of God who willingly sacrifices himself for man; the daughters of Beulah specifically hail Luvah in his robes of blood as the crucified lamb of God ("The Council of God on high watching over the Body/ Of Man clothd in Luvahs robes of blood saw & wept/ . . ./ The daughters of Beulah saw the Divine Vision they were comforted" (page 55:26–27, 29); and the one man with whom all men should identify is, of course, Jesus Christ: "Then All in Great Eternity Met in the Council of God/ as One Man even Jesus upon Gilead & Hermon" (page 99:1–2).

Further, by focusing the revised poem on the conflicts of the four zoas (Urthona-Los, Urizen, Tharmas, and Luvah-Orc), rather than on the creation of mortal man, Blake suggests that the fall may be psychological rather than physical. From this viewpoint, the human body is only the vehicle, not the cause, of damnation and salvation. Redemption can therefore occur within the human body; the form itself only manifests one's internal psychic condition, be it error or true vision. However, in *The Four Zoas* manuscript as we have it, Blake does not always disentangle his earlier insistence on spiritual regeneration only through death and a universal Last Judgment (in *Vala*) from his later idea of a spiritual regeneration on earth through imaginative vision. Consequently, the final manuscript is often contradictory or confused.

Only in the lengthy revisions to Night VIIa (which effectively eliminated the need for Night VIIb) and in the newly added Night VIII [28] does Blake clearly articulate the idea that imaginative vision can both perceive and create forms that expand to reveal the divinity of man and nature. In Night VIIa of *The Four Zoas,* Blake spells out the two modes of salvation *on earth* which the corrupted human form can achieve. First, of course, man can redeem himself through psychic integration. If he can reconcile his divided reason, emotions, and imagination and if he can overcome jealousy, distrust, and fear with love, then he can achieve on earth the harmonious being he once possessed in eternity. As Los's spectre tells the shadow of Enitharmon, "the morn of ages shall renew upon us/ To reunite in those mild fields of happy Eternity/ Where thou & I in undivided Essence walkd about/ Imbodied" (page 84:3–6). If one can annihilate one's egocentric selfhood, if one can harmoniously unite with one's emanation, then one may become on earth an "undivided Essence" or the embodiment of divine life. Los, embracing his long alien spectre "first as a brother/ Then as another Self; astonishd humanizing & in tears/ In Self abasement Giving up his Domineering lust" (page 85:29–31), learns that this process of self-annihilation has made it possible for him to reunite with Enitharmon and to become a manifest form of the divine vision. As his spectre explains,

> If we unite in one [,] another better world will be
> Opend within your heart & loins & wondrous brain
> Threefold as it was in Eternity & this the fourth Universe
> Will be Renewd by the three & consummated in Mental fires
>
> For thou art but a form & organ of life & of thyself
> Art nothing being Created Continually by Mercy & Love divine.
>
> (page 85:43–6; page 86:2–3)

Although Enitharmon is still afraid to rejoin Los, he nonetheless has learned that through love and union, one expands rather than divides one's self. Within himself, Los perceives "the Center opend by Divine Mercy inspired." When the imagination perceives that the human body

28. Margoliouth (*William Blake's Vala,* pp. xiii, 174), Bentley (*William Blake: Vala,* pp. 164–5), and Erdman (*Poetry and Prose of Blake,* p. 738) all argue convincingly that Night VIII was composed "much later" than Night IX, perhaps even as late as 1810.

and self-consciousness are but passing manifestations or formulations of the divine life that shines through them, then man can immediately give up his ego and his sense of physical imprisonment to participate more directly in this divinity.

Inspired by this regenerative awareness, Los turns to the second mode of salvation that Blake celebrates in Night VIIa, artistic creation. By "fabricat[ing] forms sublime" (page 90:22), by creating ideal outlines, the artist provides fallen man with an expansive image of the human form that he can emulate. In Blake's radical romantic reversal of mimetic theory, life imitates art. In a fallen world where existing institutions and natural forms are corrupt, man must turn to the sublime forms of the imagination manifest in works of art for a satisfying model of integration and effective organization that he can follow. Los and Enitharmon therefore work together to build Golgonooza, a utopia to replace Urizen's anti-utopia, a heavenly city on earth. Significantly, they use Blake's own artistic style of strong linear rhythms, sharp outlines, and geometric patterns as well as his watercolor medium to create their aesthetic image of the human form divine.

> And first he drew a line upon the walls of shining heaven
> And Enitharmon tincturd it with beams of blushing love
> It remaind permanent a lovely form inspird divinely human
> Dividing into just proportions Los unwearied labourd
> The immortal lines upon the heavens till with sighs of love
> Sweet Enitharmon mild Entrancd breathd forth upon the wind
> The Spectrous dead Weeping the Spectres viewd the immortal works
> Of Los Assimilating to those forms Embodied & Lovely
> In youth & beauty in the arms of Enitharmon mild reposing.

(page 90:36–44)

When life on earth begins to imitate the sublime forms of divinely inspired art, then man has begun the process of psychic reintegration and social cooperation that enables him to realize his own divinity both on earth and in heaven. The opening lines of Night VIII strikingly illustrate this. Albion, the universal man, is seemingly imprisoned in the fallen, "dead" world of Urizen's void. But two angels hover over him, offering him a vision of eternity that, if he but open his eyes and look, will inspire him to achieve divinity on earth:

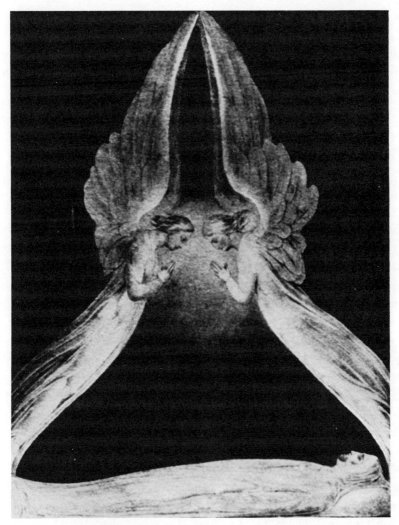

Plate 58. Christ in the Sepulchre.

The Fallen Man stretchd like a Corse upon the oozy Rock
. . . .
Two winged immortal shapes one standing at his feet
Toward the East one standing at his head toward the west
Their wings joind in the Zenith over head
Such is a Vision of all Beulah hovring over the Sleeper.

(page 99:4, 7—9, 15)

This image is an exact description of Blake's own painting of *The Angels Hovering over the Body of Christ in the Sepulchre* [*Plate 58*] executed for Butts around 1805.[29] That Blake was describing his own picture and thus identifying Albion with the soon to be resurrected Christ is even clearer in the deleted lines on page 99:

> . . . but other wings
> They had which clothd their bodies like a garment of soft down
> Silvery white shining upon the dark blue sky in silence
> Their wings touchd the heavens their fair feet hoverd above
> The swelling tides they bent over the dead corse like an arch
> Pointed at top in highest heavens of precious stones & pearl.
>
> (page 99:9–14)

Clearly, if Albion or fallen man would only imitate Christ, he could be spiritually reborn not only in an afterlife but also on earth. If fallen man patterned his own behavior after the organized outlines of romantic classicism, he would soon realize the divine vision of Innocence, the knowledge that man can be God. As Blake noted marginally in Night VIIb, Innocence, like art, must be "organized"—"Unorganized Innocence, An Impossibility/ Innocence dwells with Wisdom but never with Ignorance" (E 763).[30] Man can escape the seeming restrictions of his human form, not by becoming the "Formless indefinite" which Orc creates in Night VIIb and which Blake's marginal comment attacks, but by seeing his mortal body as a sublime and carefully organized artistic image.

In Night VIII, Blake further clarifies this moral and aesthetic distinction between a corrupt, limiting form and a divine, expansive form. Man can choose between two physical-psychological forms: the reptilian hermaphroditic monstrosity generated by Tirzah and Rahab or the human form divine woven on the looms of Cathedron by Enitharmon. Rahab and Tirzah force man to see his own body as a prison that forever separates

29. Noted by Darrell Figgis, *The Paintings of William Blake* (London, 1925), pl. 48.

30. Some critics have read this comment as Blake's condemnation of the Innocence portrayed in *Songs of Innocence,* without explaining why the vision of Innocence, of God as man, celebrated in the songs is simultaneously "unorganized" and yet "possible." I do not believe that Blake is criticizing or rejecting his earlier faith in Innocence here; rather, he is asserting that such a faith is both wise and organized or particularized, rather than ignorant, vague or abstract.

him from eternity and condemns him to the fallen world of Urizen. As long as man sees himself through such abstract rational categories, he inevitably chooses the garments prepared for him in the mills of Satan by Rahab and Tirzah—"webs of torture/ Mantles of despair girdles of bitter compunction shoes of indolence/ Veils of ignorance covering from head to feet with a cold web" (page 113:21–23). But if fallen man should expand his vision and see himself imaginatively, he would recognize his potential identity with the divine body of Christ. His body would then put on the beautiful artistic garments woven by Enitharmon.

> In soft silk drawn from their own bowels in lascivious delight
> With songs of sweetest cadence to the turning spindle & reel
> Lulling the weeping spectres of the dead. Clothing their limbs
> With gifts & gold of Eden. . . .
>
> (page 113:12–15)

Basically, Blake is defining two opposed ways of viewing the human form. When one sees through the shrunken senses imposed by Bromion on Theotormon or, as Blake feared, by Locke, Hobbes, d'Holbach, and Priestley on all eighteenth-century men, one can see the human form only as organic matter, as a "vegetated body" (page 104:37). But when one sees through the expanded and multiplied senses of the creative imagination, one sees the human form as a vehicle or image of divine humanity, as the potentially perfect body of Christ. This divine human form is vividly visualized on the last page of Night VIII; in an impressive, full-page, strongly outlined drawing, the naked Christ stands with his arms open and raised in the triumphant gesture of Innocence [*Plate 59*].

Blake made very few revisions in Night IX, however, and his original solution, the resurrection of a spiritual body only after death, remains intact. In only two lines, added on page 120, does Blake acknowledge the earthly salvation emphasized in the revised Nights VIIa and VIII. Albion now condemns Urizen not only for causing a "war within [his] members" (119:31) but also for deforming the "beautiful proportions" of the generated human form (page 120:30). But this glancing reference to a divine human form that can exist on earth as well as in heaven is not developed further here. *The Four Zoas,* for all its progress toward a satisfactory theoretical statement of Blake's solution to the problem of form,

Plate 59. Christ Triumphant, from *Vala,* Page 116, British Museum.

failed to evolve as a coherent, unified poetic structure. Wisely, Blake finally abandoned his attempts to graft his idea of a possible psychological rebirth on earth onto the traditional Christian notion of the resurrection of a spiritual body only after death. He had already begun, in 1804, a new epic, *Jerusalem,* that would fully and coherently articulate the way to salvation only fragmentarily presented in *The Four Zoas.* In order to understand the full complexity of this culminating epic, we must first study the development of the human form divine as a total symbol in Blake's late lyrics, in *Milton,* in his prose works and in his mature artistic masterpieces.

SIX

The Human Form Divine

By 1805 Blake had renewed his confidence in the vision of Innocence and Energy celebrated over a decade earlier in *Songs of Innocence*
and *The Marriage of Heaven and Hell*. He had thus rediscovered a poetic
and an artistic image that acknowledged the necessity of a bounding line
and yet allowed man to be, at least potentially, infinite. In his late poetry,
prose, and art, Blake continues to explore the possible implications of his
central symbol, the human form divine. In the figure of Christ, specifically
delineated (historically, psychologically, and artistically), Blake found an
age-old reconciliation between the constricting, because mortal, body of
Christ-the-man and the infinitely expansive, because divine, body of
Christ-the-God. In Blake's late work, the human form divine becomes a
total symbol—an image that contains all being, time, and space. It is
the artist's responsibility to recognize the infinity of this image and to
teach it to others; and he can fully communicate it only through careful
and precise distinctions, only through a strong and unwavering outline.
By presenting the human form in all its minute particularities, the artist
reveals and celebrates the holiness of every mortal limb, hand, muscle,
and hair. Blake's late poetry and prose emphasize the infinity of the
human form divine; his late art portrays the actual appearance of the divine human body.

214

To understand fully how this image of the human form divine satisfactorily solves Blake's problem with form, we must look first at the implications of this image in Blake's late poetry, prose, and art; second, at the reasons for Blake's insistence that this symbol be depicted in minute detail and with a wiry bounding line; third, at Blake's culminating artistic masterpieces and illustrations—the *Arlington Court Picture* and the designs for *Job,* the Bible, and Milton's *L'Allegro* and *Il Penseroso*—in which he visually portrays the minute particularities of the human form divine; and, finally, at the theme, narrative structure, and illustrations of *Jerusalem,* the work that most precisely articulates the full dimensions of the ultimate myth that Blake constructed around the image of the human form divine, a myth that systematizes but does not essentially alter the beliefs Blake held as a young man, a myth that is in essence a reaffirmation of Innocence and a closed, self-sufficient form.

THE INFINITE HUMAN FORM

In the poetry, prose, and art created between 1803 and 1827, Blake carefully distinguished between the fallen, degenerate human form and the expansive human form divine. The distinction is both one of vision and one of fact. The visionary eyes of Innocence, as Blake celebrates them in "Auguries of Innocence," can see "a World in a Grain of Sand" and the infinite, eternal cosmos in the human form. God "does a Human Form Display / To those who Dwell in Realms of day" (E 484). But the eye or mind already imprisoned in narrow theological conceptions sees not the human form divine, but only the vague and unsubstantial "inner light" or "Seed of God" invoked by the Quakers in the eighteenth century:

> Every Morn & every Night
> Some are Born to sweet delight
> Some are Born to sweet delight
> Some are Born to Endless Night
> We are led to Believe a Lie
> When we see not Thro the Eye
> Which was Born in a Night to perish in a Night
> When the Soul Slept in Beams of Light

> God Appears & God is Light
> To those poor Souls who dwell in Night
> But does a Human Form Display
> To those who Dwell in Realms of day.
>
> (E 484) [1]

Thus, mortality as such is no longer a prison; one can be born to "sweet delight" as well as to the sufferings of "Night." The choice is one's own, and it is a choice of vision. We can either "see With [first manuscript reading] the Eye/ Which was Born in a Night," an eye dimmed and corrupted by mind-forged manacles and self-destroying accusations, an eye ultimately destined to be destroyed by the clearer truth of day. Or we can see "thro," or beyond, this darkened eye into the "beams of light" that surround even our sleeping, night-dimmed souls.

The eye of Innocence uses these beams of light to see even farther (the beams are not themselves objects of sight, as they are for the eye of night; rather, they enable the eye of day to see the holiness inherent in all reality). The eye of Innocence sees that God has a human form and, conversely, that everything human is holy. Whenever one sees the cosmos as a man or man as both soul and solar system, one enters the divine vision Blake described in a poem to Butts on October 2, 1800:

1. These concluding lines of "Auguries of Innocence" can be read as Blake's subtle critique of the Quaker doctrine of the "inner light." The early Quakers tried to distinguish between the "Principle" or "Seed" of God that dwells in man and the actual "Essence" or "Nature" of God that is transcendent. As Robert Barclay, one of the most important early Quaker apologists, expounded this doctrine of George Fox: "By this Seed, Grace and Word of God, and Light wherewith we say everything is enlightened, and hath a measure of it, which strives with him in order to save him . . . we understand not the proper Essence and Nature of God, precisely taken, . . . but we understand a Spiritual, Heavenly, and Invisible Principle, in which God as Father, Son and Spirit dwells: a measure of which Divine and Glorious Life is in all men, as a seed which of its own nature draws, invites, and inclines to God; and this some call *Vehiculum Dei."* (*Apology for the True Christian Divinity* [London, 1676], 1736, pp. 137–38). Blake here argues that this Quaker notion of God as an inner "light" can only confuse: God either exists in man, in which case man is God, at least potentially; or he does not. Twentieth-century Quakers have also noted the truth of such criticism and no longer attempt to distinguish between the "Seed" and the "Nature" of God: the "inner light" is now considered to be the living presence of God. As Rufus M. Jones summarizes contemporary Quaker doctrine: "Its central principle is the belief in a divine light implanted in the soul of man, which convicts him of sin, condemns him when he disobeys it, and which as he obeys and follows it leads him to Christ, the living, spiritual, present Savior, who guides, inspires, empowers and sanctifies him" (*A Dictionary of Religion and Ethics,* ed. S. Mathews and G. B. Smith [New York, 1921], p. 175).

To my Friend Butts I write
My first Vision of Light
On the yellow sands sitting
. . . .
Amazd & in fear
I each particle gazed,
Astonishd Amazed
For each was a Man
Human formd . . . .
. . . .
My Eyes more & more
Like a Sea without shore
Continue Expanding
The Heavens commanding
Till the Jewels of Light
Heavenly Men beaming bright
Appeard as One Man
Who Complacent began
My limbs to infold
In his beams of bright gold
Like dross purgd away
All my mire & my clay
Soft consumd in delight
In his bosom Sun bright
I remaind . . . .

(E 683–4)

The human form is now simultaneously seen as the physical body of the individual and as the metaphoric body of the universe; defined as the body of Christ, the human form is both the macrocosmic one man and the microcosmic multitudes.

The vision of Innocence is not only analogical (one sees oneself as a metaphor for God); it is also unitive or holistic—one sees the similarities in seemingly disparate things and in so doing, links or even fuses multitudes into unity. Blake's concept of the unitive mode of vision is partly derived from his reading of Jacob Bryant and perhaps of such other syncretic mythologists as Richard Payne Knight and J. Sylvain Bailly. Blake endorsed the theosophist belief that all myths are variations of one antique, true myth and that all heroes and sublime plots derive from a single ancient epic. His poems and paintings, as he emphatically states in his *Descriptive Catalogue* (1809), recreate this primal myth in its original form. They thus embody that one unitive form which is capable of reuniting all men as one man in heaven on earth. Describing his lost painting, *The Ancient Britons,* Blake presents his theosophist notion that the hero truly depicted as Albion in British antiquities subsequently appeared in other myths and legends:

The British Antiquities are now in the Artist's hands; all his visionary contemplations, relating to his own country and its ancient glory, when it was as it again shall be, the source of learning and inspiration. . . . The giant Albion, was Patriarch of the Atlantic; he is the Atlas of the Greeks, one of those the Greeks called Titans. The stories of Arthur are the acts of Albion, applied to a Prince of the fifth century, who conquered Europe, and held the Empire of the world in the dark age, which the Romans never again recovered. (E 533–34)

Similarly, Christ was originally one man who was subsequently divided into three other parts: the sublime, the pathetic and the rational.

The Strong man represents the human sublime. The Beautiful man represents the human pathetic, which was in the wars of Eden divided into male and female. The Ugly man represents the human reason. They were originally one man, who was fourfold; he was self-divided, and his real humanity slain on the stems of generation, and the form of the fourth was like the Son of God. (E 533)

This culminating fourth form, Christ the Savior or the Urthona of *Jerusalem,* syncretically contains all modes of human existence, all modes of artistic style (sublime, beautiful, picturesque, or rational), all eras of human history. As Blake asserts, "The antiquities of every Nation under Heaven . . . are the same thing as Jacob Bryant and all antiquaries have proved. . . . All had originally one language, and one religion, this was the religion of Jesus, the everlasting Gospel" (E 534).

The distinction between the infinite form divine and the fallen, degenerate human form is not solely one of vision; it is also a fact, a state of being. The "Auguries of Innocence" acknowledge that the human form divine can be temporarily destroyed by physical conditions: "Nought can deform the Human Race/ Like to the Armours iron brace" (E 483). And in *Milton* (1804–10), Blake describes the tremendous difficulty one encounters, even after one has achieved the vision of Innocence and seen the potential infinite in man, in actually becoming the human form divine and living the life of Christ on earth. According to Blake, the poet

Milton failed to embody the divine humanity and to become a true poet-prophet because, first, he obeyed the dead literary conventions of the past, those classical Greek and Roman models that are mere "daughters of memory" rather than the living inspiration of the Old and New Testament prophecies; second, he indulged his selfish desires for fame, complete authority over his wives and daughters, and slavish devotion from his admirers (in Blake's terminology, he became a spectrous selfhood); and third, he cruelly denied the sexual and emotional needs of his wives and daughters; he neither loved nor understood his emanations. As Blake's Milton, recognizing all these errors in shame, condemns himself:

> I will go down to self annihilation and eternal death,
> Lest the Last Judgment come & find me unannihilate
> And I be seiz'd & giv'n into the hands of my own Selfhood.
>
> . . . .
>
> What do I here before the Judgment? without my Emanation?
> With the daughters of memory, & not the daughters of Inspiration [?]
> I in my Selfhood am that Satan: I am that Evil One!
> He is my Spectre! in my obedience to loose him from my Hells
> To chain the Hells, my Furnaces, I go to Eternal Death.
>
> (*M* 14:22–24, 28–32)

Blake then develops this notion of the human form divine as a potential state of being into his concept of the "states" or physical and mental conditions in which men live. His doctrine of the "states" both acknowledges the actual distinction between the fallen and the divine human form and still makes it possible for the degenerate human form to be liberated into eternity. Milton, like all fallen men dominated by Urizen, must learn to distinguish between individuals and states, between the potential infinity in every human being and the limitations of the given psychological-socio-economic state that a man inhabits at a certain time in a certain place. States cannot change, but individuals can. Blake means that, once we have objectively recognized the "state" we are in and have analyzed its potentialities and its limitations, we as individuals can reject that state for another. But the state itself, a given configuration of psychological or sociological pressures and responses, is static. A psychological syndrome or "complex" can be described and analyzed as a constant, unchanging pattern of behavior. Numerous psychiatric case histories have shown us that individuals, widely separated in time and space, enact very similar neurotic behavior patterns. Once we distinguish between states and individuals in those states we can forgive an individual for the errors or evils he commits as a result of being in that condition (that is, we condemn the state, not the individual who, at that moment, could not act otherwise). Blake's concept of states thus allows both for the recognition of a degenerate human form and also for the realization within the human form of man's potential divinity.

Blake not only distinguishes between individuals and states; he also argues that some states are better than others. Specifically, he identifies three classes, or states, of man: the "two contraries"—the reprobate and the redeemed—and the third "Reasoning Negative," the elect. The elect is the authoritarian mentality that assumes that moral absolutes exist; that every thought or action can be judged and condemned (by it) according to those absolutes; and that every intentional or unintentional attempt to thwart the dominance of those absolutes (as it defines them) must be punished with the extermination of the offender. Blake would certainly have recognized his elect mentality in two vivid portraits drawn by his contemporaries, Robert Burns's Holy Willie and James Hogg's Justified Sinner. This psychological state is wholly negative: it distorts, oppresses, murders, annihilates. This is the abstract void of disembodied intellect, an empty, soulless abyss. The state of the redeemed, in contrast, is a state of doubt, anxiety, fear, hesitation, even paralysis. The redeemed feed parasitically on the prolific Energy and imaginative vision of the reprobates, just as Theotormon's eagles feed on Oothoon in *Visions of the Daughters of Albion*. But the redeemed state does produce tension and the desire for change; and because of this, it can stimulate the development of the individual. The redeemed is thus the necessary devourer of *The Marriage of Heaven and Hell*. The reprobate state is, of course, the final state through which the individual must pass; it is the state of Innocence and vision, the state of being at one with God, of recognizing and embodying the human form divine.[2] Ultimately, the individual passes beyond all states and becomes totally free, unique, a god.

2. As Eve Teitelbaum notes, Blake sees these three states in aesthetic as well as psychological terms: Satan, the Elect, creates a purely mathematical, rational art; Palamabron, the Redeemed, copies the mistaken "blots" and "blurs" of the Dutch realists and

Blake articulates these distinctions between "fallen" and "divine" states visually as well as verbally. Man in a fallen (elect or redeemed) state is clothed; his human form divine is obscured by elaborate fashions, rigid armor, heavy and clumsy draperies. This metaphor is clearly explicated in *Milton* on Plate 18 where the shadowy female weaves a heavy, oppressive garment for the fallen Milton:

> I will lament over Milton in the lamentations of the afflicted
> My Garments shall be woven of sighs & heart broken lamentations
> The misery of unhappy Families shall be drawn out into its border
> Wrought with the needle with dire sufferings poverty pain & woe
> . . . .
> I will have Writings written all over it in Human Words
> That every Infant that is born upon the Earth shall read
> And get by rote as a hard task of a life of sixty years
> I will have Kings inwoven upon it & Councellors & Mighty Men
> The Famine shall clasp it together with buckles & Clasps
> And the Pestilence shall be its fringe & the War its girdle
> To divide into Rahab & Tirzah that Milton may come to our tents
> For I will put on the Human Form & take the Image of God
> Even Pity & Humanity but my Clothing shall be Cruelty
> And I will put on Holiness as a breastplate & as a Helmet
> And all my ornaments shall be of the gold of broken hearts
> And the precious stones of anxiety & care & desperation & death
> And repentance for sin & sorrow & punishment & fear.
>
> (*M* 18:5–9, 13–24)

The culminating image of fallen clothing is the breastplate of Aaron, an iron plaque set with twelve stones symbolizing the zodiac, the emblem, in Blake's eyes, of Urizen's reduction of heavenly infinity to a mathematical diagram of dead bodies circling automatically around a fixed, dead center, the captive sun.[3] Here, the breastplate is appropriately worn by the covering cherub.

In contrast, the reprobate in these designs is always naked (often in flames, pushing through dark, "devouring" clouds, or with limbs spread in the accepting gesture of Innocence, as on the title page and Plates 8, 13, 15, 21, 29 ["William"], and 33 ["Robert"] of *Milton*); while the tiny

---

all illusionistic, "painterly" artists; while Rintrah-Blake, the Reprobate, creates the particularizing line of "Eternal Life"; "Form as Meaning in Blake's *Milton*," *Blake Studies* 2 (1969): 37–50.

3. Northrop Frye clarifies this symbolism of the zodiac in "The Keys to the Gates," *Some British Romantics,* ed., J. V. Logan *et al.* (Athens, Ohio, 1966), pp. 13–14.

figure of William Blake on Plate 36 is clothed in a form-fitting suit. This form-revealing garment is described in the text as the female form itself; both are "A Garment of Pity & Compassion like the Garment of God" (*M* 18:35) which protects but does not constrain or diminish the human form divine. The divine relationship between man and his emanation, as Milton learns from Ololon, is that perfect visual fusion of human anatomy and flowing drapery that blends figure and garment into a single line and that is the hall-mark of Blake's personal style.

Extending this clothing metaphor to a cosmological myth, Blake contrasts the fixed, rigid, hard, and opaque "Mundane Shell" of the fallen world to the fluid, pattern-forming vortex of the world of infinite vision. As Harold Bloom has commented, the vortex is "the eddy or whirlpool of eternal consciousness, whose center is the object eternal consciousness intends" (E 829). Since both perceiver and object are aspects of a single continuum of consciousness (Blake was, like Coleridge, an epistemological phenomenologist), the human mind naturally projects its own "body-image" outward. The mind structures its experiences around the human body; thus the world becomes (that is, is known as) a giant man. If one sees the universe as a human form, rivers as veins of blood, mountains as muscles, and clouds as blood vessels, then one lives in a constantly swirling current of consciousness where every "object" is a metaphor, every simile a potential reality. Unlike Kant, who confines human perception to the categories of time, space and such modalities as causality, Blake assumes that the primal patterns of perception are structured around the image of the human form; every act of consciousness, then, approximates or "clothes" the human form divine. As Blake put it:

> The nature of infinity is this: That every thing has its
> Own Vortex; and when once a traveller thro' Eternity
> Has passed that Vortex, he perceives it roll backward behind
> His path, into a globe itself infolding; like a sun:
> Or like a moon, or like a universe of starry majesty,
> While he keeps onwards in his wondrous journey on the earth
> Or *like a human form*, a friend with whom he livd benevolent.
>
> (*M* 15:21–27) [4]

4. My italics. Martin Nurmi has drawn attention to the negative implications of Descartes' vortexes here; "Negative Sources for Blake," *Blake Essays for Damon*, ed. A. Rosenfeld (Providence, R. I., 1969), pp. 307–12. I would argue more emphatically than

From eternity, Milton perceives the fallen state of consciousness that he must enter as a giant man (Albion) asleep upon the rock of ages. Having descended into this state through the bosom of Albion, Milton then sees the world we know, a world of death, rock, fire, and war (*M* 15:36–17:20) where the human form is fragmented or shriveled up.

Milton finally casts off this erroneous vision to become what Blake is, the prophet-bard who celebrates the human form divine and, by celebrating it, actively encourages and persuades mankind to live within this form. There are two ways to achieve the human form divine: one must affirm one's own human body and live the life of Christ, and one must see the potential infinity within one's self and everything that lives. As Los says, we must take on and affirm the human form, both Bowlahoola (the digestive system, heart, lungs) and Allamanda (the nervous system), lest we become "No Human Form but only a Fibrous Vegetation/ A Polypus of soft affections without Thought or Vision" (*M* 24:37–8). Even Los's tools of creation assume a living form: "The Bellows are the Animal Lungs: the Hammers the Animal Heart/ The Furnaces the Stomach for digestion" (*M* 24:58–9).

The human form one should assume is, of course, the body of Christ (in youth) or the body of Jehovah (in maturity). That these two figures are one and the same God is revealed in the Petworth *Last Judgment,* where Christ is seated upon the throne of Jehovah, and possibly also in Blake's figure of Laocoön. In Blake's heavily inscribed engraving based on a cast of the famous Rhodian statue ([*Plate* 60], c. 1822–27), Laocoön represents both the Jehovah with whom he is identified in the captions (he is "The Angel of the Divine Presence . . . [King Jehovah]" [E 270]) and whom he physically resembles (an older man with white hair and beard—this resemblance is even more striking in Blake's earlier British Museum drawing of Laocoön) and also the Christ who mercifully sets two limits to the fall of man in *Milton.*

The Divine hand found the Two Limits: first of Opacity, then of Contraction
Opacity was named Satan, Contraction was named Adam.

(*M* 13:20–21)

Nurmi does that Blake translated Descartes' wholly materialistic vortexes into structures of a (potentially) ever-expanding consciousness (cf. John Sutherland, "Blake's 'Mental Traveller,' " *ELH* 22 [1955]:138).

Plate 60. Laocoön, Collection of Geoffrey Keynes.

Laocoön, too, in both the engraving and the drawing, resists the serpent of sin, perverted energy, and the vegetating body [5] that threatens to engulf both youths, Adam (contraction) and Satan (opacity). Like Christ, Laocoön knows both that man must fall into a vegetated body and also that man can be redeemed from that body if he recognizes its limitations, both of vision (opacity) and of form (contraction). The serpent titled "Evil" on the left of the engraving therefore consumes Satan (?)—I base these identifications of Laocoön's sons on the order in which Blake gives them in his caption, namely, "[Jah] & his two Sons Satan & Adam as they were copied from the Cherubim" [E 270]—opacity of vision must be entirely destroyed; while the serpent called "Good" on the right seemingly permits Adam (?) to escape (note that Adam is *not* being stung by the serpent)—the contraction or bounding line of the human form can be accepted. It is this "good" serpent of outline that bites Laocoön who, like Christ, must take on the contracted human form so that man may realize that divinity can exist within a mortal finite body. Still, the limitations of that finite body must be transcended by the imagination. As the caption above Adam beside the Hebraic title insists: "What can be Created / Can be Destroyed / Adam is only / The Natural Man / & not the Soul / or Imagination" (E 271). Yet the opposing legend on the left side of the engraving stresses that the natural body can be seen as infinite: "The Eternal Body of Man is The

IMAGINATION that is $\frac{\text{God himself}}{\text{The Divine Body}}$" (E 271).

In "The Everlasting Gospel" (the title is taken both from *Revelation* and from Joachim de Flora[6] and refers to the religious beliefs articulated in *Songs of Innocence* and *The Marriage of Heaven and Hell*), Blake specifically delineates the nature and life of Christ that man must imitate.

---

5. This symbolism of the serpent appeared earlier in the Tate Gallery color prints, *Europe, The Book of Ahania* and *Vala* (see above, chap. 4) and is used again in Blake's illustrations for Milton's *Paradise Lost*, Plates 2–3, 5–7, and 10–13 and the designs for *Jerusalem*, Plates 9, 62, and 72.

6. A. L. Morton may have overstressed Blake's debt to Joachim of Flora's "Everlasting Gospel" since both Joachim and Blake probably derived their Antinomian doctrines directly from St. Paul's teachings; nonetheless, Morton offers evidence of Blake's knowledge of Joachim's writings in *The Everlasting Gospel: A Study in the Sources of William Blake* (London, 1958).

Christ was a proud man who "spoke with authority," who disdained to take a bribe, who defied the leading minds of his day—"This is the Race that Jesus ran/ Humble to God Haughty to Man" (E 511). Christ was never submissive or obedient; he fought against the sneaking, hypocritical Pharisees with the righteous indignation of the true moralist. "His wrath began to burn/ In Miracles throughout the Land/ That quite unnervd Caiaphas hand" (E 511), and he violently cursed "the Rulers before the People" (E 511). In his honest anger, he affirmed his own divinity; for man, like the God of the Old Testament, must also be a wrathful and jealous God. As God told Jesus,

> If thou humblest thyself thou humblest me
> Thou also dwellst in Eternity
> Thou art a Man God is no more
> Thy own humanity learn to adore
> For that is my Spirit of Life
> Awake arise to Spiritual Strife
> And thy Revenge abroad display.
>
> (E 511–12)

Moreover, Jesus, contrary to traditional interpretations, affirmed sexual desires and the beauty of the naked body. His mother was an adulteress; he understood and forgave the woman taken in adultery; and he implicitly condemned Mary Magdalen's real sin, her secret love and false pretense to chastity. As Mary Magdalen realizes, sexual love is holy and should be openly celebrated.

> . . . O Lord this was my sin
> When first I let these Devils in
> In dark pretence to Chastity
> Blaspheming Love blaspheming thee
> Thence Rose Secret Adulteries
> And thence did Covet also rise
> My sin thou has forgiven me
> Canst thou forgive my Blasphemy.
>
> (E 514)

Blake's Jesus tacitly agrees with Mary Magdalen that it is a puritanical falsehood to call "a shame & sin/ Loves temple that God dwelleth in" and an evil repression to "hide in secret hidden Shrine/ The Naked human form divine" (E 513–14). Then Jesus forgave Mary her only sin, her coveting of a reputation for chastity to which she was not entitled. This proud, angry, sensual, merciful man is Blake's true human form divine, the body Blake himself would inhabit on earth and the character he would have all men bear. Blake's Jesus, like Blake himself, has a snub nose, hates the hypocritical, judging Pharisees, and "speaks in parables to the blind" (E 516). Blake, like Jesus, writes so that he may *not* be immediately understood; his parables or prophecies are comprehensible only to the uncorrupted eye of Innocence or the enlightened eye of the visionary. Not surprisingly, then, the human form Blake urges us to wear on earth is that of the arrogant, angry rebel against authority who celebrates the potential divinity of man through metaphor and prophecy.

In this context Blake's revised *For the Sexes: The Gates of Paradise* (ca. 1810?–18) may be read as the history of the human form in little, as the fall of man from the infinitely expansive body of the one man into the limiting body of vegetation and of his rebirth into the human form divine either through vision (the recognition of the infinite soul within) or through the fact of death, either literal (a release from the vegetative body) or psychological (a rejection of vegetating garments for the true clothing of the divine human form). The additional prologue, epilogue, touched up engravings, keys and greatly expanded captions for the seventeen emblems originally published in *For Children: The Gates of Paradise* (1793) transform Blake's earlier vision of the physical body as corrupt [7] into a vision of salvation on earth as well as after death. The title page establishes the way for the fallen, antagonistic sexes to return through the gates of paradise, which are here pictured as a rising sun flanked by two angels, while eight tiny figures float above. They must reject the false Christians who rear the dead law of Jehovah on their high altars, and live instead in the new dispensation provided by Jehovah-Christ, the God of mercy—namely, "Mutual Forgiveness of each Vice" (E 256). These fallen men and women must distinguish the covering garment from the human form divine obscured beneath it; unlike Satan, "The Accuser who is The God of This World," in the epilogue, they must recognize the infinity that is always present in the soul of man and refuse to condemn the body or acts of the individual temporarily trapped in a fallen state. They

7. See above, chapter 3.

should condemn only the *state* of Satan, not the individual in that state. Then, with Blake, they will see that "Truly My Satan thou art but a Dunce/ And dost not know the Garment from the Man" (E 266).

The added caption for the frontispiece [*Plate 9*] stresses the potential infinity of man. The child-chrysalis asleep beneath the caterpillar of generation who "Reminds thee of thy Mother's Grief" (E 265; this caterpillar also appears on the early version of Plate 28 of *Jerusalem* [*Plate 79*]) will fall into the state of Satan or rise into vision, depending on how he sees the sun—whether as the cruel shafts of an accusing God or as the human form divine revealed "To those who Dwell in Realms of day" (E 484).

> What is Man!
> [The Suns Light when he unfolds it
> Depends on the Organ that beholds it.]
>
> (E 257)

(The personification or anthropomorphizing of the sun ["he"] already subtly confirms the vision of Innocence.) But here the child remains asleep, "Born in a Night to perish in a Night/ When the Soul Slept in Beams of Light," and is plucked like a mandrake by the female will and hidden in her veil of "Serpent Reasoning" and moral absolutes [*Plate 10*]. The potential human form divine is thus condemned to the drugged sleep of the opiate mandrake. The traditional superstition that the mandrake is the generated seed of a hanged man remains an especially appropriate image for Blake's fallen, vegetating, perverted human form under the control of Vala or nature. The keys for Figures 2–5 emphasize that the child's fall is mental rather than physical. He is now trapped in the psychic prisons of his mortal body: the water of "Doubt Self Jealous watry folly"; the earth of "Melancholy"; the air of "Shame & Fear"; and the fire of war caused by "Doubt," "Self contradiction," and "Rational Truth root of Evil & Good" [*Plates 4–14*]. In these four emblems, the human form still huddles up in shrunken, foreshortened masses confined to a rocky shore within a cave or surrounded by heavy cloud banks. Only Fire breaks out of such boundaries with open arms, but he too has now become mentally manacled. Blake has significantly altered this engraving since 1793 [*Plate 61*], compare [*Plate 14*]: Fire is now blind; horned,

Plate 61. For the Sexes: The Gates of Paradise (1818), *Figure 5, Copy F.*

like the war-mongering "Horned priest," Palamabron-Pitt, described on Plate 8 of *Europe;* and scaled, like the vindictive Satan in *Satan Smiting Job with Sore Boils,* a design done between 1818 and 1825 to illustrate Plate 6 of Blake's *The Book of Job.* Here, Fire, like Blake's figures of Pitt and Nelson,[8] is a demonic parody of Energy, the embodiment of revolutionary Energy perverted into mere will to power. He is armed with spear and shield; and the flames rushing past him are now scaled. His violent rebellion against an established system—like both Orc's and Satan's —leads only to his own destruction and the channeling of greater power into the hands of Urizen. As the lengthened caption and keys emphasize, this fire is energy perverted into the "endless strife" caused by war and "Two Horn'd Reasoning Cloven Fiction/ In Doubt which is Self contradiction" (E 259, 265). Moreover, again as in *Satan Smiting Job* and Blake's *Nelson,* this erect and open-armed figure of Fire is a calculated visual parody of the Glad Day figure: Energy is here corrupted into an instrument of psychic oppression.

But in 1818 Blake offers new hope to the individual trapped in the state of Satan. The added "Keys" for the next four emblems now suggest that fallen man can return to paradise. The shell from which the winged child escapes in Figure 6 [*Plate 15*] is no longer the physical body from which the pure soul emerges but rather the "Mundane Shell . . . where the Dead dwell" (E 265), the restricted cave of the mind dominated by Urizen or the state of Ulro-Satan. The child-angel can now accept his mortal body as both a "Sexual Garment sweet"—a source of sensual pleasure—and the bounding form necessary for creative survival, without accepting Urizen's conception of the body as a fixed and final form, "a devouring Winding sheet" (E 266). Rather, he can see his physical body as an image of God, both in life and in death. The older youth in Figure 7 [*Plate 16*] now cries out, "What are these? ALAS! The Female Martyr/ Is She also the Divine Image?" He now recognizes that the divine image exists in the human form, both in the physical body at his feet and in the winged flying soul rising into the air.

8. Morton Paley discusses both *The Spiritual Form of Pitt Guiding Behemoth* and *The Spiritual Form of Nelson Guiding Leviathan* as perversions or "demonic parodies" of Energy (*Energy and the Imagination,* chap. 7).

But the closed mind of Urizen/Satan denies the child's vision. The tyrant king continues to instruct his sons (including Absalom) in the arts of war, compelled by his own "Vainglory hatcht & nurst/ By double Spectres," in arts that ultimately destroy both himself and his sons [*Plate 17*]. This fallen mind seeks escape, not by flying to the sun, but by seeking "the shadows of the Moon" in "Nights highest noon" (E 266 [*Plate 18*]). Blake now argues that to see an earthly life and one's physical body as intrinsically corrupting is a Satanic delusion which drowns the mind in "Times Ocean," in waters of doubt, fear, jealousy, and folly [*Plate 19*], and in aged ignorance [*Plate 20*]. Here the fallen mind continues to clip the wings of "all Sublunary things" and to imprison all rebellious fathers and sons in the depths of his dungeons [*Plate 21*].

Nonetheless, even this fallen mind can escape the physical and mental oppressions of the state of Satan by opening its eyes and mind, by recognizing in every human body "The Immortal Man that cannot Die" (E 266). "Fear and Hope are—Vision": by accentuating the nimbus around the old man's head in the touched up engraving for Figure 13 [*Plate 62*], compare [*Plate 22*], Blake more emphatically affirms that man can become a spiritual body in an afterlife in heaven: "The Immortal Man . . . cannot Die" (E 266). Significantly, Blake has added a tiny sketch of two figures embracing before a gate or door in the right margin of the keys at number 13; here we see two such spiritual or immortal bodies meeting before the gates of paradise. Figure 13 clearly points to a salvation *after* death; the epilogue will assure us that spiritual redemption can occur during our mortal life as well. Secure now in his conviction of holy immortality, the traveller who is everyman or, more specifically, Blake's visionary mental traveller, now hastens out of the state of Satan, the evening that perishes in a night, to enter the gates of paradise that are death to all aspects of the satanic state. Both the mental traveller and the physically crippled old man enter the tomb to be reborn on Figures 14 and 15 .[*Plates 23 and 24*]. The keys now reject only the degenerate body, pictured on the final design as a hooded, worm-wrapped figure buried in the earth [*Plate 25*]. This fallen sexual web or degenerate physical body tempts the immortal man from womb until tomb: "Thou'rt my Mother from the Womb/ Wife, Sister, Daughter to the Tomb"

Plate 62. For the Sexes: The Gates of Paradise, Figure 13, Copy F.

(E 266). So long as the "Eternal Man" sits in repose and allows the female to weave an oppressive "Web of Life" or a divided sexual garment for him, he is confined to "Dreams" and "weeping," to the restricted tomb and the hooded, crouching position of the final design.

But such temporary mental or physical descents into the state of Satan by the "Eternal Man" can be redeemed from the ten coils of the worm on the epilogue [9] by true vision and the forgiveness of sins. In the final keys, the mental traveller rejects the female will which weeps "over the Web of Life," for he recognizes that this is the state of Satan, "The Son of Morn in weary Nights decline/ The lost Travellers Dream under the Hill" (where witches live), a delusion of fading light or false vision born of night, anxiety and fear. Truly, as the epilogue shows, the "knowledge" of Satan—the assumption that human characters and thought patterns are fixed and unalterable—is ignorance. One must distinguish the external, fallen state ("the Garment") from the internal, divine soul ("the Man"). States change; individuals do not. "Every Harlot was a Virgin once/ Nor canst thou ever change Kate into Nan" (E 266). Satan's stupidity and impotence are vividly unmasked in the design Blake added with the epilogue [*Plate 63*]. Beneath the coiled worm of mortality, a grotesque sooty, bald, bat-winged Satan hovers in a painfully contorted position over the sleeping poet-traveller. As Jean Hagstrum has noted, Satan is here clearly associated with that foolish "Winking & blinking . . . Bat with Leathern wing," Dr. Johnson; and with all the closed, narrow minds hiding in the dark corners of the Royal Academy, the established Church, and the council rooms of George III.[10] His darkened body, bat wings, and the position of his arms further link him to the cruel spectre of Moloch who flees in defeat at the birth of Christ in *The Flight of Moloch,* Blake's illustration for "Hymn on the Morning of Christ's Nativity." Satan's spineless, flapping hands could never grasp a certain truth; instead, they dangle grotesquely from his wings, ludicrous appendages of a perverse mind. As David Erdman has suggested, this pathetic creature pretends to control the entire universe (the sun, moon, and stars are inscribed on his wings), but he scurries away in fear and confusion at the first glimpse of the sun rising behind the mountains. This design is Blake's *reductio ad absurdum* of the traditional icon of Satan whispering into the ear of Eve.[11] Rather than driving Adam and Eve out of paradise, this silly

9. Geoffrey Keynes suggests that the ten carefully numbered coils of the snake at the top of the epilogue associate Satan with the repressive ten commandments (*The Gates of Paradise,* London, 1968, p. 22).

10. Jean Hagstrum, *Blake, Poet and Painter* (Chicago, 1964), pp. 7–8; Plate II.

11. David Erdman, in private correspondence, August 24, 1968.

To The Accuser who is
The God of This World

Truly, My Satan thou art but a Dunce
And dost not know the Garment from the Man
Every Harlot was a Virgin once
Nor canst thou ever change Kate into Nan

Tho thou art Worshipd by the Names Divine
Of Jesus & Jehovah: thou art still
The Son of Morn in weary Nights decline
The lost Travellers Dream under the Hill

Plate 63. For the Sexes: The Gates of Paradise, Epilogue, Copy B, British Museum.

bat is himself expelled by the first hint of light in the east. Although the individual may fall under the temporary domination of Satan (this sleeping traveller's dream is clearly unpleasant, as his frown indicates; perhaps it is even the "Urizenic nightmare" Hagstrum infers [12]), he can easily escape. The sun rising behind the mountains throws a radiant nimbus around the traveller's head,[13] and his staff, although spiderwebbed with disuse, is not broken. The traveller can still awake, his imagination intact, and walk into paradise on earth. The individual, Kate and Nan, can always move beyond the nighttime hill of Satan into the daylit valley of vision, leaving Satan far behind, cowering in the darkness. Read in this way, *For the Sexes: The Gates of Paradise* is an epic in little, the epic Blake was to write with greater particularity and complexity in *Jerusalem.*[14]

The Outline of the Human Form Divine

For the divine vision of man as God to survive on earth, however, it must be imaged in a specific bounded form that can be seen and imitated by men. Only if this vision is concretely presented to the five senses will men be able to see it clearly, first as a way of life in itself; then as an actual ingredient in the makeup of other men, animals and plants; and finally, as the essence of one's own being. After one has perceived one's innate holiness, one must articulate that awareness within a unique and bounded form, a particular self-image and social role. Otherwise, Blake believed, one's consciousness of one's own divinity will fade away or be repressed; and one's Energy will be dissipated into incoherent, undirected activity. Worse yet, one will be defenseless against the imposed images of others. Every man must create his own system or personal "outline of Identity" (E 136), or he will be forced to wear the faces fashioned for him by other, alien imaginations. In his *Descriptive Catalogue* (1809), *Chau-*

12. Hagstrum, *Blake, Poet and Painter,* p. 7.

13. John Grant points out this halo in his unpublished critique of Jean Hagstrum's *William Blake, Poet and Painter,* May 1966.

14. Edward Rose has also noted the structural similarity of *For the Sexes: The Gates of Paradise* to *Jerusalem* in "The Structure of Blake's *Jerusalem*," *Bucknell Review* 11 (May 1963):44. Cf. George W. Digby, *Symbol and Image in William Blake* (Oxford, 1957), pp. 1–10.

cer Prospectus (1809), *Public Address* (1809–10), annotations to Reynolds (1798–1809), and late miscellaneous prose, Blake repeatedly asserts that a strong and determinate outline is necessary to preserve and to communicate the consciousness that man can be God.

Blake's comment on his painting of *The Bard, from Gray* in his *Descriptive Catalogue* emphatically proclaims that the authentic artistic or moral vision can be adequately conveyed to the human eye only through a "clear and determinate outline":

The Prophets describe what they saw in Vision as real and existing men whom they saw with their imaginative and immortal organs; the Apostles the same; the clearer the organ the more distinct the object. A Spirit and Vision are not, as the modern philosophy supposes, a cloudy vapour or a nothing: they are organized and minutely articulated beyond all that the mortal and perishing nature can produce. He who does not imagine in stronger and better lineaments, and in stronger and better light than his perishing mortal eye can see does not imagine at all. The painter of this work asserts that all his imaginations appear to him infinitely more perfect and more minutely organized than any thing seen by his mortal eye. Spirits are organized men: Moderns wish to draw figures without lines and with great and heavy shadows; are not shadows more unmeaning than lines, and more heavy? O who can doubt this! (E 532)

Here Blake successfully resolves the tension between an artistic reliance on outlines and a philosophical rejection of the constrictive boundaries of reason. Outline is no longer presented as Urizen's corrupting prison of infinite Energy but rather as the necessary vehicle of the imagination. Blake now gives theoretical justification for his artistic practice: outline is the basis not only of a sublime romantic classicism but also of religious salvation. Only the divine imagination can transcend the limiting categories of reason and perceive the holiness of everything that lives, but its perceptions need to be articulated in clear, specific, and carefully outlined forms if they are to survive in a sceptical world and command the allegiance of other minds. Thus the imagination uses the ordering, organizing faculties of reason to execute its chosen images. Reason and imagination are not in conflict; rather, they are—or should be—willing collaborators in the creation of a new heaven on earth. So long as reason fulfills its proper role as the dedicated apostle of the imagination, its bounding lines will reveal rather than inhibit the divinity of man.

Two further important observations should be made about Blake's insistence that a strong outline and minute particularities are necessary to the accurate depiction of the human form divine. In addition to accepting romantic classicism's theoretical demand for a precise, pristine outline style as described in chapter 4, Blake is also elevating the peculiarities of his highly developed eidetic imagination into a universally valid aesthetic and philosophical principle. Blake's well-documented capacity to see mental images as, or even more, vividly than ordinary sensory images is the essential characteristic of an abnormally intense eidetic imagination, as described in E. R. Jaensch's pioneering *Eidetic Imagery* (1930). Blake ultimately came to believe that his eidetic images, which he called "visions," were closer to an antique, uncorrupted and thus authentic mode of perception than his more blurred sensory images derived from the natural world. Since no one else received Blake's eidetic images, it was imperative that he portray them in the clearest, most definitive and detailed style possible in order to communicate them to others. Consequently, Blake condemned all religions or artistic styles based on a close imitation of nature as obstructive of true vision; he necessarily rejected the "blotting and blurring" painterly style for a precise linear style that alone could capture the minute particularities of his eidetic or "spiritual" images.[15]

Secondly, Blake's insistence upon a detailed, particularized style in painting as well as in poetry both sustained the eighteenth-century doctrine of "ut pictura poesis" in the face of growing criticism (led especially by Burke and Lessing) and also anticipated the honorific use of the pictorial analogy in the criticism of Coleridge and Hazlitt. While the nineteenth century generally rejected the "ut pictura poesis" emphasis on literary pictorialism and illustrative painting as limiting both arts too closely to an excessively detailed imitation of nature, the Romantic poets, painters, and critics still affirmed the analogous abilities of both the "sister

15. Joseph Burke has also noted Blake's correlation of eidetic imagery with a linear style and of natural images with a painterly style in "The Eidetic and the Borrowed Image: An Interpretation of Blake's Theory and Practice of Art," *Essays in Honour of Daryl Lindsay* (Melbourne: Oxford Univ. Press, 1964), pp. 110–17. Moreover, as Morton Paley has noted, Blake's reliance on the self-generated images of his own mind directly encouraged his typically "autistic," nonrational, associative modes of poetic thought (*Energy and the Imagination*, pp. 202–205).

arts" to capture the ideal in the particular, the general in the individual, and thus to communicate through symbols the presence of a spiritual world within the natural.[16] For Blake, the "ut pictura poesis" tradition had never meant the slavish imitation of nature or a literary or artistic "realism," but rather the creation of poetic images that could be visualized, on the one hand, and the creation of a visual art that communicated philosophical or "poetic" meaning, on the other.[17] Blake here clarified the sense in which the "ut pictura poesis" tradition's demand for precision or lifelike vividness (*enargeia*) in both poetry and art remained valid. Since the minute particulars of nature and humanity are "portions" of an internal Energy or divine life, they must be described in all their individuality so that no manifestation of that eternal life is obscured. And since only the poetic imagination has the ability to perceive nature sacramentally, to descry the holiness in everything that lives, the "sister arts" now became, in Blake's radical reinterpretation of "ut pictura poesis," no longer the daughters of nature but the daughters of imagination. As Blake insisted to the deluded Lord Byron "in the Wilderness," "Nature has no Outline: but Imagination has. Nature has no Tune: but Imagination has! Nature has no Supernatural & dissolves: Imagination is Eternity" (E 268). Blake thus managed to fuse a reinvigorated "ut pictura poesis" tradition with the Romantic desire to unify empiricism and idealism in poetry and art.

For the Romantic aesthetic demanded that the subjective eye of the poet or painter simultaneously record the unique particularities of his private experience (both rational and irrational) and communicate the involution of these subjective experiences within a universal spiritual, ideal, or divine power. This demand had led to Wordsworth's meticulously detailed titles and headnotes (for example, "Lines composed a few miles above Tintern Abbey on revisiting the Banks of the Wye during a Tour, July 13, 1798"), to Dorothy Wordsworth's scrupulous journal entries, to Browning's dramatic monologues; and in art, to George Stubbs' animal

16. Roy Park, " 'Ut Pictura Poesis': The Nineteenth-Century Aftermath," *Journal of Aesthetics and Art Criticism,* 28 (1969–70):155–64.

17. Jean Hagstrum has defined both the "ut pictura poesis" tradition and Blake's place within it (in *The Sister Arts* [Chicago, 1958]; in *Blake, Poet and Painter* [Chicago, 1964], and in "Blake and the Sister-Arts Tradition," *Blake's Visionary Forms Dramatic* [pp. 82–91]).

anatomies, to Joseph Wright's pictorial record of a scientific experiment, *An Experiment with an Air-Pump,* to Constable's open-air oil sketches, and to Turner's decision to lash himself to the mast of a steamship during a snowstorm at sea before painting *Steamer in a Snowstorm.* In all these cases, empiricism is the foundation upon which the artistic imagination erects its symbols. Blake, the first to articulate clearly this demand for a union of specificity with symbolic universality ("To see a World in a Grain of Sand/ And a Heaven in a Wild Flower"), thus led the way to the aesthetic theory and practice of the nineteenth century. The truths of the imagination which are the truths of life itself can be conveyed only in clear outlines, precise details, and scrupulous distinctions. To blur one's phenomenological images is to destroy them and, in so doing, to annihilate the living presence of the divine power or Energy in the human consciousness. It was for this capacity to perceive the world in a unique, subjective way and to articulate minutely the specific visions of his perception that Blake so heartily praised the drawings of young Thomas Malkin: "They are all firm, determinate outline, or identical form. . . . All his efforts prove this little boy to have had that greatest of all blessings, a strong imagination, a clear idea, and a determinate vision of things in his own mind" (E 671). As Blake summed up this empiricism in an epigram, "What is Most Grand is always most Minute" (E 505).

Outline is necessary not only to articulate and communicate the divine vision, but also to sustain one's individuality. Blake's *Catalogue* notes on "Ruth, A Drawing" explicitly identify outline with life itself. In order to live, to sustain a coherent and meaningful existence, every individual must create his own particular identity and social role since "neither character nor expression can exist without firm and determinate outline" (E 540). As Blake expands this idea:

The great and golden rule of art, as well as of life, is this: That the more distinct, sharp, and wiry the bounding line, the more perfect the work of art; and the less keen and sharp, the greater is the evidence of weak imitation, plagiarism, and bungling. Great inventors, in all ages, knew this. . . . The want of this determinate and bounding form evidences the want of idea in the artist's mind, and the pretence of the plagiary in all its branches. How do we distinguish the oak from the beech, the horse from the ox, but by the bounding outline? How do we distinguish one face or countenance from another, but by the bounding line and its infinite inflexions and movements? What is it that builds a house and plants a garden, but the definite and determinate? What is it that distinguishes honesty from knavery, but the hard and wirey line of rectitude and certainty in the actions and intentions. Leave out this line and you leave out life itself: all is chaos again, and the line of the almighty must be drawn out upon it before man or beast can exist. (E 540)

In this central statement, Blake explains the necessity of outline to artistic creation, to the structure of the personality, to the construction of a moral code, and thus to the preservation of all social order. Man cannot exist without an organized mode of personal and social behavior, without some kind of law or pattern to follow. As Huizinga has said, man is essentially *homo ludens,* a creature who plays games and who needs rules in order to survive.[18] Anticipating Huizinga, Blake urged men to create their own outlines or systems, to construct their own character and mode of expression rather than plagiarize the weakened or blurred lines of another. In the words of Blake's spokesman, Los, "I must Create a System, or be enslav'd by another Mans" (E 151). While many of us might agree that personal and social organization are necessary to survival, Blake's application of this principle to art reveals his peculiar blindness to the rigorous structures and calculated effects of the baroque, Dutch-Flemish and Venetian styles. Blake defied the popular aesthetic models of his day—Rubens, Rembrandt, Joshua Reynolds, the Venetian and Flemish schools—and demanded that contemporary artists substitute for their "blotted," "blurred" styles his own practice of "Unbroken lines, unbroken masses, and unbroken colours," that enabled him "to find form and keep it" (E 529). Only an unbroken line, argued Blake, can construct an independent personality; an original, unique work of art; or a "firm and determinate" pattern of conduct that can evolve into an entire society or political system. That political science depends on art, that "poets are the unacknowledged legislators of the world," is clearly suggested by Blake: "The wretched State of the Arts in this Country & in Europe originating in the wretched State of Political Science which is the Science of Sciences Demands a firm & determinate conduct on the part of Artists to Resist the Contemptible Counter Arts established by such contemptible Politicians as Louis XIV & originally set on foot by Venetian Picture traders Music

18. Johan Huizinga, *Homo Ludens—A Study of the Play-Element in Culture* (Boston: Beacon, 1955), *passim.*

traders & Rhime traders to the destruction of all true art as it is this Day." (E 569). Blake thus anticipates the gestalt psychologists in their findings that artistic creation, political systems, even perception itself, all depend on outline, on organized groupings of experience.[19]

Blake's ferocious attacks on Sir Joshua Reynolds' work stem directly from these two doctrines. According to Blake, Reynolds failed to see that identity, character, and ultimately truth itself depend on a distinct, organized pattern of behavior and perception, upon outline in short; and he therefore denied that precise drawing, firm lines, and definite coloring were necessary to communicate truth. For Blake, of course, a blurred line and a blurred mind are the same; to know clearly is to express oneself clearly. Blake therefore attacked Reynolds for his admiration both of blotting artists—men like Correggio, Rembrandt, Jan Steen, and the Venetians—and of blotting ideas—sweeping generalizations that ignore particular truths. "To Generalize is to be an Idiot," proclaims Blake, and again, "Distinct General Form Cannot Exist Distinctness is Particular Not General," for "Unless. You Consult. Particulars. You Cannot. even Know or See Mich: Ang.° or Rafael or any Thing Else" (E 630, 638, 634). Contrary to Reynolds' notions, Blake claims that truth cannot be learned either through inductions derived from sense-data or through deductions based on abstract hypotheses. Rather, truth is innate or intuitively grasped; it results from imagination or vision:

> Knowledge of Ideal Beauty. is Not to be Acquired It is Born with us Innate Ideas. are in Every Man Born with him. they are <truly> Himself. The Man who says that we have No Innate Ideas must be a Fool & Knave. Having no Con-Science <or Innate Science>. (E 637)

> Demonstration Similitude & Harmony [the elements of mathematic, Greek art rather than spiritual, Gothic art] are Objects of Reasoning Invention Identity & Melody are Objects of Intuition. (E 648)

Since man's capacity for true vision is innate and needs only an act of the will to be realized, it cannot be acquired (as Reynolds says taste and genius can be) from rules or judgment: "I say Taste & Genius are Not Teachable or Acquirable but are Born with us Reynolds says the Con-

19. Wolfgang Köhler, in *Gestalt Psychology* (New York, 1947), shows that "experience as such exhibits an order *which is itself experienced*" (pp. 60–1) and concludes that "the right psychological formula [for human perception] is therefore: *pattern of stimulation—organization—response to the products of organization*" (p. 165).

trary" (E 648). Vision *can* be copied, but it must be copied minutely and exactly if it is not to be corrupted in the reproduction: "Servile Copying is the Great Merit of Copying," writes Blake, for "Copying Correctly . . . is the only School to the Language of Art" (E 634, 628).

In contrast to Reynolds' neoclassicism, Blake enthusiastically affirms his own romantic classicism, a sublime art of minute discriminations, strong outlines, technically precise execution, pale and delicate coloring, vigorous linear rhythms, and tectonic structures based on the human form. "The Man who asserts that there is no Such Thing as Softness in Art & that every thing in Art is Definite & Determinate has not been told this by Practise but by Inspiration & Vision because Vision is Determinate & Perfect & he Copies That without Fatigue Every thing being Definite & determinate" (E 635). The human form divine can be seen by the eye of Innocence and worn by every individual, but it can be artistically displayed only by the hand of the visionary craftsman who can capture every subtle nuance of its expression and every slight movement of its body. Blake sums up this aesthetic theory of the bounded form in his *Catalogue* notes for *The Last Judgment:*

General Knowledge is Remote Knowledge it is in Particulars that Wisdom consists & Happiness too. Both in Art & in Life General Masses are not as Much Art as a Pasteboard Man is Human Every Man has Eyes Nose & Mouth this every Idiot knows but he who enters into & discriminates most minutely the Manners & Intentions the < *Expression* > Characters in all their branches is the alone Wise or Sensible Man & on this discrimination All Art is founded. . . . as Poetry admits not a Letter that is Insignificant so Painting admits not a Grain of Sand or a Blade of Grass < Insignificant >. (E 550)

Having theoretically defined the analogical and unitive vision of Innocence, the particular physical body of the human form divine, and the necessity for a bounding line in life as well as art, Blake confidently created the artistic masterpieces of his final years. In his illustrations for *The Book of Job,* Milton and the Bible, and in his own late paintings and drawings, Blake visually explored the myriad implications of the human form divine. And in *Jerusalem,* his culminating poetic epic, Blake spelled out— both verbally and visually—the relevance of this controlling symbol or myth for all men.

SEVEN

The Human Form Divine in Blake's Late Art

Blake's late art (1805–27) forcefully exhibits that clear and determinate outline that Blake deemed necessary both to define the "character" or identity of an individual figure or system and to communicate accurately the details of the divine vision. In such works as *Hervey's Meditations,* the illustrations to the Bible, the title page of *Genesis,* the engravings for *The Book of Job,* the *Arlington Court Picture,* and the Milton illustrations, Blake creates a coherent iconography or myth that defines the natures of Jesus, of man's epic fall and redemption, of the correct mode of perception (the divine analogy), and of Innocence in the modern world. All these designs visually celebrate the human form divine.

In addition, after 1805 Blake's art moves toward a closer union of the natural and spiritual worlds. Illusionistic details tend to reappear, as in the visionary landscapes that serve as background for some of the illustrations to *Job,* the Bible, Milton, and Thornton's *Virgil.* And Blake's palette becomes stronger and more varied, although his color effects are still limited by his watercolor and tempera media.

Blake's *Epitome of James Hervey's "Meditations Among the Tombs"*

243

(1807–10), like his various *Visions of the Last Judgment,* offers a complex visual statement of Blake's mature conception of Jehovah, of Jesus, of human history, and of man's relationship to God [*Plate 64*]. The figure of Jesus, flanked by Moses and Elias at the lower center of the design, clearly dominates the picture and fuses into a single image the various personalities and events that surround him. At the top of the design, in a circle of fire, sits God the Father, Jehovah as lawgiver with a scroll on his lap.[1] But this white-haired patriarch is not the Urizen of the Tate Gallery color-print series, the evil demiurge of the fallen body, but rather the embodiment of the sublime wrath—that "voice of honest indignation" (E 38)—that inspired the prophet-bards, Enoch and Noah, who stand or float beneath him. Blake clarifies this in his caption: "God out of Christ is a Consuming Fire." Jehovah is both the righteous anger of the just man Rintrah, who has been driven into barren wilds, and the sublime fury that inspired the creation of the tyger; he is the personification of divinely inspired "WRATH," as the inscription in the upper right corner suggests. But he is also the God of the "MERCY" inscribed in the upper left corner. The flames of the jealous Jehovah are tempered by the water of Christ's mercy, specifically the baptismal water lying in the fount at the lower left. Both anger (revolutionary Energy) and mercy (forgiveness of sins) are necessary to Blake's religious system.

The figures between Jehovah and Christ define the ways in which man can and cannot achieve the divine vision. "Abraham believed God" and this faith both in God's law and in his ultimate mercy, together with his obedience, led him to see God face to face. But the false idolatry and doubt of Aaron must be redeemed by Christ's mercy (Aaron is moving down the staircase *toward* Jesus). Significantly, Aaron wears, not the form-revealing, rhythmically linear draperies of the prophets, of Abraham, of the mother of Rebecca and the mother of Leah (two daughters of Beulah who represent the mothers of mankind), but rather the stiff robes of the covering cherub and the heavy, form-concealing breastplate orna-

---

1. Irene Tayler points out that in his illustrations to Gray, Blake "frequently opposes books to scrolls: books, squared off and hard, symbolize knowledge measured and contained (cf. "Ode to Adversity," Plate 4; "The Progress of Poesy," Plate 2); scrolls more often bear the products of inspiration" (*Blake's Illustrations to the Poems of Gray* [Princeton, 1971], p. 83n).

Plate 64. *Epitome of James Hervey's "Meditations among the Tombs,"* Tate Gallery.

mented with Newton's zodiac. Beneath Aaron stands the figure of rationality, Solomon, with crown and compasses in his right hand. Solomon is also moving down the stairs toward Christ; his critical intellect must be joined with David's inspiration—David passes at his side with crown and harp. Together they represent the majestic union of reason (the intellectual precision of the compasses) and imagination (the creative art of the harp).

And in the center, including all, stands Jesus, the transfigured "Jesus . . . alone" (*Luke* 9:36), fusing the law of Moses on the left with the divine vision of the prophet Elias, surrounded by flames, on the right. Because they are patterned on the life of Christ, the sacraments of the Christian Church (baptism, the eucharist) have created a system that forgives sins and enables the maids and mothers, fathers and children pictured in both margins to be redeemed into the divine vision, the true Christian community. Pervasive Gothic motifs emphasize the eternal truth of Hervey's vision. In Blake's late art, Gothic motifs replace Greek motifs as the vocabulary of the sublime language of primal imaginative vision. Although Blake continued to base his visual style on the idealized human figures and outlines of antique sculptures and vase-painting, he now denounced Greek and Roman art as derivative and overly restricted to rules. "Grecian is Mathematic Form   Gothic is Living Form   Mathematical Form is Eternal in the Reasoning Memory.   Living Form is Eternal Existence" ("On Virgil," 1820, E 267). Here, Abraham kneels before a medieval stained-glass window; Gothic arches support the communion table; steep Gothic arches ascend both margins of the design; and the overall structure of the design is a Gothic arch with the circle of Jehovah at its apex and Christ at the center of the "stained glass" panels within it. Hervey's vision, then, is a true, organized image of the nature of God who is both law and mercy; of man's capacity for redemption; and of Christ's forgiveness of sins that grants us life everlasting through "Living Form" and the vision of Innocence.

Christ as the reconciler of law and mercy, of Old Testament anger and New Testament love, of reason and imagination, appears again and again in Blake's late religious paintings. In *Christ Offers to Redeem Man* (*Par-*

adise Lost, 1808, Plate 4), Jehovah—who is seated in the same crouched, squared position as are Vala on Plate 51 of *Jerusalem* [*Plate 84*], Urizen on the frontispiece of *The Book of Ahania* (1795), and Albion who buries his head in the book of Mosaic law on his knees on Plate 41 [37] of *Jerusalem*—is here partially hidden behind the open arms of Christ. Here Christ has absorbed Jehovah (reason and law) in his embrace, subordinated law to imagination, and thereby conquered the accuser, Satan, who scowls in defeat beneath the pair. In the twelfth illustration to *Paradise Lost, Michael Foretells the Crucifixion* [*Plate 65*], Christ, reborn upon the cross, triumphs over all three evils prostrated at his feet. The dead, old, bearded and crowned man rotting on the ground to the left of the cross is Urizen, the spectrous perversion of law and intellect; the Scylla with three dog heads at her waist who lies in defeat at the right of the cross represents Rahab, the perversions of the church and the female will (Blake also uses this Scylla figure to represent Milton's "Sin"); and the slain serpent head of Satan, the accuser of moral sin, is nailed beneath Christ's crucified feet. Surrounding Christ are the three triumphant faculties of redeemed man. On the left is Michael, the warrior of imagination who fights with helmet and spear for the divine vision. On the right is Adam, or Albion (Christ reborn as the second Adam), the human form divine rendered incarnate in the mind, emotions and energies of mortal man. (This figure of Adam as the mortal embodiment of the human form divine also appears on both title pages of the Huntington copy of *Genesis,* where a haloed Adam reaches out to and joins both Christ at the left and Jehovah at the right.) And beneath them, bedded in the earth, sleeps Eve, the regenerative daughter of Beulah who submissively clothes the creations of Adam, giving them a determinate form and a physical substance.

In *The Christ Child Asleep on a Cross Laid on the Ground* (1805, in the collection of George Goyder), Christ strikingly combines the attributes of both the Old Testament God of law and reason and the New Testament God of love and mercy. On the right stands Joseph, holding a compass; while the L-square with which he measures the cross-shaped coffin lies on the ground. Facing Joseph on the left is Mary, her hands clasped in prayer. Her figure is backed by a living plant composed of a

Plate 65. Michael foretells the Crucifixion, from the illustrations for *Paradise Lost,* Plate 12, Museum of Fine Arts, Boston.

weeping willow, lilies, and roses, flowers that symbolize her sorrow, compassion, and love.[2] Structurally and thematically, the two figures of Joseph and Mary are linked by the trunk of the cross-coffin placed on the ground between them and by the child who voluntarily lies on this coffin, filling its shape with his body. By accepting with open arms the outline of the mortal body, the Christ child also accepts the rational laws of his father which insist that mortal man must live a corporeal life that includes physical pain and death. But because Christ is the divine imagination, he can use the outlines of the mortal body and of natural and social laws to reveal rather than deny the divine vision. (Christ's ability to use reason and bounded forms to convey his message of salvation is emphasized in *Christ in the House of the Carpenter* where the Christ child himself holds the compasses and L-square of reason, manipulating them to his own purposes.) Here his open arms also proffer the mercy of his mother, the new life of the willow tree, and the love and forgiveness of sins that make man divine on earth. This same union of law and love in the body of Christ also appears in Blake's Bible design, *Christ the Mediator*. Here again, Christ's opened arms embrace both the angelic compassion and mercy of the golden-haired woman surrounded by six angels at the left and the wrathful law of the old, white-haired and bearded Jehovah, seated on his throne, scepter in right hand, in flames at the right. The angel kneeling beside Jehovah's throne emphasizes that this law or discipline is holy; and Christ's open arms accept without despair both the outlines of the mortal body and the crucifixion and suffering entailed by mortality. Christ is serene and serious (his facial expression is much like Los's on *Jerusalem* 100); he remains confident of his capacity to mediate and reconcile the divine vision and the limits of mortality.

In addition to portraying the physical human form divine, the figure of Christ with open arms, Blake's late art frequently depicts the divine vision or "Divine Analogy" through which man sees himself as God. Blake's masterful illustrations to *The Book of Job* (1825) celebrate the expansion of Job's vision. By deliberately rejecting the single logic of the accuser,

---

2. For a detailed analysis of the symbolism of the lily and the rose in Blake's poetry and art, see John Grant's "Two Flowers in the Garden of Experience," *Blake Essays for Damon*, ed. A. Rosenfield (Providence, R. I., 1969), pp. 333–67.

Job moves from a passive faith in Jehovah into the active analogical vision of God-Christ, into the ever-present consciousness that God is man, that Job can become divine. Job's epic trial begins in the pastoral arcadia of Thel's Vales of Har: on Plate 1 [*Plate 66*], Job prays with his family in a peaceful pastoral idyll surrounded by sheep, shepherd, tents, and the Gothic church of living art. But the sun is setting and Job and his family, neglecting the musical instruments hung on the tree above them, only read "the letter" that "killeth," the Lord's Prayer, from books on Job's lap, rather than create their own vision of God.[3] Even the sheep are sleeping or sluggish, and the sheep dog snoozes, oblivious to his duties of guardianship. Job and his dependents have not yet found the way actively to realize and manifest their potential divinity or energetically to conquer the mind-forged manacles of Satan soon to be thrust upon them. Nonetheless, the marginal designs on the second plate establish that this is a valley of Innocence where Job could realize the divine vision and see that everything is holy. In the margins, sheepfolds guarded by a shepherd and shepherdess give rise to living Gothic arches filled with birds, incense, flames, and angels. But Job thinks that man shall become God only after his physical death and spiritual rebirth: "We shall wake up . . . in thy likeness." And the denier of all divine vision, Satan the accuser, already flames before Jehovah on Plate 3, eager to undermine Job's incomplete faith. And we see that Job has actually already lost the divine vision of Innocence. Rather than seeing himself as divine, Job has externalized his God into the Father. As both Northrop Frye and Ben Nelms have emphasized, the Jehovah of Plates 2, 5, and 11 *is* Satan, Job's own perverse projection of his divine humanity outward as an abstract lawgiver and omnipotent accuser.[4] The Jehovah who could permit the torments Satan executes on Job is, in Blake's eyes, the cause of them. Satan's batwings on Plate 3 clearly link him to the spectre in *Milton* and *The Four Zoas,* the voice of guilt, legalistic doubt, and despair, the rhetorician of sin and mas-

3. S. Foster Damon and Jean Hagstrum also see the silenced instruments and setting sun as signs of Job's failure to recognize the true God; *Blake's Job* (Providence, R.I., 1966), p. 12, and *Blake, Poet and Painter* (Chicago, 1964), p. 132.

4. Northrop Frye, "Blake's Reading of the *Book of Job*," *Blake Essays for Damon,* ed. A Rosenfield, p. 227; Ben Nelms, "Text and Design in *Illustrations of the Book of Job,*" *Blake's Visionary Forms Dramatic,* ed. D. V. Erdman and J. E. Grant (Princeton, 1970), p. 338.

Plate 66. *The Book of Job*, Plate 1, British Museum.

ochistic self-condemnation. Even the Herculean efforts of Job's eldest son cannot save his brethren from the tortures of this vicious Satan.

Job's sufferings in the world of fallen Experience thus test his imaginative capacity to overcome the evils that exist in contemporary society and with which all men must cope to a greater or lesser degree if the divine vision is to survive. An imagination that cannot overcome the physical sufferings, emotional griefs, and mind-forged manacles of mortality is no real imagination: the vision of Innocence, as the *Songs of Experience, The Marriage of Heaven and Hell,* and *America* showed, must be affirmed by active opposition to all forms of repression, through satire or prophetic art or political revolution.

In spite of the destruction of his flocks and children, Job continues to live the Christian life on Plate 5, generously sharing his last loaf of bread with the crippled beggar at his door. But a huge snake and briars coil along the margins of Plate 5, and a trilithon looms ominously in the left background; the cruel Jehovah has given Satan control over all but Job's death. And Job continues to worship this Jehovah, even after his children have been killed, his property destroyed, and his own body afflicted with boils. Job suffers and grieves greatly on Plate 8, especially since his friend Eliphas insists that Job alone is responsible for his sufferings (Plate 9); but he remains faithful to his mistaken notion that this Jehovah is the ultimate lawgiver and a benevolent ruler—"Though he slay me yet will I trust in him" (Plate 10).

Satan then appears before Job, first in the guise of the three "Comforters" who are actually three accusers, for they tell Job that his excessive suffering must surely be a punishment for his sins (Plate 10). For would a just God torment him so severely if he had not sinned? As Blake had written decades earlier in *The Marriage of Heaven and Hell,* "in the Book of Job Miltons Messiah is call'd Satan," Milton's messiah being of course "the Governor or Reason" and "a Ratio of the five senses" (E 34–5). Satan then reveals his identity with Job's vision of Jehovah, a jealous God of law and wrath who imposes the Ten Commandments on fallen man and who demands, in Job's dream on Plate 11, that Job submit to his authority. That this Jehovah *is* Satan is revealed both by the cloven hoof emerging from Jehovah's robes and by the serpent twining around

Jehovah's body. The composition of the design, which closely resembles that of *God Creating Adam* [*Plate 39*], also suggests that this Satan is the rationalistic demiurge of *The Book of Urizen* and the Tate Gallery color prints. Both the comforters and this satanic Jehovah impose logic and reason on human experience: if God is good and if a man suffers, then it must be his own fault, for a good God would never punish a man without sufficient cause.

Convinced of his innocence, Job resists the temptation to doubt himself; he recognizes his error in setting God above himself and insists that "in my flesh shall I see God" (Plate 11). Job will see God face to face, both the false Jehovah imaged here, and also the true God he now acknowledges to exist "in my flesh." The young Elihu further points the way to "the light of the living," where Job shall behold himself as the one man; [5] and Job now realizes that he alone has the power "to bring/ back his Soul from the pit to be enlightened/ with the light of the living" (Plate 12). Job has now become aware of the potential divinity within himself. Therefore, on Plates 13 and 14, Job perceives the divine "light of the living" face to face. God appears before him, truly revealed both in the whirlwind and as the creator of the morning stars, of the sun and moon, of heaven and earth. Throughout these engravings, Job and his God have been visually identified as white-haired, bearded, robed patriarchs with similar body structures and facial expressions.[6] Here, the revelation of the true God before the cowering Accusers signifies Job's recognition of his own divine humanity.

Job has now triumphed over the temptations of Satan. The state of Satan, of self-accusation, sin, and perverted energy—here represented by Leviathan and Behemoth, the serpent or crocodile of "the War by Sea enormous" and the hippopotamus of "the War by Land astounding" (E 249), identified with the pharaoh of Egypt (*Ezekiel* 29) and Nebuchadnezzar (*Daniel* 4), respectively—is now strictly confined to the circle of

5. Ben Nelms has demonstrated that Blake's Elihu is not another accuser, repeating the arguments of his elders, but rather a poetic genius, a persona for Blake himself, who shows Job that, not clouds, but humanized stars blaze above him, revealing the divine message that man can be god (*ibid.*, pp. 344–51). Jean Hagstrum also makes this point; *Blake, Poet and Painter*, p. 134.

6. Joseph Wicksteed makes this point in *Blake's Vision of the Book of Job* (London, 1910), Plate 13.

the fallen world (Plate 15); and Satan himself is wholly cast out (Plate 16). Job, by recognizing and rejecting his satanic tendency to see God as an abstracted power, a potential accuser and destroyer, has realized the divine vision of Innocence articulated in the New Testament and inscribed on the bottom of Plate 17: "At that day ye shall know that I am in/ my Father & you in me & I in you." Job has now consciously experienced his identity with Jesus and God: "He that hath seen me hath seen my Father also I & my Father are One." The pen and ink, brushes and palette, books and scrolls in the margins of Plate 18 now provide Job with a medium or language in which to communicate this divine vision. Knowing that the human form divine always exists potentially on earth, even amid mortal suffering, disease, and death, and knowing that a last judgment is available at all times to all men, Job now gratefully accepts the true comfort of his friends, the everlasting bounty of their love—pieces of money—and of abundant nature—roses, lilies, wheat, and pineapples blossom in the margins of Plate 19. And Job, like Oothoon, dedicates his life to teaching this divine vision to his daughters, using the symbolic structures of poetry (his hymns of praise), of painting (frescoes depicting the destruction of his sons and crops, and the appearance of the true God in the whirlwind are on the wall in Plate 20), and of music (his lyre and lute lie in the lower corners of the design). Thus Job realizes his potential divinity and achieves life everlasting: on Plate 21, we see him once again in the vales of Innocence, surrounded by his loving family, now actively playing his musical instruments of worship and singing hymns of joy as the sun rises in the east and the sheep look up expectantly [*Plate* 67]. Job's poetic genius now consciously creates and communicates the divine analogy in song and design; his Innocence is now "organized" into a firm and determinate system of perception and behavior. By learning to suffer pain without seeing it as an unjust punishment, by learning to forgive sins and to perceive the holiness of everything that lives, Job has fully realized his potential divinity; he is now the human form divine.

In addition to portraying the physical nature of the human form divine and depicting the expansion of man's (for example, Job's) vision through the divine analogy in his late art, Blake vigorously denounced the domination of the abstract rational intellect and of the female will—of a

Plate 67. *The Book of Job,* Plate 21, British Museum.

conception of the human mind and body as earthbound and constricted. The energetic rejection of the female will (the domination of chastity, sexual repression, and a conviction of sin) and of rational or empiricist thought is celebrated both in Blake's *Arlington Court Picture* and in his illustrations for Milton's *L'Allegro* and *Il Penseroso*. Blake portrays and rejects the domination of Vala in the large watercolor found at Arlington Court in 1947 and entitled *The Circle of the Life of Man* by Geoffrey Keynes [*Plate 68*].[7] In opposition to the Neoplatonic interpretation of this painting as the descent and return of souls from the sea of time and space put forth by Damon and Raine,[8] I read this design as the attempt of the veiled lady or Vala (the female will) to entice Albion (the universal man or poet) into the fallen "sleep of Ulro." Here, Vala's attempt fails. Despite her allurements, Albion vigorously rejects her circle of corrupt life and reaches instead toward another and presumably better world beyond the confines of the painting, perhaps toward the world of the divine vision.

Before I discuss further the significance of the figures in this complex painting, I would like to look at the composition of the design.[9] In contrast to Robert Simmons and Janet Warner who see the structure as a

7. Geoffrey Keynes, "Blake's Vision of the Circle of the Life of Man," *Studies in Art for Belle da Costa Greene* (Princeton, 1954), p. 205.

8. See Foster Damon, *A Blake Dictionary* (Providence, Rhode Island, 1965), pp. 86–87; and Kathleen Raine, "The Sea of Time and Space," *Journal of the Warburg and Courtauld Institutes* 20 (1957):318–37 (included in her *Blake and Tradition* [Princeton, 1968], pp. 75–98).

9. Although Northrop Frye and John Grant argue that the geometry of a (representational) painting is what we attend to last as we back away from it (in *Fables of Identity* [New York, 1963], p. 13; and "Redemptive Action in Blake's *Arlington Court Picture*," *Studies in Romanticism* 10 [1971]:22, respectively), I agree with Simmons and Warner that the composition or "blocking" of a design is what occurs to an artist first; details and color are added later. Blake's early emphasis on geometry over "minute particulars" is especially evident if we compare the preliminary drawing for the *Arlington Court Picture*, *The River of Oblivion* (reproduced by Robert Simmons and Janet Warner, "Blake's *Arlington Court Picture*: The Moment of Truth," *Studies in Romanticism* 10 [1971]) with the final design. In the drawing, the formal emphasis is placed on the right side and bottom of the design: we see a heavily blocked-in, backwards L, on whose "lap" are placed the conjurer and the veiled lady. Vaguely sketched in flying figures descend toward the conjurer from the lady's outstretched left arm, initiating the circular pattern which Blake will define more sharply in the final painting. The overall effect of the geometry of the drawing is to confine the conjurer more tightly within the three-sided frame, pushing him closer to the only open space in the drawing, at the left.

Plate 68. The Arlington Court Picture: *The Circle of the Life of Man*, National Trust.

small circle in the upper left and a large triangle in the lower right,[10] I see the geometry of the design as a large circle or, more accurately, a reversed C enclosing the left two-thirds of the painting. This reversed C is tangent to an upright rectangle that forms the right third of the work. My eye instinctively traces this backward C from upper left to lower right, beginning with the spiraling smoke or cloud wreath above the head of the "sea goddess." This wreath widens into two parallel circling movements, rounding past the chariot of the "sky god" and proceeding down the steps before the chariot. The leftward movement then descends along

10. Simmons and Warner, "Blake's *Arlington Court Picture*," pp. 5–6.

the cliffs and over the temple, and then moves left along the shoreline, behind the two major figures, and drops into the sea at the lower left. This movement is repeated in a parallel sweep to the right, circling downward from the top right frame, along the manes of the four horses, down the trunks of the two large, left-most trees (the curve from the horses to the tree trunk is strongly reinforced by the leftward arching branch of the tree to the right). The circle then sweeps back to the left along the trunk roots of both trees and through the arms of the large male figure at the bottom left, and ends at the same point as the inner circle, with the shears of Atropos, the first of the three fates. Theoretically, the circle could continue beyond the left frame of the picture and begin again with the sea goddess' wreath. But it seems significant that Blake did not define the left quarter of this circle and instead leaves the design of this portion of the painting open. What my eyes see is a reversed C with the bottom stroke curving down rather than up, very like the reversed flowing wheat stalk curling round the top of Plate 9 of *Europe* or the upside-down C-shape of the dragon in *St. Michael Binding the Dragon* [*Plate* 69]. Perhaps Blake is suggesting that there is a possible escape from this circle, rather like the visionary escape offered in "The Mental Traveller." It may also be significant that, while the circle itself seems to move clockwise, from upper left to lower right and possible escape, Vala's pointing hands try to make the circle move counterclockwise, beginning with the fates at the bottom and moving to the sea goddess at the upper left. It almost seems that Vala is trying to deny the very existence of the open left quarter.

The upright rectangle on the right is sharply outlined on the left by the large tree trunks in the right-center of the picture; on its top by the tree branches, leaves, and arbor or cave ceiling at the upper right; at the right by the frame and vertical tree trunks; and at its bottom by the steps. Although we cannot fully define the meaning of this structure until we have identified the numerous figures in the painting, it is worth noting here that the design is both severely geometrical and strongly divided into distinct segments. Even if one's eye begins with the smaller circle in the upper left described by Simmons and Warner—the sea goddess, sky god, stairs, the arms of the veiled lady, and the outstretched arms of the man in red—this smaller circle immediately spirals out into the larger

Plate 69. St. Michael Binding the Dragon, Fogg Art Museum.

circle I have traced. But the rectangle on the right remains separate from this swirling movement, fixed and static. Tentatively, I would suggest that the arms of the man in red, stretched out to the left, are rejecting the closed forms on the right for the only open area in the design.

The identity of Vala, the veiled lady in the pose of the traditional *Venus Genetrix* in the center of the painting, can be iconographically es-

tablished by reference to similar symbols and motifs in other Blake designs. This figure's diaphanous pale blue veils associate her with the figure
of Vala on Plate 32 [46] of *Jerusalem,* who is draped in a dark-blue robe
and who stands, in a reverse image of this veiled lady, with her back to us
but with her left arm also raised and her right foot similarly forward.[11]
The veiled lady's pale golden hair, which closely resembles a golden net
as it flows along her raised left arm, further links her to the golden-
haired, redeemed Vala on the final colored Plate 28 of *Jerusalem* [*Plate*
80] and, more negatively, with the "Net of Golden twine" with which
the three virgins of desire, iron repression, and sorrow trap and imprison
the helpless youth in "The Golden Net" (ca. 1803; E 474). That this
veiled lady is the sinister temptress Vala suggested by Simmons and
Warner [12] is further supported first, by the close resemblance of this lady
to the figures of Plato in *Milton and the Spirit of Plato* [*Plate* 74] and of
Juno in *The Judgment of Paris* (1817). Both Plato and the veiled lady
stand beside a seated youth and both point one hand downward—Plato
to his pernicious book and Vala to the struggling fates beneath her feet
—and the other hand upward—Plato to the domination of Venus, the
expulsion from Eden, and the triumph of the three fates and Vala to the
women towelling the horses above her head. Like Plato, this veiled lady
tries to seduce the youth beside her into believing a fallen vision of the
mortal body as evil. And Juno also points upward with her raised left
arm, offering material wealth, earthly fame, and the power to rule and repress to the seated Paris at her right who, like the youth seated beside
Vala here, rejects her gifts. This veiled lady even more closely resembles
the veiled figures of *Evening* in Blake's illustration to Cowper's "The
Task" and of Beatrice in Blake's illustration for the *Divine Comedy, Bea-*

---

11. This figure has been identified as Vala by both Keynes ("Blake's Vision," p. 205)
and Damon (*Dictionary,* p. 87). Those critics who see her as Jerusalem—George W.
Digby, *Symbol and Image in William Blake* (Oxford, 1957), p. 75; John Beer, *Blake's
Visionary Universe* (Manchester, England, 1969), p. 289; John Grant, "You Can't
Write About Blake's Pictures Like That," *Blake Studies* I (Spring 1969:199)—all fail
to explain why Jerusalem here wears a veil, is clothed in blue (in *Jerusalem* she typically wears white or is naked), or exactly resembles the sea goddess whom Digby and
Beer agree in calling Vala. Nor do they explain why, if this central female figure *is* Jerusalem the bride, the man in red turns *away* from her and reaches, not for his bride,
but for the sea or something beyond it.

12. Simmons and Warner, "Blake's *Arlington Court Picture,*" pp. 8–9, 14.

trice Addressing Dante from the Car. Evening, carrying a thorn-tipped sceptre and wearing Greek sandals and a nun's veil, draws another gray veil over her head with her raised left arm in a gesture identical with Vala's. Evening's veil is specifically described by Cowper as "the curtain of repose" that falls on bird and beast and is further linked with the "sweet oblivion" that descends on man, cutting him off from eternity.[13] Beatrice, who also stands on her car with right arm pointing down, left hand pointing up, beneath a golden net veil, her body in the *Venus Genetrix* position but swayed to the right rather than the left, closely resembles the veiled lady both visually and iconographically. As Albert S. Roe has shown, this Beatrice is Blake's female will or Rahab, the fallen state of Vala. Her spiked golden crown (substituted for Dante's olive wreath), her book of faith or law, and the self-enclosed vortex that serves as the wheel of her car all iconographically establish her negative identity as the female will incarnate.[14] Returning to the veiled lady, we see that she too points up and down, tempting the man in red to enter her curtain of oblivion and the cycle of female domination. These sinister implications of the veiled lady are iconographically emphasized in the preliminary drawing where the lady's veil is covered with at least six stars, in addition to what is perhaps an eye and four round objects (which John Grant identifies as grapes,[15] but which also look something like the body and wings of an insect). This single eye, which may represent the first eye of God, Lucifer the egotist (*Milton* 13: 17–27), this possible insect (under Rahab–Vala's domination in Blake's late poetry, man "becomes a human insect" [16]), and these six stars (which Blake usually associated with Urizen or Newton and the oppressions of reason) are distinctly inauspicious symbols. Notably, this painting is dominated by women—it contains fourteen large and over twenty small female figures and only three large and three small male figures.

13. William Cowper, "The Task," Bk. IV, ll. 248–50.
14. Albert S. Roe, *Blake's Illustrations to the Divine Comedy* (Princeton, 1953), pp. 164–71.
15. "Discussing the *Arlington Court Picture*, II," *Blake Newsletter* 4 (August 1970):23.
16. E. J. Rose has noted that, in the caterpillar-fly cycle in Blake's late poetry, "man under Rahab-Vala's rule becomes a human insect"; "Blake's Illustrations for *Paradise Lost, L'Allegro,* and *Il Penseroso,*" *Hartford Studies in Literature* 2 (1970):64.

The man in red, seated beside Vala, has been variously associated with Los or Blake as the lonely artist or rebel pictured on *Jerusalem* 30 [44] (by Simmons and Warner), with Philoctetes in *Philoctetes and Neoptolemus at Lemnos* (by Grant) and with the visionary head of the *Man Who Taught Blake Painting* (also by Grant).[17] Although of these three, only Philoctetes wears a scraggly version of the short, trimmed beard of the man in red, all three closely resemble this figure in body structure or position. Perhaps more important, we do find the same short, trimmed beard on Blake's portraits of Christ in his late works, as for instance in *Christ Girding Himself with Strength, Christ the Mediator, The Creation of Eve* (for *Paradise Lost*) and *Christ's Troubled Dream* (for *Paradise Regained*). And the knight in Blake's illustration for Chaucer's *Canterbury Tales* also wears such a short, trimmed, reddish beard. All these visual associations reinforce our initial impression that this man is the hero of the painting with whom we are asked to identify. His bright red robe and golden-red hair contrast sharply with the quieter coloring of the rest of the painting and immediately attract our eyes. Moreover, since he is the only figure in the painting with whom we can make direct eye contact, we naturally sympathize with him and see in him, quite rightly I think, an image of ourselves, of the divine human imagination or Energy contained within the mortal body.[18]

This everyman or poetic genius stretches out his arms to the left in a yearning or conjuring gesture. He is pointing or reaching to a world beyond the frame of this design and Vala's fallen world. Perhaps, in order to escape Vala's domination, he must first conjure or lay a spell upon the waters that seem to be rising.[19] Like Moses, he may need to part the waters of the (Red) sea in order to reach the promised land beyond the confines of the painting. Moreover, his outstretched hands repeat the gesture of the demonic conjurer seated on a cloud at the upper right of the title page for

17. Simmons and Warner, "Blake's *Arlington Court Picture*," p. 15; Grant, "Discussing the *Arlington Court Picture*, I," *Blake Newsletter* 3 (May 1970): 100.

18. Digby sees this male figure as Albion or Jesus (*Symbol and Image*, p. 65, fig. 60) and Geoffrey Keynes also identifies this male figure as "the ideal Man—Adam Kadmon of the Cabbala, Blake's Albion (the personification of Britain), Blake's Christ, or all three at the same time" ("Blake's Vision," p. 205).

19. Simmons and Warner first noted the rising sea, "Blake's *Arlington Court Picture*," p. 10.

Visions of the Daughters of Albion. But rather than creating and enforcing the enslaved kingdom of Bromion, this conjurer in red must, as John Grant says, "undo the damage done by his prototype" [20] and create a new Jerusalem on earth.

The fallen circle of female domination that this hero rejects begins, as I have suggested, with the sea goddess. This woman is the physical double of the central female figure and is, moreover, directly linked to Vala by an "arrow head" or double row of dots or bubbles running from her right foot to Vala's head. She is further associated with female generation by the horns of her hair—which resemble both the crescent hairstyle of a female devil in the Leconfield *Satan Calling his Legions* [21] and the crescent moon above the head of the moon-goddess on *Job* 14. Although these moon associations evoke Beulah's "moony shades and hills" (*Milton* 30:15), they take on a sinister connotation here. The moon is rising; the sun has set; night is coming. The daylit valley of vision is fading. The moon as a negative image also appears on Plate 7 of *Il Penseroso, Melancholy and her Companions* [*Plate 73*], where the female kneeling in the crescent moon on the right is drawn by two serpents with bat wings. Although the serpents function here, as they do in *Job* 14, as the traditional emblem of eternity or rebirth, their bat wings clearly indicate the satanic chastity of Melancholy. The fact that this woman rides her dark horses through the sea (her chariot and part of her body are submerged in the water)—a sea that is associated with materialism, physical generation and oppression in *The Book of Urizen*, Plate 12, in "Earth's Answer," and in *The Gates of Paradise*, Figures 2 and 10 [*Plates 11, 19*]—further links her to those fallen daughters of Beulah, Rahab, and Tirzah, who weave an imprisoning garment for the human form divine. As I have discussed in connection with *Milton*, this female garment can be either oppressive or redemptive, depending on whether it dominates or serves the male imagination.

Here, the moon goddess or Vala's handmaiden seems to triumph over the male sky god rather than submit to him. He is asleep, and the rays of the double-nimbus sun (four of which are tipped with lightning) behind

20. Grant, "Redemptive Action in Blake's *Arlington Court Picture*," p. 25.
21. Noted by Grant, *ibid.*, p. 24.

him are surrounded and perhaps in the process of being "devoured" by her dark smoke ring or clouds, as Rintrah's fiery lightning was surrounded and perhaps engulfed by the "hungry" clouds in the Argument for *The Marriage of Heaven and Hell*. Moreover, the yellow inner nimbus is circled by a blue outer nimbus; perhaps Vala's blue veil (pictured on *J* 32 [46] [*Plate 83*]) is circumscribing the yellow and "more bright" sun of the imagination. Not only is the great sun being darkened; perhaps the sun god himself is being perverted into a force of oppression as well. His recumbent position is identical with that of the half-drowned, sleeping woman in the lower right corner; and John Grant has further noted the similarity of this sky god to the tyrant-king or Jupiter in *Milton and the Spirit of Plato* [*Plate 74*]: both carry a sceptre and sit with their left foot depressed.[22] Perhaps, like the God who judges Adam from his chariot of fire [*Plate 40*], this sky god has also become a tyrannical demiurge or, at best, a passive denier of his innate creative Energy. But his facial similarity to the man in red and his physical resemblance to Christ in *Christ Girding Himself with Strength* underline the irony of this figure: he, like all men, is potentially a divine creator, but here his imaginative vision has been overwhelmed by sleep and the seductions of the daughters of Vala.[23] The music played by the horn blowers beside and behind his chariot lulls rather than wakes him. His white horses (also driven by the sun in *Job* 14) are now unharnessed and held back by four women; the women on the right even seems to be blinding her horse as she towels him. These four fiery Pegasuses are here unbridled, no longer under the control of the sky god, and further prevented from crossing the heavens by the female will (note that these horses are now seated or backed down on the steps; they are passive, exhausted). Moreover, as Simmons and Warner have suggestively noted, since this sky god or sun god is shown descending to the west at the upper left, we must assume that we are looking at him from the north; we are witnessing "not only a daily descent into night, but a seasonal descent into winter." [24] Appropriately, Vala's domain thus

22. Grant, "Discussing the *Arlington Court Picture*, I," p. 102.
23. Digby has identified the sky god's attendants as daughters of Beulah; *Symbol and Image*, p. 68.
24. Simmons and Warner, "Blake's *Arlington Court Picture*," p. 10.

lies in the wintry north, the home of Urizen and all physical and psychological oppressions.

If the sun god woke up and proceeded down the stairs on which his chariot is stationed, he would come not to the upper cave (with which the stairs do not connect) but into the rear of the lower, flaming cave where three women ply their shuttles at their looms. Their wooden-frame loom and shuttles closely resemble the industrial common carpet loom and the shuttle held by the seated woman at the left of the Persian carpet loom at the bottom of Blake's engraved advertisement for Moore & Co.'s Manufactory and Warehouse Carpeting and Hosiery (1797–98). And these female weavers with outstretched arms, shuttles in hand, also resemble the woman with her distaff and shuttle on Plate 100 of *Jerusalem* [*Plate 86*]; like her, they are weaving the "sexual garments" or physical bodies that the male imagination must wear. But unlike Enitharmon and the daughters of Beulah who weave "a Garment of Pity & Compassion" at the golden looms of Cathedron (*Milton* 18:35), these women weave the clothing of cruelty at the industrial looms of Rahab and Tirzah (*Milton* 18:20). Their association with Rahab-Tirzah is suggested both by their red hair (Blake's whore of Babylon has red hair in his Bible illustration of her triumph, 1809; there may also be a connection between the curious hair knots or crowns on the heads of these three weavers and the whore's triple-tiered papal crown) and by the configuration of their three raised arms which echoes the three pointing arms of the accusers on *Jerusalem* 93 and, more importantly, the three raised, rock-hurling arms of the men on the left in *The Stoning of Achan,* or *The Blasphemer.*

The thread that these three women weave emerges as the thread wound into a skein of yarn held by a girl at the foot of the left tree [25] and rolled into a ball of yarn by the woman standing at the left of the staircase. This thread has also been twisted into rope which is then woven into a net held by the woman standing on the right of the stairs, a net that

---

25. Unlike Grant, I do not see this girl as the "most satisfied" in the picture ("Discussing the *Arlington Court Picture,* I," p. 103). Her "half-smile" is no more marked than that of the woman standing on the right side of the staircase; and the girl's expression strikes me as one rather more of awe than pleasure. It may be worth noting that whatever she sees as she gazes upward is framed by the oval hoop of her skein; her vision is thus necessarily bounded.

seems almost to graft the small woman behind the second tree on the right to the bark of that tree. Simmons and Warner have perceptively noted that the woman holding the ball of yarn at the left, the woman with the rope and net at the right, and the woman carrying the scaled bucket between them are a parody of the three graces as they traditionally appear in Renaissance paintings, particularly in Botticelli's *Primavera*.²⁶ Here, they are the perversion of the female form divine, the triple Hecate or domination of superstition, chastity, and female will (compare [*Plate* 42]). The braided rope appears again, rolled upon the distaff held by the shell-helmeted man at the bottom, and unwound by the three fates (who closely resemble the three fates or destinies in *Milton and the Spirit of Plato* [*Plate* 74], and have also been associated with Rahab, Tirzah, and Vala ²⁷). The foremost of the three fates, Atropos, ruthlessly cuts the thread with a scissors identical to those used by Delilah to shear Samson in Blake's watercolor, *Samson Subdued* (1805), while Lachesis scowls maliciously behind her. The garments woven with this thread at these looms are garments of "anxiety & care & desperation & death" (*Milton* 18:24), garments of physical and psychological imprisonment, sexual deprivation, and despair.

But what is the significance of the procession in the upper cave, of the girl sleeping in the water at the lower right, and of the girl mounting the stairs with a bucket in her hand? Does this woman carry the water of redemptive baptism, of the pure soul, up the stairs to the procession of women in the cave above, as Simmons and Warner have suggested? ²⁸ The fact that the bucket is scaled strongly implies that its contents are evil (Satan is scaled in *Satan Smiting Job with Sore Boils, ca.* 1818); this is probably the water of death that Damon, Digby, Keynes, and Grant have all seen, ²⁹ taken from the sea of materialism. The girl at the lower right sleeps in this generated matter of the mortal body which has the ca-

---

26. Simmons and Warner, "Blake's *Arlington Court Picture*," p. 16.
27. Grant, "Discussing the *Arlington Court Picture*, I," p. 102.
28. Simmons and Warner, "Blake's *Arlington Court Picture*," p. 16.
29. Damon (*Dictionary*, p. 87), Digby (*Symbol and Image*, p. 83), Keynes ("Blake's Vision," p. 206), and Grant ("Discussing the *Arlington Court Picture*, I," p. 103) all see this water as the evil river of generation and death, variously known as storge, arnon, and pison.

pacity to drown the visionary imagination in eternal death or the "Sleep of Ulro" (as the dreamer is drowned in Figure 10 of *The Gates of Paradise,* [*Plate 19*]). But this female sleeps peacefully in the sea; it is her element and will not harm her. She may even be, as Digby has suggested, a nixie or siren, waiting there to lure sailors to their death.[30] And her visual double, the woman with the bucket and bound-up hair, proceeds up the stairs where she is greeted, rather than threatened,[31] by the two women standing on the stairwell who may recognize her as their helpmate in the subjugation of the male. Her raised left arm and position echo those of both the veiled lady here and, more strikingly, of the blue-veiled Vala on Plate 32 [46] of *Jerusalem* [*Plate 83*]: Vala assumes the same rear-view position and raised, bent left arm. Presumably, her water will sustain the weavers and the looms above (spinning thread must be dampened lest it burn). And her water may even eventually fill the buckets carried on the heads of the winged women marching in the cave; their buckets are very similar in shape to hers. These buckets are most probably the "funeral urns of Beulah" (*Jerusalem* 53:28) in which the ashes of the spiritually dead are preserved. And these walking women resemble a procession of Greek vestal virgins or caryatids, moving circularly; this may well be the "same dull round" or ratio that serves the fallen Greek or Lockean intellectual mills of reasoning. Moreover, this procession remains confined within a closed arbor or cave ("the cavern" of the five senses?), endlessly repeating the "cycle of generation," [32] like the "cold Earth wanderers" trapped in

30. Digby, *Symbol and Image,* p. 85.

31. Keynes ("Blake's Vision," p. 206), Damon (*Dictonary,* p. 87), and Grant ("Discussing the *Arlington Court Picture,* I," p. 102) all see the two women on the staircase as challenging or trying to trap the woman with the bucket. But the woman on the right makes no gesture toward the bucket carrier whatsoever, and her expression is serene, not hostile. The woman on the left does raise her left hand but this gesture, which exactly repeats the position of the left hand of the bucket carrier herself, seems more a greeting or wave of the hand than a threat. And the carrier's facial expression is not certain alarm; I see it rather as the typical Greek female profile. Notably, her face is smooth; no frowns of fear or anxiety appear.

32. Simmons and Warner, "Blake's *Arlington Court Picture,*" p. 18. John Grant doubts that this cave vision is evil and cites the "mossy cell" of Milton (*Il Penseroso,* Plate 6), as an example of a "cave of vision, not of bondage" ("Discussing the *Arlington Court Picture,* I," p. 103). The wings on the women also suggest they may be heavenly angels; but if so, they are angels who have restricted their lives to a singularly confined home and activity. Nonetheless, they *may* represent the divine as opposed to the fallen usage of the body; their head buckets may carry, not the iron garments of

the fallen cycle of "The Mental Traveller." Further, the water carried up to these caryatids in the scaled bucket finally flows back down into the sea from the river jug or culvert at the rear left of the arbor: the cycle of Vala's domination is repeated in the cycle of the water.

The culminating achievement of this perverse cycle of female domination is the wholly fallen man. At the lower end of the C I traced, at the bottom center of the design, we see the product of their looms: their distaff is held by a muscular, horned, shell-helmeted man who actively perverts his energies into aiding their oppressive system. While his right hand holds the distaff for the fates as they draw off and cut the thread of life, his left hand simultaneously scoops up the river water (which is flowing inward from the sea of materialism, to the right), and the fires that feed the looms of restraint. Here, as in the figure of Fire (*The Gates of Paradise* [*Plate 61*]), and *God Judging Adam* [*Plate 40*], the flames of revolutionary Energy have been perverted into instruments of oppression (war, wheels). Fire flows from this man's jug across the water and up into the cave of the weavers.

The Greek motifs throughout the design further emphasize that this is a false circle of life, a Grecian "Mathematic Form" eternal only "in the Reasoning Memory" (in contrast to the Gothic patterns and motifs in the *Paradise Lost* illustrations and *Hervey's Meditations*). A Greek temple stands on the shore beneath Vala's left arm; the arches of both cave and arbor are classically rounded rather than pointed; the caryatids, the chariot of the sky god, the peplos and veil of Vala,[33] the hairstyles of the bucket carrier and sleeping nixie, the figures of the fates, and the conch-shaped helmet of the youth—all help to establish an oppressive Greek environment in which Vala's domination would appropriately occur. Even

---

Rahab, Tirzah, and Vala but the holy form-fitting garments of Jerusalem. (Perhaps this divine union of male and female is represented by the naked couple lying at the left side of the cave; although the river goddess with her urn lying behind them also appears just beneath the barren-breasted, fortress-crowned, female mountain in *The Sunshine Holiday* design for Milton's *L'Allegro*). Significantly, however, these caryatids bring no salvation to the sleeping sky god; and their arbor seems almost inaccessible, except possibly by passing through and beyond the looms and their enveloping flames.

33. In this context, it may be significant that Kathleen Raine associated this veiled lady with Athena, the goddess of rational wisdom, in *Blake and Tradition* (Princeton, 1968), p. 76.

the conjurer-poet in red has a Greek key motif on the hem of his robe: he is only now emerging from Vala's control. By 1820, as he announced in "On Virgil," Blake had turned violently against his earlier adulation of Greek art and condemned the classical influence on English morality, religion, and taste as stultifying.

Parenthetically, we should remember that Blake nonetheless continued to use classical outlines, idealized human figures, strong linear rhythms, and tectonic compositions. In the *Arlington Court Picture,* as elsewhere in his late art, Blake iconographically condemned an imitative neoclassicism while using the heroic human figures, outlines, and closed constructions of romantic classicism. Blake here successfully resolves this tension between an anti-neoclassical iconography and a stylistic dependence upon a neoclassical idiom by introducing positive Gothic motifs into his compositions. In *St. Michael Binding the Dragon* [*Plate* 69], for instance, a classical Michelangelesque nude struggles within a medieval illuminated manuscript's capital letter C. In his Dante illustrations, Blake consistently and harmoniously blends classically posed and constructed figures with Gothic motifs and icons. The five muscular, closely draped classic figures in *Dante and Virgil with Saints Peter, James and John* rotate in overlapping medieval roundels. And in *The Virgin Blest,* or *Inside the Ox's Stall* (Whitworth Gallery copy), the final illustration for Milton's "Hymn on the Morning of Christ's Nativity," the ceiling of the manger rises in a carefully delineated, pointed Gothic arch framed by spandrels of medieval angel-warriors; while inside the manger, the Virgin Mary and Joseph lean beside the Christ child in classically posed and draped linearity. The manifest power and coherence of all these designs compel me to conclude, with David Irwin, that Gothic neoclassicism in Blake's late art is not a contradiction but a subtle, individual, and wholly successful synthesis.[34]

A derivative neoclassicism and this equally false circle of the life of man is vigorously rejected by the man in the red robe seated beside Vala. His arms reach out to the left, away from the seductress beside him; and his eyes stare beyond these female-dominated, nighttime events into the eyes of the viewer, into another world of active creative vision. Like the

34. David Irwin, "Gothic Neoclassicism—A Contradiction?" (paper delivered at Stanford University, April 24, 1968).

mental traveller, this visionary, with whom the spectator identifies, condemns the physical and psychological oppression of Vala's world for a more satisfying realm beyond the cold earth. Interestingly, his body and left foot never touch Vala's veil; visually, Blake has distinguished this man's liberated body from Vala's tyrannies. And Blake has lowered his gaze and the direction of his arms from the Pierpont Morgan Library preliminary drawing; the man in red now faces the reader and denies Vala even more abruptly. This man, the hero of the painting, now seems to be preparing to leap beyond the confines of the five senses into a wholly expansive world of the body and imagination.

This expansive world of imaginative Innocence is vividly depicted in Blake's designs for Milton's *L'Allegro*. In contrast to Milton's distinct preference for the pleasures of melancholy over the joys of mirth, for the contemplative over the active life, Blake chooses the open-handed, generous life of the poet-maker over the retiring, secretive life of the poet-priest. Innocence that rejoices in an ardent recognition of the holiness of everything that lives, that advocates an open, loving response to all being, is preferred to the abstract knowledge of the hermit in Blake's designs for *L'Allegro* and *Il Penseroso*. Mirth is depicted as a "buxom, blithe and debonair" woman whose blond hair ripples and flows freely, like Jerusalem's hair in the design for *Jerusalem* 32 [46] [*Plate 83*], and whose head is surrounded by a white nimbus or halo (Plate 1, [*Plate 70*]). She is accompanied in her dance by the leaping, laughing maids and youths who appear in the *Songs of Innocence* and whom Blake identifies as Milton's personifications:

> Haste thee Nymph & bring with thee
> Jest & Youthful Jollity
> Quips & Cranks & Wanton Wiles
> Nods & Becks & wreathed smiles
> Sport that wrinkled Care derides
> And Laughter holding both his Sides
> Come & trip it as you go
> On the light phantastic toe
> And in thy right hand lead with thee
> The Mountain Nymph Sweet Liberty.[35]

35. Quoted from Blake's manuscript notes which accompany these watercolors as given in *Blake: The Mystic Genius* by Adrian Van Sinderen (Syracuse, 1949), p. 57 (hereafter noted as Ms-S). This first design of *L'Allegro* is reproduced in color by Van

Plate 70. Mirth and Her Companions, L'Allegro, Plate 1, Pierpont Morgan Library.

"Jest" and "Youthful Jollity," both dressed in blue and leaping with arms raised, dance on either side of Mirth. "Quips & Cranks & Wanton Wiles"

Sinderen; the two states of the engraving are reproduced by Geoffrey Keynes in *Engravings by William Blake: The Separate Plates* (Dublin, 1956).

are at the right side of the design: "Quips" is a small dwarf with drawn up knees and ass's ears; "Cranks," just beneath him, is a fatuous-faced woman dressed in blue and sporting green bat wings; "Wanton Wiles" is the cat-faced girl in feathered bonnet and fashionable pink gown dancing at the right. Her cat face identifies her with Selima, Walpole's favorite cat, whom Blake portrayed in his illustrations to Gray's "Ode on the Death of a Favorite Cat" as a coyly wicked cat-woman who is undone by her greed for gold (fish) but who is nonetheless ultimately metamorphosed into the female human form divine and redeemed from the watery world of the fallen universe.[36] Above these three, a jolly, naked "Laughter holding both his sides" roars with joy. At the top of the design, "Nods & Becks & wreathed smiles"—four flying figures clothed in white gauze with hands or arms raised in delight—support the accusing fingers of "Sport," a flying woman in white, who drives off the wrinkled-faced, gray-haired, green-robed "Care" beneath her. Around Mirth's halo and in the upper right sky, tiny naked figures pour out libations, dance, blow bubbles that become worlds of delight, and play musical instruments. And Mirth brings with her, in her right hand, the beautiful huntress Liberty, wearing buskins and carrying a quiver of arrows (a bow is added in the final state of the engraving). Her naked right breast identifies her both with Diana, the chaste moon goddess, and the more voluptuous Venus. In the later free-line engraving of the design, Blake's affirmation of Mirth's beauty is even clearer. Blake there stretched out Mirth's left hand to support the tiny child flying in the sky, made her face broader and friendlier, and lengthened her rippling curls to the very hem of her gown. As Geoffrey Keynes notes, "the smooth conventional effect of the first state has been replaced by an exuberant freedom of drawing and design." [37] Energetic and innocent delight or "vanity" are emphatically affirmed in the caption Blake added to this plate: "Solomon says Vanity of Vanities all is Vanity & What can be Foolisher than this" (E 667). Although John Grant has argued for a negative, ironic view of Mirth,[38] her halo, her

36. Irene Tayler, "Metamorphosis of a Favorite Cat," *Blake's Visionary Forms Dramatic,* ed. Erdman and Grant (Princeton, 1970), pp. 285–303 and especially pp. 286, 294–95.

37. Keynes, *Engravings by William Blake,* p. 54.

38. Grant put heavy emphasis on the negative connotations of the cat face, bat wings, and ass's ears of "Quips & Cranks & Wanton Wiles"—all of whom he identifies as "Wanton Wiles"—and of Liberty's quiver of chastity (in a paper delivered to MLA

open-armed and dancing gesture, and the general exuberance and swirling circular movement of the design, which takes place in a golden dawn, all suggest that Mirth is an exemplar of the innocent, energetic, female form divine, that mortal joy in the good things of life, which Solomon denounced as mere vanity but which Blake celebrated as the divine vision of the holiness of everything that lives.

Blake's familiar golden-winged angel of poetic genius, Los, appears on Plate 2 as a golden-haired, golden-winged, caroling angel-lark. In opposition to Melancholy who seeks to lengthen the night, he startles the "Dull Night" (pictured on Plate 2 as the head and torso of Urizen emerging from a fortress or "Watch Tower" which closely resembles the papal prison, Castel Santangelo, in Rome and here floats on a "devouring" cloud) into the wakefulness of dawn (who is portrayed as a beautiful woman flying behind four horses). In *Milton,* of course, the lark is Los's messenger (*M* 35:63, 67). The Earth, dressed in a gray-pink robe,[39] is roused from her sleep and looks up at Los in wonder. Mirth can claim as her consort not only Los but also the golden-haired, open-armed youth with spiked crown and lily-tipped sceptre who appears in the next design as *The Great Sun* [*Plate 71*] and who is surrounded by a circle of flames containing trumpeting angels, food bearers, and libation bearers. He closely resembles both Satan in *Satan in His Original Glory* and Blake's familiar open-armed figures of Glad Day and of Christ, the divine imagination. Significantly, his flames are not confined to this circle, as are God's fires in *God Judging Adam* (compare [*Plate 40*]), but burst in exuberant freedom through the sphere at the top. The great sun beams upon the arcadian valleys of Innocence, where we can see "Milton walking by Elms on Hillocks green The Plowman. The Milkmaid The Mower whetting his Scythe. & The Shepherd & his Lass under a Hawthorne in the Dale" (E 664). The two hawthorne trees flanking this pastoral idyll are

Seminar 12: 'Illuminated Books by William Blake,' entitled "Blake's Designs for *L'Allegro* and *Il Penseroso*," on December 29, 1970). But this same buskined, bare-breasted girl reappears on Plate 8 as the beautiful moon whom the deluded Milton can view only with terror; her arrows may thus be the "arrows of desire," as E. J. Rose suggests (in "Blake's Illustrations for *Paradise Lost*, *L'Allegro*, and *Il Penseroso*: A Thematic Reading," *Hartford Studies in Literature* 2 [1970]: 62).

39. Earth may be associated with Milton here, as her light-colored robe suggests. Rose notes that in these *L'Allegro* designs of Innocence, Milton always wears light colors; in the *Il Penseroso* designs of fallen Experience, Milton always appears in a dark robe (p. 62).

Plate 71. The Great Sun, L'Allegro, Plate 3, Pierpont Morgan Library.

each imbued with a tiny winged spirit and backed by an angel holding a trumpet.

In the *Sunshine Holiday* brought by the great sun on Plate 4, the youths and maidens of the "Laughing Song" design dance gaily around a maypole, a traditional symbol of fertility and natural abundance. The children and old folk of "The Ecchoing Green" walk happily, led by a piping child, beneath a humanized tree filled with butterflies and fairies. Above, the clouds rising from the "barren breast" of a sad, sterile, gray female-mountain, crowned with dull night's fortress and accompanied by a melancholy old man-mountain, are transformed into trumpeting, food and drink-bearing figures who fly past the sun into the pink dawn of eternal poetic vision heralded by the two radiant trumpeters floating in the upper sky. In the evening that follows such a day of pleasure, imaginative tales are told. The fifth design pictures the ale-inspired fantasies: Queen Mab eating junkets on her throne in the heavens; "she" tickled and pinched by the fairies flying over her bed, "he" led astray toward a rather oppressive monastery by the false light of the friar (just as the little boy lost in *Songs of Innocence* is led astray by marsh gas, the false fire or *ignis fatuus* of that "inner light" which eighteenth-century Quakers insisted was the indwelling principle of God or *"Vehiculum Dei"* but *not* the essence of God [40]). These fanciful fairy tales and ghost stories bring no real terror but only *frissons* of delight; the huge goblin pictured here is throwing down the crop and bowl and "vanish[ing]" into thin air, just as all the evil forces represented by Moloch are vanquished by Christ's birth (in *The Flight of Moloch,* one of Blake's illustrations for Milton's "Christ's Nativity").

The young poet's final dream, inspired by Mirth or Innocence, is a vision of divine communion and creation. In the "more bright Sun of Imagination" that dominates the final design for *L'Allegro* [*Plate* 72], overwhelming the guinea-disk sun (E 555) of more conventional minds that sets at the left, the holy marriage of Mirth (who carries Hymen's torch of love) and Milton is being celebrated by a haloed Hymen or Christ. Beneath them, haloed figures with trumpets and tambourines rouse the naked figures of men, women, and children who rise in flames on each side of the sun, their newly broken or untwisted chains of harmony trailing behind (as do the chains of the liberated Orc on Plate 3 of *America*).

40. "The Little Boy lost," like the concluding lines of "Auguries of Innocence" discussed earlier, can be read as Blake's subtle critique of the Quaker doctrine of the "inner light" (see chap. 6, n. 1).

Plate 72. The Young Poet's Dream, L'Allegro, Plate 6, Pierpont Morgan Library.

That this is a holy vision, inspired by Jonson and above all Shakespeare (from whose works, in Blake's estimation, "an infinite number" of "volumes of equal value with Swedenborg's" could be produced by "any man of mechanical talents" [E 421]), rather than the false, "uncreative" world of fallen experience described by John Grant,[41] is supported by the poet's dress and gesture. Wearing a pink form-fitting suit much like those of the piper and the laughing singers of *Songs of Innocence,* the poet is visually haloed by his round gray-blue hat. Moreover, he repeats on a horzontal plane the exact gestures of Mirth on Plate 1 [*Plate 70*] : right arm stretched down, his to clasp his pen, hers to touch sweet liberty; left arm lifted, hers to the dancing joys, his to the inspiring Shakespeare (who wears the same lace collar as the poet); left foot lifted slightly above the right foot. This is a slightly less forceful version of the fully open-armed and triumphant great sun [*Plate 71*] whom the youthful poet may yet wake to become. Beneath his feet, a tiny figure runs with open arms, perhaps to announce the great vision; a couple lovingly embrace; and three women float upon the "Haunted Stream." The first of these spirits points up toward the poet's vision; the second looks directly at us, possibly inviting us to enter this vision; the last looks back in distress, apparently frightened by what she sees beyond the right side of the picture. Is it the advent of Melancholy on the next design that disturbs her?

In contrast to this joyful, truly visionary poet, the contemplative poet, a man like Blair or Young or Milton whom Blake admired but did not wish to emulate, seeks the constrained imagination of the black-robed Melancholy: the folded hands of a devout nun rather than the exuberant embraces of a mirthful maid. Melancholy is depicted in the first design for *Il Penseroso* [*Plate 73*] as Vala, the dark-veiled embodiment of chastity and the female will (compare the veiled Vala on *Jerusalem* 32 [46] [*Plate 83*]) who keeps her closest companions, the gaunt "Spare Fast" at her left and the praying "Quiet" at her right, under her thumbs. Rather than lifting her arms in welcome, as Mirth does, Melancholy keeps them close to her sides, her hands opened downward in a gesture not so much of benediction as of oppression. It may be worth noting that "Peace," the beautiful woman with flowing golden locks, a radiant red halo and a shepherdess' crook at the far left, turns her body away from Melancholy. In the world dominated by Vala-Melancholy, we see familiar aspects of the realm of fallen Experience: [42] in the sky at the left, surrounded by devour-

41. John Grant, "From Fable to Human Vision," *Blake's Visionary Forms Dramatic,* ed. Erdman and Grant, pp. xi–xiv.

42. E. J. Rose also identifies Mirth and Melancholy with the states of Innocence and Experience, respectively, in some of the designs; "Blake's Illustrations," p. 62.

Plate 73. Melancholy and Her Companions, Il Penseroso, Plate 7, Pierpont Morgan Library.

ing clouds, the old hag "Mute Silence" scowling at the tiny naked figure ("Philomel") who tries to delight her; in the sky at the right, the moon-goddess of chastity, drawn by two bat-winged serpents in a cloud; and above, the "Cherub Contemplation," a white-haired, white-robed figure, kneeling on the marble platform of a chariot with wheels of fire, with opened arms and golden wings. And to the right of Melancholy, we see the Muses circling in a ring around a flaming altar. Rather than leaping through the air like Mirth's visionary joys, they move sedately back and forth, wheel within wheel. Only "retired Leisure," isolated in "trim gardens" at the far right, is free to find his own pleasures among the lilies and the roses, the traditional emblems of the Virgin Mary, growing beside him.

The student-poet Milton prefers to follow this perverse vision of Vala-Melancholy rather than chasing the buskined, bare-breasted, golden-haired moon who closely resembles "Sweet Liberty" of *L'Allegro*, Plate 1 [*Plate* 70]. Both the design and Blake's manuscript notes comment ironically on Milton's verse:

> To behold the wandring Moon,
> Riding near her highest Noon,
> Like one that has been led astray
> Thro the heavens wide pathless way.
>
> (*Il Penseroso*, ll. 67–70)

Blake reads and illustrates these lines ironically as "Milton in his Character of a Student at Cambridge. Sees the Moon terrified as one led astray in the midst of her path thro heaven" (E 665).

Looking at Blake's design, we note that the moon does not look particularly "terrified": her expression is calm as she moves through the sky. Perhaps it is Milton to whom Blake intended the adjective "terrified" to be applied: his hand is raised and his expression registers some slight dismay. Perhaps Milton is trapped in the "character" or the state [43] of the student who, afraid to face life directly, escapes into his books. Similarly, it may be Milton rather than Blake who sees the moon "as one led astray": the moon herself seems to be moving purposefully forward, in har-

---

43. For Blake's use of the word "character" to denote an eternal state of being or psychological complex, see his *Descriptive Catalogue* notes on his painting of Chaucer's Canterbury Pilgrims: "The characters of Chaucer's Pilgrims are the characters which compose all ages and nations: as one age falls, another rises, different to mortal sight, but to immortals only the same; . . . . Of Chaucer's characters, as described in his Canterbury Tales, some of the names or titles are altered by time, but the characters themselves for ever remain unaltered, and consequently they are the physiognomies or lineaments of universal human life, beyond which Nature never steps. Names alter, things never alter" (E 523–4).

mony with the star flowers or constellations surrounding her. But the moon is clearly threatened by Milton's rational rejection: the devouring clouds send up icy spears beneath her feet and ring her round, just as the crescent moon itself is ringed by a spiky cloud-halo. Still, it appears that the moon could leap out of these devouring clouds and embrace Milton, if only he would open his arms to her; perhaps then the drooping red flowers (roses?) at the lower left would revive.

But this pensive poet prefers a dream of death, sin, law, and fate to a dream of the human form divine. Blake vigorously rejects this melancholy vision in the ninth design, entitled *Milton and the Spirit of Plato* [*Plate 74*]. Plato, a Urizenically old, white-haired and bearded, white-robed man, imposes his fallen vision of reason and repression on the exhausted Milton. Plato's learning is dominated by three classical gods: Venus, Mars, and Jupiter. In the left circle above Plato's head, we see the reign of Venus, the domination of the female will. The vegetating web growing, Daphne-like, from Venus' left hand first binds both Adam and Eve to the tree of generation and thus leads to their expulsion from the paradise of the human form divine. In this delusion created, appropriately Blake thought, by the writer of *The Republic,* Mars, the god of war or energy perverted, presides tyrannically over an oppressed political state. Here, a helmeted Mars rules with spear in left hand, stone decalogue before him and bat-winged spectre hovering over his right shoulder in the upper central circle. The final circle of Plato's closed system is dominated by pure mathematics and abstract reason. The philosopher-king turned tyrant-Jupiter holds the compass and spear of rational repression, while his slave rolls the mill wheel of Locke's "ratio" or of mathematic computation behind him.[44] Inexorably controlling all three spheres, the three fates or "Destinies" spin and cut the thread of life at the top of the design. Blake himself described the design thus: "The Spirit of Plato unfolds his Worlds to Milton in Contemplation. The Three destinies sit on the Circles of Platos Heavens weaving the Thread of Mortal Life these Heavens are Venus Jupiter & Mars. Hermes flies before as attending on the Heaven of

44. John Grant has also stressed Blake's emphatic anti-Platonism in this design: "In Plato's scheme the three Fates are above the realms of the three sinister Great Gods and are thus dominant in the universe" ("Discussing the *Arlington Court Picture*, I," p. 102).

Plate 74. Milton and the Spirit of Plato, Il Penseroso, Plate 9, Pierpont Morgan Library.

Jupiter the Great Bear is seen in the sky beneath Hermes & the Spirits of Fire Air Water & Earth Surround Miltons Chair" (E 666). These three circles also illustrate episodes in Milton's *Paradise Lost:* the expulsion from Eden, the rebellion of Satan, and God the Father using his golden compasses to construct the world with "number, weight and measure." Milton's and Plato's visions are spiritually similar. And Plato's "Worlds," his fixed spheres or wheels-within-wheels, systematically eliminate all sexual pleasure. Plato rejects the female sensuality proffered by earth (the enrooting woman beneath Milton's chair) as totally corrupting, sinful physical flesh; he thus condemns man to the chastity enforced on him by water or the female will (the bat-winged woman behind Milton's chair traps the man in a net beneath the sea). Moreover, Plato blocks the poet's vision of fire (the naked creatures rising in flames from the grave or corpses at the left) and thus cuts him off from his own imaginative energies, although the fact that the upper figure in these flames is lashing those below him with thongs may indicate that this is the fire of the *Gates of Paradise* (1818, [*Plate 61*]), namely, revolutionary Energy perverted into mere will to power. And Milton himself bends his head, oblivious to the gaily circling figures of air over his head or the noble constellation of the Great Bear behind him.

Milton, thus misled by Plato's pernicious teachings and encouraged in his delusion by Melancholy, retreats from the flaring sun (the "Great Sun" of *L' Allegro*) in *Milton Led by Melancholy.* Instead, he seeks cover under the shade of oak trees inhabited by serpents (a snake winds around the left arm of the man who is the personification of the tree at the right) and authoritarian figures (the old man in the tree at the left holds a sceptre tipped with an acorn over three huddled figures), and dominated by bat-winged or antennaed insects. As E. J. Rose notes, these two humanized bugs "should remind us of the caterpillar-fly cycle in Blake's work where man under Rahab-Vala's rule becomes a human insect." [45] Milton can see the sun only as malign (it hurls spear-beams down at him) and hastens to escape, hand in hand, with Melancholy. The unusually dark, grim coloring of this design emphasizes his error. *Milton's Dream* focuses on the oppressive, law-giving Jehovah-Urizen who floats above Milton's head,

45. Rose, "Blake's Illustrations," p. 64.

hands raised in a gesture of prohibition, flanked by two huddled youths (the head-grasping youth on his right repeats the arm gesture of the snake-encircled, bat-winged, fallen head at the bottom of the preludium for *Europe*). Moreover, this red-haloed Urizen, who is backed by a seated, meditating carbon copy of himself, floats within a rainbow-sphere, very similar to that concentrically lined circle surrounding the torso of the punishing, law-giving God who expells Adam and Eve from Paradise in Lorenzo Ghiberti's first panel on the Porta del Paradiso of the Baptistery in Florence. Rather than the covenant of hope promised by the rainbow arch, this full rainbow circle focuses all dreams of the future exclusively on Jehovah-Urizen. Milton's dream, as Blake notes, is a "Strange Mysterious Dream . . . of Scrolls & Nets & Webs" (E 666). On the wings of sleep appear women strangled in nets, embracing lovers trapped beneath a scroll and seven eyes. These seven eyes may represent the seven eyes of God listed in *Milton* (13:18–27) and *Jerusalem* (55:31): the six eyes of the fallen tyrants—Lucifer, the egotist; Molech, the executioner; Elohim, the judge; Shaddai, the accuser; Pahad, the terrified one; and Jehovah, the lawgiver—and the seventh eye of Jesus, the forgiver of sins and redeemer of mankind. If so, Milton still has the opportunity to escape his sleep of delusion and awake to see with the eighth eye of the redeemed poet. His three wives and three daughters float beside him, bringing him new worlds of vision if he will only open his eyes and leap, like the tiny figures on the scroll soaring above Urizen's fixed rainbow-sphere, beyond the predestined prophecies of a rationalistic God. He will then truly become the eighth eye described in *Milton* 15:4, the individual whose "Sleeping Body . . . now arose and walk'd with them in Eden, as an Eighth/ Image Divine tho' darken'd; and tho walking as one walks/ In sleep; and the Seven comforted and supported him" (E 108).

Clearly then, Penseroso's or Milton's fall into satanic error is not final. As in Blake's *Milton,* the state of sin and error can be abandoned and the sin forgiven. On the final plate of *Il Penseroso,* a mother nurses two children while a third looks on (at the lower right), two friends reunite even from the grave beneath lilies of resurrection, while lovers embrace in a rose garden of Innocence beneath the open blessing arms of the redeemed poet. Milton's "Peaceful Hermitage" or "mossy cell" has become a "home of vision, not of bondage." [46] Above Milton's cell, the sky is filled with the constellations of Cancer, Gemini, Orion, Taurus, and Aries which, as a group, are visible in the skies of the northern hemisphere only in the winter and spring. In the leafy foliage or earth above Milton's cell, six women raise their arms in desire, while a seventh huddles nearby. Milton, in old age, has passed through the winter skies of self-deception to the springtime rebirth of the prophetic imagination. He can now celebrate the sensual and creative joys of Innocence rather than Plato's or Melancholy-Vala's dream of power and violence. Throughout these designs, Blake affirms the human form divine and its innocent joys of sensual pleasures, sexual desire, procreation, the loving care of the young, and imaginative creation over the more abstract and ultimately cruel satisfactions of the Platonic philosopher.[47]

Thus Blake's late artistic masterpieces celebrate the physical appearance and expansive analogical vision of the human form divine and, further, portray the capacity of this finite/infinite form to triumph over the limited vision and body of Urizenic reason and Vala's materialism. In *Je-*

46. Grant, "Discussing the *Arlington Court Picture*, I," p. 103.

47. Since they may lend credence to this interpretation of Blake's *L'Allegro* and *Il Penseroso,* it is worth noting some interesting correlations between Blake's portrayals of Mirth and Melancholy and the descriptions of Venus and Saturn given in Alexander Browne's *Ars Pictoria* (London, 1669), a school text in drawing, painting, limning, and etching which Blake used as a youth and from whose final plate he derived his donkey in *Hecate.* Discussing the impact of astrology on human appearances, Browne describes those born under Venus in terms almost identical to Blake's Mirth. Venus is the "Queen of all *joy,*" the "Mother of love and beauty," and "her motions are *pleasant* and *mirthful,*" being given to *sports, dalliance, dancing,* and *embracings,* she makes the countenance *aimiable, pleasant,* and *merry,* working a kind of *whiteness* in the Body . . . yet prettily mixed with *red*" (p. 61). Notably, Blake's Mirth is given white and red skin tones. The influences of Saturn, which closely resemble Blake's Melancholy, on the other hand, "are partly *good,* and partly *bad,* according to the disposition of him that receiveth them, as weeping, *melancholy,* etc.; he causeth religious *actions,* as to *bow* the *knee,* look down upon the *earth, pray* and such like *motions* of the *Breast* and *Face,* common to all those which pray, or other *austere* and *satyrical* Fellows" (pp. 61–62). On the one hand, Saturn is "the *seed of great profundity,* the *Auctor* of secret *contemplation,* the *imprinter* of *weighty thoughts* in Men" (p. 58). On the other, "he makes a Man *subtil, witty,* a *way-layer* and murtherer" (p. 62). Further, he "causeth a complexion of color between black and yellow, meager, . . . small eyes, . . . with looks cast down, an heavy Gate" (p. 58). At least some of the influences of Saturn can be seen in Blake's Melancholy and may reinforce my suggestion that Melancholy is a dangerous mistress to follow, a potentially destructive Vala or female will.

rusalem, as we shall see in the next chapter, Blake summed up his culminating myth, the epic fall and regeneration of the one man, Albion, who is all human men. And in one of the most archetypal of his late designs, *Christ in the Lap of Truth,* Blake triumphantly portrays the eternal validity of the vision of Innocence as the energetic recognition of the human form divine in all men at all times.

EIGHT

Jerusalem

The structure, plot, imagery, and designs of Blake's last poetic epic, *Jerusalem* (1804–20), explore the nature and significance of the human form divine. Can this image successfully communicate the divine vision of man as God? And can it provide a viable psychological and social structure in terms of which every man can realize and sustain his potential divinity within a bounded finite form? The apocalypse presented on the final plates of the poem is an overwhelming affirmation of the capacity of the human imagination to create and sustain the fusion of man and God in a time beyond time.

The designs for *Jerusalem,* as everywhere in Blake's art, are composed almost without exception around a distinctly outlined human figure. Imposing Michelangelesque men and women, often nude or clothed in clinging draperies, walk, sit, run, crouch, and leap through undefined spaces or non-illusionistic landscapes. Their motion, when impeded, is obstructed by other human figures or by flames, roots, wings, or animal heads and limbs growing out of their own bodies. In these designs, as elsewhere, Blake's artistic image of evil is "the sight of the human body surrendering its unique form and dissolving into a non-human landscape." [1] The visual

1. W. J. T. Mitchell, "Blake's Composite Art," in *Blake's Visionary Forms Dramatic,* ed. D. V. Erdman and J. E. Grant (Princeton, 1970), p. 71.

world of *Jerusalem,* then, is the human form: here the human body creates its own pictorial space, its own compositional relationships. Both in its designs and in its narrative structure, *Jerusalem* is Blake's ultimate apotheosis of the human form divine as the necessary shape of all temporal, spatial, and imaginative reality.

The structure of *Jerusalem* is, of course, fourfold—there are four chapters of exactly twenty-five plates each—and is organically patterned on the outline of the human body. After introducing his major characters and epic theme—the fall and regeneration of Albion, the universal man—in the first chapter, Blake thematically organizes the rest of the poem around the four major aspects of the human form: the body, the rational mind, the emotions, and the imagination. The last three chapters define the three basic errors or sins that can separate the human form from its own divinity. The first error, described in the second chapter and attributed to the Jews, is the misuse of the *body.* The second error, depicted in the third chapter and ascribed to the Deists, is the abuse of the *mind* and the *emotions.* And the third error, portrayed in the last chapter and addressed to the Christians who are most responsible for it, is the corruption of the *imagination.* But all these errors can be corrected; the last chapter concludes with a sudden apocalypse, Blake's ecstatic affirmation of the human form divine, the resurrected man in whom body, mind, emotions, and imagination are purified through the "divine vision" that Los has sustained throughout the poem. Thus, the end is the beginning. Blake does not believe in a Miltonic or Wordsworthian "fortunate fall"; man is born with the capacity for perfect Innocence, for that ideal balance of Energy and reason that creates an Eden of holy creativity, mercy, pity, love, and peace. Any separation from such heavenly self-fulfillment is a denial of one's potential divinity, a real evil or error that must be overcome as quickly as possible. Since *Jerusalem* has not been read in precisely these terms,[2] I shall study in each section of the poem

2. I do not think that either Karl Kiralis or Edward Rose have satisfactorily analyzed the fourfold structure of *Jerusalem,* although both their attempts have illuminated aspects of the poem. Karl Kiralis, in "The Theme and Structure of William Blake's *Jerusalem,*" included in *The Divine Vision: Studies in the Poetry and Art of William Blake,* ed. Vivian De Sola Pinto (London: Gollancz, 1957), links the three final chapters to the three ages of man. The Jews represent childhood; the Deists, adolescence;

Blake's exploration of the human form divine as a viable union of Energy and reason, the infinite and the finite, to which fallen man must return.

The frontispiece of chapter 1 [*Plate 75*] establishes the epic pattern of the entire poem and of this chapter in particular. Los or Blake, the poet-prophet of the Second Coming and the Last Judgment, here humbly dressed as an eighteenth-century English watchman in blue workcoat and felt hat (Los is identified as "Albion's Watchman" on *J* 56:32) and carrying a fiery globe of light, steps into the tomb or fallen world constructed by the degenerated Albion, to bring the saving light of the divine vision to lost mankind. Significantly, Los steps through a Gothic arch and wears Greek sandals. He brings Blake's own artistic idiom of Gothic-romantic classicism: a vision of "Living" Gothic motifs blended with sharply outlined figures and tectonic compositions. As Los goes, a wind from within the arch blows his coat back to the left: Henry Lesnick has shown that this is the wind of time or mortality blowing from the fallen world into heaven (this same wind blows the old man *toward* death's door in Blake's design for *The Gates of Paradise*, Figure 15 [*Plate 24*]).[3] The effect of

---

and the Christians, maturity (p. 147). Although reference to the three ages of man appears in *Jerusalem* on pl. 98:28–40, it does not occur earlier and does not seem central to Blake's structure. Nor do the three "states," Judaism, Deism, and Christianity, seem to reflect the "growth" of man, as Kiralis asserts; rather, they seem to be three equally fallen states from which the individual must free himself.

Edward Rose's analysis of the structure of *Jerusalem* seems more perceptive; "The Structure of Blake's *Jerusalem*," *Bucknell Review* 11 (May, 1963): 35–54. Rose correctly points to a quest structure reminiscent of *Milton* and to the theme of the fall of man from Eden (p. 38). As he suggestively writes, "*Jerusalem* combines the fall of man from unity with the poet's, or the imagination's, quest to redeem error by recreating man or reuniting him with eternity" (p. 38). But Rose's analysis of the fourpart structure of *Jerusalem* is less convincing. He links each chapter to a "state dominated by an appropriate Zoa": the first chapter is dominated thematically and imagistically by Tharmas, the second by Luvah, the third by Urizen and the fourth by Los (Urthona) (p. 49). Unfortunately, Rose offers no specific quotation or imagery to support these identifications; nor does a close reading of the text seem to uphold these ascriptions. If anything, as my reading attempts to show, the *second* chapter belongs to Tharmas (the body), the third to *both* Urizen and Luvah (the mind and emotions), and the fourth to Urthona (the imagination).

Perhaps the most illuminating comment on the poem's structure has been made by Northrop Frye. Dividing the four chapters into the fall, man's struggle in the fallen world, redemption, and apocalypse, respectively, Frye notes the fundamental structural antithesis in each chapter: "Each part of *Jerusalem* presents a phase of imaginative vision simultaneously with the body of error which it clarifies"; *Fearful Symmetry* (Boston, 1962), p. 357.

3. Henry Lesnick, "The Function of Perspective in Blake's *Jerusalem*," *Bulletin of the New York Public Library* 73 (1969): 49–55.

the wind here is to thrust Los back from the fallen world, thus making his self-sacrificing descent even more difficult. The divine vision that Los brings is, of course, both a way of seeing—the "divine analogy"—and a way of living—the forgiveness of sins. The poem follows the archetypal Christian epic pattern of descent and return, of loss and recovery. The agent of redemption is clearly the artistic imagination; the ultimate goal is participation in the light or vision carried by the artist; the object to be saved is fallen man, now imprisoned in a dark graveyard. This imagery is specified in the writings above and on the sides of the Gothic archway in the early print of the frontispiece in the collection of Geoffrey Keynes [*Plate* 75]. The arch leads to that "Void, outside of Existence, which if entered into/ Englobes itself & becomes a Womb, such was Albions Couch." This is the abyss of the fallen world where man is separated from his true existence, the full realization of his potential divinity. Los carries the two-pronged message of Christ: his merciful self-sacrifice to save mankind and the promise of final forgiveness and redemption:

> Half Friendship is the bitterest Enmity said Los
> As he enterd the Door of Death for Albions sake Inspired
> The long sufferings of God are not for ever there is a Judgment.

> (E 143)

But Los, addressing the forces of reason and potential self-repression within every man (his spectre), acknowledges that every potentially divine faculty of the human form is capable of corruption: "Every Thing has its Vermin O Spectre of the Sleeping Dead!" It is the poet's task to destroy these vermin, these mental and physical manacles of division and self-destruction, and to restore man to the divine vision.

The first chapter is addressed "To the Public" because it portrays the universal fall of man and presents a general introduction to Blake's epic theme and characters. To help his readers unravel the complexities of his analysis of human experience, Blake briefly summarizes his plot, the nature of his protagonist, the nature of the fallen world of Ulro, the way to salvation, and finally the goal of life itself—ultimate reunion with the human form divine. Both the opening lines of *Jerusalem* and the illustration on Plate 4 [*Plate* 76] narrate Blake's plot, the willful fall and difficult redemption of Albion from "the sleep of Ulro" into "the awaking to

Plate 75. Jerusalem, Frontispiece, early print, Collection of Geoffrey Keynes.

Chap: 1

Of the Sleep of Ulro! and of the passage through
Eternal Death! and of the awaking to Eternal Life.

This theme calls me in sleep night after night, & every morn
Awakes me at sun-rise, then I see the Saviour over me
Spreading his beams of love, & dictating the words of this mild song.

Awake! awake O sleeper of the land of shadows, wake! expand!
I am in you and you in me, mutual in love divine:
Fibres of love from man to man thro Albions pleasant land.
In all the dark Atlantic vale down from the hills of Surrey
A black water accumulates, return Albion! return!
Thy brethren call thee, and thy fathers, and thy sons,
Thy nurses and thy mothers, thy sisters and thy daughters
Weep at thy souls disease, and the Divine Vision is darkend:
Thy Emanation that was wont to play before thy face,
Beaming forth with her daughters into the Divine bosom.
Where hast thou hidden thy Emanation lovely Jerusalem
From the vision and fruition of the Holy-one?
I am not a God afar off, I am a brother and friend;
Within your bosoms I reside, and you reside in me:
Lo! we are One: forgiving all Evil; Not seeking recompense!
Ye are my members O ye sleepers of Beulah, land of shades!

But the perturbed Man away turns down the valleys dark:

Phantom of the over heated brain! shadow of immortality!
Seeking to keep my soul a victim to thy Love! which binds
Man the enemy of man into deceitful friendships:
Jerusalem is not! her daughters are indefinite:
By demonstration, man alone can live, and not by faith
My mountains are my own, and I will keep them to myself!
The Malvern and the Cheviot, the Wolds Plinlimmon & Snowdon
Are mine, here will I build my Laws of Moral Virtue!
Humanity shall be no more: but war & princedom & victory!

So spoke Albion in jealous fears, hiding his Emanation
Upon the Thames and Medway, rivers of Beulah: dissembling
His jealousy before the throne divine, darkening, cold!

Plate 76. *Jerusalem,* Plate 4, Copy E(TP), Paul Mellon Collection.

Eternal Life," when Jesus becomes "not a God afar off" but "a brother and a friend" (*J* 4:1, 2, 18). As Jesus calls to the sleeping (fallen) Albion:

> . . . wake! expand!
> I am in you and you in me, mutual in love divine:
> . . . .
> Within your bosoms I reside, and you reside in me:
> Lo! we are One; forgiving all Evil; Not seeking recompense!
> Ye are my members O ye sleepers of Beulah, land of shades!
>
> (*J* 4:6–7, 19–21)

The design on Plate 4 repeats this movement from sleep or delusion to wakefulness or vision. A crouching, blank-faced, blue-robed figure spreads her heavily draped arms oppressively over two youths who gaze longingly upward. To the upper left, a beautiful, naked, winged woman with golden hair guides three female figures through the dark clouds toward a waning moon that frames the Greek inscription, Μονος ὁ Ἰεσους. This design seems to represent the domination of the female will or the veiled Vala (a similar hooded figure was identified as the "Mother . . . Wife Sister & Daughter" of the grave-worm on the final design for *The Gates of Paradise* [*Plate* 25]); of the devouring cloud of reason that swags heavily around the title and down upon the man on the right; and of the web of mystery (a spider web or net runs down the right margin) over Albion. He can be freed from these oppressions only with the aid of Los and Jerusalem, the true female form divine who leads the other three emanations of the four Zoas into the starlit vision of Jesus. The Greek inscription, Μονος ὁ Ἰεσους, may refer to Luke 9:36, as Joseph Wicksteed suggested,[4] although the Greek text there reads Ἰησοῦς Μόνος. The disciples first saw Jesus, transfigured, accompanied by Moses and Elias; but in their final vision, they saw "Jesus alone." Blake's use of the inscription might thus suggest that Jesus fuses the law and prophecy of the Old Testament with the forgiveness of sins promised in the New Testament. More likely, however, Blake's inscription is taken from the only passage in the Greek Bible of his day that contained the exact phrase, Μόνος ὁ Ἰησοῦς:

4. Joseph Wicksteed, *William Blake's Jerusalem* (New York: Beechhurst Press, 1955), p. 117.

John 8:9.[5] The phrase occurs during John's description of Jesus' response to the woman taken in adultery: the Pharisees, "convicted by their own conscience, went out one by one, beginning at the eldest, even unto the last: and *Jesus was left alone,* and the woman standing in the midst" (italics mine). Blake's use of this source would then suggest that the rejected Jerusalem, along with all falsely accused women, will be forgiven by Jesus and restored to perfect harmony with Albion. "Jesus alone," or the divine vision that he embodies, has the capacity to see beyond the perversions of the female will and to redeem the emanations of all men.

The protagonist of this epic plot is, of course, Albion. Albion is the Cabbalistic Adam Kadman, the Christian Adam, the Pythagorean man-as-the-measure-of-all-things. He is, in the expansions of this poem, all men at all times: the twelve tribes of Israel, the twelve prophets of the Old Testament, the twelve accusers of Blake at his trial in Chichester in 1804, the leaders of present-day England. He is England and, beyond the England of 1800, the England in which, according to the syncretic mythographers of Blake's day, all religions originated. Albion therefore becomes the twenty-eight cathedral cities of England; and his sons are the fifty-two counties of England and Wales, the thirty-six counties of Scotland, and the thirty-four counties of Ireland. And finally, Albion is the cosmos, both the vegetating polypus of organic matter (*J* 15:4–5) and the radiating wheel within wheel of spiritual powers—of stars, galaxies, and heavens immaterial. Albion as the cosmos is vividly depicted on Plate 25 [*Plate* 77]. Here, Rahab (with red hair, on the right), Tirzah (on the left, with her hair prudishly bound in a knot), and Vala (above, weaving her veil or web of matter with her arms spread as on Plate 4 [*Plate* 76])—the three fallen daughters of Ulro—draw out the veins of organic nature like an umbilical cord from Albion's spiritual energies. The sun, moon, and several constellations—including Orion's belt—are contained in Albion's cosmic body. Albion is here being forced to sacrifice his poten-

5. Though some recent editions of the Greek testament offer a different reading here, Μόνος ὁ 'Ιησοῦς would almost certainly have been in Blake's text. That reading is given by Stephanus in his edition of 1550 which became the *textus receptus* and as such the basis for most popular editions through the eighteenth century. Likewise, the important editions of Erasmus (Basel, 1514), Wittstein (Amsterdam, 1733), and the London Polyglot of 1657 report the same reading of John 8:9. I am indebted to Professor Ronald Mellor of the Stanford Classics Department for this information.

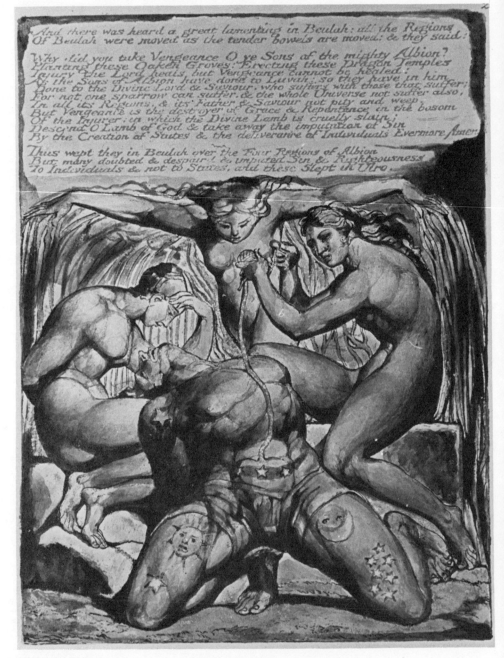

Plate 77. Jerusalem, Plate 25, Copy E(TP), Paul Mellon Collection.

tially infinite Energy to the creation of a limited, materialistic universe, just as St. Erasmus was martyred by having his living intestines drawn out on a windlass in Poussin's *The Martyrdom of St. Erasmus,* the visual source for this design.[6] Albion's intestines are the life or substance of the entire physical universe, as Blake announces to the Jews on Plate 27:

"All things Begin & End in Albions Ancient Druid Rocky Shore."

You have a tradition, that Man anciently contain in his mighty limbs all things in Heaven & Earth: this you received from the Druids. "But now the Starry Heavens are fled from the mighty limbs of Albion." (E 169–70)

Albion, then, is man, England, the universe, infinity itself; and his fate is the fate of both man and God.

Albion's fallen state is the world we live in, the world without the divine vision, the void dominated by reason. Blake portrays this as "An orbed void of doubt, despair, hunger & thirst, & sorrow" (*J* 18:4). It is a psychic state of alienation, paranoia, and psychosis, in which man is cut off from those he needs most, in which his emanation flees from him in jealousy and suspicion. It is a world dominated by the concepts of law and order, of sin, guilt, and punishment. As Albion moans,

> The disease of Shame covers me from head to feet: I have no hope
> Every boil upon my body is a separate & deadly Sin.
> Doubt first assaild me, then Shame took possession of me
> Shame divides Families. Shame hath divided Albion in sunder!
> (*J* 21:3–6)

Normal emotions of affection, generosity, anger, and fear are perverted into neurotic syndromes of frustration and vindictive cruelty: the "Hounds of Nimrod," "War and deadly contention" systematically annihilate love and liberty. Here

> . . . All bold asperities
> Of Haters met in deadly strife, rending the house & garden
> The unforgiving porches, the tables of enmity, and beds
> And chambers of trembling & suspition, hatreds of age & youth
> And boy & girl, & animal & herb, & river & mountain
> And city & village, and house & family. . . .
> (*J* 18:21–25)

6. This source was pointed out to me by Morton Paley in a lecture entitled "Word and Image in *Jerusalem:* Some Problems," given at the University of California at Berkeley on May 4, 1971.

In such a world, Albion disintegrates into a "chaotic non-entity," a schizophrenic state of self-hatred, nonidentity, incoherence, terror, and a frantic grasping after secure routines, laws, and dogma.[7]

Albion can escape this void only by following the dictates of Los, his own imagination. Los's role is threefold. First, he must reawaken Albion to the divine vision and force him to recognize the true relationship between man and God, between man and woman, between man and his environment. Blake again pictures this awakening as a process of expansion, of liberation from constricting forms of thought and action, of "opening the centre" to find the "wheel within wheels" from which all being radiates. Edward Rose has articulated some of the implications of this image:

The opened center is the destruction of the selfhood, the egoistic "white Dot" (*J* 29:19). When a center opens it dilates, expanding into infinity: the "Globe of Blood" contains the *Word* and expands to become the *human form divine*.

. . . The Centre of the wheel through its productive action rather than egoistic contraction reaches infinity at every point on its everexpanding perimeter; that is, there are wheels *within* wheels. Creative centers are cornucopias, not vortices —dilating eyes of plenty, not shrunken orbs. (*J* 77) [8]

With opened eyes and mind, Albion can perceive the potential harmony between man and woman, man and city. Blake again uses a clothing metaphor to describe this divine relationship. The woman and the city should be the garments of the man: ideally, they are environments or vehicles that surround him, that gently follow the lines of his body and the patterns of his thought, that provide the material substance which manifests his creative will and vision. The linking of woman and city as the outward embodiment of man's imaginative vision is clear in the image of the "building of pity and compassion" constructed by "those golden builders" near "mournful ever weeping Paddington": [9]

7. For perceptive studies of schizophrenia that support Blake's analysis, see Erik Erikson's *Identity: Youth and Crisis,* (London, 1968), ch. 4, and *Childhood and Society* (New York, 1950); R. D. Laing's *The Divided Self* (Baltimore; Penguin 1965); and Hannah Green's *I Never Promised You a Rose Garden* (London, 1964).

8. Edward J. Rose, "The Symbolism of the Opened Center and Poetic Theory in Blake's *Jerusalem,*" *Studies in English Literature* 5 (Autumn 1965): 587.

9. Paul Miner has accounted for Paddington's "ever weeping" by the fact that "at this time St. George's Burying Ground occupied a large portion of the Paddington area near the intersection of Edgeware, Bayswater, and Oxford roads. This also was the loca-

The stones are pity, and the bricks, well wrought affections:
Enameld with love & kindness, & the tiles engraven gold
Labour of merciful hands: the beams & rafters are forgiveness:
The mortar & cement of the work, tears of honesty: the nails,
And the screws & iron braces, are well wrought blandishments,
And well contrived words, firm fixing, never forgotten,
Always comforting the remembrance: the floors, humility,
The ceilings, devotion: the hearths, thanksgiving:
Prepare the furniture O Lambeth in thy pitying looms!
The curtains, woven tears & sighs, wrought into lovely forms
For comfort. there the secret furniture of Jerusalems chamber
Is wrought: Lambeth! the Bride the Lambs Wife loveth thee:
Thou art one with her & knowest not of self in thy supreme joy.

(*J* 12:30–34)

The union of woman and city is realized most completely, of course, in
the dominating figure of Jerusalem, the bride of the lamb and the city of
God.[10]

Having revived the divine vision, Los must next teach Albion how to
follow Christ. Albion must live the life of Christ: he must rebel against
his spectre; defy and refute the rhetoric of reason, sin, and despair; and
annihilate his own selfhood—that "mighty Hand" of self-interest who
"Condensed his Emanations into hard opake substances; / And his infant
thoughts & desires, into cold, dark cliffs of death" (*J* 9:1–2).

Finally, Los must help Albion to create his own system, lest he "be en-
slavd by another Mans" (*J* 10:20). Such a system must rise from the foundations laid in *The Marriage of Heaven and Hell:* love and hate, Energy
and reason, are not moral polarities or absolutes but rather "contraries"
that are both necessary to create an image combining human limitations
and divine infinity, man and God. The only absolute evil is what Los calls
a "negation," an empty abstraction that never existed, a meaningless con-

---

tion of the Tyburn gallows, Blake's fatal rood tree." Nearby were Tirzah's looms, the
Asylum for female orphans ("Visions in the Darksom Air," *Blake Essays for Damon,*
ed. A. Rosenfeld [Providence, R.I., 1969], pp. 256–57). Moreover, in 1812, Paddington was a slum inhabited by poverty-stricken Irish laborers (David Erdman, *Blake:
Prophet Against Empire,* rev. ed. [Garden City, N.Y., 1969], p. 474).

10. For an excellent study of the image of the city in *Jerusalem* and in earlier Blake
poems, see Kenneth R. Johnston's "Blake's Cities: Romantic Forms of Urban Renewal,"
Blake's Visionary Forms Dramatic, ed. Erdman and Grant, pp. 413–42.

cept such as "sin" that can only destroy the potential divinity within man, his imagination and his capacity for pleasure. As Los explains:

> . . . this is the manner of the Sons of Albion in their strength
> They take the Two Contraries which are calld Qualities, with which
> Every Substance is clothed, they name them Good & Evil
> From them they make an Abstract, which is a Negation
> Not only of the Substance from which it is derived
> A murderer of its own Body: but also a murderer
> Of every Divine Member: it is the Reasoning Power
> An Abstract objecting power, that Negatives every thing
> This is the Spectre of Man: the Holy Reasoning Power
> And in its Holiness is closed the Abomination of Desolation
> Therefore Los stands in London building Golgonooza
> Compelling his Spectre to labours mighty; trembling in fear
> The Spectre weeps, but Los unmovd by tears or threats remains.

(J 10:7–19)

Los, then, is both poet-prophet and politician: he both reveals the divine vision and enables Albion to construct the state of Jerusalem on earth. He both teaches the life of Christ, the forgiveness of sins, and the fourfold understanding of man and actively *saves* Albion by showing him how to live that life and see that vision. And Albion, too, must expand his personal awareness of his fall and of the last judgment into a total apocalypse, a universal salvation for all mankind. Chapter I ends with Albion's recognition of his responsibility not only to follow Los back to the divine vision but to lead all men into the ultimate apocalypse.

But to reunite with the divine vision, Albion must first overcome the four primary errors or fallen states of man: the corruption of the body, the mind, the emotions, and the imagination. Chapter 2 depicts the body in its pure and defiled states. It is addressed to the Jews, who, in Blake's view, originally affirmed the beauty of the body and its sensuality in Solomon's *Song of Songs* and in their Cabbalistic and Hasidic sects, but who also repeatedly denied the body, denigrated women, and pharisaically condemned the woman taken in adultery. The frontispiece to chapter 2 [*Plate* 78] shows Hand, the stern lawgiver and Mosaic judge who perverts the flames of Energy into controlled serpentine instruments of oppression,[11] angrily rejecting the gentle advances of Jerusalem. Here Hand is a

---

11. David Erdman derives the name Hand from the accusing "indicator" or printer's fist of Leigh Hunt's editorial signature in the *Examiner,* a journal which had attacked Blake's "bad drawings" in 1808; *Blake,* rev. ed., pp. 457–58.

Plate 78. Jerusalem, Plate 26, Copy E(TP), Paul Mellon Collection.

grotesque parody of the crucified savior: he bears stigmata on his hands and ankles, spreads his arms in the cruciform position, and radiates a demonic flame-halo from his head. Rather than welcoming the bride of the lamb, Hand denounces Jerusalem as "liberty" which, to Hand's compulsively ordered mind, can mean only "unbridled license." As Hand exclaims,

> SUCH VISIONS HAVE APPEARD TO ME
> AS I MY ORDERD RACE HAVE RUN
> JERUSALEM IS NAMED LIBERTY
> AMONG THE SONS OF ALBION.
>
> *(J 26)*

If one assumes that these words are spoken by Blake rather than by Hand, they become even more subtle. Blake's race is now "orderd;" he is creating his own system. And his vision perceives that Jerusalem is both denounced as "license" by the deluded sons of Albion and simultaneously hailed as genuine freedom by the redeemed sons of Albion. Perhaps this ambivalence in speaker and meaning is intentional: it shows us how two opposed views of man's relation to Jerusalem's sexuality can be simultaneously held in the mind. Such irony forces the reader's mind to expand beyond the narrow structures of Aristotelian logic and prepares him for Blake's ultimately analogical thinking.

In immediate contrast to Hand's rejection of the female body is the affirmation of feminine beauty pictured on Plate 28. The first and last states of this plate, the final version printed in Copy E and all posthumous copies of *Jerusalem* and a trial proof found in the Pierpont Morgan copy of *Jerusalem,* present Blake's image of ideal feminine beauty and sensuality. In the earlier proof [*Plate* 79], a man, his back to us, with short hair, a thick left arm, and knotted back muscles copulates beneath a net or stamen upon a mammoth lily with a woman facing us who has hair in locks and long thighs.[12] A large caterpillar, the emblem of generation that also appears on the frontispiece for *Gates of Paradise* [*Plate* 9] emerges from

12. Although they do not discuss the sexes of the figures on the proof plate specifically, both S. Foster Damon and John Grant seem to see the figure on the right (whom David Erdman and I see as male) as a woman, the figure in the rear as male (in *A Blake Dictionary* [Providence, Rhode Island, 1965], p. 240; and "Two Flowers in the Garden of Experience," *Blake Essays for Damon,* p. 356, respectively). I agree that the forward figure has very delicate fingers on its right hand—but the rear figure's left-hand fingers seem almost as delicate. The muscles of the upper arms seem equally powerful on both figures. Finally, the clearly shorter hair, more heavily accentuated back muscles and seemingly more aggressive forward thrust of the pelvis of the forward figure persuade me of its masculinity. Nor do the embracing couple at the lower left of *The Day of Judgment,* Blake's final design for Blair's *Grave,* to whom Grant draws attention, seem as "decisive" a clue as Grant assumes (p. 359). There, the woman at the front is clearly turned sidesaddle, as are *both* figures in the final version of Plate 28, but neither figure in the proof plate is so seated (unless, possibly, the rear figure is—the proof is confusing here—which would support a *feminine* identification for it). The rear male figure in the *Grave* design extends his *left* knee, as does the *forward* figure in the proof. And the male figure in the *Grave* design clasps *both* hips of the woman with both hands, a motif not repeated in the proof design. But if the rear figure is *male* in the proof, as Damon and Grant assume, then my subsequent argument for the femininity of *both* figures in the final plate is strengthened, since the rear figure exhibits no visible genitals in the final design.

David Erdman in "The Suppressed and Altered Passages in Blake's *Jerusalem,*" *Studies in Bibliography* 17 (1964): 18 also sees a forward male and a rear female copulating in the Morgan proof, but he thinks the two figures on the revised plate remain the same (opposite) sexes. This analysis, although plausible, does not explain why Blake smoothed out the back muscles of the figure on the right, nor why the lovers are no longer copulating.

Plate 79. *Jerusalem*, Plate 28, early proof, Copy F, Pierpont Morgan Library.

their union. This design seems to depict a fruitful sexual consummation, perhaps that of Albion and Vala described on Plate 20: "Albion loved thee: he rent thy Veil: he embraced thee: he lov'd thee!" (*J* 20:36). The lovers create a potential butterfly and their union takes place on a lily that may well be the Lilly of Havilah, that Biblical land of abundance and beauty that Blake in a letter to Hayley (March 12, 1804) compares to "Heaven, . . . Eden & all the countries where Jewels abound" (*K* 837).

In the final, revised engraving of this plate [*Plate 80*], Blake focused more specifically on the beauty of the female body, that feminine sensuality so perversely denied by Hand. He carefully erased the back muscles, slimmed down the pelvis, lengthened the thighs, and turned the lower torso of the forward figure toward the right; he defined the smooth *mons veneris* and added a right thigh to the rear figure; and he removed the caterpillar. The deliberate emasculation of the forward figure and the accentuated femininity of the long-haired figure at the rear, together with the fact that the two figures no longer copulate, suggest to me that Blake changed the sex of the forward figure. What I see here, in the Paul Mellon colored copy, are two women embracing beneath Vala's golden net, that gentle "veil of tears/ Weeping in pleadings of Love" (*J* 29: 3–4). This may portray the ideal union of Vala and Jerusalem, of the physical and spiritual female form, that takes place in Havilah or Beulah and that Vala later denies after her fall from eternity:

> I was a City & a Temple built by Albions Children.
> I was a Garden planted with beauty I allured on hill & valley
> The River of Life to flow against my walls & among my trees
> . . . .
> . . . why loved I Jerusalem!
> Why was I one with her embracing in the Vision of Jesus
> Wherefore did I loving create love. . . .
>
> (*J* 29:36–8, 43–5)

But Albion has already seen this perfect female form on the river of his own city:

> He found Jerusalem upon the River of his City soft repos'd
> In the arms of Vala, assimilating in one with Vala
> The Lilly of Havilah: and they sang soft thro' Lambeths vales,

Plate 80. *Jerusalem*, Plate 28, Copy E(TP), Paul Mellon Collection.

In a sweet moony night & silence that they had created
With a blue sky spread over with wings and a mild moon,
Dividing & uniting into many female forms: Jerusalem
Trembling! then in one comingling in eternal tears,
Sighing to melt his Giant beauty, on the moony river.

(*J* 19:40–48)

Here, in Havilah and in moony Beulah, the two aspects of woman—
her physical, sensual beauty and her capacity for spiritual and emotional
comfort—are fused into a single, ideal female form, the proper garment
or golden net for the creative male imagination. Significantly, in the Paul
Mellon colored copy, the half visible faces of both women blend into a
single full-face portrait, thus emphasizing their perfect unity. These fused
females also blend into the stamen of the lily, the generative seed of Havilah that procreates, clothes, and nourishes the male human form divine.

But this ideal vision of the female has been corrupted into the fallen female body in the designs on Plates 35 [31] and 37 [33]. As in *Genesis,*
the woman on Plate 35 [31] divides from the ribs of the man, rather
than blending with him in a perfect Blakean union of the sexes [*Plate
81*]; at the bottom of Plate 37 [33], Jerusalem herself vegetates and
roots herself around a stony coffin rather than a living male body [*Plate
82*]. Blake and the eternal ones cry out against this perversion of male
and female sexuality into separated, hostile bodies:

Have you known the Judgment that is arisen among the
Zoa's of Albion? Where a man dare hardly to embrace
His own Wife, for the terrors of Chastity that they call
By the name of Morality. their Daughters govern all
In hidden deceit! they are Vegetable only fit for burning:
Art & Science cannot exist but by Naked Beauty displayd.

(*J* 36 [32]:44–9)

So that fallen, sexually divided man may be capable of returning to the
human form divine, Christ in his mercy established limits to the corrupti-
bility of the mortal body. In *Jerusalem,* as in *Milton* and the *Laocoön,*
these limits are Satan and Adam, opacity and contraction. Satan is the
boundary of delusion: mortal vision cannot become so blinded, so opaque,
that man is physically unable to imagine or see the human form divine.
What he will see, at the extreme of error, is Satan, the false human form,

Then the Divine hand found the Two Limits, Satan and Adam,
in Albions bosom; for in every Human bosom those Limits stand.
And the Divine voice came from the Furnaces, as multitudes without
Number! the voices of the innumerable multitudes of Eternity.
And the appearance of a Man was seen in the Furnaces,
Saving those who have sinned from the punishment of the Law.
In pity of the punisher whose state is eternal death,
And keeping them from Sin by the mild counsels of his love.

Albion goes to Eternal Death: In Me all Eternity
Must pass thro' condemnation, and awake beyond the Grave:
No individual can keep these Laws, for they are death
To every energy of man, and forbid the springs of life;
Albion hath enterd the State Satan! Be permanent O State!
And be thou for ever accursed! that Albion may arise again:
And be thou created into a State! I go forth to Create
States: to deliver Individuals evermore! Amen.

So spake the voice from the Furnaces, descending into Non-Entity

Plate 82. Jerusalem, Plate 37 [33], Copy E(TP), Paul Mellon Collection.

the psychology of sin and self-annihilation. But even Satan is capable of being seen as a figure of great beauty, as Blake's impressive watercolor in the Tate Gallery, *Satan in His Original Glory,* demonstrates. And Adam is the limitation of physical substance itself. Significantly, in *Jerusalem,* the physical body is no longer the "solid obstruction" that it appeared to Los in *The Book of Urizen.* Rather, the human body, despite its necessary boundaries, can become the vehicle of salvation. Through the mercy of Christ, man can realize his divinity in the mortal body, both by seeing that body as potentially divine and by using his body to perform acts of forgiveness, love, and creative mental warfare.

Blake here articulates and sustains the distinction between a necessary, beneficial contraction—the bounding outline—and the excessive, harmful contractions of Urizen. When Albion descends to the outermost limit of contraction, he has closed his eyes to the potential infinitude of the human form. The danger is always present that fallen man will mistake the form itself for its function. Form is good insofar as it enables man to perceive and embody the divine vision on earth; it is evil whenever it becomes an end in itself: a fixed, dead object or an absolute law.

Blake vividly depicts this distinction between the merciful bounding line and the self-destructive contraction in terms of the feminine form on Plate 32 [46] [*Plate 83*]. Here, we see the choice that Albion must make: between the beautiful but veiled Vala at the left and the even more lovely naked Jerusalem at the right. The design is Blake's parody of traditional representations of Hercules at the crossroads. Whereas Hercules was asked to choose the modestly veiled virtue, who conventionally stands before her temple of honor, over the lasciviously naked vice and her accompanying city of lust, Albion is asked to reject this traditional submission to chastity and the female will. He should choose, not the veiled Vala standing before the dome of St. Paul's, the temple of state religion, but the naked Jerusalem and the Gothic spires of Westminster Abbey, the "Living Form" of "Eternal Existence." The configurations as well as the iconography of the design subtly affirm Jerusalem's glorious sensuality and realization of divine Energy. Whereas Vala stands rather stiffly at the left, enclosed in the cylinder of her blue veil, Jerusalem is flanked by three naked pubescent girls. One presses tightly to her right

Plate 83. Jerusalem, Plate 32 [46], Copy E(TP), Paul Mellon Collection.

hip; the second leans against her left hip with right arm lifted to Jerusalem's shoulder and left arm supporting the third girl, who dramatically leaps off this girl's left hip into the air, her left leg bent and her right arm vigorously pointing toward the top of the plate. Janet Warner has defined this particular gesture as "one of Blake's favorite means of depicting forces of spiritual or physical energy, from joy or delight to its more sinister aspect as a destructive force." [13] The beauty and vitality of this figure, here called Erin, is a representation of joy, inspiration, and freedom, as it is on the Argument of *Visions of the Daughters of Albion.*

The movement of the composition is even more significant. Structured roughly as an isosceles triangle laid on its side with its apex at the right, the thrust of the design is clearly from the static Vala at the left, rightward and upward, to the leaping Erin at the upper right. As our eyes move to the right over the four naked figures, we can see an increasing fluidity and linear rhythm in their bodies. The small girl at the right sandwiched between Vala and Jerusalem, stands stiffly, her body pressed against Jerusalem's, her arms huddled to her breast. Jerusalem herself stands calmly in the traditional *Venus Genetrix* position. The girl at her left repeats this pose, but in a more attenuated contortion: her breasts are turned to the left, her left hip juts more forcefully to the right, and both her arms are raised. Furthest to the right, the leaping Erin defies all the laws of gravity and anatomy, thrusting her body outward and upward and back upon itself in a dramatic gesture of complete liberation. This compositional diagonal thrust toward freedom is underlined both by the golden clouds that swirl upward and rightward from Jerusalem's feet and by Jerusalem's flowing golden hair, which lies flatly along her right, Vala side, but is lifted, coiling and flaming, upward and toward Erin on her left, liberated side.

But Albion, in chapter 2, rejects this liberated female form divine. Having lost both his poetic vision and his true human body, he becomes "but a Worm seventy inches long/ That creeps forth in a night & is dried in the morning sun" (*J* 29:6–7). He assumes the fallen, condensed body of Satan, a parody of the human form divine. Satan has

13. Janet Warner, "Blake's Use of Gesture," *Blake's Visionary Forms Dramatic*, ed. Erdman and Grant, p. 190.

> . . . a white Dot called a Center from which branches out
> A Circle in continual gyrations. this became a Heart
> From which sprang numerous branches varying their motions
> Producing many Heads three or seven or ten, & hands & feet
> Innumerable at will of the unfortunate contemplator
> Who becomes his food [:] such is the way of the Devouring Power
> . . . .
> Albions Emanation which he had hidden in Jealousy
> Appeard now in the frowning Chaos prolific upon the Chaos
> Reflecting back to Albion in Sexual Reasoning Hermaphroditic.
>
> (*J* 29:17–24, 26–8)

In place of the infinitely expansive center of the human form divine is the circumscribed "white Dot" of the great selfhood, Satan, which moves outward only in strictly concentric circles. In place of the divine analogy, which reveals to man that he is both an individual and potentially the cosmos, is the satanic abstraction, which blurs all minute particulars into an indefinite generalization that can only reduplicate the same blotch over and over (as are Satan's head, hand, and foot). In place of the true union of the sexes, in which the female is a garment for the male, is the unnatural begetting of an abstraction upon chaos that engenders only an impotent hermaphrodite. Edward Rose has further analyzed this sodomy:

The false appropriation of universality . . . is the basis of the selfhood's power —abstraction. . . . Any attempted unity upon fallen principles, therefore, is necessarily hermaphroditic, since it is the yoking of the unlike upon the basis of partial likeness or upon the indefinite doubled. That is to say, two abstract and therefore indefinite or general ideas, no matter how similar they may be, can never produce one concrete, definite, or particular reality which is true unity. . . . In moral terms the products of hermaphroditic or mistaken unity, that is, generalization, are cruelty and law; in aesthetic terms, the products are fable and allegory.[14]

This grotesque satanic blotch of a human form is strikingly pictured on Plate 50, where Hand the accuser sits confined to a narrow stony island in the midst of a raging sea. Hand has become the grotesque "Devouring Power" described on Plate 70:

> And this the form of mightly Hand sitting on Albions cliffs
> Before the face of Albion, a mighty threatning Form.
> His bosom wide & shoulders huge overspreading wondrous

14. Rose, "Symbolism," p. 591.

Bear Three strong sinewy Necks & Three awful & terrible Heads
Three Brains in contradictory council brooding incessantly.
Neither daring to put in act its councils, fearing each-other,
Therefore rejecting Ideas as nothing & holding all Wisdom
To consist. in the agreements & disagree [me]nts of Ideas.
Plotting to devour Albions Body of Humanity & Love.
Such Form the aggregate of the Twelve Sons of Albion took; & such
Their appearance when combind: but often by birth-pangs & loud groans
They divide to Twelve: the key-bones & the chest dividing in pain
Disclose a hideous orifice; thence issuing the Giant-brood
Arise as the smoke of the furnace, shaking the rocks from sea to sea.
And there they combine into Three Forms, named Bacon & Newton & Locke,
In the Oak Groves of Albion which overspread all the Earth.

(*J* 70:1–16)

The monster depicted on Plate 50 has three heads—Bacon's, Newton's
and Locke's, all wearing spiky crowns and contorted with hatred or dismay. A twofaced body crawls out of Hand's neckbone, appropriately originating between Bacon (who took Janus as his emblem) and Newton (the
measurer and divider). This figure further proliferates into two more tor-
sos and heads in turn, which fly in sickly yellow flames out over the sea,
toward the setting sun and waning moon on the right (significantly, the
lighted side of the moon is *away* from the sun in this cosmically disori-
ented universe). Lightning flashes at the left past another pale white
moon or sun.[15] Under the rule of this satanic Hand, Albion becomes the
reasoning, shrunken, vegetated body of Reuben, his tongue folded "between Lips of mire & clay," his ear bended "in a spiral circle outward"
(with no center), his eyelids "narrowed."

The appropriate consort for Albion's shrunken "Sexual Machine" is
Vala, the female denier of love and sex, the "Aged Virgin Form"
(*J* 39:25), the "paragon of virtue," the embodiment of chastity, the accuser
of harlots, and self-righteous murderess of "children of whoredoms"
(*J* 45:64). Vala is now hermaphroditically united with the spectre and
uses his perverse rhetoric to persuade Albion that she alone embodies
true female love and beauty:

15. I think Henry Lesnick is mistaken in seeing this lightning as a bird's beak; the
Paul Mellon colored copy shows only a flash of lightning originating from a small
moon or circular object (a meteor or comet?) in the sky ("Narrative Structure and the
Antithetical Vision of *Jerusalem,*" *Blake's Visionary Forms Dramatic,* ed. Erdman and
Grant, p. 397).

Vala was Albions Bride & Wife in great Eternity
The loveliest of the daughters of Eternity when in day-break
I emanated from Luvah over the Towers of Jerusalem
And in her Courts among her little Children offering up
The Sacrifice of fanatic love! . . .

. . . .

Know me now Albion: look upon me I alone am Beauty
The Imaginative Human Form is but a breathing of Vala
I breathe him forth into the Heaven from my secret Cave
Born of the Woman to obey the Woman O Albion the mighty
For the Divine appearance is Brotherhood, but I am Love.

(*J* 33 [29]:39–43, 48–52)

And Albion is corrupted by Satan and Vala. By the end of chapter 2, he
has become the fallen human body, oblivious to the loving cries of Jerusalem and the daughters of Beulah.

The Eye of Man, a little narrow orb, closd up & dark,
Scarcely beholding the Great Light; conversing with the Void:
The Ear, a little shell, in small volutions shutting out
True Harmonies, & comprehending great, as very small:
The Nostrils, bent down to the earth & clos'd with senseless flesh.
That odours cannot them expand, nor joy on them exult:
The Tongue, a little moisture fills, a little food it cloys,
A little sound it utters, & its cries are faintly heard.

(*J* 49:34–41)

Close on the fall of the human body comes the fall of the mind and the
emotions—of their respective capacities for reason and for faith. Chapter 3 is addressed to the eighteenth-century Deists who glorified the
mind's rage for order, law, and logic and then denied the value of the
imagination and existence of the soul. The frontispiece of chapter 3, Plate
51 [*Plate 84*], exposes the unholy trinity of the Deist faith: Vala, the
huddled woman at the left with a crown of spikes and a fleur-de-lis
sceptre; Hyle, the crouching, impotent figure in the center with bowed
head; and Scofield, the bald, chained figure slouching off to the right
who is a mirror image of the dagger-bearing, suicidal figure of despair in
The House of Death [*Plate 44*]. All three figures are massive and dark,
compositionally confined within two static boxes and a cylinder. These figures are frozen and dead, huddled beneath heavy, swagging black-red

Plate 84. Jerusalem, Plate 51, Copy E(TP), Paul Mellon Collection.

clouds and pale yellow, enclosed flames. Vala is the perversion of God the Father, the domination, not of Old Testament law or New Testament mercy, but of nature and the female will. Hyle (or Hayley) is her "Son," the impotent prime minister of her rule of materialism and hair-splitting moral absolutism. And Scofield is the spirit or "Unholy Ghost" of Vala's reign, the incubus of accusation, self-doubt, and despair. Historically, of course, Scolfield was the accuser at Blake's trial for sedition in Chichester in 1804; in *The House of Death* he is the accuser of the fallen body, the hanging judge who condemns mortal men to unrelieved suffering, disease, and suicidal despair.

Repeating the structure of the previous chapter, Blake poses the divine use of the mental faculties and the emotions—man's capacity for reason, pity, desire, and wrath—against the Deist perversions of the human mind. By "Deists," of course, as Harold Bloom notes, Blake did "not mean Toland, Collins, Tyndal and the other controversialists who argued for a religion of Nature against the Anglican orthodoxy of *their* day. Blake means the orthodoxy of *his* day, a Church of England that had covertly assimilated many Deist attitudes. Primarily, he means Rahab, the Eternal State Religion, the organized violence carried out in the names of Jesus and Jehovah" (E 855). The Deists' perversions are basically threefold. They believe in (1) the existence of an absolute order, law, or mathematical explanation of the universe; (2) the punishment of sin, where sin is defined as any deviation from this absolute order; and (3) the worship of the female will or Rahab, the embodiment of female chastity, sexual repression and frustration, strict social mores, and the total denial of physical and spiritual desire. This Rahab is portrayed in the design on Plate 53 as a pouting queen, crowned with the triple-tiered papal crown and seated upon the sunflower of frustrated sexual desire (an image established in Blake's earlier poem from *Songs of Experience,* "Ah! Sunflower," and used again for the ninety-ninth illustration to Dante's *Paradiso,* where the queen of heaven, Beatrice as the female will, sits on a huge sunflower, her tyrant's fleur-de-lis sceptre in one hand and a narcissistic looking glass in the other). Here, Rahab is flanked by the *closed* butterfly wings of female beauty and "winged joy" (as opposed to the open wings of the sexually gratifying Jerusalem or queen of the fairies who appears on the title page) and inscribed on these wings are the sun, moon, and stars; she rules the material universe (compare [*Plate 63*]).

The social and psychological results of these Deist beliefs are manifold and harmful. A belief in law leads to a reverence for the state over the individual, for the collective over the minute particular, for the good of the whole over the growth of the self. The end always justifies the means and the result is the accusation and incarceration of the individual, mass executions, and war. All these punishments are inflicted by the Druids, the primitive practitioners of black magic, idolatry, human sacrifice and cannibalism. Led by Gwendolen, the naked woman coiled round by massive worms beneath the bat-winged beams of a bloody moon on Plate 63, and sanctioned by the traditional religious rituals performed at Stonehenge and beneath other Druid trilitha,[16] modern Druid rites of witch hunting, sadistic tortures, and mass executions proliferate. These tortures and slaughters are eagerly performed by the vampire daughters of Albion and Rahab who "divide & unite at will/ Naked & drunk with blood . . . dancing to the timbrel/ Of War" (*J* 58:1–3). It is they who sit in judgment on men's crimes, "naked upon the Stone of trial"; it is they who carry out the ceremonial brainwashings and executions. They pass "the Knife of flint . . . over the howling Victim"; they mock him with a cruel crown of iron thorns; they erect "a temple & an altar" in the very center of his heart, destroying forever his capacity to love; and they "obscure the sun & the moon," completely blocking out the divine vision (*J* 66:19, 23, 29, 34). Men are either murdered or reduced to Milquetoasts, completely submissive to the female will.

Constantly at war with its external enemies, this Deist state must vigorously suppress all dissent within its own ranks. No one escapes scrutiny; consequently, every member of the state lives in continual paranoic fear, distrust, resentment, and hatred. In this prevision of Orwell's *1984,* all political and sexual unions are marriages of policy, never of love. They are thus inherently perverse or, in Blake's terminology, hermaphroditic. Vala's union with the spectre sets the pattern for all these sadistic relationships:

> Then the Spectre drew Vala into his bosom magnificent terrific
> Glittering with precious stones & gold, with Garments of blood & fire
> . . . .
> A dark Hermaphrodite they stood frowning upon Londons River.
>
> (*J* 64:25–6, 31)

16. John Beer discusses Blake's use of the trilitha to symbolize the Druids' cruel idolatry of law: "Rock always symbolized the hardness and opacity which he regarded as the antithesis of true vision, while the simple geometric shapes of circle and trilithon aptly symbolized that reduction to simple order and mathematical design which resulted from the exact thinking of the rationalists"; *Blake's Visionary Universe* (Manchester, England, 1969), p. 21. Although Beer fails to explain why Blake used equally simple geometric shapes and a rigorous symmetry in his own true visions, the Butts Bible illustrations, he accurately identifies the trilithon as an image of repression.

For an account of Druid rites, English literary images of the Druids, and Blake's use of traditional Druid lore, see A. L. Owen, *The Famous Druids* (Oxford, 1962). The savagery of the Druids is emphasized in Hugh Last's "Rome and the Druids: A Note," *Journal of Roman Studies* 39 (1949). But see Nora K. Chadwick's *The Druids* (Cardiff, 1966) for a sympathetic account of Druid learning and lore.

The body politic of the Deists is at best a random collection of atomistic individuals joined only by fear or self-interest, never by a genuine spiritual communion. It is the grotesque seven-headed human-serpent or polypus pictured on the bottom of Plate 75, Blake's culminating image of the fallen physical world. For Blake, the apparently parasitic rooting of the colonial forms of the hydroid polyp (of the *Cnidaria* family), its menacing and proliferating tentacles, and its poison combined to make it an appropriate image of the endlessly multiplying, self-devouring, vegetated world. In *Jerusalem,* the polypus is specifically pictured as a collection of rocks fragmented from eternity, "Opake hardnesses covering all Vegetated things" (*J* 67:5), which the Deists hail as the "Atomic Origins of Existence" (*J* 67:12). And it is the spiritual state of the Deists as well:

> Then all the Males combined into One Male & every one
> Became a ravening eating Cancer growing in the Female
> A Polypus of Roots of Reasoning Doubt Despair & Death.
>
> (*J* 69:1–3)

This is a body politic schizophrenically divided against itself: "Envying stood the enormous Form at variance with Itself/ In all its Members" (*J* 69:6–7).

In this self-divided, paranoic kingdom, the human intellect itself is destroyed. The creative imagination is reduced to mere fancy, what Coleridge called "no other than a mode of Memory emancipated from the order of time and space," [17] an arbitrary associater of fixed, dead objects. As a result, the art of the Deists degenerates into empty mathematical formulas or mystifying complexities. It is the art of the machine, of war and death. The sons of Urizen pervert

> . . . all the Arts of Life . . . into the Arts of Death in Albion.
> The hour-glass contemnd because its simple workmanship.
> Was like the workmanship of the plowman, & the water wheel,
> That raises water into cisterns: broken & burnd with fire:
> Because its workmanship. was like the workmanship of the shepherd.
> And in their stead, intricate wheels invented, wheel without wheel:
> To perplex youth in their outgoings, & to bind to labours in Albion
> Of day & night the myriads of eternity that they may grind
> And polish brass & iron hour after hour laborious task!

17. S. T. Coleridge, *Biographia Literaria,* ed. J. Shawcross (London, 1907), I, p. 202.

Kept ignorant of its use, that they might spend the days of wisdom
In sorrowful drudgery, to obtain a scanty pittance of bread:
In ignorance to view a small portion & think that All,
And call it Demonstration: blind to all the simple rules of life.

(*J* 65:12–28)

This is the false art of Rome and Greece which only ornaments an already perverted vision of nature. Blake emphatically denounces this mimetic celebration of tyranny and war in "On Virgil" (1820):

Sacred Truth has pronounced that Greece & Rome as Babylon & Egypt: so far from being parents of Arts & Sciences as they pretend: were destroyers of all Art . . . Virgil in the Eneid Book VI. line 848 says Let others study Art: Rome has somewhat better to do, namely War & Dominion

Rome & Greece swept Art into their maw & destroyd it a Warlike State never can produce Art. It will Rob & Plunder & accumulate into one place, & Translate & Copy & Buy & Sell & Criticise, but not Make. Grecian is Mathematic Form Gothic is Living Form Mathematic Form is Eternal in the Reasoning Memory. Living Form is Eternal Existence. (E 267)

In contrast to his earlier affirmations of the Greeks in his letters to Cumberland in 1795–96, Blake now rejects the moral and political systems of the Greeks and especially of the Romans. In both these cultures, aesthetic creations were at best but derivative imitiations of the primal visions of the artists of Atlantis. At worst, the Greeks and Romans reduced their art to mathematic formulas and arbitrary rules and forbade originality of content and form. Although Blake himself continued to use neoclassical figures, linear rhythms, clear outlines, and calculated symmetries, he does so not in obedience to rules but in response to his private and highly organized visions. He creates his own system; the Romans only imitated the Greeks' system, and the Greeks in turn copied theirs readymade from their ancestors.

Genuine religious faith is also destroyed by the Deists. To increase their control over the minds of mankind, Rahab-Vala and Urizen systematically root out true Christian worship and replace it with the complex, arbitrary ceremonies of mystery that are designed to confuse, frighten, and thus further subjugate the devout. The fallen trinity of mystery replaces the holy Trinity of vision; contentions of chastity, "Deceit & Fraud," jealousy, "Revenge & deadly Murder" (*J* 69:11, 13) replace the love and mercy of Jesus and the saving doctrine of states; and the "Tabernacle in the Wilderness" where men must worship Rahab's "Religion of Chastity, forming a Commerce to sell Loves,/ With Moral Law, and Equal Balance" (*J* 69:34–5), replaces the Gothic cathedral of Christ, that true "Sanctuary of Eden" which "in the Camp: in the Outline,/ In the Circumference: & every Minute Particular is Holy" (*J* 69:41–2). Under this barrage of contradictions, reason itself is destroyed. The warrior sons of Albion cry out on their way to battle:

> Once Man was occupied in intellectual pleasures & energies
> But now my soul is harrowd with grief & fear & love & desire
> And now I hate & now I love & Intellect is no more.
>
> (*J* 68:65–7)

In such a totalitarian regime, even the most independent, rebellious individual begins to doubt his own sanity, as do Winston Smith in *1984* and McMurphy in *One Flew over the Cuckoo's Nest.* The elect, of course, maintain their single, certain truth and are secure in their unquestioned conception of the universe; but everyone else is tortured by uncertainty, anxiety, and self-distrust. Even Jerusalem begins to doubt the validity of the divine vision:

> O Lord & Saviour, have the Gods of the Heathen pierced thee?
> . . . .
> Art thou alive! & livest thou for-evermore? or art thou
> Not: but a delusive shadow, a thought that liveth not.
> Babel mocks saying, there is no God nor Son of God
> That thou O Human Imagination, O Divine Body art all
> A delusion. but I know thee O lord when thou arisest upon
> My weary eyes even in this dungeon & this iron mill.
> . . . .
> And altho I sin & blaspheme thy holy name, thou pitiest me;
> Because thou knowest I am deluded by the turning mills.
> And by these visions of pity & love because of Albions death.
>
> (*J* 60:52, 54–9, 62–4)

In opposition to these Deist perversions of the mind, the emotions, and the imagination, Los celebrates the divine use of the mind—the constant awareness of the "Divine Similitude." This is the vision of Innocence that sees God as father, shepherd, and lamb; the flock as children, men, and gods; the garden as "The fields of Cows by Willans farm" (*J* 27:15), Eden, and Jerusalem. Los defines this analogical mode of perception thus:

> We live as One Man: for contracting our infinite senses
> We behold multitude; or expanding: we behold as one,
> As One Man all the Universal Family; and that One Man
> We call Jesus the Christ: and he in us, and we in him,
> Live in perfect harmony in Eden the land of life,
> Giving, receiving, and forgiving each others trespasses.
>
> (*J* 38 [34]:17–22)

The form in which this divine analogy is realized on earth is language. The words and syntax of poetry and everyday discourse that correlate objects and actions through nouns and verbs determine the conceptual framework within which our thoughts, actions, and conscious existence take place. Kant first emphasized that human perception occurs only within the pre-existing forms or modalities of time, space, simplicity, and causality that he called categories; Shelley attributed this experience-shaping power directly to language, that "perpetual Orphic song,/ Which rules with Daedal harmony a throng/ Of thoughts and forms, which else senseless and shapeless were" (*Prometheus Unbound,* IV:414); and both Ernst Cassirer and Benjamin Lee Whorf have argued that language itself constitutes the mental system, the Kantian categories, through which all conscious human experience is filtered.[18] For these neo-Kantians and linguistic anthropologists, as for Shelley and Blake, all conscious experience presupposes a symbolic language. Blake asserts that all human experience is shaped by pre-existent image patterns, be they gestural, pictorial, or verbal. Communicating the "Divine Similitude" (the analogical perception that reveals the holiness of man and nature), Blake first acknowledges the linguistic structures that make his visions possible:

> (I call them by their English names: English, the rough basement,
> Los built the stubborn structure of the Language, acting against
> Albions melancholy, who must else have been a Dumb Despair.)
>
> (*J* 36 [40]:58–60)

18. Ernst Cassirer, *An Essay on Man* (Garden City, N.Y.: Doubleday, Anchor, 1944), p. 176 and pt. 2, chap. 8; Benjamin Lee Whorf, *Language, Thought, and Reality,* ed. J. Carroll (Cambridge: M.I.T. Press, 1956), pp. 247–52 and *passim.*

Finally, however, Blake goes even further than the linguistic anthropologists and asserts that all mental experience is fundamentally shaped by a single visual form, the human body. Analogy ultimately becomes universal reality for Blake: ideally, we will not only see ourselves and all men as one man, we will actually "live as One Man." The content or structure of this ultimate "Divine Similitude" or analogy is the sum of man's authentic relationships with the cosmos, with woman, with the fourfold aspects of his own being. The eternals explicitly define Blake's ultimate vision of the individual as infinite, as both soul and solar system, on Plate 55:

> Let the Human Organs be kept in their perfect Integrity
> At will Contracting into Worms, or Expanding into Gods
> . . . .
> Every one knows, we are One Family: One Man blessed for ever.
>
> *(J* 55:36–7, 46)

> The Infinite alone resides in Definite & Determinate Identity.
>
> *(J* 55:64)

The genuine fusion of male and female, as we have seen before, is the union of a physical body with its clothing. The garment is the external manifestation or coloring of a spiritual energy or perfect outline. As Blake summarizes:

> In Great Eternity, every particular Form gives forth or Emanates
> Its own peculiar Light, & the Form is the Divine Vision
> And the Light is his Garment. This is Jerusalem in every Man
> A Tent & Tabernacle of Mutual Forgiveness Male & Female Clothings.
>
> *(J* 54:1–4)

This relationship of masculine energy to feminine form is visually displayed in Blake's drawing of *The Last Judgment* owned by J. L. Rosenwald. Here, the two pillars of the throne of God are represented by Jachin and Boaz, who symbolize the two sexes both in Cabbalist and Freemason traditions. As Albert S. Roe explicates, "In Blake's system he conceives the essential harmony of creation to be the vital balance between the creative imagination, which he characterizes as masculine, and its reflection in the feminine world of material existence." [19] And everywhere in

19. Albert S. Roe, "A Drawing of the Last Judgment," *The Huntington Library Quarterly* 21 (1957–58):45.

Blake's mature art, clinging (feminine) draperies function to define and extend the outlines of the human form divine.

The character of the individual human being at the center of this cosmic universe and feminine garment is fourfold. As Blake puts it pictorially on Plate 54, the human mind divine should be ruled by the integrated faculties of reason, desire, wrath, and pity. Imagination should order man's desire for the infinite and the pleasurable, his rebellious anger at the restrictions of the fallen world, and his pitying forgiveness of sins into a single, rational character or personality. Whenever this occurs, man becomes organized; he can create a new system, a true art based on melody, outline, and the visions of the imagination (as opposed to a fallen art based on "Harmonies of Concords & Discords," "Lights & Shades," and "Abstraction" [*J* 74:24–6]). He can then create the ideal artistic image pictured on Plate 75, a clearly defined but infinitely expanding line of interlocking circles of open-winged angels, rather than the blurred confusion of serpent, male and female at the bottom of this plate that is the artistic product of Rahab's—or Blake's archenemy Joshua Reynolds'—disunity misunited.

The last chapter of *Jerusalem* describes the corruption and regeneration of the most essential of human attributes, the imagination. Addressed to the Christians who have been given—and lost—the divine vision in its original purity, this chapter, paralleling the others, contrasts the true divine vision sustained by Los to the distorted vision proclaimed by the fallen church. The frontispiece to this chapter, Blake's famous engraving of Albion worshipping Christ [*Plate 85*] vividly defines man's true relationship with Christ. Jesus and Albion are identical in body structure and size, and both spread their arms open in the traditional cruciform pattern. Christ, of course, is nailed to the double-branched tree of mystery (the false religion of the establishment Church upheld by the "Human Abstract"), and his crown of thorns radiates a brilliant light that illuminates the entire scene. Albion, standing with left leg out and head lifted in adoration, is a mirror image of Blake's Glad Day figure [*Plate 37*], the image of Energy or Innocence reborn and triumphant. The reuse of the Glad Day figure here in spite of its parodic appearance as perverted energy in *The Spiritual Form of Nelson Guiding Leviathan,* in *Fire* [*Plate 61*] (*The*

Plate 85. Jerusalem, Plate 76, Copy E(TP), Paul Mellon Collection.

Gates of Paradise), and in *Satan Smiting Job with Sore Boils* demonstrates Blake's faith that divine Energy can transcend the Orc cycle and escape the corruptions of reason. Christ and Albion can become one: in the ultimate achievements of his human capacities for creation, mental warfare, action, and vision, man is God; God is man. As Blake cries to the deluded "Christians," "I know of no other Christianity and of no other Gospel than the liberty both of body & mind to exercise the Divine Arts of Imagination" (*J* 77).

The Christians have denied the divine vision in two ways. They have perverted a forgiving, accepting love into a vengeful law "of sin, of sorrow & of punishment" presided over by such accusers as Caiaphas, "the dark Preacher of Death" (*J* 77:19, 18); and they have rejected sexual pleasure and love. Blake merges these two perversions into his striking image of the covering cherub. The cherub is the antichrist incarnate; he incorporates all those Pharisees, scribes, Sadducees, and men of the cloth who do not practice what they preach. He is the hermaphroditic, egoistic selfhood; a disorganized, chaotic nonentity; a mere show of outward ceremony and empty allegoric pomp; a human dragon who serves the whore of Babylon; a contracted body imprisoned beneath a veil and net of veins. In every way, the cherub is a grotesque parody of the human form divine. Blake devotes all of Plate 89 to the construction of this image, using his familiar techniques of allusion, analogy, lists, and categorization:

> Tho divided by the Cross & Nails & Thorns & Spear
> In cruelties of Rahab & Tirzah [,] permanent endure
> A terrible indefinite Hermaphroditic form
> A Wine-press of Love & Wrath double Hermaph[r]oditic
> Twelvefold in Allegoric pomp in selfish holiness
> The Pharisaion, the Grammateis, the Presbuterion,
> The Archiereus, the Iereus, the Saddusaion, double
> Each withoutside of the other, covering eastern heaven
>
> Thus was the Covering Cherub reveald majestic image
> Of Selfhood, Body put off, the Antichrist accursed
> Coverd with precious stones, a Human Dragon terrible
> And bright, stretchd over Europe & Asia gorgeous
> In three nights he devourd the rejected corse of death
>
> His head dark, deadly, in its Brain incloses a reflexion
> Of Eden all perverted: Egypt on the Gihon many tongued

And many mouthd: Ethiopia, Libya, the Sea of Rephaim
Minute Particulars in slavery I behold among the brick-kilns
Disorganiz'd, & there is Pharoh in his iron Court:
. . . .
Above his Head high arching Wings black filld with Eyes
Spring upon iron sinews from the Scapulae & Os Humeri.
There Israel in bondage to his Generalizing Gods
Molech & Chemosh, & in his left breast is Philistea
In Druid Temples over the whole Earth with Victims Sacrifice,
. . . .
His Loins inclose Babylon on Euphrates beautiful
And Rome in sweet Hesperia . . .
. . . .
But in the midst of a devouring Stomach, Jerusalem
Hidden within the Covering Cherub as in a Tabernacle
Of threefold workmanship in allegoric delusion & woe [.]
. . . .
A Double Female now appeard within the Tabernacle,
Religion hid in War, a Dragon red & hidden Harlot
Each within other . . .
For multitudes of those who sleep in Alla descend . . .
Wandering in that unknown Night beyond the silent Grave
They become One with the Antichrist & are absorbed in him.

(*J* 89:1–18, 28–32, 38–9, 43–5, 52–4, 58, 61–2)

In opposition to this freakish fancy of a diseased imagination, Los celebrates the visionary creation of a pure imagination, that image of the
human form divine that is both a way of life and a mode of perception.
One lives in Innocence:

Go, tell them that the Worship of God, is honouring his gifts
In other men: & loving the greatest men best, each according
To his Genius: which is the Holy Ghost in Man; there is no other
God, than that God who is the intellectual fountain of Humanity.

(*J* 91:7–11)

and one sees analogically:

He who would see the Divinity must see him in his Children
One first, in friendship & love; then a Divine Family, & in the midst
Jesus will appear; so he who wishes to see a Vision; a perfect Whole
Must see it in its Minute Particulars; Organized. . . .

(*J* 91:18–21)

Los is aided in his efforts to redeem the human imagination by both Jerusalem and the daughters of Beulah. Jerusalem reminds Albion of the true visions of the night of Beulah, those moments of sexual ecstasy and creation when man unites with the daughters of Beulah to regenerate the divine humanity in time and space (*J* 79:72–77, *J* 85:6–9). Only through such sexual communion with one's divine female emanation can the individual male procreate the human form divine, the mortal bodies of his sons and daughters that are nonetheless vehicles of infinity. Since the true daughters of Beulah never lose this vision of their children as holy, they can teach the divine vision both to their mates and to their offspring. With their help, Los confidently predicts that a universal last judgment will come, a time when all men will simultaneously acknowledge their divine humanity, when all sexual conflicts will cease, when all sins will be forgiven and thus rendered nonexistent.

And the prediction of Los comes to pass. With the suddenness of vision, with the instantaneous illumination of a finally understood truth, the ultimate apocalypse takes place. As in the fourth act of Shelley's *Prometheus Unbound* or Wordsworth's climactic vision on Mount Snowden in *The Prelude,* Blake's apocalypse occurs both in and out of time. It happens *in* time whenever an individual perceives the divine analogy, the presence of God within himself. But the apocalypse, the moment when all men simultaneously realize their divine humanity, happens *out* of time, or rather, *beyond* time. This is that ultimate moment which is potential within time (in the sense that it is possible for it to occur at any instant) but which, should it actually take place, immediately leaps out of time into eternity. For the moment that all men see themselves and each other as gods is the moment when earth becomes heaven, the particular becomes infinite, and time becomes eternity. When all distinctions between the finite and the infinite are merely modes of perception, capable of being reperceived and recreated simultaneously, then such distinctions no longer "exist" in any meaningful sense. Reality is then pure flux, motion, energy.

> To see a World in a Grain of Sand
> And a Heaven in a Wild Flower

> Hold Infinity in the palm of your hand
> And Eternity in an hour

(E 481)

is to live in a realm both within and beyond time and space.

Vegetable nature thus becomes the manifestation of infinity; its "concrete" objects are but momentary perceptions of the infinite energy that exists only as motion. Blake's metaphysics, despite George Harper's and Kathleen Raine's arguments,[20] are not Platonic; Blake does not believe in a static, objective, ideal world of permanent forms or ideas that are manifested in a lesser "reality" in nature. Rather, Blake seems to hold a concept not unlike that behind modern physics: "matter" or "reality" is essentially energy (compare $e = mc^2$) and the forms or "objects" we perceive are only the temporal modes of energy. In other words, vision (perception) is creation; it is a process of imposing form on energy. Thus, reality —the external forms we perceive—is wholly dependent on the imagination: "If Perceptive Organs vary: Objects of Perception seem to vary" (*J* 30:55) and "the Eye altering alters all" (E 476). Blake sums up this metaphysics in his catalogue entries for *A Vision of the Last Judgment:*

Vision or Imagination is a Representation of what Eternally Exists. Really and Unchangeably. . . . I have represented [*The Last Judgment*] as I saw it [.] to different People it appears differently as every thing else does for tho on Earth things seem Permanent they are less permanent than a Shadow as we all know too well. (E 544)

This world of Imagination is the World of Eternity it is the Divine bosom into which we shall all go after the death of the Vegetated body This World [of Imagination] is Infinite & Eternal whereas the world of Generation or Vegetation is Finite & Temporal There Exist in that Eternal World the Permanent Realities [that is, eternal energies] of Every Thing which we see reflected in this Vegetable Glass of Nature. (E 545; bracketed material is mine)

To see beyond the finite and temporal orderings both of one's own mind and of the collective minds of others (the world of generation or vegetation) is to liberate one's imagination completely. One can then see one's "self" as only a momentary image that is always in the process of flowing and changing, of entering into new metaphorical relationships

20. George Mills Harper, *The Neoplatonism of William Blake* (Chapel Hill: University of North Carolina Press, 1961), p. 81 and *passim;* Kathleen Raine, *Blake and Tradition* (Princeton, 1968), I, pp. 1–332.

that transform one's self-consciousness. Whenever an individual sees his "self" in this way, he immediately gains total control over his ontological and psychological worlds: he can "be" whatever he chooses to "be." This liberation of the imagination or "freedom of choice" is another way of saying what Blake means by divinity. To be "God" is to *know* that the finite objects or "natural world" that surround us are only constructions of the human imagination and that beyond these temporal orderings lies that pure creative Energy (what Blake calls "mental things") that *is* being. As soon as one knows this truth, one is freed from all "mind-forg'd manacles" and impowered to create one's own images or orderings. And since one knows that no one image is any more absolute than another, one will constantly create new images and "selves," for the sheer pleasure that the creative act brings. But each image, as an image or "object," exists "really & unchangeably": it has its own unique identity and cannot be blurred or confused with any other image. Blake does not mean that a given world of pure Platonic forms exists eternally; but rather that, as each individual imagination creates its own images or metaphors, whether they had been articulated before or had existed only potentially, it perceives each image's minute particularity and articulates it in its unique, determinate, and unchanging specificity. The liberated imagination can sketch any line it chooses around the dynamic pulsations of Energy, but that line, once selected, should be drawn clearly, sharply, and definitively, and the images it outlines should be unique and unmistakeable identities. In this way, the imagination uses reason to clarify and organize its ever new images.

Blake's climactic ending of *A Vision of the Last Judgment* triumphantly celebrates this freedom and creative power:

Mental Things are alone Real what is Calld Corporeal Nobody Knows of its dwelling Place [it] is in Fallacy. . . . Error or Creation . . . is Burnt up the Moment Men cease to behold it I assert for My self that I do not behold the Outward Creation & that to me it is hindrance & not Action it is as the Dirt upon my feet No part of Me. What it will be Questiond When the Sun rises do you not see a round Disk of fire somewhat like a Guinea O no no I see an Innumerable company of the Heavenly host crying Holy Holy Holy is the Lord God Almighty I question not my Corporeal or Vegetative Eye any more than I would Question a Window concerning a Sight I look thro it & not with it. (E 555)

Blake's very language demonstrates the imagination's capacity to construct both the vegetative world and the liberated visions of the man-god. Whereas most men see the sun (a "corporeal object") as the dead metaphor of traditional speech, as "a round Disk of fire somewhat like a Guinea," Blake prefers to create his own image or metaphor for the sun, "an Innumerable company of the Heavenly host crying Holy Holy Holy is the Lord." Blake is surely right to assert that there is no more absolute reality in the traditional metaphor than in his: both are subjective projections of a human imagination. The average man who submits blindly to the conventional metaphor has not gained a *truer* understanding of the sun; he has only sacrificed his own creative freedom to the collective will of society and tradition. Blake refuses to submit to the dead metaphors of others; he looks straight through their corporeal windows, which seem solid doors ("realities") to their eyes (which are "Born in a Night to perish in a Night"), and beyond into the "Realms of day" where man is simultaneously finite and infinite.

This is the vision Blake celebrates, both pictorially and poetically, in the triumphant closing pages of *Jerusalem*. Suddenly, at line 23 on Plate 94, the apocalypse occurs: "Time was finished!" With this moment of universal vision comes the end of time, the beginning of eternity. Albion revives under the divine breath; inspired by his imagination, he strides forth, "clothed in flames of fire," to compel the fallen mind, body, and emotions to return to their rightful functions. He energetically compels "Urizen to his Furrow; & Tharmas to his Sheepfold;/ And Luvah to his Loom: Urthona he beheld mighty labouring at/ His Anvil" (*J* 95:16–8). The separated female will repents and returns to Albion's bosom in love and humility, "Adoring his wrathful rebuke" (*J* 95:23). This ecstatic union of male and female is pictured on Plates 96 and 99, where Albion as Jehovah-Urizen-Jesus ardently embraces the beautiful, naked Britannia-Jerusalem in flames of desire and Energy. The design on Plate 99 is based on Marten de Vos's *The Prodigal Son:* [21] the reunion of Albion with Jerusalem is ultimate testimony to the mercy of the Father-Jesus-Jehovah and is moreover the climactic homecoming of the poem. As

21. Sir Anthony Blunt, *The Art of William Blake* (New York, 1959), Plate 49, a and b.

Albion is reunited both with his emanation and with his four Zoas (the
four perfections of body [Tharmas], mind [Urizen], emotion [Luvah],
and imagination [Urthona]), Jesus appears before him as the human
form divine, "The Good Shepherd" of Innocence who forgives and re-
unites with the repentant Albion.

Albion is now one man, both the fourfold universal man and the savior
Christ. "Urizen & Luvah & Tharmas & Urthona arose into/ Albions
Bosom" (*J* 98:21–2); he is both a specific identity and a participant
in the one man. Albion now lives in a community of vision, a society in
which everyone perceives the infinite within the particular. Like the lily,
cloud, and clod in Thel's Vales of Har, all men now speak

. . . in Visionary forms dramatic which bright
Redounded from their Tongues in thunderous majesty, in Visions
In new Expanses, creating exemplars of Memory and of Intellect
Creating Space, Creating Time according to the wonders Divine
Of Human Imagination, throughout all the Three Regions immense
Of Childhood, Manhood & Old Age [;] & the all tremendous unfathomable Non
    Ens
Of Death was seen in regenerations terrific or complacent varying
According to the subject of discourse & every Word & Every Character
Was Human according to the Expansion or Contraction, the Translucence or
Opakeness of Nervous fibres such was the variation of Time & Space
Which vary according as the Organs of Perception vary & they walked
To & fro in Eternity as One Man reflecting each in each & clearly seen
And seeing: according to fitness & order.
                        (*J* 98:28–40)

Thus Blake sums up his theories of language, art, and metaphysics. Poetry
and painting, music and dance—whose very words, images, notes, and
gestures are "visionary forms dramatic"—create the universe in which
men perceive, think, and act. Time, space, social organizations, and the
conceptual structures of human thought are all constructs of the imagination realized in language and specifically in the ultimate image and body
of the human form, which extends throughout "the three Regions
immense/ Of Childhood, Manhood & Old Age." And these linguistic
and visual images or "visionary forms" are themselves dramatic symbols:
they exist both as temporal realities and as expressions or inspirations of
the imagination. Man uses symbolic forms to structure the world he imag-

ines; but these structures constantly expand beyond themselves, suggesting alternative forms and thus liberating the imagination to create ever new systems, "according to fitness & order."

Once man has entered this state of visionary awareness, he need never fear his mortal life or body. He can always choose—to live with the eternals in a dynamic game of mental warfare, or to take on the human form and accept for a moment the contractions of mortality. In Blake's final vision of man as both mortal and divine, both temporal and eternal,

> All Human Forms [are] identified even Tree Metal Earth & Stone. all
> Human Forms identified, living going forth & returning wearied
> Into the Planetary lives of Years Months Days & Hours reposing
> And then Awaking into his Bosom in the Life of Immortality.
> And I heard the name of their Emanations they are named Jerusalem.
>
> (*J* 99:1–5)

The danger of descending into Beulah to clothe one's imaginative creations in physical form, to repose in the city of Jerusalem or in "Planetary lives," is, of course, that your imagination may submit to reason, harden into the closed state of Satan, and mistake the garment for the man. And even if one does keep faith with the divine vision on earth, one must still cope with the cruelties of other men, natural disasters, diseases, and physical death. Still, we probably neither can nor should avoid our planetary lives; even the eternal imagination or Energy requires a circumscribing form to prevent it from dissipating itself into stasis (what modern scientists call entropy). A clear and determinate outline, a bounded form, is life itself, or at least it is the life Blake and his readers know. But even as we live in our mortal bodies, we can always choose: to see a grain of sand or the infinite world within it, to hold a wild flower (and treasure its own minute, particular beauty) or the eternal heaven within it.

The final design restates both the structure of *Jerusalem* and the way to salvation, both within and beyond time [*Plate 86*]. Los, in his eternal form of Urthona, stands proudly in the center, holding the tools of creation. His left hand grasps the tongs of the blacksmith which also resemble a compass, an association reinforced by the fact that Los-Urthona, like the Ancient of Days, holds them between thumb and fore-finger. Tongs seize and shape molten metal into new images; compasses circumscribe,

Plate 86. Jerusalem, Plate 100, Copy E(TP), Paul Mellon Collection.

dissect, or measure already existing materials. This iconographic fusion of tongs and compasses therefore embodies Blake's conception of the union of imagination and reason in the creative process. The imagination continually shapes new images from the transforming pulsations of divine Energy; reason then clarifies, organizes, and more minutely particularizes these images by drawing the "outline of Identity." His right hand holds the hammer that both destroys restrictive conceptions and forges its own images. On the left, the Los of the frontispiece or the redeemed Albion of Plate 97 bears off the round golden globe of true vision. Behind Urthona coils the serpentine temple of Avebury, composed of numerous trilitha placed side by side in a perfect circle with two symmetrical tails. On the right, a dark female (Enitharmon or Jerusalem) holds the spindle (in her left hand) and the blood-red threads or fibers (falling from her right hand) of the looms of Cathedron beside the crescent moon of Beulah (the land of physical and artistic creation). All three background images represent aspects or phases of the artist's or imagination's task. First, Urthona must redeem the imagination of fallen man by sending the light of vision into the dark void of Ulro, as Los-Blake does on the frontispiece [*Plate* 75]. Second, Urthona must annihilate the perverse laws of corrupted minds and diseased emotions—he must demolish the false religions, self-righteous codes, and serpentine temples of the accusers, be they the Druids at Avebury or the Deists of the eighteenth century. He can do this by transforming the fallen temples of the Druids into the perfectly organized city of Golgonooza, the golden city of art. As Kenneth Johnston has perceptively noted, the trilitha of the serpentine temple are here regularly ordered, whereas elsewhere in Blake's designs they always "stand separately, at odd angles to each other, some fallen or indistinguishable from massive unhewn rocks nearby, never in a complete circle." [22] Moreover, these trilitha rise from luxuriant foliage, colored gold and green in the Paul Mellon copy, in contrast to the dark, barren surroundings in which Blake usually sets them. Here, Urthona has successfully completed his project of urban renewal. And finally, the imagination must welcome both the female body and the human body itself as a loving, outlining garment or darkening, defining color (rather than a cruel, constricting armor) for its divine Energy, accepting the limitations of "planetary lives" as nothing more than modes of vision. Los-Urthona dominates the design, confidently sustaining, as he has done throughout the poem, the divine vision of Innocence that transforms mortal man into the human form divine.[23]

Blake's ultimate affirmation of Innocence and Energy as a total identification with Christ both physically, in the human form divine, and imaginatively, through the divine analogy, is celebrated in Blake's Bible illustration, *The Holy Family,* or *Christ in the Lap of Truth* [*Plate* 87]. Analogically, the painting fuses two levels of experience, the human and

22. Kenneth R. Johnston, "Blake's Cities," p. 436.
23. Here, I disagree with Karl Kiralis who sees a "look of dejection" on Los's face ("Correspondence," *Blake Studies* 1 [Spring 1969]: 213). Los's expression in Copy E appears to me to be earnest, serious, but serene and confident rather than dismayed. I agree with Kiralis that man must re-enter the "Planetary lives" on Plate 98, but I do not see this return into a mortal body, as Kiralis does, as a necessary fall from fulfillment.

Plate 87. The Holy Family, or *Christ in the Lap of Truth.*

the divine. At the literal, historical level of single vision, Jesus stands in
the lap of his mother Mary; his father Joseph sits on the left, his grand-
mother Anne on the right. At his feet, a small naked child plays happily
with a lamb. Three angels frame the scene; two stand praying at either

side, the third watches serenely from above. At the allegoric level of two-fold vision (to use Dante's fourfold method of exegesis laid out in his letter to Can Grande della Scala,[24] a method similar to Blake's notion of "fourfold vision" in his November 22, 1802, letter to Butts), this scene represents the Holy Family, and the physical creation of the Son of God. Morally, or "three fold in soft Beulah's night" (E 693), the scene signifies the willingness of Christ to assume a human body and to sacrifice himself in order to redeem mankind from the state of Satan. He appears here in the cruciform position, palms out, left foot over right. And at the highest, fourfold, anagogic level—what Blake calls the divine analogy—the scene depicts the one man seated, with his arms spread in the accepting gesture of Innocence, in the lap of the divine mother, truth. The child playing at the Christ child's feet looks much like him and also clearly evokes the child playing with a lamb on the second plate of "Spring" in the *Songs of Innocence*. Analogically, this child of Innocence is Christ —man is God, God is man; and this divine vision of Innocence is the ultimate and holy truth, blessed and confirmed by the angel hovering above.

Significantly, both the "naive" child of Innocence and the fully conscious Christ share this divine truth. Both the child's instinctive, "thought-less" trust in the love and care of God (as in "The Fly" where the child is "happy" whether he lives or dies [25]) and the consciousness of oneself as the human form divine, which Christ and Job achieve, are equally valid ways of participating in the one true divine vision. Unlike Wordsworth, Blake did not believe that the acquistion of self-consciousness and consciousness-of-consciousness (what Wordsworth called "the philosophic

24. Charles Sterrett Latham, *A Translation of Dante's Eleven Letters* (Cambridge, Mass., 1891), p. 193.

25. In contrast to John Grant who sees the speaker of "The Fly" as a calloused "man *in* Experience" ("Interpreting Blake's 'The Fly,' " *BNYPL* 67 [1963]:596) and also to Jean Hagstrum who sees "thought" in the fourth stanza as a positive value ("The Fly," *Blake Essays for Damon*, pp. 376–80), I read "thought" as a negative, Urizenic attribute, an attempt to divide and categorize human experience, which the innocent speaker rightly rejects. The echo of Descartes' rationalistic credo, "Cogito, ergo sum," in "If thought is life/And strength and breath" may lend credence to this reading. I would therefore explicate the fourth stanza thus: "If (according to you, Descartes, Urizen or the voice of rational Experience) thought is life . . . ," then truly am I free and "happy," so long as I ignore or deny your assumptions.

mind" [26]) is an absolute value in itself. The innocent little boy of "A Little Boy Lost" knows as surely as Job comes to know that

> Nought loves another as itself
> Nor venerates another so.
> Nor is it possible to Thought
> A greater than itself to know:
>
> And Father, how can I love you,
> Or any of my brothers more?
> I love you like the little bird
> That picks up crumbs around the door.
>
> (E 28)

The little boy's intuitive knowledge of his own and everything's innate holiness is as profoundly true as the adult's hard-won, conscious recovery of that innocent vision. But since most of Blake's readers, like Albion, Job, and Blake himself, have not been able to sustain the child's intuition and have had to struggle to regain complete conviction of their own capacity for divinity, they naturally look upon the adult's consciousness of the human form divine as more important and meaningful, for them. And perhaps the fact that in *The Holy Family,* Christ is *above* the child in the very lap of truth rather than at her feet indicates that Blake himself preferred a conscious, "organized" Innocence to an unconscious, intuitive (but not necessarily "disorganized") Innocence. Certainly, his late poetry and art is a supremely complex and self-aware exploration of the implications of his central metaphor, the human form divine. But, in contrast to many of Blake's critics, I do not believe that Blake, like Wordsworth and Milton, regarded the fall from Innocence into Experience as either necessary or fortunate.[27] As *Jerusalem* so vividly shows, the fall into error and the

---

26. William Wordsworth, "Ode: Intimations of Immortality," I. 187.

27. Blake's comments on good and evil, as reported by Henry Crabb Robinson, seem to support this reading. On December 10, 1825, Blake declared, "There *is* no use in education. I hold it to be wrong. It is the great sin. It is eating of the tree of the knowledge of good and evil. This was the fault of Plato. He knew of nothing but the virtues and vices, and good and evil. There is nothing in all that. Everything is good in God's eyes." Earlier that evening, Blake had told Crabb Robinson that Jesus Christ "is the only God. But then," he had added, "and so am I and so are you." And a week later, he returned to this belief in the innate holiness of man to criticize Milton's notion of the Fall as fortunate. As Blake said to Robinson, "I saw Milton, and he told me to be-

state of Satan, a disintegration into "chaotic non-entity," is horribly pain-
ful, even self-destructive. Blake never condemned man to such a living
hell if it could be avoided. His spokesman, Los, devotes all his time and
energies, first, to preventing such a fall and, second, to rescuing the fallen
and leading them back into eternity where the one man waits with the
eternals and Jehovah to welcome all men back into the human form divine (*J* 98–99). For man *can* avoid the fall into the sleep of Ulro
and eternal death, albeit rarely; the Savior who walks, awake and expansive, in eternal life has been able to sustain the divine vision without
doubt or despair (*J* 4:1–7). The fall into error and contraction is not
for Blake an inevitable phase in the growth of the self, as it is for Wordsworth, for whom the years necessarily bring the "inevitable yoke" and
"earthly freight" of custom, "heavy as frost, and deep almost as life".[28]
Rather, for Blake, the fall occurs whenever, but *only* when, an individual
permits his reason to usurp control over his imagination, whenever he allows himself to question, doubt, or deny his potential divinity. The men of
Innocence who never doubt their holiness remain all life long in touch
with this absolute truth and are to be envied their certainty. Those of us
who cannot sustain the purity of their vision must, like Milton and Albion and Job, relearn—and in the process perhaps come to appreciate
more intensely—the ultimate truth that we *are* the human form divine. At the moment we know this, we pass through a last judgment and
beyond time into eternity; at that moment, for each and ultimately for all
of us, the divine Energy, imagination, and love of Christ are clothed on
earth by our bodies, by the bridal garments and the city of Jerusalem.

---

ware of being misled by his 'Paradise Lost.' In particular, he wished me to show the
falsehood of the doctrine, that carnal pleasures rose from the Fall. The Fall could not
produce any pleasure." (All quotations from Blake as reported by Henry Crabb Robinson, *Diary, Reminiscences, and Correspondence,* ed. Thomas Sadler, London, 3rd ed.,
1872, Vol. II, December 10, 1825, p. 8, and December 17, 1825, p. 11, respectively.)
  28. "Ode: Intimations of Immortality," ll. 125–29.

Index